"Would You Mind Repeating That?"

Uncork a Mint of Phrases and Timeless Sayings in Your Brain.

Richard A. Delia

Find and use the wit and wisdom of 15,000+ Americanisms, adages, aphorisms, bromides, clichés, colloquialisms, epigrams, figures of speech, idioms, maxims, platitudes, proverbs, tongue twisters, spoonerisms and memorable doggerel to entertain and amuse you and your friends.

(Grouped by similarity of meaning for easy reference.)

ISBN-10: 0989812405
ISBN-13: 978-0-9898124-0-5
Library of Congress Control Number: 2014915003
4² Forced Square Publishing
Berkeley Heights, NJ

Printed in the United States of America

First Edition

Affiliated websites:
http://www.wittydittees.com – (visualized clichés, idioms, etc. on T-shirts)
http://www.moneygraffiti.com – (drawings and spontaneous writings on U.S. banknotes)

Cover collage and photography by author.

Typefaces:
Interior text—11/ *Minion Pro*
Cover headline— 47/ *Impact*
Rear cover headline—24/ *Minion Pro*

Direct orders of this book:
ranje_rover@yahoo.com
$25./postpaid (in Continental USA)

A long time coming . . .

Illustrations here by Jon Buelow

. . . but worth the wait!!

ACKNOWLEDGMENTS

If it is true that defeat is an orphan, but victory has a thousand fathers, this book is a hands-down victory. For surely it has thousands if not millions of authors. To make a long story short, it is a joint effort by the human race since time immemorial.

In compiling this work, I acknowledge the great contribution of a friend who many years ago, in a manner I shall explain, inspired me to write this book. Also, to the many hundreds of people all across America who have since contributed to the work through their own kind submissions and recommendations both in person, by mail (and later by email), my appreciation runneth over. I hope this collection does justice to your expectations.

I am especially appreciative to *The New York Times, Advertising Age* and to other publications who in the course of my research saw fit to publish my author's inquiries, and to each reader who in the spirit of the scope and depth of this book responded to my call from all across America. I wish it were possible to thank everyone individually.

To my many friends, whose opinions I sought on various creative choices to be made ranging from cover colors and layout, to illustration design, to the book's title, your patient help and encouragement were key.

I gratefully acknowledge the invaluable contributions to this book in its final form by Richard J. Noyes, in both his astute creative recommendations and technical advice, and for sharing his publishing expertise.

To my family, for their moral support and creative input, I express especial thanks. Above all, I thank God. And to my former wife, Marjorie, and our daughter, Marisa, who with the patience of saints, waited through so many hours of isolation while daddy was off in his corner and played word games, I dedicate this book with my love and gratitude.

INTRODUCTION

Once (a pun a time), a dear friend named Hugh Clay Paulk, out of a clear blue sky and apropos of nothing, gave me a list of some 300 sayings. The list had no categories, nor order, nor apparent rhyme or reason. Yet I found it to be at once delightful, inspirational, witty, pithy, provocative and instructive. To me as a lover of language it radiated its own unique and almost magical charm.

In Hugh's words, this was the "wisdom of the ages." He called it a collection of "adages, clichés, aphorisms, homilies, gems of knowledge, essences of experiences, old saws and sayings." To that we may add epigrams, allusions, idioms, proverbs, platitudes, bromides, banalities, similes, metaphors, benedictions, maledictions, limericks, shibboleths, *bon mots* and whatnots. Most were familiar expressions, your bedrock Americanisms, from rolling stones, gift horses and wells run dry, to barn doors, last laughs and stitches in time. None was vulgar or offensive. Some I had never heard before and some may be also new to you.

But, alas, the more I read these sayings and thought about them, the more I found them only a teaser. Not only was the list too snow-white for my particular tastes, it was a mere snowflake in a blizzard.

So I got to thinking. The more I pondered the idea, the merrier it got. Why not a comprehensive book of clichés? Why not a compendium? Bit by bit, day by day, I began to compile my own list. Every time I caught myself using a cliché, or heard anyone do it, I would write it down. Never to be caught without pencil and pad nearby, almost all the time, even next to the bed, I writ with a flick of the wrist every witticism, banality, platitude, proverb, truism and all other specie of word to the wise that crossed my eye, ear, mind and mind's eye. Every time I found a shoe that fit, I wore it. When something hit it on the head, I nailed it.

Paying closer attention than usual to what people were saying, I soon found that all in love and war, rather than being fair, is often quite foul. Be forewarned that some of these entries may get the hackles up of even a sworn trooper. Which does not alter the fact that this is how certain people—who shall remain nameless—actually speak. Please note that I have excluded what are, in my judgment, the most scurrilous (largely sexual) entries from this collection which at a future time I may offer in a separate book.

In the course of my phrase-collecting for this compendium, the scope of the material seemed to take on a mind of its own and gradually broadened itself to include many obscure but memorable sayings from my own experience, both as a veteran of the U.S.M.C., and the Ulcer Gulches of Madison Avenue, to as far back as memory would take me. Some phrases are from my boyhood recollection, high school taunts and challenges, hurled at one another by adolescents, catcalls and buzzwords, insults and general doggerel. Whether kids still talk this way I don't know. It is a likely topic for someone's future investigation.

Whatever you want to call the word marriages you will find in this potpourri, you will have them coming out your ears. I tend to think of them all, collectively, as clichés. If much of it has a familiar ring, don't be surprised.

Clichés are everywhere. Even in the high-tech 2000's, they remain the mainstay stock-in-trade of movies, music, business, news media, advertising, and just us ordinary folk who want to get our point across as shortly and sweetly as we can.

Believe You Me

Before the sun sets tonight, you yourself are apt to utter at least one phrase in this book—maybe three, five, ten, depending on your level of consciousness. You will do this without batting an eyelash, without a second thought. Without even having read this book.

The reason you will speak these expressions is that already many of them are second nature to you. They are, really, efficient little units of thought, combinations of words that belong to one another, married in the mind, ear and soul for all eternity.

Beyond that, they are dynamic communicators. They convey a precise image or shade of meaning no other combination of words quite matches. When you say "tit for tat" (possibly a derivative of "this for that," though some believe it descends from *tip for tap*, "a blow for a blow") it immediately suggests reciprocation. In the general stream of everyday life, such phrases serve us well. If your train of thought runs in a certain track you can hardly entertain an idea—or communicate it—without couching it in these familiar terms.

Clichés are so popular because they are insidious, rarely calling attention to themselves, and so easy to use because they are often the first thoughts to spring to mind. They offer comfort, reassurance, the counsel of an old and wise friend. They are ready-made answers to life's most complex traumas and problems. They provide smiles to the sour, hope to the despairing, reason to the senseless. Usually they work like a charm.

Just listen to the dialogue around you; read your magazines, newspapers, watch TV, Facebook and Twitter. You'll find that the great preponderance of human discourse consists of what I call platification (platitudinous oversimplification).

This is not offered as a scholarly work, nor does it purport to be a definitive collection of scrupulous quotations. It contains only essential ideas, with little crossing of the t's and doting on i's. Besides its basic resource value, it is intended as a book for fun. It is hoped that it will bring you light moments for a lifetime, maybe to kindle some nostalgia, or perhaps every now and again to recharge your creative batteries.

Still, the linguist will find here a fertile field for etymological exploration and possible food for thought in new dimensions. It is fascinating to reflect, for example, that some sayings offer contradictory advice. "Look before you leap," counsels caution, while "He who hesitates is lost" urges action. "To thine own self be true," indeed; but "When in Rome do as the Romans do." "Absence makes the heart grow fonder," may in fact be, "out of sight, out of mind." (Come to think of it, could that be a definition for a blind madman)?

You may hear the same idiom used to convey different meanings. "All over the place," in one context, could mean uncontrolled, unpredictable or inconsistent, while in others it could indicate anything from ubiquitous to commonplace to comprehensive. In contrast, "All over the lot," suggests confusion or poor organization.

Not uncommonly, you will hear the same saying used to defend different sides of the fence, modified to suit the situation, e.g. "There is honor among thieves," or "There is no honor among thieves. "All is grist that comes to the mill," and "All is not grist that comes to the mill," are also of that genre. You decide what's right.

Some expressions go about in a cloak of uncertainty. Is it "No rest for the weary," or "No rest for the wicked"? Some say it's, "No rest for the weary and the wicked need none." Is it "Water over the dam," or "Water under the bridge"? Is it "Possession is nine-tenths of the law" or "Possession is nine points of the law"? We hear it both ways. And we hear that: "They say there are but eleven points to the law and possession is nine of them."

Once, many years ago, I saw the actor Tony Randall on a TV talk show expound on this very subject. He said that he had a collection of such protean and contradictory sayings. Didn't offer them for publication or even hint that they might become available. In any event, I had long been intrigued by the idea of contacting him to propose swapping notes with him. But, alas, Tony Randall has gone to his final reward. Moral for me: he who hesitates is lost.

Famous Lost Words

Like contractions, familiar sayings are also subject to shrinkage. "The proof of the pudding is in the eating," the saying goes; but when the mayor of your town or the president of the United States says, "The proof is in the pudding" the electorate gets his/her drift. Frequently you'll hear a speaker preface a remark with, "Long story short," a compact version of "To make a long story short." Whatever works; whatever you find useful.

This book makes no attempt to split semantic hairs. It simply presents what people have said, are saying, and in all probability will continue to say long after you and I turn up our toes.

It is tempting to disregard my own advice and to hold some of these little gems up to the light. Some phrases do cry out for closer analysis. Their origins are as fascinating as their ubiquity. Writers in "the language dodge" often devote entire columns to the etymology of one or two particular sayings, and I wish that time and space would permit me to do the same for many of these entries. A reader tells me that "dingbat" comes from the cattle range, and that a dingbat is a small ball of dried dung on an animal's tail. If this is so, I wonder why didn't they call it "dungbat"? It would be nice to hit the roundup trail to find out.

Words of a Feather (or, Like Goes with Like)

One major aim in organizing this collection was to classify the entries not necessarily by keywords or alphabetically but by their intent or meaning. A word about my categories: to corral these expressions into classifications is a stickler's wicket. To impose arbitrary boundaries on them is akin to mooring fenceposts in the ocean. The terrain is vast and constantly shifting. Then too, many expressions could rightfully be placed not in one but in several categories. Does "to break even" belong under Uneventful or Tie? Or is it a form of Reciprocation, with "even Steven"? Does "You sound like a broken record" belong under Bore, Monotonous, or Repetition? Should "From all indications" go under Appearance or Obvious? My categories stretch like fences across a marsh and admittedly are imprecise.

In some cases I place an entry into more than one category, usually because of its usage in several senses, e.g. "To take a chance," which in one sense can mean "Risk" or in another can indicate "Gambling." For idioms like "take to," with upwards of 4 meanings, I list the most familiar. Also, if the phrase has a key word, I often list it under both its common meaning and its distinguishing word. Thus, you will find "To take it on faith" under both "Acceptance" and "Faith."

This compendium neither provides definitions of entries nor speculates on their origins, inasmuch as many other reference works already do, sometimes with conflicting or tautological advice. Some define clichés with other clichés, e.g. explaining that "the name of the game" is "the crux of the matter."

Often, to arbitrarily decide which classification any particular expression belongs in becomes a flip of the coin. For example, does the phrase, "And there the similarity ends" belong under "Alike" or "Different"? A logical argument could be made either way. Reasoning that up until that phrase was uttered, the items being compared were similar, I chose the former. However, an equally valid argument could be made that once that phrase was said, whatever came afterwards was different, so it belongs under "Different." Similarly, should "the lesser of two evils" be placed under "Inferiority" or "Advantage"? I flipped many a coin.

In some cases an expression naturally belongs in one classification because of a key word, "family," for example, but also has a widely known meaning in another sense. In such instances, I have included it under both. Thus, you will find "In a family way" under both "Family" and "Pregnant" or "Don't look a gift horse in the mouth" under both "Gratitude" and "Horse," etc. And when I couldn't choose between classifications I put it in several. Feel free to suggest changes for future editions.

As evidence of how elusive even the most familiar expressions can be, consider that after 30+ years of cliché-collecting, I had not included "a babe in the woods," "against all odds," "to be all smiles," "to be continued," "in between paychecks," "scared to death" and the classic, "I wouldn't wish it on my worst enemy," all of which didn't make the cut until early 2013 and which in usage today are still as common as cow pies/meadow muffins in a pasture. (Did I include "make the cut"? If not, I need to!)

Claim to Fame

One perennial function of clichés in popular culture (or their key words) has been to inspire titles for books, movies, songs and even advertising campaigns. Many a familiar set of words, after centuries in circulation as a proverb or cliché, gets "re-branded" by being affixed to, or adapted for, a novel or film, e.g. *A Hole in the Head* (1959), *A Stitch in Time* (1963), *In Cold Blood* (1967), *Blue in the Face* (1995), *Still Waters Run Deep* (1996), *Liar Liar* (1997), *Wag the Dog* (1997), *Pushing up Daisies* (2005) and countless others, a tradition that carries through to this writing, with a movie titled *Few and Far Between* set for release in 2014. Many famous advertising slogans have similar roots, e.g. "When it rains it pours" (Morton Salt); "Out of this World" (Mars Candy); "Nothing comes closer to home." (Stouffer's). This phenomenon also can work the other way around. A book or film title can quickly become a cliché, as with *Catch-22* (1970), which has since come to describe any paradoxical or quirky dilemma. I think it safe to say that many future multimillion-dollar ad themes, book or movie titles are tucked between the covers of *Would You Mind Repeating That?*

Many familiar expressions are immutable; their word order is so fixed and their meaning so precise that the amalgam of words has almost come to serve as a word itself. A test I often use is to remove one word from a phrase to see if we might substitute any other word, such as, "a step in the right _____." In this case, the word "direction" leaps into the breach and no suitable alternate would dare to step forward. Similarly, with "his _____ is worse than his bite" no other word comes so readily to mind as "bark." There may be a term to describe the linguistic function for such a tight-knit and bulletproof unit of words; if so, I am unaware of it.

Other expressions allow for more flexibility, such as "once in a while," which may be modified with an intensifier to become "once in a *great* while," denoting an even greater rarity. In recording such phrases, rather than to include both side by side, I enclose the variable word in parentheses, so that the entry reads, "Once in a (great) while," indicating that the phrase may be used with or without the designated word to convey essentially the same meaning.

Some words I have enclosed in brackets, e.g. [it]. This indicates that the expression may be used with the bracketed word or that other descriptive words may be substituted; so that, "To love [it] to pieces" may be used as "I love it to pieces" or "I love that new song to pieces."

For Any and all Reasons

Throughout these pages you will also find some fill-in-the-blank entries, e.g. "As [adj.]* as they come," which is to say that it is not the particular words that have become embedded in the language but more so the syntactical structure. Thus, you might say, "As smart as they come," "As dumb as they come" or "As cool as they come" to convey your meaning. Similarly, "The only good [n.] is a dead [n.] or "To [v.] for the sake of [n.]" can take meaning by inserting the desired part of speech, as in "The only good snake is a dead snake," "The only good crow is a dead crow," "To argue for the sake of arguing," "To run for the sake of running," etc. You picks your words and you takes your choices.

* [adj.] = adjective, [adv.] = adverb, [n.] = noun, [p.] = pronoun, [v.] = verb, [sb] = somebody, [so] = someone

Caution, Learners of English: Some of the expressions presented in this book, though commonly used in everyday discourse, are considered crude, profane, vulgar or otherwise offensive in polite society. In such cases, these expressions show an asterisk within the objectionable word or words, e.g. "Go f*ck yourself" and "Up your *ss." Expressions containing asterisked words should not be carelessly used.

One category is devoted to puns, and throughout this volume I have interspersed many original puns, as I have heard them or thought of them. Punning upon the familiar is nothing new. When James Thurber said, in the 1930's, "It is better to have loafed and lost than never to have loafed at all," it gave a new teeth to an old saw, and a bite still sharp in the 2000's that is likely to sustain itself into the 2100's and beyond.*

* My elaboration on contemporary pun and ink appears in William Safire's book, *I Stand Corrected* (pg. 358). N.B. Many of the bad puns in this volume (*sans* attribution) are my own; the better ones I take credit for.

An Oronym by Any Other Name

Instead of saying the wrong word, you may occasionally mishear a word or phrase. This has come to be known as a Mondegreen, generally from misheard song lyrics. Linguistically, such sound-alike phrases are known as oronyms or homophones. The term was originally coined by an author who heard the lyrics of *The Bonny Earl of Murray* (a Scottish ballad) as:

Ye highlands and ye lowlands
Oh where hae you been?
Thou hae slay the Earl of Murray
And Lady Mondegreen.

What the actual lyrics said was that they "slay the Earl of Murray and laid him on the green." Lady Mondegreen existed only in the hearer's mind. And to this day Lady Mondegreen's name has been used to describe all mishearings of this ilk. Some classic misheard lyrics:

"Excuse me while I kiss this guy."
("Excuse me while I kiss the sky.")
Purple Haze, Jimi Hendrix

"The girl with colitis goes by."
("The girl with kaleidoscope eyes.")
Lucy in the Sky with Diamonds, The Beatles

A fine source of amusement for some is to play games with the sayings. You can mix and match them—like silly putty—for some delightful wordplay. Just one tiny juxtaposition is enough to open somebody's eyes. Next time you want to acknowledge that somebody is right, try, "You hit the nail right between the eyes" and watch the expression. Other examples: The Waltz Street Journal. The wild and wooly vest. Home is where the hearth is. These are what I call plays on clichés. What might the word-pundits name a cliché that has so punned it?

A *punché? Piché? Clun?* It moggles the bind—oops, boggles the mind. Ah yes, this collection also offers a selection of classic spoonerisms.

I have listed most entries with no attribution of authorship, particularly the classic ones which can easily be researched by Google, Yahoo, Bing or other popular search engines. Those that I believe to be my own originals, or from family members or friends, I have credited accordingly. Please feel free to challenge any attributions, and also to recommend entries for inclusions in future editions.

Having now compiled and organized this volume of more than 15,000 accretions of our language, idiomatic idiosyncrasies, pairings of words, thoughts and concepts, I feel a little as I did after reading Hugh Paulk's list decades ago.* What I have here now is maybe a snowball in Alaska. Of all the sayings I have set out to record—many, I believe, making their debut in written form in this compilation—inevitably some elusive ones have managed to escape.

There is always room for improvement. I could spend a lifetime refining this book, but it would be twice as long and still far from complete. In going to publication at this time, I am guided by some of the advice in the book itself: "Progress, not perfection" and "Don't make the best the enemy of the good." Things change, people change, and the vitality of our language and the resourcefulness of its speakers are an ever-renewing source of joy and amazement. Even as we go to press, I can think of other sayings that should be included and I hear a voice somewhere calling, "I've got one for you." Hold the presses!

ABOUT THE AUTHOR

Photo: Stanley W. Fine

A native New Jerseyan, Richard A. Delia served for 3 years in the U.S.M.C., graduated *magna cum laude* from Fairleigh Dickinson University in Madison, NJ, worked on Madison Avenue for 10 years at several of the world's major agencies, including as a copywriter at NH&S in Chicago (now Omnicom) and as V.P. and Creative Supervisor at Ted Bates & Co. Advertising, Inc. in Manhattan. For 15 years afterwards, he headed his own advertising agency in NYC, P.F.P. Advertising, Inc., (Projects for Peace) where he represented many educational institutions, including M.I.T. Center for Advanced Engineering Study and Westinghouse Learning Corporation. He produced an instructive filmstrip on language, *A Turn of the Phrase*, which was distributed to schools nationwide. Delia subsequently devoted 11 years to screenwriting and has completed 12 satiric screenplays largely based on his varied life experiences, including *Jinglehearts, A Free Country, Death by Design, Police Navidad, Wholly Smokin' and The Seven DWFs*. Besides his screenplays, Mr. Delia has authored numerous short stories, poems and 2 novels, *Medicine Avenue* and *Poison Ivy,* scheduled for publication in 2015.

Abandonment

Abandon all hope, ye who enter here. ♦ Left bed and board. ♦ Left high and dry. ♦ Left in the lurch. ♦ Left out in the cold/in the street/to twist in the wind. ♦ Out in left field. ♦ Put up for adoption. ♦ Rats desert the sinking ship. ♦ The girl I left behind me. ♦ To bail out. ♦ To be left standing with one's d*ck in one's hand. ♦ To drop [it]/[so] like a hot potato. ♦ To get stood up. ♦ To get/give the kiss-off. ♦ To hang [so] out to dry. ♦ To hit the silk. ♦ To jump ship. ♦ To kick [so] to the curb. [see also Attack] ♦ To leave [so] holding the bag/in the lurch. ♦ To leave [so] to the tender mercies of [n.]. ♦ To shake the dust off one's clothes. ♦ To be/get stood up. ♦ To stand somebody up. ♦ To throw [so] to the dogs/to the wolves/under the bus. ♦ To walk out on [so].

Absence

A woman absent is a woman dead. ♦ Absence, which doth make the heart grow fonder, makes the mind wander. ♦ Absence makes the heart grow fonder. ♦ Absentee management. ♦ AWOL (absent without official leave). [military] ♦ Conspicuous by one's absence. ♦ Conspicuously absent. ♦ Far from the eye, far from the heart. ♦ Gone but not forgotten. ♦ Going, going, gone! ♦ Gone with the wind. ♦ Has stepped away for a moment. [see also Telephonese] ♦ Long gone. ♦ Long since forgotten/gone. ♦ I miss you so much. ♦ It's history. ♦ Not at his/her desk. ♦ Not in today. ♦ Out of sight, out of mind. ♦ Please don't talk about me when I'm gone. ♦ Separation anxiety. ♦ The absent are always at fault. ♦ They stayed away in droves. ♦ They are good that are away. ♦ To absent oneself. ♦ To be a no-show. ♦ To cut class. ♦ To play hookey. ♦ When the cat's away, the mice will play.

Abstain

A teetotaler. ♦ Best birth control: one aspirin, held firmly between the knees. ♦ Complete abstinence is easier than perfect moderation. ♦ I'd rather not. ♦ Just say no (to drugs). ♦ Let this cup pass from me. ♦ Lips that touch alcohol will never touch mine. ♦ Never again. ♦ Swear off (the sauce). ♦ Thanks but no thanks. ♦ To be on the wagon. ♦ To go on the water wagon. ♦ To go to AA. ♦ To take a pass on [it]. ♦ To take a vow of chastity/poverty.

Abundance

A bumper crop. ♦ A bushel and a peck (and some in a gourd). ♦ A chicken in every pot. ♦ A cornucopia of [n.]. ♦ A good/great many. [see also Crowding] ♦ A little [n.] goes a long way. ♦ A mess of [n.]. ♦ A passel of [n.] ♦ A sh*t load of [n.]. ♦ A slew of [n.]. ♦ A treasure trove (of) [n.]. ♦ A (whole) bunch (of). ♦ An embarrassment of riches. ♦ An inexhaustible supply. ♦ Brimming over (with). ♦ Chock full. ♦ Crawling with [n.]. ♦ Filled/stuffed to the gills. ♦ Filled to capacity. ♦ Full to the brim. ♦ He/she is not the only fish in the sea/pebble on the beach. ♦ I could go on all day. ♦ I've got a million of 'em. ♦ It never rains but it pours. ♦ More [n.] than one knows what to do with. ♦ More [n.] than you can shake a stick at. ♦ More than enough (to go around). ♦ More than one can handle. ♦ My cup runneth over. ♦ Plenty to go around. ♦ Quite a bit/few/lot. ♦ Surfeit is the father of many fasts. ♦ The bases are loaded. ♦ The groaning board. ♦ The Horn of Plenty. ♦ There are plenty of (other) fish in the sea. ♦ There's (plenty) more where that came from. ♦ To be riddled/rife with [n.]. ♦ To have [it] coming out the gazoo/wazoo. ♦ To have [it] out the *ss. ♦ To be long on [it]. ♦ To be up to one's ears/eyeballs/eyes/neck/wazoo in [it]. ♦ To have [it] aplenty. ♦ To have [it] coming out (of) one's ears. ♦ To have [it] out/up the wazoo. ♦To have [it] out/up the ying yang. ♦ To have [it] up to one's eyeballs. ♦ To want for nothing. ♦ Wait, there's more! ♦ When it rains it pours. ♦ Will it ever/never end?

Acceptance
(also accord)

A roundtable discussion. ♦ A meeting of the minds. ♦ (All) very well. ♦ (All) well and good. ♦ An article of faith. ♦ Come to terms (with). ♦ Good enough for me. [see also Enough] ♦ Great minds run in the same channels. ♦ Great minds think alike. [Great minds like a think.] ♦ Hold still for. ♦ I can just/only imagine. ♦ I'll take that as a compliment. ♦ I'll take your word for it. [see also Belief] ♦ In the ballpark. ♦ Let go and let God. ♦ Love me for who I am. ♦ Make allowances/ apologies/excuses for. ♦ Might as well. ♦ Not to repent of a fault is to justify it. ♦ Not one to argue. ♦ Objection sustained. [see also Agree] ♦ Of that persuasion. ♦ Of that school of thought. ♦ Put up with. ♦ Resigned to (the fact). ♦ So be it. ♦ Sure, why not. ♦ Take a leap of faith. ♦ Take it as a given. ♦ Take it as is. ♦ Take it at face value. ♦ Take it lying down. ♦ Take it with the proverbial grain of salt. ♦ Take [it]/[so] for granted. ♦ Take, with all its warts. ♦ The ayes have it. [see also Vote] ♦ The (Good Housekeeping) seal of approval. ♦ To abide by the law/rules. ♦ To adopt the party line. ♦ To agree in principle. [see also Agree] ♦ To be in synch (with). ♦ To be of one mind. ♦ To be on the receiving end. ♦ To be on the same page/wavelength. ♦ To buy into [it]. ♦ To get used to. ♦ To resign oneself (to one's condition/fate). ♦ To seal the deal. ♦ To speak the same language. ♦ To stand for [it]. ♦ To subscribe to [n.]. ♦ To take a/the hint. ♦ To take a meeting. ♦ To take it on faith. [see also Faith] ♦ To take kindly to. ♦ To take one's word for it. ♦ To take one at one's word. ♦ To take [so] up on [it]. ♦ With a wink and a nod. ♦ Within acceptable limits/tolerances. ♦ You don't have to ask me twice. ♦ You have my (complete) sympathy.

happen. ♦ As luck would have it. [see also Luck] ♦ By a strange quirk of fate. ♦ By (sheer) happenstance. ♦ By (sheer) serendipity. ♦ Even a broken watch is right two times a day. ♦ Every once in a while even a blind hog comes up with an acorn. ♦ I get more [n.] by accident than you do on purpose. ♦ If you leave a monkey in a room with a typewriter long enough, it'll write a novel/the entire works of Shakespeare. ♦ It just so happens. ♦ Most accidents happen in the home. ♦ Nothing with God is accidental. ♦ On a collision course. ♦ Serendipity is looking for the needle in the haystack and finding the farmer's daughter. ♦ To be accident prone. ♦ To come/ happen/ run across. ♦ To crack up. ♦ To cream in. ♦ To cross [so]'s path. ♦ To happen upon. ♦ To just happen along. ♦ To have a fender-bender. ♦ To rack up. ♦ To stumble upon. [see also Discovery] ♦ To total one's car. ♦ To walk into a pole. ♦ To zig when you should have zagged.

Accident

A chance encounter. ♦ A head-onner. ♦ A head-on collision. ♦ Accidentally on purpose. [see also Contrive] ♦ Accidents will happen. ♦ An act of God. ♦ An accident waiting to

Accompany
(also corollaries)

Arm in arm. ♦ Ask a dumb question and you get a dumb answer. ♦ At the same time. ♦ Cheek by jowl. ♦ Cheek to cheek. ♦ Collateral damage. ♦

Diamond cuts diamond. ♦ Go along for the ride. ♦ Hitch one's wagon to a star. ♦ Hitchhike on somebody else's coattails. ♦ In the same breath. ♦ Inextricably linked. ♦ Iron sharpens iron. ♦ It goes with the territory. ♦ Ride piggy-back. ♦ Scissor cuts string, rock dulls scissor, paper wraps rock. ♦ Shoulder to shoulder. ♦ Side by side. ♦ Side effects. ♦ Skill and assurance are an invincible couple. ♦ Stick with me and you'll go far. ♦ Tag along. ♦ The house of a tall man must have high ceilings. ♦ To go hand in glove/hand in hand. ♦ To go together like hand and glove. ♦ To go together like pirates and parrots. ♦ To keep company (with). ♦ To live common law. ♦ To ride shotgun. ♦ To shack up (with). ♦ To sit in the suicide seat. ♦ With your looks and my brains, we'll go far. ♦ We are not alone. ♦ You can't have one without the other.

Accuracy

A bow-by-blow (description). ♦ A crack shot. ♦ A direct hit. ♦ As Wyatt Earp said, "Fast is fine, but accuracy is final." ♦ Bullseye. ♦ Dead center. ♦ Dead on. ♦ Deadeye Dick. ♦ Ground zero. ♦ Just so. ♦ No more, no less. ♦ Pinpoint accuracy. ♦ Right/smack between the eyes. ♦

Right on. ♦ Right on target. ♦ Right on the money. ♦ Right on the nose. ♦ Right on the old schnozzola. ♦ Spot on. ♦ That's the ticket. ♦ The beginning of wisdom is to call things by their right names. ♦ To a T. ♦ To be case sensitive. ♦ To be on course. ♦ To be on the right tack/track. ♦ To hit home. ♦ To hit it right on the button. ♦ To hit it right on the nose. ♦ To hit the nail on the head. ♦ To hit it right on the screws. ♦ To hit one's mark. ♦ To keep good time. ♦ To the letter. ♦ True to form. ♦ True to life. ♦ True to the mark.

Accuse

An outstanding warrant (for [so]'s arrest). ♦ Before you sweep the street, dust your own house. ♦ First drive the flies off your head. ♦ How do you plead? ♦ I wouldn't talk if I were you. ♦ I don't see any halo over your head. ♦ I wouldn't say that if I were you. ♦ If it weren't for you. ♦ It takes one to know one. ♦ It's all your fault. ♦ Incriminating evidence. ♦ Indicted by a/the Grand Jury. ♦ Let he who is without sin among you cast the first stone. ♦ Look who's talking. ♦ People who live in glass houses shouldn't throw stones. ♦ Point the accusing finger (at). ♦ The frying pan calling the kettle black. ♦ The pot calling the kettle/skillet black. ♦ To be charged with [n.]. ♦ To be painted/tarred with the same brush. ♦ To beg the question. ♦ To call for[so]'s head. ♦ To file a grievance (against). ♦ To finger [so]. ♦ To level/ prefer/press charges. ♦ To point the accusing finger (at). ♦ To put the finger on [so]. ♦ To stand accused (of). ♦ You have no room to talk. ♦ You should talk. ♦ You're projecting (like crazy).

Action

A contact sport. ♦ A course of action. ♦ A deed done is a race won. ♦ A man of action. ♦ A man of words and not deeds is a garden full of weeds. ♦ A mile wide and an inch deep. ♦ Actions speak louder than words. ♦ Affirmative action. [see also Initiative] ♦ All hat and no cattle. ♦ All show and no go. ♦ All talk and no action. ♦ An action figure. ♦ And . . . action! ♦ Any plan of action, however ill-conceived and im-plemented, is better than no action at all. ♦ Deeds are males and words are females. ♦ Do something about it. ♦ Do well is better than say well. ♦ Fine words butter no parsnips. ♦ In desire, the thought is seed to the deed. ♦ *In medias res.** ♦ In the thick of (it).* ♦ In the throes of. *[see also Now] ♦ Intentions which die are pretensions which lie. ♦ It is better to light one candle than to curse the dark. ♦ It is harder to turn word to deed than deed to word. ♦ Lights, camera, action! ♦ Roasted pigeons will not fly into your mouth. ♦ Swing, batter, swing! ♦ The road to hell is paved with good intentions. ♦ To act on. ♦ To bring to bear. [see also Attack] ♦ To get into the act. ♦ To go about it. ♦ To go that route. ♦ To go to it. ♦ To make it happen. ♦ To see one's way (clear) to. ♦ To take the ball and run with it. ♦ Trouts are not caught with dry breeches. ♦ Well done is better than well said.

Adequacy

A man's legs should be long enough to reach the ground. ♦ A bird in the hand is worth two in the bush.

◆ Better to be a big fish in a little pond than a little fish in a big pond.* ◆ Better to have a smaller piece of a bigger pie. *[see also Relativity] ◆ Better the leader in a village than second in Rome. ◆ Don't give up your day job. ◆ Either you have it or you don't. ◆ Enough to go around. ◆ Half a loaf is better than none. ◆ I got shoes; you got shoes; all God's chillun got shoes. ◆ It's better to be the head of the lizard than the tail of the dragon. ◆ The Lord provides. ◆ You can only wear one suit at a time.

Admire
(also awe)

A distant admirer. ◆ A mark of respect. ◆ A real piece of work. ◆ Adoring fans/public. ◆ Hold above all others. ◆ Hold in high esteem/regard. ◆ Mutual admiration society. ◆ O come, let us adore Him. ◆ Put a premium on. ◆ To be stagestruck/starstruck. ◆ To be a stage-door Johnny. ◆ To be duly/favorably impressed. ◆ To have stars in one's eyes. ◆ To look up to [so]. ◆ To pay homage (to). ◆ To think the sun rises and sets on [so]. ◆ To think a lot/highly of. ◆ To think the world of [so]. ◆ To place [so] on a pedestal. ◆ To take one's hat off (to). ◆ To worship the ground [so] walks on.

Adorned

A clotheshorse. ◆ A fashion plate. ◆ A suit of clothes. ◆ (All) decked out. ◆ (All) dolled up. ◆ All dressed up with nowhere to go. ◆ (All) gussied up. ◆ (All) wrapped up with a bow on top. ◆ Decked out like Lady Astor's horse. ◆ Dressed in one's Sunday best. ◆ Dressed to a T. ◆ Dressed to kill. ◆ Dressed to the nines. ◆ Eye candy. ◆ In a monkey suit. ◆ In one's glad rags. ◆ In one's best bib and tucker. ◆ In one's Sunday-go-to-meeting clothes. ◆ In one's Sunday best/suit. ◆ In (white) tie and tails. ◆ Rings on her fingers, bells on her toes. (She shall have music wherever she goes.) ◆ The frosting/icing on the cake. ◆ The wearing of the green. ◆ To top it all off. ◆ To clean up/scrub up real nice. ◆ To paper [it] over. ◆ To put a happy face on it. ◆ To put on the finishing touches. ◆ To top it (all) off. ◆ To touch [it] up. ◆ Tricked out. ◆ Understated elegance. ◆ Window dressing. ◆ With a cherry on top. ◆ With all the bells and whistles/trappings/trimmings. ◆ With all the hoopla and hullabaloo.

Advantage

A cheat sheet/crib sheet. ✦ A dwarf on a giant's shoulder sees the farther of the two. ✦ A rich man's problem. [see also Bonus] ✦ A Sunday punch. ✦ (All) to the good. ✦ An ace in the hole/up one's sleeve. ✦ Get/have a leg up (on). ✦ Get/give a head start. ✦ Get/have the edge on. ✦ Get/have the upper hand. ✦ In the country of the blind, the one-eyed man is king. ✦ Insider information. ✦ Location, location, location. ✦ Play one's long suit/trump card. ✦ Redeeming qualities. ✦ Saving grace. ✦ (Sitting) in the catbird seat. ✦ Some men have it, some men don't. ✦ Specialty of the house. ✦ Tell them [n.] sent you. ✦ That's a plus. ✦ That's the beauty of [it]. ✦ The home court/home field advantage. ✦ The sweet spot. ✦ To be better off. ✦ To be in the national/public interest. ✦ To count [it] to the good. ✦ To deliver a knockout punch. ✦ To fish in troubled waters. ✦ To get the jump on. ✦ To have an inside track. ✦ To have every advantage. ✦ To have [it]/[so] in the palm of one's hand. ✦ To have [so] by the shorts/short hairs/short and curlies. ✦ To have [so] over a barrel. ✦ To level the playing field. ✦ To press one's advantage. ✦ To show [it] to (its best) advantage. ✦ To steal a march (on). ✦ To take full advantage (of). ✦ To tip the scales in one's favor. [see also Decisive] ✦ One's stock in trade. ✦ One's strong suit.

Adversity

A stumbling block. ✦ A broken bone knits stronger. ✦ Adversity builds character. ✦ Adversity breeds virtue. ✦ Adversity has no friends. ✦ Adversity successfully overcome is the highest glory. ✦ Every adversity carries the seed of opportunity. ✦ Evil comes to us by ells and goes away by inches. ✦ He's a better man for it. ✦ In one's way. ✦ It comes at a price. ✦ It was the best of times, it was the worst of times. ✦ In the way. ✦ Misfortune arrives on wing and departs by foot. ✦ Prosperity makes friends and adversity tries them. ✦ Sacrifice is good for the soul. ✦ Smooth seas do not make skilled sailors. ✦ Staunch in the face of adversity. ✦ Sweet are the uses of adversity. ✦ The stronger a kite against the wind, the higher it soars. ✦ These are the times that try men's souls. ✦ Things are tough all over. ✦ To fall on hard times. ✦ To take one for the team. ✦ What doesn't kill you makes you stronger. ✦ When the going gets tough, the tough get going. [see also Perseverance] ♦ Your hour of need.

Advertising

A diamond is forever. ♦ A little dab'll do ya. ♦ An advertising agency is 85 percent confusion and 15 percent commission. ♦ A word from your local station. ♦ And now a word from our sponsor. ♦ Ask the man who owns one. ♦ Be all that you can be. ♦ Builds strong bodies eight ways. ♦ Do you make these common mistakes in English? ♦ Does she or doesn't she? Only her hairdresser knows for sure. ♦ Double your pleasure, double your fun. ♦ Fluffy not stuffy. ♦ Fly the friendly skies. ♦ Good to the last drop. ♦ Half of my advertising budget is wasted; the problem is, I don't know which half. ♦ Hasn't scratched yet. ♦ He who has a thing to sell and goes and whispers in a well, is not so apt to get the dollars as he who climbs a tree and hollers. ♦ Honest-to-goodness goodness. ♦ I can't believe I ate the whole thing. ♦ I'd walk a mile for a Camel. ♦ It cleans your breath (what a toothpaste!) while it cleans your teeth. ♦ It pays to advertise. ♦ It takes a licking and keeps on ticking. ♦ It's the next best thing to being there. ♦ It's not how it is but how people think it is that matters. ♦ Join the Navy and see the world. ♦ Let your fingers do the walking. ♦ Melts in your mouth, not in your hand. ♦ Mmmm, mmmm, good; mmm, mmm good; that's what Campbell's Soups are; mmm, mmm good. ♦ Munch a bunch. ♦ Nickle, nickle, nickle, roody ah, dat, da da. ♦ 99 and 44/100% pure: it floats. ♦ Not a cough in a carload. ♦ Plop, plop, fizz, fizz; oh, what a relief it is. ♦ Progress is our most important product. ♦ Say it with flowers. ♦ Sell the sizzle, not the steak. ♦ Shave and a haircut, two bits. ♦ Snap, crackle, pop. ♦ So round, so firm, so fully packed; so free and easy on the draw. ♦ Somewhere west of Laramie. ♦ Take tea and see. ♦ Tan, don't burn. ♦ The beer that made Milwaukee famous. ♦ The codfish lays a thousand eggs,/The humble hen but one,/The codfish never cackles/To show you what she's done,/And so we scorn the codfish/While the humble hen we prize,/Which only goes to show you,/It pays to advertise! ♦ The Marine Corps Builds Men. ♦ There's a Ford in your future. ♦ They laughed when I sat down at the piano. But when I started to play! ♦ Think small. ♦ To get the word out. ♦ To put a plug in for. ♦ We try harder. ♦

When you care enough to send the very best. ♦ When you have nothing to say, sing it. ♦ Which twin has the Toni? ♦ Word of mouth advertising is the best. ♦ You don't have to be Jewish to love Levy's. ♦ You can be sure if it's Westinghouse. ♦ You'd think I had . . . bad breath. ♦ You'll get a kick out of Kix. ♦ You'll wonder where the yellow went. ♦ You've tried the rest, now try the best.

Advice
(also kibitz)
A backseat driver. ♦ A Monday morning quarterback. ♦ A sidewalk superintendent. ♦ A word to the wise is sufficient. ♦ Advice you get for free may be priceless; but usually it's worthless. ♦ Advice and consent. ♦ Advise and consent. ♦ An armchair general/ quarterback. ♦ Here's what you should do: ♦ If I were you . . . [see also If] ♦ It is easier to give advice than to follow it. ♦ Ladies and gentlemen, take my advice; take off your bloomers and slide on the ice. ♦ Talk to [so] like a Dutch uncle. ♦ To have a talk/word with [so]. ♦ To play 25-cent psychologist. ♦ Unsolicited advice. ♦ When I want your advice I'll ask for it. ♦ When people ask for advice, often what they really want is praise. ♦ Words of wisdom. ♦ Words to live by/profit by. ♦ You ought to [v.] why don'tcha.

Affability
A good egg. ♦ A good ol' boy. ♦ A good Samaritan. ♦ A good skate. ♦ A prince among paupers. ♦ A good-natured slob. ♦ A gentleman and a scholar. ♦ A kindly soul. ♦ A regular guy. ♦ A rose among the thorns. ♦ As nice a chap as you could ever hope to find/see. ♦ For he's a jolly good fellow. ♦ Hail-fellow-well-met. ♦ Just one of the boys. ♦ Men of good cheer. ♦ My good man. ♦ Now there's a good fellow. ♦ Old buddy/chum/pal. ♦ The salt of the earth. ♦ To have one's best interests at heart.

Affectation
A city slicker. ♦ Airy-fairy ♦ Artsy-fartsy. ♦ Charles of the Ritz. ♦ Fancy-schmancy. ♦ Glitter/glitz and glamor. ♦ Just too precious for words. ♦ La-di-da. ♦ To put on airs. ♦ To put on the dog/Ritz. ♦ What are you posing for, animal crackers? ♦ To strike a pose.

Affinity
A [n.] after one's own heart. ♦ Cotton to/take to [it]. ♦ Cut from the same

cloth. ♦ It grows on you. ♦ Just my cup of tea. ♦ Kindred souls/spirits. ♦ Kissin' cousins. ♦ Like a brother/sister to me. ♦ Made for each other. ♦ My kind of girl/guy. ♦ My kind of [n.]. ♦ Near and dear to one's heart. ♦ Next-door neighbor. ♦ Pen pals. ♦ Soul mates. ♦ Take a liking/shine to. ♦ To be cut out for [it]. ♦ To be inclined to. ♦ To be leaning in that direction. ♦ To be partial to [it]/[so]. ♦ To be right up one's alley. ♦ To be so inclined. ♦ To click with [so]. ♦ To have a penchant/predilection/propensity (for). ♦ To have a tendency (to). ♦ To go together like hand and glove. ♦ To go together like [n.] and [n.]. ♦ To have every intention (to). ♦ To have something in common. ♦ To like the cut of [so]'s jib. ♦ To have a soft spot in one's heart (for). ♦ To have an eye for. ♦ Two hearts beat as one. ♦ To tend to. ♦ We've got it going on.

Age

A dirty old man. ♦ A little old lady. ♦ Age and treachery will always overcome youth and skill. ♦ Age before beauty. ♦ Age is just a number/only a number. ♦ Age will tell. ♦ Along/on in years. ♦ An old bat/buzzard/coot/cuss/duffer/fart/fogy/fossil/fuddy-duddy/geezer/gizzard. ♦ At the tender age (of). ♦ Been around since the Flood. ♦ Been around forever. ♦ Been around since Jesus left Philadelphia. ♦ Been around since the Year One. ♦ Been around since Christ was a carpenter's mate. ♦ Do not resent growing old—many are denied the privilege. ♦ Fifty is the new thirty. ♦ George Washington slept here. ♦ Getting old ain't for sissies. ♦ Getting on in years. ♦ He's [n.] if he's a day. ♦ He's old enough to be your father. ♦ If I wake up without something hurting someplace I know something's wrong. ♦ If only I were twenty years younger. ♦ In one's second childhood. ♦ Just because there's snow on the roof doesn't mean there isn't fire in the furnace. ♦ Live to a ripe old age. ♦ Long in the tooth. ♦ Many a good tune was played on an old fiddle. ♦ Many moons ago. ♦ No spring chicken. ♦ Now I'm dating myself. ♦ Now you're showing your age. ♦ Of a certain age. ♦ Of childbearing age. ♦ Of (legal) age. ♦ Oh, to be young again. ♦ Old as dirt/ water. ♦ Old as the hills. ♦ Old as Methuselah. ♦ Old enough to be her father. ♦ Old enough to know better. (But young enough to want to anyway — R.D.). ♦ Old folks are twice children. ♦ Old golfers never die; they just lose their balls. ♦ Old soldiers never die, they just fade away. ♦ Older than dirt. ♦ Older than God. ♦ Old wine and friends improve with age. ♦ Respect your elders. ♦ She's thirty if she's a day. ♦ Since day one. ♦ Since the dawn of creation/time. ♦ Since time out of mind/immemorial. ♦ Still going/growing strong. ♦ The (legal) age of consent. ♦ The older you grow, kid, it's harder to brush off them knocks. ♦ The terrible twos. ♦ To be well preserved. ♦ To be young at heart. ♦ To be young at heart is to be an old fart. ♦ To come of age. ♦ To grow old before one's time. ♦ To grow old gracefully. ♦ To have it all behind you. ♦ To improve with age. ♦ To mellow over the years. ♦ Up in years. ♦ Up there (in age). ♦ When I was young and in my prime I used to do/get it all the time; but now that I am old and grey I only do/get it once a day. ♦ When I was your age . . . ♦ You can't stay old forever. - Debra Maria Delia ♦ You'll never be younger than you are today. ♦ You're not getting older; you're getting better. ♦ You're not getting any younger. ♦ You're only as old as you feel.

Agitation

(All) bent out of shape. ♦ (All) riled up. ♦ (All) steamed up. ♦ Better to be p*ssed off than p*ssed on. ♦ Blow a fuse. ♦ Blow one's cork/top/stack. ♦ Boiling mad. ♦ Do a slow burn. ♦ Fighting mad. ♦ Fit to be tied. ♦ Fit to kill. ♦ Frothing at the mouth. ♦ Fuming and a-fussing. ♦ Get one's balls/bowels in an uproar. ♦ Get one's nose out of joint. ♦ Have a fit ♦ Have a hemorrhage. ♦ Have a wild hair up one's *ss. ♦ Have conniptions. ♦ Hot under the collar.

♦ Hotter than a 50-cent African soup bowl. ♦ I could spit nails. ♦ I'm mad as hell (and I'm not going to take it anymore). ♦ Itching/spoiling for a fight. ♦ In a blind rage. ♦ In a tizzy. ♦ Mad as a hornet/wet hen. ♦ Moral indignation. ♦ On the warpath. ♦ Really ticked. ♦ Rip-roaring mad. ♦ Road rage. ♦ Rompin' stompin' mad. ♦ Sh*t a brick. ♦ Sh*t rivets. ♦ Sh*t nickels. ♦ Sh*t a banana. ♦ Sh*ttin' and a-spittin'. ♦ Shock value. ♦ Spring-loaded to the p*ssed-off position. ♦ That (really) burns my *ss. ♦ To be hopping mad. ♦ To be in a huff. ♦ To be p*ssed off. ♦ To be P.O.'d. ♦ To be (really) p*ssed. ♦ To be ticked off. ♦ To blow up like a balloon. ♦ To burn one up. ♦ To fly into a terrible rage. ♦ To fly off the handle. ♦ To fume and fuss. ♦ To get all steamed/worked up. ♦ To get medieval. ♦ To get one's dander up. ♦ To get one's knickers in a twist/panties in a bunch. ♦ To get one's nose out of joint. ♦ To give [sb] *agita*. ♦ To go ballistic/bananas/bonkers/caveman/postal. ♦ To go through the roof. ♦ To have a bee in one's bonnet. ♦ To have a bug up one's *ss. ♦ To have/throw a fit/tantrum. ♦ To have/throw a sh*t fit. ♦ To have an axe to grind. ♦ To have one's *ss upon one's shoulders. ♦ To hit the ceiling. ♦ To see red. ♦ To throw a hissy-fit. ♦ To go through the roof. ♦ To raise the roof. ♦ To swell up like a toad. ♦ To work oneself up (to a fever pitch). ♦ To work oneself into a frenzy/lather. ♦ Up in arms.

Agree

A meeting of the minds. ♦ A yes man. ♦ And how! ♦ Ain't it/that the truth? ♦ Alright already. ♦ All those in favor of [n.], say "Aye." ♦ Amen to that. ♦ As well you should. ♦ Awright aw-rootie. ♦ Behind you 100%. ♦ By mutual agreement/consent/understanding. ♦ Can't say's I blame you. ♦ Check and double check. ♦ Count me in. ♦ Ditto for me. ♦ Don't feel like the Lone Ranger. ♦ Don't feel lonesome. ♦ Don't I know it. ♦ Don't you (just) know it. ♦ Fine by me. ♦ For sure. ♦ From your lips to God's ears. ♦ Hear, hear! ♦ Have it your way. ♦ (How) right you are. ♦ I can dig it. ♦ I can relate. ♦ I couldn't agree (with you) more. ♦ I couldn't've said it better myself. ♦ I heartily heart that. ♦ I hope to tell you. ♦ I second the motion. ♦ I was thinking the same thing (myself). ♦ I'd/I'll be the first to admit it. ♦ I'll do just that. ♦ I'll drink to that. ♦ I'll give [p.] that. ♦ I'll say! ♦ I'm all for it/that. ♦ I'm game. ♦ I'm good with it/that. ♦ I'm inclined to agree (with you). ♦ I'm with you there. ♦ I'm with you all the way. ♦ If you insist. ♦ It's a deal. ♦ It's something I would do. ♦ Join the club. ♦ Let's shake on it. ♦ Me too. ♦ More than you know. ♦ More than you'll ever know. ♦ My sentiments exactly. ♦ Music to my ears. ♦ Now that's a fact. ♦ Now you're talking. ♦ Now you're talking my language. ♦ Now you're cooking (with gas). ♦ Now you're saying something (Jim). ♦ Objection sustained. [see also Acceptance] ♦ Okay—be that way. ♦ Okey-doke.* ♦ Okey-dokey.* [see also Superlatives] ♦ Pass me an oar. ♦ Point well taken. ♦ Put 'er there. ♦ (Right) back atcha. ♦ Right on. ♦ Right you are. ♦ Same here. ♦ See eye to eye/eyeball to eyeball. ♦ Sho 'nuff (sure enough). ♦ So say you all? ♦ Solid on that. ♦ Sounds good to me. ♦ Sounds like a plan. ♦ Spoken like a trooper. ♦ Sure thing. ♦ Sure, why not? ♦ Tacit agreement. ♦ Tell me about it! ♦ That makes two of us. ♦ (That's) fine by/with me. ♦ That's exactly/just what I had in mind. ♦ That's for (damn/darn) sure. That's more like it. ♦ That's putting it mildly. [see also Tact] ♦ That's the understatement of the year/decade/century. ♦ That's saying something. ♦ The ayes have it. ♦ The feeling is mutual. ♦ There you go. ♦ There's something to be said for that. ♦ To abide by. ♦ To agree in principle. [see also Acceptance] ♦ To agree to disagree. [see also Disagree] ♦ To be disposed to. ♦ To be down with [it]. ♦ To be on the same page/wavelength. ♦ To be more than happy to. ♦ To be only too happy to. ♦ To be so inclined. ♦ To be sold on [it]. ♦ To be sure. ♦ To be up for [it]. ♦ To bear [so] out. ♦ To buy into [it]. ♦ To come around (to [so]'s point of view). ♦ To cut/make a deal. ♦ To echo those sentiments. ♦ To get along, go along. ♦ To get/have one's own way. ♦ To go along with (the program). ♦ To make a positive ID/identification. ♦ To put it mildly. [see also Tact] ♦ To reach an accord/agreement/understanding. ♦ To reach an amicable settlement. ♦ To say the same thing. ♦ To see things the same way. ♦ To settle on/upon. ♦ To strike a bargain. ♦ To strike a sympathetic chord. ♦ To take up the cry. ♦ To yes [so] to death. ♦ True that. ♦ Truer words were never spoken. ♦ When you're right, you're right. ♦ Who am I to argue? ♦ Why didn't I think of that? ♦ Works for me. ♦ Yessiree, Bob. ♦ You and me both. ♦ You ain't just whistling Dixie. ♦ You ain't lying! ♦ You bet! ♦ You bet your *ss. ♦ You bet your Bayer aspirin. ♦ You betcha! ♦ You/you'd better believe it. ♦ You bet your bippy/boots. ♦ You bet your (everlovin'/sweet lovin') *ss. ♦ You better honk. ♦ You can say that again. ♦ You could/might say that. ♦ You couldn't be more right/righter. ♦ You dad well better believe. ♦ (You) damn straight. ♦ You damn well told. ♦ You durn tootin'. ♦ You f*cking A (well told). ♦ You f*cking well right. ♦ You know it. ♦ You said a mouthful (in a few words). ♦ You said it! ♦ You said that right. ♦ You tell 'em. ♦ You took the words (right) out of my mouth [plagiarism? — R.D.] ♦ You won't get any argument from me. ♦ You're absolutely right. ♦ You're calling the shots. ♦ You're darn/durn tootin'. ♦ You're dadblamed/ dadburned/dang/doggone right. ♦ You're OK in my book. ♦ You're so right. ♦ You're telling me! ♦ You're the doctor. ♦ You've got a point (there) ♦ You've got that right.

Aid

A hands-on approach. ♦ A nurse's aide. ♦ Aid and abet. ♦ Anything you need, let us know. ♦ Every little bit helps. ♦ (How) may I/we help you? ♦ I need all the help I can get. ♦ If you can't help don't hurt. ♦ Just because you've helped (me) doesn't allow you to hurt (me). ♦ Lend moral support. ♦ May I/we be of assistance? ♦ Mother's little helper. ♦ Thanks for your help; (I'll take it from here). ♦ To come to [so]'s defense. [see also Ally] ♦ To get behind [it]/[so]. ♦ To give aid and comfort to the enemy. ♦ To help [so] out. ♦ To hold the candle (for). ♦ To lend a (helping) hand. ♦ To roll up one's sleeves and pitch in. ♦ To rally to the cause. ♦ To see one through. ♦ To

take [it] off [so]'s hands. ♦ What can I/we do for you? ♦ [What can I/we do you for? —var., humorous] ♦ When you carry the torch for the other fellow, the glow of your own lamp is brighter.

Aim

Bombs away! ♦ Get [it] in one's crosshairs/peepsights. ♦ Keep your eyes on the prize. ♦ Ready, aim, fire! ♦ Take aim. ♦ Target practice. ♦ To draw a bead on. ♦ To focus on. ♦ To home in/hone in on. ♦ To make a point of [it.] ♦ To narrow it down. ♦ To pinpoint it. ♦ To put one's finger on. ♦ To set one's sights on. ♦ To take deadly aim. ♦ To zero in on. ♦ We aim to please.

Alert
(also attentive, observant)

A first-hand account. ♦ At the ready. ♦ Be on the lookout for. (BOLO) ♦ Cheese it, the cops! ♦ Chickie, the cops! ♦ Eagle-eye Fleagle. ♦ Eyewitness testimony. ♦ Heads up! ♦ I know what I saw. ♦ If you see something, say something. ♦ If you snooze, you lose. ♦ Keenly aware. ♦ Keep a sharp lookout. ♦ Keep an ear to the ground. ♦ Keep an eye out (for). ♦ Keep one's antennae out/up. ♦ Keep one's eye on the ball. ♦ Keep one's eyes peeled. ♦ Keep one's mouth shut and eyes open. ♦ Look alive! ♦ On full/

high alert. ♦ On the job. ♦ On the *qui vive.* ♦ Pay (close) attention. ♦ Powers of observation. ♦ Ramrod straight. ♦ Snap to attention. ♦ Stop, look and listen. ♦ The shepherd must not fall asleep counting sheep. ♦ To be all ears. [gibe: Like a jackass!] ♦ To be all eyes. ♦ To be aware of one's surroundings. ♦ To be eagle-eyed/sharp-eyed. ♦ To be/get on the ball/beam/stick. ♦ To be/keep on one's toes. ♦ To have a keen eye. ♦ To have a lot on the ball. ♦ To have keen powers of observation. ♦ To have/keep one's feelers out. ♦ To have one's finger on the pulse (of). ♦ To have one's wits about one. ♦ To issue an all-points bulletin. [see also Announcement] ♦ To keep a weather eye out. ♦ To keep an eye on. ♦ To keep one's eyes peeled. ♦ To keep tabs on. ♦ To keep watch. ♦ To not miss a trick. ♦ To pay (close) attention. ♦ To play chickie. ♦ To prick up one's ears. ♦ To sit bolt upright. ♦ To sit up and take notice. ♦ To watch like a hawk. ♦ Watch it. ♦ Watch out. ♦ Watch yourself. ♦ Wide awake. ♦ You need to have eyes in the back of your head.

Alibi
(also excuses)

A bad excuse is better than none. ♦ A cover story. [see also Best, Conceal] ♦ A plausible explanation. ♦ A poor workman always blames his tools. ♦ A(n) airtight/bulletproof/ironclad/ solid alibi. ♦ An Alibi Ike. ♦ Driving drunk and claiming you were too intoxicated to know right from wrong. ♦ Everybody has his faults. ♦ Everybody makes mistakes (that's why they put erasers on pencils). [see also Err] ♦ Excuses are like *ssholes: everybody's got one. (And they all stink!) ♦ Excuses, excuses (all I ever hear are excuses). ♦ Friends don't need explanations; enemies will never believe them. ♦ I didn't know the gun was loaded. [see also Guns] ♦ I didn't realize that I was going so fast. ♦ I forgot to duck. [see also Injury] ♦ I got it from a toilet seat. ♦ I had car trouble. ♦ I must be losing my touch. ♦ I must be slipping. ♦ I never got the memo. ♦ I only work here. ♦ I ran into a doorknob. ♦ I think I'm getting the flu. ♦I was just keeping up with traffic. ♦ I'm only human. ♦ If it doesn't fit, you must acquit. ♦ It could happen to anyone. ♦ It is a good horse that never stumbles. ♦ Killing your parents then asking for mercy on the grounds that you are an orphan. ♦ Lucy, you got some 'splainin' to do. ♦ My alarm didn't go off. ♦ No excuse. ♦ Nobody in here but us chickens. ♦ Never explain—your friends do not need it, and your enemies will not believe it anyway. ♦ Nobody's perfect. ♦ Not my doing. ♦ Not tonight, dear, I have a headache. [riposte: But I don't want to f*ck your head]. ♦ Tell it to the judge. ♦ That's what they all say. ♦ The devil made me do it. ♦ The dog ate my homework. ♦ The train broke down. ♦ This better be/ought to be good. ♦ To cop a plea. ♦ To explain [it] away. ♦ To make allowances/apologies/excuses for. ♦ To make up a cockamamie story. ♦ To play [it] down. ♦ To soft pedal [it]. ♦ To talk one's way out of [it]. ♦ To tell one's side of the story. ♦ What have you got to say for yourself? ♦ What is the meaning of this? ♦ We are all manufacturers—some make good, others make trouble and still others make excuses. ♦ We've all done it at one time or another. ♦ Who hasn't done that? ♦ You'd better have a good excuse.

Alike

(also equal, equivalent, similar)
A boilerplate [n.]. ♦ A chip off the old block. ♦ A carbon copy. ♦ A cookie-cutter [n.]. ♦ A mirror image. ♦ A parallel universe. ♦ A parity product. ♦ A reasonable facsimile thereof. [see also Imitation] ♦ A splinter group. ♦ A striking similarity. ♦ A strong resemblance. ♦ All is grist that comes to the mill. ♦ All men are created equal. ♦ Along the lines of. ♦ Along the same lines. ♦ An alternate reality. ♦ And the like. ♦ Any sufficiently advanced technology is indistinguishable from magic. ♦ As good as any. ♦ At night all birds are black. ♦ Berries from the same stem. ♦ Birds of the same feather. ♦ By the same token. ♦ Can't tell one from another. ♦ Can't tell the difference. ♦ Can't tell which is which. ♦ Chickens don't make ducks. ♦ Conform to the norm. ♦ Cut from the same cloth. ♦ He puts his pants on (in the morning) the same way you do—one leg at a time. [see also Commonplace] ♦ Identical twins. ♦ I do that too. ♦ I have one just like it/ that. ♦ I like [n.] as much as the next guy. ♦ In a similar vein/way. ♦ In like manner. ♦ In the dark they're all alike. [see also Women] ♦ Like begets like. ♦ Like father, like son. ♦ Like his father before him. ♦ Like two peas in a pod. ♦ Lying down they're all alike. ♦ Martyr and persecutor are usually cut from the same cloth. ♦ No matter how you slice it, it's still baloney. ♦ No two people are alike. ♦ On a similar note. ♦ One and the same. ♦ Parts is parts. ♦ People are alike everywhere. ♦ People are people wherever you go. ♦ People are people. ♦ Rabbits always have children with long ears. ♦ Same difference. ♦ Samey-same. ♦ Six feet of earth make all men

of one size. ♦ Some semblance of [n.]. ♦ Something like [it]. ♦ Stamped from the same mold. ♦ Tastes like chicken. ♦ The apple doesn't fall far from the tree. ♦ The Bobbsey twins. [see also Sidekicks] ♦ The (exact) same thing. ♦ The likes of. ♦ The same thing happened to [n.]/[p.]. ♦ The spit and image. ♦ The spitting image. ♦ There's a lid for every pot. ♦ There the similarity ends. ♦ They all look alike (to me). ♦ Tigers of the same stripe. ♦ To be a dead ringer. ♦ To bear a (striking) resemblance (to). ♦ To fit the description. ♦ To have the same effect. ♦ To take after [so]. ♦ To that effect. ♦ Two of a kind. ♦ We are all brothers under the skin. ♦ You men are all alike. ♦ You have only one thing on your mind. ♦ You're just like all the rest.

Ally

(also applause, approval)

A joint venture. ♦ A lot in common. ♦ A Kumbaya moment. ♦ A lot in common. ♦ A lot to be said for [it]. ♦ A peer group. ♦ A ringing endorsement. ♦ A round of applause. ♦ A sort of chemistry between us. ♦ A sparring partner. ♦ A staunch supporter. ♦ A vote of confidence. ♦ All signals/systems (are) go. ♦ Are you thinking what I'm thinking? [see also Opinion] ♦ Best friends forever. (BFF) ♦ Bosom buddies. ♦

Brothers/comrades in arms. ♦ Cast/throw in one's lot with. ♦ Friends in high places. ♦ Get along famously. ♦ Get in good/in tight with. ♦ Get in step (with). ♦ Get on the good/right side of [so]. ♦ Give a big hand (to). ♦ Give high marks (to). ♦ Give the go-ahead (to). ♦ Give the nod/the OK. ♦ Hear, hear! ♦ In cahoots (with). ♦ In harness with. ♦ In league with. ♦ In perfect harmony. ♦ In tandem (with). ♦ In unison. ♦ Join forces. ♦ Joined at the hip. ♦ Kindred spirits. ♦ Like the ball brothers: they hang together. ♦ Mitting. ♦ On good terms (with). ♦ One's fellow man. ♦ Pitch one's tent with. ♦ Play nice. ♦ Put your hands together for. ♦ Smoke 'em if you've got 'em. ♦ Team up (with). ♦ The best of friends. ♦ The brotherhood of man. ♦ The old-boy network. ♦ The two of us just clicked. ♦ To be all for [it]. ♦ To be *sshole buddies. ♦ To be in bed with. ♦ To be in lockstep with. ♦ To be in [so]'s corner. ♦ To be OK with [it]. ♦ To be on [so]'s side. ♦ To bestow one's blessing (on). ♦ To be (well) connected. ♦ To buddy up (with). ♦ To cement relations (with). ♦ To cling to each other/one another. ♦ To come to [so]'s defense. [see also Aid] ♦ To compare notes. ♦ To cozy up (to). ♦ To find favor (with). ♦ To get/give a heads-up/thumbs up. ♦ To get/give the green light/final approval. ♦ To get/give the seal/stamp of approval. ♦ To go hand in hand. ♦ To greenlight [it]. ♦ To hit it off. ♦ To make a goodwill gesture. ♦ To make a show of (good) faith. ♦ To make nice. ♦ To mend fences. ♦ To pal around (with). ♦ To pool resources. ♦ To present a united front. ♦ To put heads together. ♦ To reach across the aisle. ♦ To rubber-stamp [it]. ♦ To see fit (to). ♦ To show solidarity (with). ♦ To side with [so]. ♦ To sign off on [it]. ♦ To strike up a friendship. ♦ To take [so]'s side. ♦ The smoking lamp is lit. ♦ We're in it/this thing together. ♦ Under the aegis/auspices of. [see also Protection]

Almost
(also proximity)

A close call/shave. [see also Close, Marginal] ♦ A close second. ♦ A distant second. ♦ A glancing blow. ♦ A margin of error. ♦ A miss is as good as a mile.

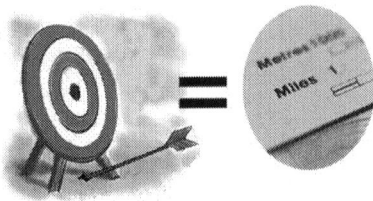

♦ A near-death experience. ♦ A near miss. ♦ A runner-up. ♦ A second-class citizen. ♦ A second-stringer. ♦ A work in progress. ♦ Almost but not quite. ♦ Almost doesn't count. ♦ Almost doesn't count except in horseshoes (and hand grenades). ♦ Always a bridesmaid, never a bride. ♦ An also-ran. ♦ An honorable mention. ♦ An understudy. ♦ And I use the term loosely. ♦ As it were. ♦ By a cat's whisker. ♦ By a gnat's eyebrow. ♦ Close but no cigar. ♦ Close enough. ♦ Close to home. ♦ Come off second best. ♦ Damn/damned/darn/ durn near. ♦ Finish out of the money. ♦ In a manner of speaking. ♦ In a sense. ♦ In a way. ♦ In one/some sense. ♦ In one's own way. ♦ Just about. ♦ Just missed it. ♦ Just shy of (the mark). ♦ Kinda sorta. ♦ Never show a fool a job half finished. ♦ Nice try. ♦ Nigh on (to). ♦ Not what I had in mind. ♦ Of sorts. ♦ Off by a (red) c*nt hair. ♦ Off center. ♦ Only scratches/skims the surface. ♦ Or thereabouts. [see also Approximately] ♦ Or words to that effect. ♦ Out of network. ♦ Out of one's league. ♦ Pretty near. ♦ Put a little hair around it. ♦ Right church, wrong pew. ♦ Second banana. ♦ Second in command. [see also Command] ♦ So close/ near, yet so far. ("*Tan prope. Tan proculque.*") ♦ So to speak. ♦ Something of a [n.]. ♦ Somewhat of a [n.]. ♦ The next best thing. ♦ To be within one's grasp/reach. ◆ To come in second. ◆ To come off second best. ◆ To come pretty close. ◆ To come within a gnat's whisker/hair's breadth (of). ◆ To dodge the bullet. ◆ To hit close to home. ◆ To play second fiddle. ◆ To take second place. ◆ To verge on. ◆ To warm the bench. ◆ Up to a point. ◆ Waiting in the wings. ◆ You missed a spot. ◆ You missed your calling.

Ambition

A mover and a shaker. ◆ A star in its ascendancy/on the rise. ◆ A young Tiger. ◆ A young Turk. ◆ Bright-eyed and bushy-tailed. ◆ Bubbling with enthusiasm. ◆ Busy as a beaver/bee. ◆ Champing at the bit. ◆ Feeling one's Cheerios/oats/ Wheaties. ◆ Frisky as a newborn colt. ◆ Full of beans. ◆ Full of pepper and prune juice. ◆ Full of p*ss and vinegar. ◆ Full of pith and vigor. — R.D. ◆ Full of vim and vigor. ◆ Highly motivated. ◆ Naked ambition. ◆ On the come. ◆ Put some elbow grease into it. ◆ Raring to go. ◆ Sassy as a jay. ◆ Still going strong. ◆ Straining at the leash. ◆ To be a go-getter. ◆ To be an eager beaver. ◆ To be up and coming. ◆ To eat 'em up alive. ◆ To have get-up and-go. ◆ To hustle one's bustle. ◆ To take on the world. ◆ Up and at 'em.

Amorous

A bitch in heat. ◆ (All) hot and bothered. ◆ Booty call. ◆ Come on to. ◆ Cop a feel. ◆ Getting hot and heavy. ◆ Have a crush on. ◆ Have hot rocks. ◆ He was all over her like a cheap suit. ◆ He'd f*ck a snake if he could hold it. ◆ Horny as a dog with three dicks. ◆ Horny as a three-balled cat/billy goat. ◆ Horny as a toad. ◆ Horny as f*ck/hell. ◆ Hot to trot. [see also Readiness] ◆ If you can't be near the one you love, love the one you're near. ◆ In the heat of passion. ◆ Keep a cool tool, fool; I'm wise to that rise in your Levis. ◆ Looking for love (in all the wrong places). ◆ On the make. ◆ Put the make on. ◆ Put the moves on. ◆ To be all over [so] (like a cheap suit). ◆ To be hard up. ◆ To be hot for/on somebody. ◆ To be smitten with [so]. ◆ To come courting. ◆ To dance attendance on. ◆ To have (goo goo) eyes for. ◆ To have hot rocks. ◆ To have Roman eyes and Russian fingers. ◆ To have the hots for [sb]. ◆ To lust after [sb]. ◆ To feel [so] up.

Anatomy
(physical references)

Arm of the law. ◆ Belly of the beast. ◆ Chest of drawers. ◆ Crook of the elbow. ◆ Ear of corn. ◆ Ears of the pitcher. ◆ Elbow of the pipe. ◆ Eye/teeth of the storm. ♦ Eyes of the potato. ♦ Finger of fate. ♦ Foot/head of the bed. ♦ Foot of the hill. ♦ Hand of bananas. ♦ Hand of cards. ♦ Hands of the clock. ♦ Head of cabbage/lettuce. ♦ Heel of the boot. ♦ Hollow of one's hand. ♦ Jaws of the vise. ♦ Lap of luxury. ♦ Leg of the journey. ♦ Lip of the jug. ♦ Mouth of the river. ♦ Neck of the bottle. ♦ Neck of the woods. ♦ Nose of the plane. ♦ Roof of the mouth. ♦ Shoulder of the road. ♦ Spine of the book. ♦ Tongue of the shoe.

Anger

An angry young man. ♦ Anger is but one short stroke from danger. ♦ Anger is never without a reason, but seldom with a good one. ♦ Count to ten when angry; your tongue is in a wet place and may slip. ♦ Foaming/ frothing at the mouth. ♦ In high dudgeon. ♦ More in sorrow than in anger. ♦ Nor say nor do that thing that anger prompts you to. ♦ Not the fastest horse can catch a word spoken in anger. [Chinese proverb.] ♦ To throw a tantrum. ♦ Whatever is begun in anger ends in shame.

Animals

Beast of burden ♦ Blind as a bat. ♦ Carrier pigeon. ♦ Cash cow. ♦ Chattering like a magpie. ♦ Cool cat. ♦ Crazy like a fox. ♦ (Crazy) old coot. ♦ Dirty bird. ♦ Dirty dog. ♦ Doe-eyed beauty. ♦ Eager beaver. ♦ Fleet as a deer. ♦ Frisky as a newborn colt. ♦ Healthy as a horse. ♦ King of beasts. ♦ Lord of the jungle. ♦ Moo cow. ♦ Meek as a lamb. ♦ Seeing eye dog. ♦ Slippery as an eel. ♦ Slow as a turtle/snail. ♦ Sly as a fox. ♦ Stool pigeon. ♦ Stubborn as a mule. ♦ To cat around. ♦ To outfox [so]. [see also Outwit] ♦ To squirrel it away. ♦ Trained seal. ♦ Ugly duckling. ♦ Weasel in the henhouse. ♦ Wise old owl. ♦ Wolf in sheep's clothing. [see Dupe, Imitation]

Announcement

All rise! ♦ Attention, please. ♦ Avast, ye swabs. ♦ Calling all cars. ♦ Hear ye, hear ye! ♦ Know ye by these presents. ♦ Look! Up in the sky! It's a bird . . . it's a plane . . . it's Superman! ♦ Make one's presence known. ♦ May we have your attention, please. ♦ Now hear this. ♦ Stand by for this important announcement. ♦ The public address system. ♦ The town crier. ♦ Throw one's hat in the ring. ♦ To come over the bitch-box/PA (system)/squawk box. ♦ To deliver an address. ♦ To establish contact with. ♦ To get in touch with [so]. ♦ To hold court. ♦ To issue an all-points bulletin. [see also Alert]

♦ To leave one's calling card. ♦ To make an announcement. ♦ To put [so] on notice. ♦ To reach out to [so]. ♦ To serve notice. ♦ To serve papers on [so]. ♦ To shout it from the rooftops. ♦ We interrupt this program for an important message. ♦ Wait'll you hear this. ♦ You wonder why I've brought you all together. ♦ Listen up.

Anonymity

A certain somebody/someone. ♦ A complete unknown. ♦ A face in the crowd. ♦ A man of mystery. ♦ A mystery man. ♦ A perfect stranger. ♦ A whatchamacallit. ♦ An old so-and-so. ♦ I'll never forget old what's-his-name? ♦ Jane/John Doe. ♦ Joe Blow. ♦ Joe Doakes. ♦ Joe Schmo. ♦ Joe Six-pack. ♦ John Q. Public. ♦ Mr. Everyman. ♦ Mr. Nobody. ♦ The Unknown Soldier. ♦ Tomb of the unknowns. ♦ Unsung heroes. ♦ Who shall remain nameless. ♦ Whoozywhatsis. ♦ You know who you are.

Anticipation

A watched pot never boils. ♦ Anticipation is often greater than realization. ♦ Couldn't you just die? ♦ Getting there is half the fun. ♦ Pulling for a full house/a royal flush/an inside straight. ♦ To await with bated breath. ♦ To be a clock-watcher. ♦ To have a funny feeling. ♦ Tune in next week. ♦ Waiting for the other shoe to drop. ♦ Waiting for the punchline. ♦ With an eye to.

Anytime

Any old day. ♦ Any (old) day of the week. ♦ Any (old) time. ♦ Any time, day or night. ♦ Anytime, anywhere. ♦ Around the clock. ♦ At all hours (of the day or night). ♦ At the time and place of one's choosing. ♦ At your convenience. ♦ On any given day. ♦ 24/7. ♦ 24/7/365. ♦ The city never sleeps. ♦ Wherever, whenever.

Anywhere

Anywhere and everywhere. ♦ East Side, West Side, all around the town. ♦ From all corners of the earth. ♦ From every walk of life. ♦ Helicopters are for people who want to fly but don't want to go anywhere. ♦ If you can make it there you can make it anywhere. ♦ On the face of the earth. ♦ This side of creation. ♦ This side of the Mississippi.

Apologies

A thousand pardons. ♦ An act of contrition. ♦ Beg pardon. ♦ Dreadfully/terribly sorry. ♦ Excuse me (for breathing). ♦ Excuse the expression. ♦ Excuse the interruption. ♦ He who excuses himself accuses himself. ♦ I beg your pardon. ♦ I meant nothing by it. ♦ My humble apologies. ♦ No offense intended. ♦ Pardon me. ♦ Pardon my French. ♦ Please forgive me. ♦ 'Scusey *moi*. ♦ Sorry about that. ♦ Sorry to say. ♦ Sorry for the interruption/intrusion. ♦ Sorry, you're not my type. ♦ Sorry I asked. ♦ (Well), excuse the hell out of me. ♦ (Well), excuse me all to hell. ♦ What can I say, after I've said I'm sorry?

Appearance
(also glamorize)

A killer view. ♦ A welcome sight. ♦ Always keep your house at its best, for the unexpected guest. ♦ Always put your best foot forward. ♦ (Always put your best foot floorward. — R.D.) ♦ Clothes make the man. ♦ (Clothes help the man make the woman! — R.D.) ♦ For appearance sake. ♦ From all indications. ♦ From all (outward) appearances. ♦ I've got an image to uphold. ♦ Good clothes open all doors. ♦ Image is everything. ♦ It's all in the presentation. ♦ It's not what it looks like. ♦ Keep the greasy side down. ♦ Keep up appearances. ♦ Looks are/can be deceiving. [see also Dupe] ♦ Looks aren't everything. ♦ Never let them see you sweat. ♦ On you it looks good. ♦ Please the eye and pick the purse.

♦ Presentation is everything. ♦ Sell the sizzle, not the steak. ♦ The cut of one's jib. ♦ The eyes are the mirror of the soul. ♦ Things are not always what they seem. (And that goes double for people! — R.D.) ♦ To avoid the appearance of impropriety. ♦ To come across (as). ♦ To make an appearance. ♦ To make an impression. ♦ To paint a glowing picture. ♦ To paper over the cracks. ♦ To see [it] in a favorable/good light. ♦ To show [it] in its best light. ♦ What is true by lamplight is not always true by sunlight. ♦ You can't judge a book by its cover. ♦ You don't get a second chance to make a first impression. ♦ You wear it well.

Apple

An apple a day keeps the doctor away. ♦ An apple for the teacher. ♦ An apple in one's stomach at bedtime lies like lead. ♦ Apple of one's eye.

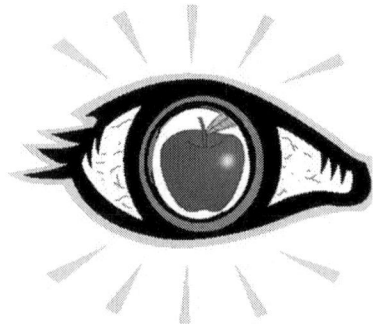

♦ He is a bad apple. ♦ How about them apples? ♦ If you don't like my apples, don't shake my tree. ♦ In apple-pie order. [see also Organize] ♦ One rotten apple spoils the whole barrel. ♦ The apple does not fall far from the tree. ♦ To be an apple-polisher. ♦ What's worse than biting into an apple and finding a worm? Biting into an apple and finding half a worm! ♦ You can't mix oranges and apples.

Appreciation

A token of appreciation. ♦ Bless your (little) heart. ♦ Customer Appreciation Day. ♦ For that good deed you deserve a star on your wand and to be called the Good Fairy. ♦ How thoughtful of you! ♦ I am forever in your debt. ♦ I can't thank you enough. ♦ I don't know how to (begin to) thank you. ♦ Many thanks. ♦ Much obliged. ♦ Really, you shouldn't have. ♦ Right neighborly of you. ♦ Thanks a bunch. ♦ Thanks a lot. ♦ Thanks a million. ♦ That really wasn't necessary. ♦ That's mighty kind of you. ♦ That's right nice of you. ♦ That's sporting/white of you. ♦ To be eternally grateful. ♦ Two, four, six, eight! Who do we appreciate? ♦ You

have my undying gratitude. ♦ You (really) shouldn't have.

Approximately

A couple o' three. ♦ Give or take (a few). ♦ As near as I can estimate/reckon. ♦ For want of a better word. ♦ In a manner of speaking. ♦ In so many words. ♦ In the ballpark. ♦ In the vicinity. ♦ More or less. ♦ Or around that. ♦ Or so. ♦ Or thereabouts. [see also Almost] ♦ Plus or minus (a couple). ♦ To a greater or lesser degree/extent. ♦ Yay many.

Apt

A good/perfect fit. ♦ All in good season. ♦ Age-appropriate. ♦ An opportune time. ♦ Custom made. ♦ Don't cast your pearls before swine. ♦ Good and proper. ♦ If the shoe fits, wear it. ♦ In order. ♦ Just so. ♦ Just my cup of tea. ♦ Just the ticket. ♦ Just what I need (ed). ♦ Just what the doctor ordered. ♦ Made to order. ♦ Render to Caesar the things which are Caesar's. ♦ Right up one's alley. ♦ Suit the action to the word, the word to the action. ♦ Suited to a T. ♦ Sweets to the sweet. ♦ That suits me (just) fine. ♦ The right man comes at the right time. ♦ The very thing. ♦ There's a time and a place for everything. ♦ Timing is everything in life. ♦ To be age-appropriate. ♦ To be ideally suited. ♦ To do [it] justice. ♦ To do justice (to). ♦ To fill/fit the bill. ♦ To fit like a glove. ♦ To fit like a second skin. ♦ To lend itself to. ♦ To suit one to a "T."

Armed

A lean, mean fighting machine. ♦ Armed and dangerous. ♦ Armed conflict. ♦ Armed to the teeth. ♦ In full battle regalia. ♦ Forewarned is forearmed. [see also Caution] ♦ Live ammo. ♦ Loaded for bear. ♦ Locked and loaded. ♦ Pistol-Packin' Mama. ♦ Thrice armed is he who knows his cause is just. ♦ To arm oneself. ♦ To be packing. ♦ To be packing heat/iron. ♦ To be trigger happy. ♦ To have an itchy trigger finger. ♦ To take up arms.

Arrival

A public appearance. ♦ Arrive alive. ♦ Here come(s) the judge. ♦ Look what the cat dragged in. ♦ Lookie, lookie, here comes Cookie. [see also Discovery] ♦ Make an appearance. ♦ Make the scene. ♦ To rear its ugly head. [see also Happen] ♦ Show one's face. ♦ To appear in public. ♦ To blow into town. ♦ To burst onto the national scene. ♦ To come a-calling. ♦ To come calling. ♦ To make an entrance. ♦ To show up. ♦ To show up on one's doorstep. ♦ Visits always give pleasure—if not the arrival, the departure.

Arrogance

A know-it-all. ♦ A smart Alec. ♦ A wiseass. ♦ A wisenheimer. ♦ Arrogance diminishes wisdom. ♦ Cruisin' for a bruise. ♦ Don't let it go to your head. ♦ He thinks he's all that. ♦ He thinks that his *ss weighs a ton. ♦ If you walk with your head held high, you will never find lost coins in the street. ♦ Smartass: an intelligent donkey. ♦ Smarty-pants. ♦ Spoiling for a fight. ♦ To be a legend in his own mind. ♦ To be a smartass. ♦ To be high and mighty. ♦ To be stuck up. ♦ To be too [adj.] for one's own good. ♦ To get on one's high horse. ♦ To grab hold of God's balls. ♦ To have a big/swelled head. ♦ To have a chip on one's shoulder. ♦ To have a lot of cheek. ♦ To have an in-your-face attitude. ♦ To have one's *ss upon one's shoulders. ♦ To let it go to your head. ♦ To look down one's nose (at). ♦ To think the world owes you a living. ♦ Too big for one's boots/britches. ♦ Who do you think you are? Anyhow? ♦ Who do you think you are, king Tut?

Ass

An ass calls another "long ears." ♦ An ass between two haystacks starves. ♦ An ass will deny more in an hour than a hundred philosophers. ♦ Ask an ass and you're bound to get a bray. ♦ Every ass likes to hear himself bray. ♦ He who makes an ass of himself must not take it ill if men ride him. — R.D. ♦ Jawbone of an ass. ♦ Never assume: it makes an ass out of u and me. ♦ Not every ass has long ears. ♦ The ass that brays the most eats the least.

Assault

(also beat, injure, whip)

Give a knuckle sandwich. ♦ Grab by the scruff of the neck. ♦ Give 'em the old one-two. ♦ To beat [so] within an inch of his/her life. ♦ To beat/kick the (living) crap/daylights/sh*t/tar out of [so]. ♦ To beat [so] like a drum. ♦ To beat [so] up. ♦ To beat the pants off [so]. ♦ To box [so]'s ears. ♦ To do bodily harm to. ♦ To get/give a sound drubbing. ♦ To go on the attack. ♦ To hand [so] his/her head. ♦ To hit/smack/whack/ whomp [so] upside the head. ♦ To kick the (living) sh*t out of [so]. ♦ To knock [so]'s block off. ♦ To mop/wipe the floor with [so]. ♦ To pin [so]'s ears back. ♦ To skin [so] alive. ♦ To take after [so] with a [n.]. ♦ To take a pot shot (at). ♦ To tan [so]'s hide. ♦ To whale the tar out of [so]. ♦ To work [so] over. ♦ To wring [so]'s neck.

Association

(also affiliation, company, insepara-bility, togetherness)

A get-together. ♦ A meet and greet. ♦ A necessary evil. ♦ A package deal. ♦ A spelling bee. ♦ A standing member. ♦ A sweat lodge. ♦ Any club that would have me, I wouldn't want to belong to. ♦ All together now. ♦ All told. ♦ All in a heap like Satan sent the sixpence. ♦ An *omnium gatherum*. ♦ At a/one clip. ♦ Birds of a feather flock together. ♦ Band of brothers. ♦ Brothers in arms. ♦ Class reunion. ♦ Come on in; the water's fine. ♦ Dearly beloved, we are gathered here. ♦ Engaged to be married. ♦ Every path hath a puddle. ♦ Free association. ♦ Gather round the campfire, boys and girls. ♦ Going steady. ♦ Guilt by association. ♦ Honey is sweet but the bee stings. ♦ If you lie down with dogs, you'll get up with fleas. ♦ If you walk with the lame, you may begin to limp. ♦ In a committed relationship. ♦ Into each life a little rain must fall. ♦ It comes/goes with the territory. ♦ Join the Navy and ride the waves. ♦ Joined at the hip. ♦ Keeping company. ♦ Love me, love my dog. ♦ Members only. ♦

Misery loves company. ◆ Mixed emotions: when your mother-in-law drives your new Cadillac off a cliff. ◆ Part and parcel (of). ◆ Seeing someone (at the moment). ◆ The pleasure of your company. ◆ There are good and bad in every race. ◆ There are pros and cons to everything. ◆ They came/gathered from near and far. ◆ To be in good company. ◆ To be in league (with). ◆ To be painted/ tarred with the same brush. ◆ To fall/get in with the wrong crowd. ◆ To form an alliance/association. ◆ To hold hands. ◆ To keep company (with). ◆ To keep [so] company. ◆ To put one's arm around. ◆ To rub elbows/shoulders with. ◆ To run with the pack. ◆ To team up with. ◆ Two's company; three's a crowd. ◆ We are as good as company any day. ◆ Welcome to the club. ◆ You are known by the company you keep. ◆ You can judge a man by the company he keeps. ◆ (You can judge a man by the company that keeps him. — R.D.) ◆ You have to take the bad with the good. * ◆ You have to take the bitter with the sweet. *[see also Forbearance]

Assurance

As God is my witness. ◆ As sure as I'm standing here talking to you. ◆ As sure as night follows day. ◆ Assurance is two-thirds success. ◆ Believe it or not. ◆ Believe (you) me. ◆ Fifty million Frenchmen can't be wrong. ◆ Honest Injun. ◆ Honest to God. ◆ Honest to goodness. ◆ Honest to Pete. ◆ I cheat you not. ◆ I kid you not. ◆ I raise my right hand to God. ◆ I sh*t you not. ◆ I swear on my mother. ◆ I swear to God. ◆ I'll stake my reputation on it. ◆ It can't miss. ◆ It's a sure thing. ◆ It's like money in the bank. ◆ Never fear, [n.] is here. ◆ Not to worry. ◆ On my word of honor. ◆ Or your money back. ◆ Rest assured. ◆ So help me, God. ◆ Take it from one who knows. ◆ To allay one's fears. ◆ To put/set one's mind at ease. ◆ The check is in the mail. ◆ To swear by all that's holy. ◆ To swear on a stack of Bibles.

◆ Trust me on this one. ◆ Would I kid you? ◆ Would I sh*t you? ◆ Yes, Virginia, there is a Santa Claus. ◆ You bet your life. ◆ You can bank/count/

depend/make book on it. ◆ You can take it/that to the bank. ◆ (You can) take it from me. ◆ You can't go wrong. ◆ You have my (solemn) word.

Astonishment

(also exasperation, surprise)

A small wonder. ◆ A wow factor. ◆ As I live and breathe. ◆ Bless my bones/soul. ◆ By cracky. ◆ By gar. ◆ By God. ◆ By golly. ◆ By gosh. ◆ By gosh and by golly. ◆ By gum. ◆ By Jove's beard. ◆ Close your eyes and open your mouth. ◆ Dagnabit. ◆ Egad! ◆ Eyes as wide as saucers. ◆ Eyes bug out. ◆ For crying out loud. [see also Dismay] ◆ Forget about it. ◆ For God's/Pete's /pity's sake. ◆ For the love of God/Pete. ◆ Gadzooks! ◆ Gawd love a duck. ◆ Gee whiz. ◆ Golly gee whillikers/ whiskers/whittakers. ◆ Golly gee whiz. ◆ Good God. ◆ Good gosh (almighty). ◆ Good golly, Miss Molly. ◆ Good grief (Charlie Brown). ◆ Gosh awrooty. ◆ Great balls of fire. ◆ Great gobs of goose grease. ◆ Great day in the morning. ◆ Great God almighty. ◆ Great golly gee. ◆ Great guns! ◆ Heavens to Betsy. ◆ Holy cannoli/cow/crap/God/ guacamole/Hannah!/Jesus/mackerel/moley/Moses/Savannah/sh*t!/smoke/Toledo. ◆ Holy mackell, Andy. ◆ I swanee! ◆ I swow! ◆ I wouldn't've believed it if I didn't see it (with my own eyes). ◆ I'll be a dirty bird. ◆ In a state of (total) shock. ◆ It blows my mind. ◆ It never ceases to amaze me. ◆ Jesus, Mary and Joseph. ◆ Jiminy crickets ◆ Jiminy split. ◆ Jumping Jehosephat ◆ Jumping Jesus. ◆ Jumping jimminy. ◆ Knock/throw [so] for a loop. ◆ Land o'goshen. ◆ Land sakes alive. ◆ Leaping lizards. ◆ Man alive! ◆ Man oh man! ◆ Mercy me. ◆ Mother of mercy. ◆ Mouth agape. ◆ My everlovin' *ss! ◆ Never in all my born days. ◆ Never in all my years. ◆ Of all things. ◆ Oh, my. ◆ Oh, (my) God. ◆ Never saw it coming. ◆ Swanee to goodness! ◆ Tarnation and thunderation. ◆ That does it. ◆ That takes the cake. ◆ To be all eyes. ◆ To be taken aback. ◆ To drop a bombshell. ◆ To set [so] back on his/her haunches/heels. ◆ What in the Sam Hill. ◆ What to my wondering eyes did appear. ◆ Well, butter my butt and call me a biscuit. ◆ Well, what do you know! ◆ What a pleasant surprise. ◆ What do you know about that! ◆ Will wonders never cease? ◆ Wonder of wonders. ◆ You could not pick my jaw up off the floor with a shovel. ◆ You had to be there. ◆ You'll never guess what/who I saw (today).

Attack

A banzai attack. [see also Suicide, Surprise] ◆ A clenched fist. ◆ A full frontal assault/attack. ◆ A hail of bullets/gunfire. ◆ A Parthian shot. ◆ A parting shot. ◆ A preemptive strike. ◆ A punch in the mouth. ◆ A shot in the breadbasket. ◆ A surprise attack. ◆ Aim to maim. ◆ An unprovoked attack. ◆ Bring out/up the big guns. ◆ Cut to the quick. ◆ Get one's licks in. ◆ Go for the jugular. ◆ Go for the nuts. ◆ Go for the soft underbelly. ◆ Hit them where they live. ◆ Hit them with all you've got. ◆ Leap into the fray. ◆ Let 'em have it with both barrels. ◆ Storm the Bastille/ palace/ramparts. ◆ Throw a haymaker/roundhouse. ◆ Throw a sucker punch. ◆ Throw in the heavy artillery. ◆ To ambush/dry gulch [so]. [see also Surprise] ◆ To be/get in [so]'s face. ◆ To be under attack. ◆ To bean [so]. ◆ To beat/cuff/cudgel [so] about the head. ◆ To bitch-slap. ◆ To bring to bear. [see also Action] ◆ To cold-cock [so]. ◆ To come after/go after [so]. ◆ To cut [n.]/[p.] off at the knees. [see also Rescue] ◆ To deliver a knockout blow. ◆ To draw (the first) blood. ◆ To fire a broadside. ◆ To go on the attack. ◆ To kick [so] to the curb. [see also Abandonment] ◆ To land/throw a punch. ◆ To lash out (at). ◆ To leap into the breach. ◆ To lay/light into [so]. ◆ To make an attempt on one's life. ◆ To open fire. ◆ To paste [so] in the mouth. ◆ To pick a fight/quarrel. ◆ To punch [so] out. ◆ To step on [so]'s toes. ◆ To strike a blow. ◆ To strike the first blow. ◆ To take a poke/swing at [so]. ◆ To take potshots at [so]. ◆ To throw the first punch. ◆ To throw one's Sunday punch. ◆ To whale away. ◆ You really know how to hurt a guy, don't you? ◆ With guns blazing.

Attitude

An attitude adjustment. ◆ As is our confidence, so is our capacity. ◆ Check/leave your attitude at the door. ◆ I think I can; I think I can; I think I can. ◆ If you think you're beaten, you are. ◆ In the right frame of mind. ◆ It's all in your mind. ◆ Mind over matter. ◆ The little engine that could. ◆ To cop an attitude. [see also Oppose] ◆ To exercise (tremendous) willpower. ◆ To have a negative/positive attitude. ◆ You can if you think you can. ◆ You have some 'tude on you, dude.

Attraction

A fatal attraction. ◆ A (good) drawing card. ◆ A magnetic personality. ◆ Animal magnetism. ◆ Drawn like bees to honey. ◆ It brings out the animal in me. ◆ Like a moth to a flame.

♦ Like flies to meadow muffins. ♦ Opposites attract. ♦ The call of the wild. ♦ To go for [it] (in a big way). ♦ To gravitate towards [it]/[so]. ♦ To rear back on one's hind legs.

Attractive
(also cute)

A dapper Dan. ♦ A feast for the eyes. ♦ A head-turner. ♦ A knockout. ♦ A (real) cutie-pie. ♦ A show-stopper. ♦ A sight for sore eyes. ♦ A sight for sore eyes is never an eyesore. – R.D. ♦ A vision of loveliness. ♦ An eye-opener. ♦ Are there any more at home like you? ♦ Cute as a bug/button. ♦ Cute as a bug's/hog's ear. ♦ Cute as a cootie. ♦ Cute as a speckled pup. ♦ Don't get cute with me. ♦ Drop-dead gorgeous. ♦ Easy on the eyes. ♦ Gee, you're cute when you're mad. ♦ He/she can park his/her shoes under my bed anytime. ♦ I'd let her/him eat crackers in my bed any day. ♦ I wouldn't throw her/him out of bed. ♦ Looking good. ♦ Looks good enough to eat. [see also Temptation] ♦ Movie-star handsome/pretty. ♦ Pretty as a picture. ♦ Pretty as you please. ♦ Take the scenic route. ♦ To catch one's eye. ♦ To cut a dashing figure. ♦ To have curb appeal. ♦ To have drool appeal. ♦ To have sex appeal. ♦ To make a good (first) impression. ♦ To turn heads. ♦ You ought to be in pictures.

Authority

A father figure. ♦ By the authority/ power vested in me ♦ Smokey the Bear. ♦ The cop on the beat. ♦ The cop on the corner. ♦ The landed gentry. ♦ The powers that be. ♦ The privileged few. ♦ The proper authorities. ♦ The pushiest people often wind up with the most pull. ♦ The town fathers. ♦ Those in high places. ♦ To be an authority on (the subject). ♦ To carry a lot of weight. ♦ To have a lot of pull. ♦ To have clout. ♦ To have it on good authority. ♦ To have street cred.

Available

A roadside stand. ♦ Anything's for sale—at the right price. — Dominick P. Delia ♦ At hand. ♦ At one's beck and call/disposal/fingertips. ♦ Buy or lease. ♦ Everything has its price. ♦ Everything must go. ♦ Fire sale. ♦ On hand. ♦ On the agenda. ♦ On the (auction) block. ♦ On the docket. ♦ On the market. ♦ On the menu. ♦ There for the taking. ♦ To go begging. ♦ To go under the gavel/hammer. ♦ To put up stock. ♦ Up for grabs. ♦ Within (easy) reach. ♦ Yours for the asking/taking.

Avoid

A hands-off policy. ♦ At a remove from. ♦ At arm's length. ♦ Do not disturb.

♦ Don't fix what ain't broke. (also, If it ain't broke don't fix it.) ♦ Don't go there. ♦ Don't start that (business/ stuff) again. ♦ Have no truck with. ♦ I don't want to get involved. ♦ Keep a respectful distance. ♦ *Laissez faire.* ♦ Leave/let well enough alone. ♦ Leave me out of this. ♦ Let sleeping dogs lie. ♦ Let's not get into/talk about that. ♦ Make a hole! ♦ Never kick a fresh dog turd around on a hot day. [Harry Truman's philosophy of life] ♦ To avoid [it] like the plague. ♦ To distance oneself (from). ♦ To dodge the bullet. ♦ To dodge the issue/ question. ♦ To get/keep out of the way. ♦ To give a wide berth (to). ♦ To go over [so]'s head. ♦ To leave/ let [it] alone/be. ♦ To make way. ♦ To shy away (from). [see also Oppose] ♦ To steer clear (of). ♦ To step aside. ♦ To studiously avoid. ♦ To ward off. ♦ To wave off. ♦ Wouldn't touch it with a ten-foot pole.

Bachelorhood

(see also Womanize)

A bachelor pad. ♦ A bachelor party. ♦ A confirmed bachelor. ♦ A gay blade. ♦ A lewd bachelor makes a jealous husband. ♦ A pick-up line. ♦ Alas and alack, to be lacking a lass. ♦ Chasing pony tails has made a horse's *ss of many a man. — R.D. ♦ Do you come here often? ♦ Excuse me, is this your handkerchief? ♦ Going steady—with Ex-Lax. ♦ Had any lately? ♦ He thinks he's God's gift to women. ♦ It's not like we're losing a daughter; we're gaining a son. ♦ Man about town. ♦ Man of the world. ♦ May I ask you a personal question? ♦ Mr. Right. ♦ Pardon me, miss, your slip is showing. ♦ The time I've lost in wooing, in finding and pursuing, the light that lies in women's eyes has been my heart's undoing. ♦ To come onto a girl. ♦ What're you doing New Years? ♦ What's a nice girl like you doing in a place like this? ♦ Where have you been all my life? ♦ Why bring a ham sandwich to a banquet? ♦ Why buy the boar/pig when all you want is a little sausage? [bachelorette's version] ♦ Why buy the cow when milk is so cheap? ♦ Why buy the cow when you can get the milk for free?

Bald

A bald eagle. ♦ A bald head is soon shaved. ♦ A bald-faced lie. ♦ Bald as a billiard. ♦ Bald as a billiard ball/ cueball. ♦ Bald men are sexier. ♦ I'm not bald; I'm just taller than my hair. ♦ Said one bald-headed man to the other, "Let's put our heads together and make an *ss of ourselves." ♦ Seize opportunity by the beard, for it is bald behind. ♦ To look like a plucked chicken.

Beauty

A beauty queen. ♦ A long-stemmed, American beauty rose. ♦ A raving beauty. ♦ A thing of beauty is a joy forever. ♦ Age before beauty. ♦ Beauty is as beauty does. ♦ Beauty is in the eye of the beholder. ♦ Beauty is only skin deep. ♦ Beauty without character is nothing but a morning glory faded at noon; character without beauty is a hardy perennial. ♦ Black beauty. ♦ Black is beautiful. ♦ Handsome is as handsome does. ♦ High, wide and handsome. ♦ Oh, beautiful, for spacious skies. ♦ Queen of the hop. ♦ That's the beauty part (of it). ♦ The face that launched a thousand ships.

Begin

A fresh start. ♦ A good beginning makes a good ending.—[English saying] ♦ A new beginning. ♦ Anchors aweigh. ♦ And so it begins. ♦ And thereby hangs a tale. ♦ And they're off! ♦ Begin at the beginning. ♦ Begin today what you'd do tomorrow. ♦ Call the meeting to order. ♦ Court is now in session. ♦ For openers. ♦ From day one/the word go. ♦ Game on. ♦ Get it off the ground. ♦ Get off on the right foot. ♦ Get off to a jackrabbit start. ♦ Get the ball rolling. ♦ Get the show on the road. ♦ Good morning, Glory (what's your story?). ♦ Ground-breaking ceremony. ♦ He who begins many things finishes but few. – [Italian saying] ♦ Heigh yo, Silver, away! ♦ Hit the deck/ground running. ♦ I have not yet begun to fight. ♦ I'm just hitting my stride. ♦ In the beginning was the Word. ♦ In the first place. ♦ In the formative stages. ♦ Just getting warmed up. ♦ Kick things off. ♦ Let 'er/it rip. ♦ Let the games begin. ♦ Life begins at forty. ♦ Off to a rocky start. ♦ Off to the races. ♦ On the count of three: one . . . two . . . ♦ Once begun, it's half done. ♦ Once upon a time. ♦ One for the money, two for the show, three to get ready, four to go! ♦ Off to a flying start. ♦ On your mark, (get) set, go! ♦ Opening ceremonies. ♦ Opening night. ♦ Plunge in with both feet. ♦ Ready, set, go! ♦ Right off the bat.

♦ Right from the get-go/the hit/the start. ♦ Right out of the gate. ♦ Rise and shine. ♦ Spring has sprung. ♦ Strike up the band. [see also Music] ♦ That's good, for openers. ♦ The battle is joined. ♦ The Big Bang theory. ♦ The inaugural address. ♦ The kickoff. ♦ The longest journey begins with a single step. ♦ The man who moves mountains begins by carrying away small stones. ♦ The opening bell. ♦ The opening salvo. ♦ The point of entry. ♦ To advance a hypothesis/proposition/theory. ♦ To begin with. ♦ To bring [it]/[so] into the world. ♦ To burst onto the scene. ♦ To come into play. ♦ To come out fighting/swinging. ♦ To come out with guns blazing. ♦ To crank up. ♦ To dive in head first. ♦ To get going. ♦ To get it on. ♦ To get off to a false start. ♦ To get one's rear in gear. ♦ To go into business. ♦ To go into/take effect. ♦ To let the genie out of the bottle. ♦ To make a grand entrance. ♦ To make/take a headlong plunge. ♦ To make the first move. ♦ To open the floodgates. ♦ To put [it] into effect/practice. ♦ To set out (to). ♦ To shove off/tee off/weigh anchor. ♦ To (make a) start. ♦ To start off/start up. ♦ To strike out (on).

♦ Well begun is half done. ♦ You have to crawl before you can walk. ♦ You've gotta start somewhere.

Behavior

A moral imperative. ♦ Be a good boy/girl for daddy/ mommy. ♦ Be on one's best behavior. ♦ Clean up one's act. ♦ Fall in line. ♦ Follow the crowd. ♦ Get a life. ♦ Get one's act/sh*t together [see also Organize]. ♦ Hear no evil; see no evil; speak no evil. ♦ I can't take you anyplace. ♦ Is that any way to run an airline? ♦ Keep one's nose clean. ♦ Mind one's manners. ♦ Pay one's respects. ♦ Play it the company way. ♦ Pull oneself together. ♦ Remain above the fray. ♦ Shape up or ship out. ♦ Show common courtesy. ♦ Straighten up and fly right. ♦ Time off for good behavior. ♦ To be a model citizen. ♦ To be straight-arrow. ♦ To behave oneself. ♦ To calm down. ♦ To change one's ways. ♦ To exercise self-control/willpower. ♦ To get a grip (on oneself). ♦ To get in/into shape. ♦ To get one's head on straight. ♦ To get oneself together. ♦ To go straight. ♦ To kick a/the habit. ♦ To mend one's ways. ♦ To mind one's Ps and Qs. ♦ To set a good example. ♦ To toe the line/mark. ♦ To toe the party line. ♦

To walk the straight and narrow. ♦ When he/she was good, he/she was very, very good.

Behind

At the tail end (of). ♦ Behind schedule. ♦ Behind the times. ♦ In arrears. ♦ Like a donkey's tail—always behind. ♦ Past due. ♦ Playing catch-up ball. ♦ Running from behind. ♦ The line forms to the rear. ♦ The trailing edge. ♦ To bring up the rear. ♦ To close/narrow the gap. ♦ To fall behind. ♦ To come in/finish dead last. ♦ To be in/fall into arrears. ♦ To have a lot of catching up to do. ♦ To make up for lost time. ♦ To suck hind tit/titty.

Belief

A firm believer. ♦ Believe only half of what you see and nothing of what you hear. ♦ Believe that and I'll tell you another one. ♦ Believe (you) me. ♦ Don't believe everything you hear/read/see. ♦ Give [so] the benefit of the doubt. ♦ I'll take your word for it. [see also Acceptance] ♦ Lend credence to. ♦ Put stock in. ♦ Seeing is believing. ♦ Take my word for it. ♦ To have every reason to believe. ♦ To make a believer (out) of [so]. ♦ To set store by. ♦ To take [it] at face value.

♦ To take [so] at his/her word. ♦ To take [so]'s word for it. ♦ Would I lie to you?

Best

(also superiority)

A cover story. [see also Alibi, Conceal] ♦ A cut above (the rest). ♦ A force to be reckoned with. ♦ A plum assignment. ♦ A *tour de force.* ♦ A work of art. ♦ A world-beater. ♦ All others pale by comparison. ♦ All that/this and more. ♦ At a premium ♦ At the peak of perfection. [see also Superlatives] ♦ At the top of one's game. [see also Excel] ♦ Best bar none. ♦ Best by far. ♦ Best in show. ♦ Better by far. ♦ Better than a poke in the eye with a sharp stick. ♦ Can't beat it (with a stick). ♦ Couldn't be better. ♦ Far and away the best. ♦ He/she ain't got nothing on you. ♦ Head and shoulders above the rest. ♦ In a class by itself. ♦ In full bloom/flower. ♦ In top form. ♦ Light years ahead. ♦ Look no further. [see also Win] ♦ Nothing short of sensational. ♦ On one's game. ♦ One of the all-time greats. ♦ Passed him like he was standing still. ♦ Right up there with the best of them. ♦ Second to none. ♦ Takes a back seat to no one. ♦ The be-all-and-end-all. ♦ The best of the best. ♦ The best of the west. ♦ The best that ever came down the pike. ♦ The cream of the crop. ♦ The *creme de la creme.* ♦ The Eighth Wonder of the World. ♦ The feature attraction. ♦ The finer things in life. ♦ The gold standard. ♦ The great grandaddy of them all. ♦ The greatest invention since the wheel. ♦ The greatest thing since sliced bread. ♦ The high water mark. ♦ The main event. ♦ The mother of all [n.]. ♦ The *piece d' resistance.* ♦ The quintessential [n.]. ♦ To be a [n.] and a half. ♦ To beat [it]/[so] by a country mile. ♦ To break all records. ♦ To break/ hold the record. ♦ To have perfect pitch. ♦ To hit one's stride. ♦ To leave the others at the starting gate/in the dust. ♦ To make others look sick/pale (by comparison). ♦ To run circles/rings around (all others). ♦ To save the best for last. ♦ To take precedence. ♦ To tower over. ♦ Top drawer/echelon/shelf. ♦ Top of the line. Topnotch. ♦ Who could ask for anything more? ♦ You couldn't ask for more.

Bet

A friendly bet. ♦ A small wager. ♦ Bet you a dollar to a donut. ♦ Double or nothing. ♦ Even money. ♦ Five will get you ten. ♦ How much do you want to bet? ♦ I'll bet you any amount of money. ♦ Lay you ten to one (odds). ♦ To make book on. ♦ Wanna bet? ♦ Wanna lay some money on it? ♦ Would you care to make a (small) wager on it/that? ♦ You (can) bet your bottom dollar. ♦ Your best bet. [see also Choices]

Betray

A dastardly act. ♦ A turncoat. ♦ Betray a confidence. ♦ Break ranks (with). ♦ *Et tu,* Brute? ♦ High treason. ♦ Play ball with us and we'll stick the bat up your *ss. ♦ Stick it to [so]. ♦ The Stockholm Syndrome. ♦ To cross party lines. [see also Vote] ♦ To cross someone up. ♦ To do [so] wrong. ♦ To doublecross. ♦ To fraternize with the enemy. ♦ To go rogue. ♦ To sell [it] out from under [so]. ♦ To stab [so] in the back. ♦ To sell [so] out. ♦ To sell [so] down the river. ♦ To throw [so] to the lions/under the bus. ♦ To two-time [so]. ♦ Toss to the wolves. ♦ Twin crucifix: double cross.

Big
(also mostly, roomy)

All wool and a yard wide. ♦ Beyond measure. ♦ Big as a house. ♦ Big as all outdoors. ♦ Big shoes to fill. ♦ By (sheer) force/weight of numbers. ♦ Go big or go home. ♦ In large measure. ♦ Is it bigger than a bread box? [see also Question] ♦ It's humongous.

♦ Of epic/ staggering proportions. ♦ Of the highest order. ♦ Of this magnitude. ♦ On a grand scale. ♦ The large economy size. ♦ The lion's share. ♦ The majority rules. ♦ The wide open spaces. ♦ Think big. ♦ To have breathing room/elbow room/ wiggle room. ♦ We can't fight it; it's bigger than both of us. ♦ With room to spare. ♦ You could drive a Mack truck through there.

Birth

A Caesarian birth. ♦ A C-section. ♦ And baby makes three. ♦ Another mouth to feed. ♦ Baby on board. ♦ Born to be wild. ♦ Break out the cigars. ♦ It's a boy! ♦ It's a girl! ♦ Leaders are not made, they're born. ♦ Man born of woman. ♦ The blessed event. ♦ The kicking is always hardest before the birth. ♦ The miracle of creation. ♦ To come into the world. ♦ To give birth (to). ♦ To have a baby. ♦ Yessir, that's my baby.

Blab
(also confess)

A blabbermouth. ♦ A dirty rat fink. ♦ A snitch/stool pigeon. ♦ A tell-all book. ♦ A whistleblower. ♦ Bear witness. ♦ Blow the whistle (on). ♦ By one's own admission. ♦ Claim responsibility. ♦ Confession is good for the soul. ♦ Face the music. ♦ For a good time, call this number. ♦ I'll tell teacher on you. ♦ Insider information. ♦ Kiss and tell. ♦ Let the cat out of the bag. ♦ Make a Freudian slip. ♦ Make a slip of the tongue. ♦ Me and my big mouth. ♦ Sing like a bird. ♦ Spill the beans. ♦ Talk out of turn. ♦ To air one's dirty laundry (in public). ♦ To bare one's soul. ♦ To be a tattletale. ♦ To blurt it out. ♦ To break one's silence. ♦ To call the cops/police. ♦ To carry/tell tales (out of school). ♦ To clue [so] in (on). ♦ To come clean. ♦ To drop a dime on [so]. ♦ To get it off one's chest. [see also Confide] ♦ To have a big mouth. ♦ To let [so] in on [it]. ♦ To fink/ rat/squeal on [so]. ♦ To flap one's yap. ♦ To kiss and tell. ♦ To make a clean breast of [it]. ♦ To make a (full) confession. ♦ To name names. ♦ To open one's big (f*cking) yap. ♦ To "out" [so]. ♦ To own up (to). ♦ To put one's foot in it/in one's mouth. ♦ To rat [so] out. ♦ To spill one's guts. ♦ To talk out of turn. [see also Outspoken] ♦ To tell on [so]. ♦ To turn state's evidence. ♦ To turn [so] in.

Blame

By one's own admission. ♦ If you're going to get the blame, you may as well get the gain. ♦ If I'm going to go to jail for stealing, it'll be for something big. ♦ In for a penny, in for a pound. ♦ It wasn't me nor Albert, it might have been Sally. ♦ It's on her/him/me/you/them. ♦ Might as well be hanged for the sheep as for the lamb. ♦ Penetration, however, slight, is sufficient to complete the offense. [Uniform Code of Military Justice] ♦ The butler did it. ♦ To be the fall guy. ♦ To be the scapegoat. ♦ To be to blame (for). ♦ To claim/take responsibility (for). ♦ To 'fess up. ♦ To hold [it] over [so]'s head. ♦ To hold [so] accountable. ♦ To lay the blame at [so]'s doorstep. ♦ To lay the blame on. ♦ To own up to. ♦ To pin something on [so]. ♦ To point the accusing finger (at). ♦ To put the blame where it belongs. ♦ To take the blame/fall/rap (for). ♦ To take responsibility for. ♦ To play patsy.

Bonus

A baker's dozen. ♦ A bargain at twice the price. ♦ A chaser. ♦ A double dip. ♦ A doubleheader. ♦ A double whammy. ♦ A double-edged sword. ♦ A kicker. ♦ A little bit on the side. ♦ A [n.] and a half. ♦ A rich man's problem. [see also Advantage] ♦ A second helping. ♦ A twin bill. ♦ A two-fer. ♦ All that—and more! ♦ An added attraction. ♦ And furthermore. ♦ And on top of that. ♦ And one for good measure. ♦ And one for the pot. ♦ And one to grow on. ♦ And then some. ♦ As if that weren't enough. ♦ As well. ♦ At that. ♦ BOGO (Buy One Get One). ♦ But wait! There's more! ♦ Double dipping. ♦ Get the best of both worlds. ♦ In addition. ♦ In the bargain. ♦ Kill two birds with one stone.

♦ Make it a double. ♦ More bang for the buck. ♦ More than one bargained for. ♦ Not to mention. ♦ On top of everything else. ♦ So much the better. ♦ Take two, they're small. ♦ The frosting/icing on the cake. ♦ The gift that keeps on giving. ♦ There's always room for one more. ♦ To be double-jointed. ♦ To boot. ♦ To double up. ♦ To draw flight skins. [military] ♦ To get hazardous duty pay. ♦ To get paid double time/ overtime/time and a half. ♦ To get two bites (out) of the apple. ♦ To go back for more/seconds. ♦ To go into overtime. ♦ To go (you) one better. ♦ To have it both ways. ♦ To have the best of both worlds. ♦ To have two strings to one's bow. ♦ To say nothing of. ♦ To sweeten the kitty/pot. ♦ To throw [it] in (for free). ♦ Twice as nice at half the price. ♦ Two for the price of one. ♦ What do you want? Egg in your beer? ♦ What's more. ♦ With interest.

Bore
(also blasé, monotonous)

A crashing bore. ♦ A Johnnie one-note. ♦ A long, drawn-out affair. ♦ A mind like a locomotive: one-track. – R.D. ♦ A one-hit wonder. ♦ A one-trick pony. ♦ A party pooper. [see also Disappointment] ♦ A real stiff. ♦ A wet blanket. ♦ A yawn is at least an honest opinion. ♦ *Ad nauseam.* ♦ As exciting as watching grass grow. ♦ As exciting/thrilling as watching paint dry. ♦ Been there, done that. ♦ Bored out of one's gourd. ♦ Bored stiff. ♦ Bored to death/distraction/tears. ♦ Cast a jaundiced eye (on). ♦ Does nothing but eat, sleep and breathe. ♦ Dull as dishwater. ♦ Have a one-track mind. ♦ He who is bored easily is a bore. ♦ I've seen it all. ♦ In a rut. ♦ Is there no end? ♦ It's all been done before. ♦ It's been done. ♦ It's been done to death. ♦ It's *déjà vu* all over again. ♦ I've heard it all before. ♦ Kilroy was here. ♦ Like a bump on a log. ♦ Limp as a dishrag. ♦ Same old, same old. ♦ Same old sh*t/stuff. ♦ Same old song and dance. [see also Dance] ♦ Show me a beautiful woman and I'll show you a guy who's tired of f*cking her. ♦

Sick and tired. ♦ Sick and tired of being sick and tired. ♦ (So) what else is new? [see also News] ♦ Tell me something I don't know. ♦ The daily grind. ♦ The man whose life is an open book makes dull reading. ♦ The rat race. ♦ The thrill is gone. ♦ There are no boring subjects; only boring writers. ♦ To be a(n) (old) stick in the mud. ♦ To belabor the point. ♦ To sound like a broken record. ♦ To stare at the four walls. ♦ You're no fun anymore. ♦ What a drag. ♦ What did you take up in college, time and space? ♦ Wake me (up) when it's over. ♦ Will this never end? ♦ World weary.

Borrow

A two-bit chiseler. ♦ Borrowed interest. ♦ If borrowing was good, every man would lend out his wife. ♦ Living on borrowed time. ♦ May I borrow a cup of sugar? ♦ Neither a borrower nor a lender be. ♦ On the cuff. ♦ Put it on the arm. ♦ Put the arm/bite on. ♦ Something old, something new, something borrowed and something blue. ♦ To hit you up. ♦ To run up a tab.

Boss

A bigwig. ♦ A controlling interest. ♦ A czar of industry. ♦ A druglord. ♦ A kingpin. ♦ A slumlord. ♦ A straw boss.

♦ A V.I.P. (very important person). ♦ An alpha male. ♦ At the helm/wheel. ♦ At the top of the food chain. ♦ Big brass. ♦ Big Man on Campus. ♦ Boss and underboss. ♦ Boss of all bosses (*capo di tutti capi*). ♦ Brass hat. ♦ Chief cook and bottle washer. ♦ Cock of the walk. ♦ Commander-in-chief. [see also Command] ♦ Head honcho. ♦ Head of household. ♦ I may not always be right but I'm always the boss. — Dominick P. Delia ♦ In command. ♦ In the Number One slot. ♦ It's good to be king. ♦ King of the Hill. ♦ King/ruler of the roost. ♦ Large and in charge. ♦ Leader of the pack. ♦ Many a King of the Hill now lies under it. ♦ Master of all you survey. ♦ The big cheese/wheel. ♦ The big kahuna. ♦ The big/high muckety-muck/muck-a-muck/mucky-muck. ♦ The boss does not go for the water. ♦ The driving force. ♦ The first thing a smart secretary types is the boss. ♦ The lady/man of the house. ♦ To be holding all the cards. ♦ To be in (full) control. ♦ To be in charge. ♦ To be on top of the situation/things. ♦ To be one's own boss. [see also Independent] ♦ To boss [so] around. ♦ To buffalo/cow [so]. ♦ To control the purse strings. ♦ To delegate authority. ♦ To farm [it] out. ♦ To give (the) orders. ♦ To reign supreme. ♦ To rule the roost. ♦ To wear the pants (in the family). [see also Dominate] ♦ Top banana. ♦ Top brass. ♦ Top dog. ♦ Top gun. ♦ Top in one's area of expertise. ♦ What he/she says goes. ♦ Who died and left you boss? ♦ Who's minding the store? ♦ You can't play king of the hill unless there's a hill. ♦ You're not the boss of me. ♦ You're the boss.

Boys

A bouncing baby boy. ♦ A boyish grin. ♦ A mama's boy. ♦ Boys will be boys. ♦ Every man is a boy at heart. ♦ Fair-haired boy with cheeks of tan. ♦ Mama's little boy. ♦ Never send a boy to do a man's job. ♦ See what the boys in the back room will have. ♦ Snips and snails and puppy dogs' tails—that's what little boys are made of. ♦ The boy is father to the man. ♦ The only difference between a boy and a man is the price of his toys.

Brag

A b.s./bullsh*t artist. ♦ A (big) blow-hard/bag of wind/windbag. ♦ A paper tiger. ♦ A show of force. ♦ All hat and no cattle. ♦ All talk and no action. ♦ All wind and no sail. ♦ Anything you can do I can do better. ♦ Are you bragging or complaining? [riposte: I don't know whether to brag that I have nothing to complain about or complain that I have nothing to brag about. — R.D.] [see also Complain] ◆ Don't let your alligator mouth over-load your tadpole *ss. ◆ Feet of clay. ◆ From the empty well comes the loud-est echo. ◆ If we don't have it you don't need it. ◆ I'll huff and I'll puff and I'll blow your house in. ◆ Not bad, if I do say so myself. ◆ One penny in the money box makes more noise than a whole boxful. ◆ Sabre-rattling. ◆ 'Tis wise not to brag—it isn't the whistle that pulls the train. ◆ Talk is cheap. ◆ The empty barrel makes the most noise. ◆ The steam that blows the whistle doesn't move the train. ◆ To be a bullsh*t artist. ◆ To be all mouth. ◆ To blow smoke. ◆ To have bragging rights. ◆ To talk a good ballgame. ◆ To talk out of one's *ss. ◆ To talk the talk. ◆ To talk through one's hat.

Brave

(see also Courage)

A coward dies a thousand deaths; a brave man but one. ◆ A death-defy-ing feat. ◆ All bravery stands upon comparisons. ◆ Be brave, my son, and let who will be clever. ◆ Books should be no better nor braver than their authors. ◆ Brave actions never want a trumpet. ◆ Brave men and good wines last but a short time. ◆ Discretion is the better part of valor. ◆ Don't be afraid to take a big step when one is indicated: you can't cross a chasm in two small jumps. ◆ Faint heart never won fair maid. ◆ Fortune favors the bold/brave. ◆ Many brave souls are asleep in the deep. ◆ Not born in the woods to be scared by an owl. ◆ Only the brave deserve the fair. ◆ There is a fine line between brav-ery and stupidity. ◆ 'Tis more brave to live than to die. ◆ To laugh danger in the face. ◆ To take on all comers.

Brief

A day in the life. ◆ A one-liner. ◆ A quick study. ◆ A short round. ◆ A thumbnail sketch. ◆ An elevator pitch/speech. ◆ As big as a minute. ◆ Brevity is the soul of wit. ◆ If brevity is the soul of wit, the half-wit is a genius. ◆ In 25 words or less. ◆ No comment. ◆ Short and sweet. ◆ Short, sweet and to the point. ◆ Slice of life. ◆ The shorter of two words is often the better one. ◆ The true art of words: never use two when one will do! ◆ To paint with a broad brush. ◆ To say the least.

Britain

Britannia rules the waves. ◆ Britannia waives the rules. ◆ Cheerio, old chap.

♦ Dear Old Blighty. ♦ Fish and chips. ♦ Great Britain. ♦ John Bull. ♦ I say there, guv'nor. ♦ On whose dominions the sun never sets. ♦ Rule Britannia. ♦ The British are coming! ♦ The British Empire. ♦ There will always be an England. ♦ Veddy veddy British.

Bureaucracy

Go through a lot of Mickey-mouse/red tape/rigmarole. ♦ In development hell. ♦ Lost in the shuffle. [see also Confused] ♦ Make a big to-do. ♦ Make a production out of [it]. ♦ Pass it from department to department. ♦ To adhere to the letter of the law. ♦ To come across one's desk. ♦ To follow protocol. ♦ To go through (proper) channels. ♦ To jump through hoops. ♦ To kick it upstairs. ♦ To make a big megillah. ♦ To make a federal case out of it.

Burn

A case of arson. ♦ Burned to a crisp. ♦ Burst into flame. ♦ Catch (on) fire. ♦ Go up in flames/smoke. ♦ Go up like a match/kindling wood/tinder. ♦ Put a match to (it). ♦ Struck by a firebug. ♦ To crash and burn. ♦ To torch.

Business

A cottage industry. ♦ A going concern. ♦ A pleasure doing business with you. ♦ Anything is for sale at the right price. ♦ Business and pleasure don't mix. ♦ Business as usual. ♦ Business before pleasure. ♦ Business is booming. ♦ Business is business. ♦ Do a booming business. ♦ Do a land-office/landslide business. ♦ Drum up business. ♦ Everybody's business is nobody's business. ♦ Fair trade. ♦ For sale (cheap). ♦ Hang out one's shingle. ♦ High finance. ♦ In the market for. ♦ I've got a business to run here. ♦ On company time. ♦ On the Big Board. ♦ On the auction block. ♦ On the market. ♦ Shop talk. ♦ Strictly business. ♦ Supply and demand. ♦ Taking care of business. ♦ The customer is always right. ♦ The majority of the best trades are the ones not made. ♦ The open market. ♦ The principal business of life is to enjoy it. ♦ There's no business like show business. ♦ To be about my father's business. ♦ To do business (with). ♦ To get down to business. ♦ To ply one's trade. ♦ To set up shop. ♦ To take care of the business/matter/task at hand. ♦ To take one's business elsewhere. ♦ Unfinished business. ♦ You cannot mix business with pleasure.

Busy

A beehive of activity. ◆ Busier than a one-armed paperhanger (with the crabs/hives). ◆ Busier than a one-eyed cat watching two mouseholes. ◆ Busier than a one-legged man in an *ss-kicking contest. ◆ Busier than a three-legged cat in a dry sandbox. ◆ At the height of rush hour. ◆ Busy as a beaver/bee. ◆ Grass never grows on a busy street. ◆ I only have two hands. ◆ If I had any more to do, I'd stick a broom up my *ss and sweep while I'm running. ◆ It's like Grand Central Station in here. ◆ To be on the go. ◆ To be short-handed. ◆ To have a lot on one's plate. ◆ To have one's hands full. ◆ To keep oneself busy. ◆ To run one ragged. ◆ Out and about. ◆ Up and about/around/doing. ◆ Up to one's eyeballs. ◆ What's all the commotion? ◆ Where everybody goes, grass never grows.

Capability

A heavy hitter. ◆ A natural born [n.]. [see also Nature] ◆ A past master. ◆ A well-rounded individual. ◆ Capability Brown. ◆ Core competencies. ◆ Crack troops. ◆ Either you have it or you don't. ◆ Equal to the task. ◆ In capable hands. ◆ Has knowledge and know-how. ◆ He/she got game. ◆ My able assistant. ◆ My gal/guy/man Friday. ◆ Ready, willing and able. ◆ Right-hand man/right-hand woman. ◆ Some people have it, some people don't. ◆ Sure-footed as a mountain goat. ◆ The go-to gal/guy. ◆ To bat in the cleanup spot. ◆ To be good at [it]. ◆ To be in good hands. ◆ To be suited for [it]. ◆ To be thoroughly/well versed in. ◆ To be up for anything. ◆ To be up for [it]. ◆ To have a command of. ◆ To have a head for [it]. ◆ To have a flair/knack for [it]. ◆ To have a (pretty good) shot at it. ◆ To have a way with [it]. ◆ To have an eye for. ◆ To have it in you. ◆ To have the right stuff. ◆ To have what it takes. ◆ To know what you're doing. ◆ To know your stuff. ◆ To lend itself to. ◆ To walk the walk. ◆ To work wonders. ◆ Up to par/snuff. ◆ When you're hot you're hot (and when you're not you're not). ◆ When you've got it, you've got it.

Carefree
(also relief)

A devil-may-care attitude. ◆ A free spirit. ◆ A good-time Charlie. ◆ A load off one's mind. ◆ A wackadoodle. ◆ A welcome relief. ◆ As if nothing had happened. ◆ As though the weight of the world had been lifted from one's shoulders. ♦ Breathe/ heave a (great) sigh of relief. ♦ Caesar fiddled while Rome burned. ♦ Don't worry; be happy. ♦ Don't worry (your pretty little head) about it. ♦ Feel a great weight lifted from one's shoulders. ♦ Footloose and fancy-free. ♦ Happy-go-lucky. ♦ It always happens to somebody else. ♦ It's the gypsy in me. ♦ Loose as a goose. ♦ Loosey-goosey. ♦ Not a care/worry in the world. ♦ Soldier of fortune. ♦ Take a load off. ♦ To get the monkey off one's back. ♦ To be lighthearted. ♦ To play the field. [see also Comprehensive] ♦ What, me worry? ♦ Wherever the wind blows/takes me. ♦ Whew, you had me going there. ♦ Worry is interest you pay on troubles you don't have yet. [see also Worry]

Catch

Catching is before hanging. ♦ Caught dead to rights. ♦ Caught in a compromising position. ♦ Caught in the act. ♦ Caught/nabbed red-handed. ♦ Caught with the smoking gun. ♦ Incriminating evidence. ♦ *In flagrante delicto.* ♦ Nailed cold. ♦ To be caught with one's fingers in the till/ hand in the cookie jar. ♦ To catch/be caught flatfooted/red-handed. ♦ To catch a bird, put a little salt on its tail.

– Marcantonio Serritella. ♦ To catch [*so*] in a lie. [see also Proof] ♦ To get the goods on [*so*]. ♦ To leave a paper trail.

Causality

A chain letter. ♦ A chain of events. ♦ A chain reaction. ♦ A cumulative effect. ♦ A daisy chain. ♦ A little spark may cause a titanic flame. ♦ A product of one's environment. ♦ A rolling ball is followed by a running child. ♦ A vicious circle. ♦ As a consequence of. ♦ As Maine goes, so goes the nation. ♦ By virtue of (the fact). ♦ Cause and effect. ♦ Every litter bit hurts. ♦ Every little bit helps. ♦ Every oak must be an acorn. ♦ For (good) cause. ♦ Goodwill is built by many small things but undone by one. ♦ It all adds up. ♦ Liking leads to loving, loving leads to kissing, kissing leads to f*cking and you ain't going to f*ck me, brother. ♦ Little leaks sink big ships. ♦ Little sparks cause big fires. ♦ Little things mean a lot. ♦ One rotten apple will spoil the whole barrel. ♦ One thing leads to another. ♦ *Post hoc ergo propter hoc.* ♦ Take care of the little things and the big things will take care of themselves. ♦ The domino effect. ♦ The more you itch, the more you scratch. ♦ The ripple effect. ♦ The trickle-down effect. ♦

There goes the neighborhood. ♦ To bring [it] about. ♦ To give birth (to). ♦ To give rise to. ♦ To show probable cause. ♦ What's good for General Motors is good for the U.S. ♦ When one door closes, another opens. ♦ When the elephants fight, the grass gets trampled.

Caution

A cause to pause. ♦ A prenup. ♦ A prenuptial agreement. ♦ Be good; and if you can't be good be careful; and if you can't be careful name it after me. ♦ Beware of Greeks bearing gifts. ♦ Beware the shoemaker with no shoes. ♦ Beware the young doctor and the old barber. ♦ Caveat emptor. (Buyer beware). ♦ Close cover before striking. ♦ Cross on the green not in between. ♦ Check and double check. ♦ Don't do anything I wouldn't do (and if you do, name it after me). ♦ Don't give her/him/me/them/any ideas. ♦ Don't put all your eggs in one basket.

TLC Dec 13

♦ Don't speak to strangers. ♦ Don't step into a dead man's shoes. ♦ Double check. ♦ Draw the wagons in a circle. ♦ Drive carefully: don't expire before your license does. ♦ Drive safely. The life you save may be your own. ♦ Enjoy present pleasures in such a way as not to injure future ones. ♦ Exercise all due caution. ♦ Forewarned is forearmed. [see also Armed] ♦ Go not over the water when you cannot see the bottom. ♦ I always choose my words with care/ I keep them short and sweet;/you never know from day to day/which ones you'll have to eat! ♦ Katy, bar the door! ♦ Keep out of the reach of children. ♦ Let the watchword be caution. ♦ Look before you leap. ♦ Look both ways even when crossing a one-way street. ♦ Never buy cloth from a naked person. ♦ Never go shopping on an empty stomach. ♦ Never laugh when a hearse goes by; you may be the next to die. [see also Death] ♦ Never put anything smaller than your elbow in your ear. ♦ Never test the depth of a river with both feet. ♦ Not for the faint of heart. ♦ Parental/ viewer discretion is advised. ♦ Play it cagey. ♦ Play it/one's cards close to the vest. ♦ Play it safe. ♦ Shake well before using. ♦ Sleep with one eye open. ♦ Take care. ♦ Take/use only as directed. ♦ Those who fear snakes must not overturn rocks. ♦ To choose one's battles carefully. ♦ To do due diligence. [see also Investigate] ♦ To keep at a safe distance. ♦ To pick one's way. ♦ Watch your step. ♦ When you jump for joy, beware no one pulls the rug out from under you — R.D. ♦ You break it, you've bought it. ♦ You buy it, you break it. (sign in a piñata store).

Cavil

A niggler. ♦ A nitpicker. ♦ A motor mouth. ♦ Belabor the point. ♦ My, how you do run on. ♦ To nitpick. ♦ To put too fine a point on (it). ♦ To spell out. ♦ To split hairs. ♦ To tell a shaggy dog story. ♦ When the lion is attacking, do not worry about catching fleas. ♦ When you put your head in the lion's mouth, you don't worry about his bad breath.

Censored

Adults only. ♦ Banned in Boston. ♦ Blue movies. ♦ Purple passages. ♦ Rated PG. Parental discretion is advised. ♦ Stag films. ♦ The Iron Curtain. ♦ The expurgated version. ♦ Under 17 not admitted. ♦ Unmentionable acts. ♦ "X" rated.

Certainty

A put pilot. [film jargon] ♦ A safe assumption. ♦ A safe bet. ♦ A standing offer. ♦ A sure cure. ♦ A sure thing. ♦ Absolutely, positively. (absitively, posolutely). ♦ An airtight case. ♦ An ironclad guarantee. ♦ As surely as night follows day. ♦ Backed by the full faith and credit of the United States government. ♦ Bank on it. ♦ Beyond a reasonable doubt. ♦ Beyond a shadow of a doubt ♦ Beyond a/any doubt. ♦ Can be counted on. ♦ Certainly not. [see also Oppose] ♦ Count on [it]. ♦ For certain/sure. ♦ In no uncertain terms. ♦ It's only a matter/question of time. ♦ It's safe to say. ♦ Make no mistake (about it). [see also Clarification] ♦ No bout a-doubt it. ♦ No doubt (about it). ♦ No getting around it. ♦ No ifs ands or buts. ♦ No maybes about it. ♦ No question about/of it. ♦ No two ways about it. ♦ Nothing is certain in this world but death and taxes. ♦ Or I'll eat my hat. ♦ Or I'll pay for lying. ♦ Really and truly. ♦ Sure as God made little green apples. ♦ Sure as heck/hell. ♦ Sure as sh*t. ♦ Sure as shooting. ♦ Sure enough. ♦ Sure thing. ♦ That's a fact. ♦ (That's) for sure. ♦ To be a shoo-in. ♦ To be secure in the knowledge. ♦ To be supremely confident. ♦ To be sure. ♦ To leave nothing to chance. ♦ To make (absolutely) certain. ♦ To make (doubly) sure. [see also Precaution, Proof] ♦ To say/state without fear of contradiction. ♦ To see to it. ♦ To set (great) store by. ♦ You bet your boots.

Used with permission from Microsoft.

♦ (You can) count on it. ♦ You can set your watch by it. [see also Dependable] ♦ You can take it/that to the bank. [see also Assurance] ♦ When all else fails. ♦ When all else fails, read the directions/manual. ♦ Without a doubt. ♦ Without fail. ♦ Without question. ♦ You bet your bippy. ♦ You bet your (sweet) *ss/tucas.

Challenges

All right for you. ♦ Come outside and say that. ♦ Come over here and say that. ♦ Do you want to make something of it? ♦ Don't make me come back/over there. ♦ Halt, who goes there? ♦ Go ahead, make my day. ♦ How'd you like a bust in the mouth? ♦ I can whip you with one arm/hand tied behind my back. ♦ I dare you to step over that line. ♦ I double (dog) dare you. ♦ I'll belt you one in the mouth. ♦ I'll break every bone in your body. ♦ I'll chew you up and spit you out for breakfast. ♦ I'll deck you and dick you before you can throw me and blow me. ♦ I'll give you a fat lip. ♦ I'll go you one better. ♦ I'll hit you so hard it'll jar your whole family. ♦ I'll hit you so hard you'll starve to death from spinning. ♦ I'll kick the living sh*t out of you. ♦ I'll kick your *ss all over town. ♦ I'll kick your *ss around the block. ♦ I'll kick your *ss so hard your teeth will rattle. ♦ I'll knock your block off. ♦ I'll p*ss on your grave. ♦ I'll put your headlights out. ♦ I'll knock/smack you into the middle of next week. ♦ I'll slap you nekkid and hide your clothes. ♦ I'll turn you every way but loose. ♦ Lay/lead on, Macduff. [see also Leadership] ♦ My old man can whip your old man any old time. ♦ Not to be outdone. ♦ One of these days, pow!, right in the kisser. ♦ Say that again and you'll be spitting your teeth out. ♦ Three, six, nine, the fight is mine, and I can lick you any old time. ♦ To draw a line in the sand. ♦ To throw down the gauntlet. ♦ Wait till I get my hands on you. ♦ Why, for two cents I'd punch you right in the nose. ♦ You couldn't fight/ punch your way out of a (wet) paper bag. ♦ You got a problem with that? ♦ You want a piece of me? ♦ You'll wind up flat on your *ss. ♦ Your *ss is grass and I am the lawnmower.

Change

A cataclysmic upheaval. ♦ A change for the better. ♦ A change of clothes. ♦ A change of fortune hurts a wise man no more than a change of the moon. ♦ A change of pace. [see also Varied, Different] ♦ A change of venue. ♦ A life-changing experience. ♦ A paradigm shift. [see also Progress] ♦ A (real) Dr. Jekyll and Mr. Hyde. ♦ A sea change. ♦ A seismic shift. ♦ A sign of the times. ♦ A revolving door. ♦ A dual/split personality. ♦ A wolf may change his coat but not his ways. ♦ All change is not growth. ♦ An agent of change. ♦ An alter ego. ♦ Consistency is the hobgoblin of little minds. ♦ Culture shock. ♦ Don't change/switch horses in midstream. [see also Horse] ♦ Fashion: in one year and out the other. ♦ God made heads round so thoughts could change direction. ♦ Going through the change (of life). [see also Progress] ♦ In all change there is opportunity. ♦ In new digs. ♦ Inconsistency is the only thing in which men are consistent. ♦ It's never too late to change. ♦ It's the same, only different. ♦ Just when you have all the answers, they change the questions. ♦ Like sex, it's never the same. ♦ Lord, give me the ability to change the things I can change, the strength to endure the things I cannot change and the wisdom to know the difference. —The Serenity Prayer [see also Endurance] ♦ Only fools never change their minds. ♦ Only the highest and lowest characters don't change. ♦ Only the names have been changed to protect the innocent. ♦ Play musical chairs. ♦ Presto chango. ♦ Prices/terms/dates/times subject to change. ♦ The dice are always rolling. ♦ The ebb and flow. ♦ The more things change, the more they remain the same. ♦ The only permanent thing in life is change. ♦ The shifting sands (of time). ♦ The times they are a-changin'. ♦ The ups and downs. ♦ The vagaries/vicissitudes of life. ♦ The seeds/winds of change. ♦ Times change, tastes change. ♦ To be a changed man/woman. ♦ To change one's tune. ♦ To change partners. ♦ To go through the change (of life). ♦ To grow out of it. ♦ To have a change of heart. [see also Withdraw] ♦ To have mood swings. ♦ To switch gears.

◆ To turn into (something). ◆ You can change the course of history but not the history of courses. ◆ You can't dip your hand into the same stream twice.

Chat

Chew the fat. ◆ Chew the rag. ◆ Idle chitchat. ◆ Strike up a conversation. ◆ To bandy about. ◆ To chat [so] up. ◆ To have a word with [so]. ◆ To jaw with [so]. ◆ To jaw [so] down. ◆ To make small talk. ◆ To pass the time of day. ◆ To pick [so]'s brain. ◆ To shoot the breeze. ◆ To shoot the bull. ◆ To shoot the sh*t. ◆ To swap yarns.

Child

A child prodigy. ◆ A half-pint. ◆ A little bundle of joy. ◆ A little nipper. ◆ A little shaver. ◆ A little squirt. ◆ A young whippersnapper. ◆ A wild child. ◆ Children found in church or Sunday school are seldom found in jails. ◆ Children should be seen and not heard. ◆ Children should be seen and not hurt. ◆ Children should speak only when spoken to. ◆ Daddy's little girl. ◆ First comes love, then comes marriage; then comes baby in a baby carriage. ◆ God bless the child who has his own. ◆ It's a wise child that knows its own father. ◆ Knee-high to a grasshopper.

◆ Out of the mouths of babes comes wisdom. ◆ Suffer the little children to come unto me. ◆ Snips and snails and puppy dogs' tails—that's what little boys are made of. ◆ Sugar and spice and everything nice—that's what little girls are made of. ◆ The boy is father to the man. ◆ The pitter-patter of little feet. ◆ The young'ns. ◆ What do you want to be when you grow up? ◆ You know what happens to children who mock their parents? She-bears come out of the woods and devour them. ◆ You spend the first 2 years of children's lives teaching them to walk and talk. Then you spend the next 16 years telling them to sit down and shut-up.

Chitchat

And to what (may I ask) do I owe this honor? ◆ Any time. ◆ Are you married/single? ◆ Can't kick. ◆ Did you go anywhere special for the weekend? ◆ Doing anything special for the weekend? ◆ Don't mention it. ◆ Don't trouble yourself. ◆ Fine thank you (and you?) ◆ Fine thanks, and you? ◆ Gimme some skin. ◆ Good to see you. ◆ Good to see you, too. ◆ Greetings and salutations. ◆ Hanging in there (like an old pair of nuts). ◆ Have a nice day/weekend. ◆ How about you? ◆ How are you (today)? ◆ How do you do? ◆ How now, brown cow (grazing in the green, green grass). ◆ How was your weekend? ◆ How you doing? riposte: anybody I can and the easy ones twice!] ◆ How's it going? ◆ How's the family? ◆ How's tricks? ◆ Hey, good lookin', whatcha got cookin'? ◆ Hi/howdy, neighbor. ◆ How goes the war? ◆ How's by you? ◆ How's every little thing? ◆ How's the missus/wife? [riposte: Better than nothing!] ◆ How's the world treating you? ◆ How's your hammer hangin'? ◆ How they hanging? ◆ I daresay. ◆ I must say. ◆ Long time no see. ◆ 'Morning, Glory, what's your story? [rejoinder: That don't rhyme, Frankenstein.] ◆ Good/nice to meet you. ◆ No bother at all. ◆ No complaints, thanks. ◆ No problem. ◆ No trouble at all. ◆ No sense/use complaining. ◆ Not at all. ◆ Not to worry. ◆ Please allow me to introduce myself. ◆ Pleased to make your acquaintance.

◆ Say hey. ◆ Some weather we're having, isn't it? ◆ (That's O.K.)—no harm done. ◆ That's what friends are for. ◆ The pleasure is/was all mine. ◆ Think nothing of it. ◆ Think the rain'll hurt the rhubarb this year? ◆ Top of the morning (to you). ◆ Whaddya say? ◆ What are friends for? ◆ What do you do for a living? ◆ What gives? ◆ What's bugging/eating you? ◆ What's cooking? ◆ What's new (with you)? ◆ What's on your mind? ◆ What's shakin' bakin'? ◆ What's the (good) word? ◆ What's the matter? ◆ What's the sense/use of complaining? ◆ What's the word? Thunderbird. What's the price? Twenty cents twice. ◆ What's up? ◆ What's your line (of work)? ◆ What've you /whatcha been up to? (No good, I'll bet.) ◆ Whazzup? ◆ Where (are) you from? [rejoinder: From my mother. (ironic/sarcastic)] ◆ Where did you go to school? ◆ Where do you hail from? ◆ You'd do the same for me, wouldn't you? ◆ You'd've done the same (thing) for me. ◆ You're (more than/most/quite/very) welcome.

Choices

Among the favored few. ◆ Anything your (little) heart desires. ◆ As you see fit. ◆ At the time and place of your choosing. ♦ Boxers or briefs? ♦ Choose your battles carefully. ♦ Coffee, tea or milk? (Coffee tea or me)? ♦ Draw your own conclusions. ♦ Either-or. ♦ Freedom of choice. ♦ Get it if it's hot; forget it if it's not. — R.D. ♦ He who hoots with the owls at night cannot expect to soar with the eagles in the morning. ♦ If that's the way you want it, that's the way you'll get it. ♦ If you want to play you've got to pay. — Dominick P. Delia ♦ It's either or. ♦ It's up to you. ♦ It's your funeral. ♦ Make of it what you will. ♦ Name your poison. ♦ Out of options. ♦ Or what? [see also Question] ♦ Pick a card—any card. ♦ Suit yourself. ♦ Take it or leave it. [see also Settle] ♦ Take your choice/pick. ♦ The choice is yours. ♦ The [adj.]/[adv.] the better. ♦ The pick of the litter. ♦ To choose/pick sides. ♦ To go that route. ♦ To leave one no choice (in the matter). ♦ To one's liking. ♦ To pick [so] out of a lineup. ♦ To shop around. ♦ To weigh one's options. ♦ What other choice did I/do I have? ♦ What else is on? ♦ Where to, buddy? ♦ You asked for it. ♦ You can't burn the candle at both ends.

♦ You can't have it both ways. ♦ You can't have your cake and eat it too. ♦ You have 2 choices—slim and none. ♦ You have 2 choices: 1). Take it. 2). Leave it. ♦ You name it, you've got it. ♦ You pays your money and you takes your chances/choices. ♦ Your best bet. [see also Bet]

Christmas

A secret Santa. ♦ As full of sh*t as a Christmas goose. [see also Skepticism] ♦ Christmas comes but once a year. ♦ Face lit up like a Christmas tree. ♦ Green Christmas, white Easter. ♦ Green Christmases make fat graveyards. ♦ Home for the holidays. ♦ Lit up like a Christmas tree. ♦ It's beginning to look a lot like Christmas. ♦ Naughty children get coal in their stocking for Christmas. ♦ One good reason Santa is so jolly is because he knows where all the bad girls live. ♦ Peace on Earth, goodwill to men. ♦ 'Tis the season (to be jolly). ♦ Why doesn't Santa have any children? Because he only comes once a year and only down chimneys.

Cigar/Cigarette

A cigarette is a cigarette, but a good cigar is a smoke. ♦ A pack of butts/smokes. ♦ Can I borrow a cigarette? ♦ Cancer sticks. ♦ Cigarettes will stunt your growth. ♦ Every cigarette you smoke is another nail in your coffin. ♦ No smoking (on premises). ♦ Second-hand smoke. ♦ Smokers are a dying breed. ♦ Smoking is a pleasure you can get carried away with. (In a coffin). ♦ Smoking stunts your growth. ♦ To blow smoke rings. ♦ To bum/grub a cigarette. ♦ To smoke like a chimney.* ♦ To smoke like a fiend. *[see also Excess] ♦ What this country needs is a good five-cent cigar. ♦ What this country needs is a good no-scent cigar. ♦ You're coughing better.

Clarification

A talking point. ♦ A textbook example. ♦ Apropos of [it]. ♦ Are you talking to me? [see also Rejoinders] ♦ By way of example/illustration. ♦ Case in point. ♦ Contrary to popular belief/opinion. [see also Public] ♦ Don't get me wrong. ♦ *Exempli gratia*/e.g./for example. ♦ For your information. ♦ For your information and edification. ♦ I have only one thing to say (about that). ♦ I'll have you know: ♦ If you need further details/explanation/facts/information, just ask. ♦ In case you haven't noticed. ♦ In other words. ♦ Let me hasten to add. ♦ Let me say this about that. ♦ Let's make one thing (perfectly) clear. ♦ Make no mistake (about it). [see also Certainty] ♦ Never let it be said. ♦ Not to be confused with. ♦ That explains everything. ♦ That is/*id est*/i.e. ♦ That is (to say). ♦ That's what I'm talking about. ♦ To bring [it] into sharper focus. ♦ To disabuse [so] of the idea/notion. [see also Conflict] ♦ To dispel the notion. ♦ To draw a clear/sharp distinction. ♦ To fill in the blanks. ♦ To firm [it] up. ♦ To get back to [so]. ♦ To get down to/into the nitty gritty. ♦ To get down to the nuts and bolts. ♦ To issue a (flat) denial. ♦ To let [so] know. ♦ To make sense. ♦ To mention just/only a few. ♦ To report (all) the gory details. ♦ To set the record straight. ♦ To spell it out. ♦ To wit. ♦ What did you mean by that? ♦ What would you say a thing like that for? ♦ Why (on earth) would you say such a thing? ♦ You. Yes, you!

Clean

A new broom sweeps clean. ♦ Clean as a hound's tooth/pig's whistle. ♦ Cleanliness is next to godliness. ♦ Clear the decks. ♦ Make a clean sweep. ♦ No evidence of foul play. ♦ No sign of a struggle. ♦ So clean you could eat off the floor. ♦ Spick and span. ♦ Spit and polish. ♦ Spruce up. ♦ Squeaky clean. ♦ The washed pot never spoils. ♦ To clean house. To clean up. ♦ To give a G.I. shower to [so]. [military] ♦ To go on a cleaning jag. ♦ To have a field day. [military] ♦ To police the area. ♦ To redd up. ♦ To scrub up. ♦ To swab down. ♦ To sweep up/tidy up.

Clear

A clear conscience is a good pillow. ♦ Clear a path. ♦ Clear across the land. ♦ Clear as a bell. ♦ Clear as crystal. ♦ Clear through. ♦ Crystal clear. ♦ Let's make something perfectly clear. [see also Clarification] ♦ The coast is clear. ♦ To be in the clear. ♦ To clear the air. ♦ To clear the decks. ♦ To clear [it] up. ♦ To have a clear conscience. ♦ To have a clear shot (at). ♦ To make it abundantly clear. ♦ To see one's way clear (to).

Close

A brush with death. ♦ A clinging vine. ♦ A close call/shave. [see also Almost, Marginal] ♦ A hanger-on. ♦ A heartbeat away from [n.] ♦ A narrow escape.

EMERGENCY
EXIT

♦ A near miss. ♦ A tight squeeze. ♦ As close as your skin. ♦ At point-blank range. ♦ Close but no cigar. ♦ Close quarters. ♦ If you can read this you're too close. [Bumper sticker]. ♦ Not room enough to swing a cat. [see also Crowding] ♦ One grenade can get you all. ♦ To cling tenaciously. ♦ To cut it close. ♦ To feel as if the walls are closing in. ♦ To hit close to home. ♦ To latch onto. ♦ To stick to you like glue. ♦ To tailgate. ♦ Too close for comfort. ♦ Up close and personal. ♦ Within shouting/spitting/ striking distance. [see also Distance]

Clumsy
(also awkward)

A noisy cat catches no mice. ♦ All *ssholes and elbows. ♦ Butterfingers! [see also Loss] ♦ Like a bull in a china shop. ♦ Like a cow p*ssin' on a flat rock. ♦ Like a herd of turtles. ♦ The elegance of elephants. ♦ To be all thumbs. ♦ To be ham-handed. ♦ To do [it] with a heavy hand. ♦ To be ill at ease. ♦ To be off balance. ♦ To have two left feet. ♦ To trip over one's own feet. ♦ To walk like one has a corn cob up one's *ss.

Coincidence

As chance/luck would have it. ♦ As it turned out. ♦ By pure/sheer coincidence. ♦ Coincidence, Einstein said, is God's way of remaining anonymous. ♦ Fancy meeting you here. ♦ Funny you should ask/mention it. ♦ Glad you brought it/that up. ♦ I just happened to be in the neighborhood. ♦ I was just going to say that/the same thing (myself). ♦ It just so happens. ♦ It's a small world. ♦ Just the man/woman I want to see. ♦ Small world, isn't it? ♦ Speak of the devil and he appears. [see also Devil, Gossip] ♦ The world gets smaller every day. ♦ To come up with [it] independently. ♦ What a coincidence. ♦ What brings you here?

Cold

A cold snap. ♦ A cold spell. ♦ A sheet of ice. ♦ A winter wonderland. ♦ Baby, it's cold outside. ♦ Bitter cold. ♦ Chilled to the bone. ♦ Cold and clammy. ♦ Cold as an Eskimo's nose. ♦ Cold enough for you? ♦ Cold enough to freeze the balls off a brass monkey. ♦ Cold hands, warm heart. ♦ Colder than a well digger's *ss (in Montana). ♦ Colder than a whore's heart. ♦ Colder than a witch's tit. ♦ Colder than a witch's titty in a brass bra. ♦ Feed a cold; starve a fever. ♦ Frozen stiff. ♦ In the dead of winter. ♦ It's [n.] degrees below (zero). ♦

Jack Frost. ♦ Like an icicle. ♦ So cold it'd freeze the balls off a pool table. ♦ Sub-zero. ♦ The best thing to take for a winter cold is vitamin C. Take it all the way to Florida. ♦ The mercury's dropping. ♦ The thermometer's falling. ♦ To catch one's death of cold.

Collaboration

A bucket brigade. ♦ A camel is a horse put together by a committee. ♦ A group grope. ♦ A joint effort. ♦ All chiefs and no Indians. (also, Too many chiefs and not enough Indians). ♦ Collective wisdom. ♦ Let's synchronize watches. ♦ The buddy system. ♦ The division of labor. ♦ The dream team. ♦ There is no "I" in team/teamwork. ♦ To gang up (on). ♦ To have a gang bang. ♦ Too many cooks spoil the broth/soup. ♦ Two captains sink the ship. ♦ Two heads are better than one. (But not faces./But not on coins. — R.D.) ♦ When many roosters crow, the dawn is slow in coming. ♦ Where there are six cooks, there is nothing to eat.

Combat

A casus belli. ♦ A declaration of war. ♦ A knock-'em-down, drag-'em-out fight. ♦ A contest of the wills. ♦ A tug of war. ♦ An armed conflict/

struggle. ◆ Counter revolution. ◆ Dire situations call for dire solutions. ◆ Fight fire with fire. ◆ Hand-to-hand combat. ◆ (Locked in) mortal combat. ◆ Shake hands and come out fighting. ◆ The big fish eat the little fish. ◆ The horrors of war. ◆ To battle it out. ◆ To do battle. ◆ To come to grips (with). ◆ To go a few rounds. ◆ To go to the mat. ◆ To go to war. ◆ To have it out (with). ◆ To match wits (with). ◆ To confront/meet/tackle head-on. ◆ To put up a (good) fight. ◆ To stand up to [so]. ◆ To take [so] on. ◆ Two can play the same game. ◆ War does not determine who is right—only who is left.

Command

A command performance. ◆ A commanding lead. ◆ A commanding presence. ◆ Assume the position. ◆ Second in command. [see also Almost] ◆ That's an order. ◆ That's not a request, it's an order. ◆ The chain of command. ◆ The commander-in-chief. [see also Boss] ◆ The Ten Commandments. (They are not called the Ten Suggestions). ◆ To kick *ss and take names. ◆ To command a high salary. ◆ To command attention/ respect. ◆ To do it on command. ◆ To have

a command of one's subject. ◆ To take command. ◆ Up against the wall, motherf*cker. ◆ Your wish is my command.

Commonplace

A common, garden-variety [n.]. ◆ A dime a dozen. ◆ A plain Jane. ◆ All over the place. ◆ All around the house. ◆ Common as catsh*t and twice as nasty. ◆ Every time you turn around. ◆ Generally speaking. ◆ He puts his pants on (in the morning) the same way you do—one leg at a time. [see also Alike] ◆ If you've seen one, you've seen them all. ◆ In all other ways unremarkable. ◆ In everyday conversation. ◆ It ain't fancy but it's good. ◆ It's all in the game. ◆ It's just another day. ◆ Just an ordinary guy. ◆ Just another day at the office. ◆ Just one of the guys. ◆ Just plain folks. ◆ Kilroy was here. ◆ Like horseh*t, it's all over. ◆ Middle class. ◆ No big whoop. ◆ No frills. ◆ No great shakes. ◆ Nothing out of the ordinary. ◆ Nothing that I haven't seen before. ◆ Of modest means. ◆ Off the shelf. ◆ On (the) average. ◆ One on every streetcorner. ◆ Par for the course. ◆ Plain Vanilla. ◆ Run-of-the-mill. ◆ There's a lot of that going around. ♦ Try to curb your enthusiasm. ♦ Underwhelming.

Comparison

A basis of comparison. ♦ A study in contrasts. ♦ Comparisons are odious. ♦ Diametrically opposed. ♦ Dollar for dollar. ♦ In stark contrast. ♦ Let's compare apples to apples. ♦ Lilies white look best among roses. ♦ On the other hand. ♦ Pound for pound. ♦ Shall I compare thee to a summer day? ♦ The standard by which (all) others are judged. ♦ There's none so fair as can compare to the Marine Corps infantry. [military chant] ♦ To pale by comparison. ♦ To stack up against. ♦ You can't compare oranges to apples. ♦ You should see the other guy.

Compel

A shotgun wedding. [see also Marriage] ♦ Bring pressure to bear. ♦ Dragged kicking and screaming. ♦ Forced to act against one's will. ♦ If you know what's good for you. ♦ To be hardwired (to). ♦ To force [it] down [so]'s throat. ♦ To force [so]'s hand. ♦ To force the issue. [see also Pressured] ♦ To make you an offer you can't refuse. ♦ To twist [so]'s arm. ♦ We have our ways. ♦ We have ways to make you talk. ♦ You have your work cut out for you.

Complain

(also lament)

A crank call. ♦ A crying towel. ♦ A grim reminder. ♦ A hard luck story. ♦ A list of grievances. ♦ A pity party. ♦ A sad tale of woe. ♦ A sob sister. ♦ Bawl/cry one's eyes out. ♦ Care and woe. ♦ Cry on [sb] 's shoulder. ♦ Crying like a baby. ♦ For gripe's sake. ♦ In sackcloth and ashes. ♦ Kick against the pricks. ♦ Kick up a fuss. ♦ Make a scene/stink. ♦ Mouth off. ♦ My, how you do go on. ♦ Not that I'm complaining, mind you. ♦ Of all the gin joints in all the towns in all the world, she walks into mine. ♦ Oh, my aching back. ♦ Sob story. ♦ Some people would complain even if you hung 'em with a brand-new rope. ♦ Sound off. ♦ To air one's grievances. ♦ To bellyache. ♦ To bitch and moan/p*ss and moan. ♦ To blow/let off steam. ♦ To break down and cry. ♦ To cause/make a scene. ♦ To cry in one's beer. ♦ To cry like a baby. ♦ To cry/sing the blues. ♦ To feel sorry for oneself. ♦ To file/lodge a complaint. ♦ To hang one's head and cry. ♦ To have a beef with [so]. ♦ To kvetch. ♦To make a big to-do/whoop dee doo. ♦

To p*ss and moan. ♦ To pitch a bitch. ♦ To poor mouth [it]/[so]. ♦ To rend your garments. ♦ To run off at the mouth. ♦ To shoot your mouth off. ♦ To sound the death knell. ♦ To spiel off. ♦ To spout off. ♦ To squawk. ♦ To tear one's hair out (by the roots). ♦ To turn on the tears/waterworks. ♦ To vent one's spleen. ♦ To wallow in self-pity. ♦ To wring one's hands in despair. ♦ Trouble and woe. ♦ Weeping and gnashing of teeth. ♦ What have I done to deserve this? ♦ What's your beef? ♦ Where did I/we go wrong? ♦ Where did I/we fail? ♦ Why me, Lawd/Lord? ♦ Woe is me.

Complicity

It takes two to tango. ♦ Just the two of us. ♦ One lies, the other swears to it. ♦ Partners in crime. [see also Crime] ♦ Running mate. ♦ To side with. ♦ To be party to. ♦ To take sides. ♦ To vouch for [so]. ♦ When one says jump, the other says, "how high?" ♦ When one says sh*t, the other squats. ♦ You and me against the world.

Comprehensive
(also completely)

A cohesive whole. ♦ A meal in itself. ♦ (All) across the board. ♦ All in all. ♦

All over the place. ♦ All over [it] like a cheap suit. ♦ All present and accounted for. ♦ All shapes and sizes. ♦ All that happy horsesh*t. ♦ All the gory/sordid details. ♦ All the way around. ♦ All things, wise and wonderful. ♦ All under one roof. ♦ All-inclusive. ♦ Any way, shape or form. ♦ Any way you look at it. ♦ At every turn. ♦ At length. ♦ Bag and baggage. ♦ Carpet bombing. ♦ Clean/clear through. ♦ Every [n.] in the book. ♦ Every [n.] known to man. ♦ Every inch a [n.]. ♦ Every step of the way. ♦ Everything but the kitchen sink. ♦ Everything in creation. ♦ Everything under the sun. ♦ Everything you always wanted to know about [n.] but were afraid to ask. ♦ From [n.] to [n.] (and everything in between). ♦ From head/tip to toe (and everywhere in between). ♦ From A to Z. ♦ From aardvark to zebu. ♦ From the cradle to the grave. ♦ From the dreidel to the grave. ♦ From soup to nuts. ♦ From start to finish. ♦ From stem to stern. ♦ He/she is nothing if not [adj.] ♦ Head over heels. ♦ In full force. ♦ In every quarter. ♦ In every respect. ♦ In every/the truest sense of the word. ♦ (In every sentence of the Word. – R.D.) ♦ In/into every nook and cranny. ♦ It's all part of our service. ♦ It's all there. ♦ Leaves nothing to be desired. ♦ Lock, stock and barrel. ♦ One-stop shopping. ♦ Out and out. ♦ Right down to one's toes. ♦ Root and branch. ♦ Something for everyone. ♦ That's all the [n.]-ier it gets. ♦ The be all and end all. ♦ The full force and effect. ♦ The whole ball of wax. ♦ The whole enchilada. ♦ The whole kit and caboodle. ♦ The whole *megillah*. ♦ The whole nine yards. ♦ The whole schmear. ♦ The whole *schmeggege*. ♦ The whole shebang. ♦ The whole shooting match. ♦ The whole sordid affair. ♦ The whole *tchotchke*. ♦ The (whole) works. ♦ Through and through. ♦ To and fro. ♦ To be all things to all people. ♦ To cast a wide net. ♦ To cover a lot of ground. ♦ To cover the field/territory/waterfront. ♦ To dot all one's I's and cross all one's T's. [see also Thorough] ♦ To play the field. [see also Carefree] ♦ To see it through to completion. ♦ To the best of one's [n.]. ♦ To take a blanket/scattergun/shotgun approach. ♦ To the full/ fullest (extent). ♦ To the max. ♦ To work up a full head of steam. ♦ Toe, knee, chest, nut! ♦ Up and down the line. ♦ Wall to wall. [see also Crowding] ♦ Warts and all.

Compromise

A meeting of the minds. ♦ Come to an understanding. ♦ Come to terms. ♦ Find common ground. ♦ Give and take. ♦ Hammer out the differences. ♦ Hash it out. ♦ Hug it out. ♦ In the middle of the road. ♦ Life is just a series of trade-offs. ♦ Like Solomon, to split the baby. ♦ Meet in the middle. ♦ Meet [*so*] halfway. ♦ Split the difference. ♦ Strike a balance. ♦ Strike a happy medium. ♦ Talk it out/over. ♦ To compromise oneself/ one's principles. ♦ To reach an accord/agreement. ♦ To settle out of court. ♦ To strike a compromise. ♦ To talk it out/over. ♦ To work it (on) out.

Conceal

A cover story. [see also Alibi, Best] ♦ A dog in the manger. ♦ A hidden agenda. ♦ Cover a multitude of sins. ♦ Draw a veil over. ♦ Lay down/ throw up a smoke screen. ♦ Put lipstick on a pig. ♦ Statistics, like bikinis, are often more shocking in what they conceal than what they reveal. ♦ To cover one's tracks. ♦ To do a cover-up. ♦ To double back on one's own tracks. ♦ To hide one's light under a bushel. ♦ To mask the truth. ♦ To put a happy face on [it]. ♦ To put on a happy face. ♦ To sweep [it] under the rug. ♦ To take cover. ♦ To throw [*so*] off the track. ♦ To touch [it] up. ♦ Under wraps. ♦ You're not leaving the house in *that*.

Confide

A heart-to-heart talk. ♦ A hot tip. ♦ A slip of the lip can sink a ship. ♦ Don't let this go any further. ♦ For your eyes only. ♦ Forget you ever heard it. [riposte: Heard what?]. ♦ Get it off one's chest. [see also Blab] ♦ Get it straight from the horse's mouth. ♦ I'll let you in on a little secret. ♦ Insider information/ trading. ♦ (Just) between you and me. ♦ Just so's you know. ♦ Keep this *entre nous*. ♦ Lay it on me. [see also Defy] ♦ Let it all (hang) out. ♦ Let one's hair down. ♦ Little pitchers have big ears. [and mouths! – R.D.] ♦ Off the record. ♦ Privileged information. ♦ Take [so] into one's confidence. ♦ Talk turkey. ♦ The inside scoop. ♦ The walls have ears. ♦ There's something I have to tell you. ♦ This is just between the two of us/you and me. ♦ To be in on [it]. ♦ To clue [so] in (on). ♦ To get the 411 on. ♦ To get/give the inside poop/scoop/ skinny. ♦ To get the lowdown (on). [see also Investigate] ♦ To let [so] in on it. ♦ To put it (all) out there. ♦ To take [so] aside/to one side. ♦ To take

[so] into one's confidence. ♦ To talk man to man/woman to woman. ♦ Top secret clearance. ♦ To whisper into [so]'s ear. ♦ You didn't hear it from me.

Conflict

(also disagree, incompatibility)
A barroom brawl. ♦ A battle for the hearts and minds of men. ♦ A battle royal. ♦ A bone/point of contention. ♦ A contradiction in terms. ♦ A duel to the death. ♦ A fight to the finish. ♦ A formidable opponent. ♦ A free-for-all. ♦ A generation gap. ♦ A "he says/she says" situation. ♦ A heated argument. ♦ A hot-button issue. ♦ A hot potato. ♦ A knock-em-down, drag-em-out fight. ♦ A lover's quarrel. ♦ A moot point. ♦ A personality conflict. ♦ A p*ssing contest. ♦ A pitched battle. ♦ A political football. ♦ A (real) Dr. Jekyll and Mr. Hyde. ♦ A screaming/shouting match. ♦ A split personality. ♦ A stormy/tempestuous relationship. ♦ A turf war. ♦ A war of nerves. [see also Nervous] ♦ All-out war/ warfare. ♦ Arch enemy. ♦ At cross purposes. ♦ At each other's throats. ♦ At issue. ♦ At loggerheads. ♦ At odds [with]. ♦ Beat/kick the (living) crap/sh*t out of [so]. ♦ Choose

your weapons. ♦ Come to blows. ♦ Cross swords (with). ♦ Cutthroat/ fierce competition. ♦ Draw first blood. ♦ Dog eat dog. ♦ Duke/slug it out. ♦ East is east and west is west and never the twain shall meet. ♦ Feudin', a-fightin' and a-fussin'. ♦ Fight fair and square. ♦ Fight like a man. ♦ Fight the good fight. ♦ Fight to the last ditch. ♦ Fight tooth and nail. ♦ Go at it hammer and tongs. ♦ Go *mano a mano*. ♦ Go toe to toe. ♦ Gunfight/shootout/showdown at the O.K. Corral. ♦ Have a bone/crow to pick with [so]. ♦ Have a falling out (with). ♦ Have a run-in (with). ♦ Have a showdown. ♦ His word against hers. ♦ Hotly contested. ♦ In the trenches. ♦ Irreconcilable differences. ♦ It takes two to quarrel but only one to end it. ♦ In the thick of battle. ♦ My worthy opponent. ♦ No love lost between them. ♦ Oil and water do not mix. ♦ On/ to the contrary. ♦ On opposite sides of the fence. ♦ On the front lines. ♦ Out of step/synch (with). ♦ Pistols at ten paces. ♦ Put up a good fight. ♦ Psychological warfare. ♦ Put up your dukes. ♦ Put your dukes up. ♦ Swords at sunrise. ♦ That's debatable. ♦ The battle lines are drawn. ♦ The manly art of self-defense. ♦

The theaters of war. ♦ The fight of one's life. ♦ This is/means war. ♦ To bang/butt heads. ♦ To bump egos/ heads. ♦ To challenge/question authority. ♦ To engage in (the fine art of) fisticuffs. ♦ To exchange/have words (with). ♦ To fight it out. ♦ To fight like cats and dogs. ♦ To fly in the face of conventional wisdom. ♦ To go at it. ♦ To go head to head. ♦ To go nose to nose. ♦ To go toe to toe. ♦ To go up against. ♦ To have a dust-up/faceoff/run-in. ♦ To have an axe to grind. ♦ To have it out. ♦ To lock horns (with). [see also Impasse] ♦ To meet pockets of resistance. ♦ To mix it up. ♦ To pit one against the other. ♦ To put up a (good) fight. ♦ To stave off. ♦ To square off. ♦ You can't put a square peg in a round hole. ♦ You said it, I didn't! – Debra Maria Delia ♦ You said it, not me! ♦ Your word against mine.

Confucius Say:

Confucius say: is better to lose a lover than to love a loser. ♦ Confucius say: Man who is all wet a lot, soon is all washed up. ♦ Confucius say: man with head up *ss can't see for sh*t. ♦ Confucius say: Woman with dress up run faster than man with pants down. ♦ Confucius say: Man who lose key to woman's apartment get no new key. ♦ Confucius say: Man who make love on ground have piece on earth. ♦ Confucius say: Woman who fly upside down have crack up. ♦ Confucius say: Man troubled by wet dream wake up with solution in hand. ♦ Confucius say: Woman who is tainted even in part has impure whole. ♦ Confucius say: Man who is over a barrel soon in a pickle. ♦ Confucius say: Man who walk through turnstile sideways going to Bangkok. ♦ Confucius say: Man with tongue in cheek cannot speak straight talk. ♦ Confucius say: Man with split personality beside himself. ♦ Confucius say: Man who chase two hares catch neither. ♦ Confucius say: Man who engage in horseplay make ass of himself in end. ♦ Confucius say: Man who call spade a spade may dig own grave. ♦ Confucius say: Man who scratch *ss should not bite fingernails. ♦ Confucius say: Man who think success but a stone's throw away has rocks in head. ♦ Confucius say: Woman who put husband in doghouse soon find him in cathouse.

Confused

(All) bollixed up. ♦ (All) discombobbled/ discombobulated. ♦ All mixed up. ♦ All screwed up. ♦ As confused as a baby in a topless bar. ♦ At sixes and sevens. ♦ Blowing smoke. ♦ Can't make heads nor tails of it. ♦ Doesn't know what he/she is talking about. ♦ Doesn't know which end/way is up. ♦ Don't know if you're coming or going. ♦ Don't have a clue. ♦ Get one's signals/ wires crossed. ♦ Harum-scarum. ♦ Higgeldy-piggeldy. ♦ It's clear as mud. ♦ It's all Greek to me. ♦ Just plain corn-fused. ♦ Legal mumbo-jumbo. [see also Law] ♦ Legalese. ♦ Like a Chinese fire drill. ♦ Lost in the shuffle. [see also Bureaucracy] ♦ Not wrapped too tight. ♦ So noisy I can't hear myself think. ♦ The right hand doesn't know what the left hand's doing. ♦ To be fershimmel/ meshuggah. ♦ To blur the lines. ♦ To get/give mixed signals. ♦ To lose one's bearings. ♦ To muddy the waters. ♦ To not know what to do. ♦ What to do, what to do? ♦ What's a body to do? ♦ Where the Fugawi? ♦ Willy nilly. ♦ You crazy, mixed-up kid. ♦ You've lost me.

Consideration

After due consideration. ♦ All things (duly) considered. ♦ Do unto others as you would have them do unto you. [see also Reciprocation] ♦ Do unto others before they do unto you. ♦ Follow the golden rule. ♦ He who has the gold, makes the rules. ♦ Put yourself in the other guy's shoes. ♦ See what the boys in the back room will have. ♦ To take [it] into consideration. ♦ To take [it]/others others into account.

Contract

A binding contract. ♦ A deal's a deal. ♦ A gentleman's agreement. ♦ At the stroke of a pen. ♦ Gimme five. ♦ Gimme some skin. ♦ Let's shake on it. ♦ Party of the first part. ♦ Party of the second part. ♦ Put 'er there, partner. ♦ Sign on the dotted line. ♦ Signed in blood. ♦ Signed, sealed and delivered. ♦ To ink a deal. ♦ To make a pact. ♦ To put one's John Hancock/John Henry. (on). ♦ To sign on/up.

Contrive

(also coy)

A master manipulator. ♦ A method to one's madness. ♦ A stage whisper. ♦ A stalking horse. ♦ Accidentally on purpose. [see also Accident] ♦ As a means to an end. ♦ Bobbing and weaving. ♦ Dazzle 'em with footwork. ♦ For tax purposes. ♦ Heads I win, tails you lose. ♦ In cahoots (with). ♦

May I carry your books home? ♦ Play both ends against the middle. ♦ Set a thief to catch a thief. ♦ Something up one's sleeve. ♦ The fix is in. ♦ The oldest trick in the book. ♦ To cook the books.

♦ To juggle the books. ♦ To do/make an end run. ♦ To hatch a plot. ♦ To have ulterior motives. ♦ To lie in wait. ♦ To mess with [so]'s head. ♦ To perpetrate a hoax. ♦ To play cat and mouse. ♦ To play footsie(s) (with). ♦ To play good cop/bad cop. ♦ To play hard to get. ♦ To play head games/mind games. ♦ To play one against the other. ♦ To play politics. ♦ To run with the fox and hunt with the hounds. ♦ To set [so] up. ♦ To set up a straw man. ♦ To spring a/the trap. ♦ To throw in a red herring. ♦ To use reverse psychology. ♦ Under an assumed name.

Cool

A measured response. ♦ Calm, cool and collected. ♦ Calm down.

◆ Chill (out). ◆ Cold and calculating. ◆ Compose yourself. ◆ Cool as a cucumber. ◆ Cool it. ◆ Cool, man, cool. ◆ Devoid of emotion. ◆ Get a grip (on oneself). ◆ Let cooler heads prevail. ◆ One cool customer. ◆ The voice of reason. ◆ Self-composed. ◆ Self-possessed. ◆ To be a cold fish. ◆ To betray no emotion. [see also Emotion] ◆ To have ice water in one's veins. ◆ Unflappable. ◆ When everybody around you is losing their heads, keep yours. ◆ Without batting an eye/eyelash. [see also Quickly]

Cooperation

A member in good standing. ◆ And so you see between them both, they licked the platter clean. ◆ Between consenting adults. ◆ Get with it. ◆ Get with the program. ◆ Go along with the program. ◆ If you can't beat 'em, join 'em. [see also Powerless] ◆ If you can't join 'em, beat 'em. ◆ Never bend so far over backwards you have your head up your *ss. ◆ Play ball with. ◆ To bend over backwards (for). ◆ To get along, go along. ◆ To get on the bandwagon. ◆ To go along. ◆ To take to it (like a duck to water). ◆ When you jump on somebody else's bandwagon, don't upset your own applecart. — R.D.

Correct

A sound argument. ◆ A step in the right direction. [see also Progress] ◆ Be sure you're right, then go ahead. ◆ If that's what you're looking for you came to the right place. ◆ It's either right or wrong. ◆ It's the right thing to do. ◆ Like one's spectacles: right on the nose. ◆ Moving in the right direction. ◆ On the right track. ◆ Right as rain. ◆ Right makes might. ◆ Right on the money. ◆ Right side up. ◆ There is no such thing as being half right. ◆ To be dead right. ◆ To be onto something. ◆ To be politically correct. [see also Politics] ◆ To set [so] straight. ◆ To take a turn for the better. ◆ To the point. ◆ We must be doing something right. ◆ What would Jesus do? [see also Religion] ◆ What's right is not always popular and what's popular is not always right. ◆ What's right is. ◆ What's right is right. ◆ When you're right, you're right. ◆ You came to the right place. ◆ You're right, the world is wrong.

Courage
(also bravery)

A cast-iron stomach. ◆ A major pair of *cojones*. ◆ Be just and fear not. ◆ Brass balls. ◆ Buck up. ◆ He without courage is a knife without an edge. ♦ Intestinal fortitude. ♦ Keep a stiff upper (lip). ♦ Keep your chin up. [but don't lead with it or get hit on it. — R.D.] ♦ Keep your spirits up. ♦ Laugh fear in the face. ♦ Nerves of steel. ♦ Take heart. ♦ The courage of one's convictions. ♦ To get up the nerve (to). ♦ To beard the lion in his den. ♦ To brave it. ♦ To brave the elements/ storm. ♦ To bring oneself to [it]. ♦ To conquer one's fears. ♦ To cowboy up. ♦ To man up. ♦ To muster (up) one's courage. ♦ To screw up/work up one's courage/nerve. ♦ To show courage/ grace under fire. ♦ To show true grit. ♦ To steel one's nerves. ♦ Whistling in the dark. ♦ Whistling past the graveyard. ♦ Who's afraid of the big, bad wolf?

Cowardice

A gutless wonder. ♦ A yellow stripe up one's back. ♦ Afraid of one's own shadow. [see also Fear] ♦ Are you a man or a mouse? ♦ Better to be a live dog than a dead lion. ♦ Better to be a live coward than a dead hero. ♦ Come on, you sons of bitches, do you want to live forever? ♦ Conscience doth make cowards of us all. ♦ He who fights and runs away, lives to fight another day. ♦ Him you can judge by

his cover: spineless. ♦ In fear of one's life. ♦ In mortal fear. ♦ Mother, oh, mother, oh what shall I do? My needs they are many, my pleasures are few. I married a man who is handsome and tall, but to my disappointment has no balls at all. No balls at all; no balls at all; I married a man who has no balls at all. ♦ The coward calls himself cautious, the miser thrifty. ♦ To be a lily-liver. ♦ To be a yellow-bellied, lily-livered coward. ♦ To be chicken sh*t. [see also Strict] ♦ To chicken out. ♦ To get/have cold feet. ♦ To not have a hair on one's *ss. ♦ To see right and not do it is cowardice. ♦ To the frightened warrior, every bush moves. ♦ To the thief on the run, each knock's an alarum. ♦ To wimp out. ♦ Weak in the knees. ♦ You ain't got an ounce of gumption in you. ♦ You dassn't do/say such a thing. ♦ You wouldn't dare (say that to his/her face).

Cozy

Comfortable as an old shoe. ♦ Comfortable in one's (own) skin. ♦ Creature comforts. ♦ In one's comfort zone. ♦ In the comfort of one's own home. ♦ Snug as a bug in a rug. ♦ To be comfy-cozy. ♦ To cozy up (to). ♦ To curl up with a good book.

♦ To make oneself comfortable. ♦ Warm as toast.

Crazy
(also dull, dimwitted)

A few bricks shy of a load. ♦ A few fries shy of a Happy Meal. ♦ A few inches short of a foot. ♦ A few ounces shy of a pound. ♦ A looney-tune. ♦ A mad scientist. ♦ A twisted/ warped mind. ♦ A twisted/ warped/ sense of humor. ♦ A bubble off plumb. ♦ Absolutely bonkers. ♦ As crazy as a peach-orchard pig. ♦ As mad as a March hare. ♦ Certifiably insane. ♦ Crazy as a bedbug/coot/ loon. ♦ Crazy as a Betsy Bug. ♦ Crazy as a sh*thouse rat. ♦ Crazy like a fox. ♦ Crazy little mama. ♦ Crazy, man, crazy. ♦ Crazy old coot. ♦ Doesn't have both oars in the water. ♦ Everyone's crazy except thee/you and me—and I'm not so sure about thee/you. ♦ Freaked out. ♦ Have you gone (completely) daft/mad? ♦ He who the gods wish to destroy they first make mad. ♦ I don't know if there's a method to his madness, but surely there's a madness to his method. — R.D. ♦ In la-la/ lala land. ♦ In Never-Never land. ♦ It feels as though there are only two sane people left on earth—me and thee—and sometimes I wonder about thee. ♦ In Cloud Cuckoo Land (var. Cuckoo Cloud Land). ♦ In the crazy house/looney bin/nut house. ♦ Mad as a hatter ♦ Mad as cheese. ♦ Not a hundred percent. ♦ Not all there. ♦ Not dealing with a full deck. ♦ Not the sharpest knife in the drawer. ♦ Not the sharpest tool in the shed. ♦ Not too tightly wrapped. ♦ Nuts. ♦ Nutsy Fagin ♦ Nutty. ♦ Nutty as a fruitcake. ♦ Nutty as a squirrel turd. ♦ Off one's nut/rocker/trolley. ♦ Out of one's bird/gourd/mind/nut/skull/tree. ♦ Out of touch with reality. [see also Fantasize] ♦ Played a few games too many without his helmet. ♦ Slightly daft. ♦ Stark raving mad. ♦ Stir crazy. ♦ Temporary insanity. ♦ The elevator doesn't go all the way to the top floor. ♦ The lights are on but there's nobody home. ♦ The mind is the first thing to go. ♦ The train has left the station. ♦ There's a thin line between genius and madness. ♦ They'll send the man with the net for you. ♦ They're coming to take me away. ♦ To be a raving lunatic. ♦ To be animal crackers. ♦ To be certifiable. ♦ To be cracked. ♦ To be in a drug-induced delirium/frenzy. ♦ To be in a fog. ♦ To be in never

never land. ♦ To be looney tunes. ♦ To be off one's nut. ♦ To be off the wall. ♦ To be one fry short of a happy meal. ♦ To be out of it. ♦ To be out of one's mind. ♦ To be possessed by demons. ♦ To be punch drunk. ♦ To be punchy. ♦ To be slap-happy. ♦ To be soft/touched in the head. ♦ To be touched. ♦ To be totally out of it. ♦ To be whacked out/wigged out. ♦ To cart you off to the Funny Farm. ♦ To come unhinged. ♦ To crack up. ♦ To drive [so] bananas/batty bonkers/crazy/nuts/up the wall. ♦ To flip out. ♦ To flip one's lid/wig. ♦ To freak out. ♦ To froth at the mouth. ♦ To go ape/apesh*t/batty/ bonkers/ buggy/dingy/gaga/insane/ kerflooey/nuts/off the deep end/off one's trolley/off the rails/stir crazy. ♦ To have a cow. ♦ To have a (few) screw(s) loose. ♦ To have bats in one's belfry. ♦ To lose touch with reality. ♦ To lose one's marbles. ♦ To plead (temporary) insanity. ♦ To take leave of one's senses. ♦ To wig out. ♦ To wind up cutting out paper dolls. ♦ To wind up in Bellvue/ Greystone. ♦ To wind up in the loony bin. ♦ Totally out of it. ♦ Touched in the head. ♦ What are you, some kind of nut? ♦ You must be out of your cotton-picking mind. ♦ You ought to have your head examined. ♦ You're as crazy as Dick's hat band. ♦ You've got rocks in your head.

Credit

A 21-gun salute. ♦ A credit to the race. ♦ A feather in one's cap. ♦ A hat tip (to). ♦ A letter of commendation/ recommendation. ♦ A ticker tape parade. ♦ An honorable mention. ♦ A job well done. ♦ A pat on the back. ♦ A tip of the hat. ♦ Author, author! ♦ Attaboy!/ Attagirl! ♦ Clever fellows, these Japanese. ♦ Compliments to the chef. ♦ Get/give high marks. ♦ Give a big hand (to). ♦ Give credit where credit is due. ♦ Give that man a cigar. ♦ Go to the head of the class. ♦ Good for you! ♦ Hear, hear! ♦ I knew you had it in you. ♦ I've got to hand it to you. ♦ It couldn't've happened to a nicer gal/guy. ♦ It'll look good on your record/resume. ♦ Let's hear it for [n.]. ♦ Nice going/job! ♦ Pride of authorship. ♦ Rah, rah, sis boom bah! ♦ Score one for [n.]. ♦ Stand up and take a bow. ♦ That's telling 'em. ♦ The edge does all the cutting but the blade takes all the credit. — R.D. ♦ Three cheers! ♦ To be in the Hall of Fame. ♦ To be the brainchild (of). ♦ To clap [so] on the back. ♦ To get/give A for effort. ♦ To give [so] a (well-deserved) pat on the back. ♦ To give [so] his/her due. ♦ To pay tribute to. ♦ To take hats off to. ♦ Way to go! ♦ What do you want, a medal? ♦ You done good. ♦ You're a better man than I am, Gunga Din. ♦ You've got to give [p.] that.

Crime

A crime against the state. ♦ A crime of opportunity/ passion. ♦ A crime spree. ♦ A criminal history. ♦ A lesser included offense. ♦ A life of crime. ♦ A little bit of larceny. ♦ A minor infraction (of the law). ♦ A rap sheet. ♦ An actionable offense. ♦ Crime and punishment. ♦ Crime does not pay. ♦ Crimes against humanity. ♦ Don't do the crime if you can't do the time. [see also Imprisonment, Punishment] ♦ Grand larceny. ♦ Partners in crime. [see also Complicity] ♦ Petty larceny. ♦ Society prepares the crime; the criminal commits it. ♦ The act is not criminal unless the intent is criminal. ♦ The scene of the crime. ♦ Where there is no law there is no crime/transgression. [see also Law]

Critical

A lot at stake. ♦ A lot riding on it. [see also Decisive] ♦ A tiebreaker. ♦

A matter of life and death. ♦ A watershed moment. ♦ At a crossroads. ♦ Can make you or break you. ♦ Drive as though your life depended upon it. It does. ♦ Failure is not an option. ♦ It all hinges on [it]. ♦ No margin for error. ♦ Sink or swim. ♦ That's all that matters. ♦ The moment of truth. ♦ The pivot man. ♦ The tipping point. ♦ To cast the deciding vote. ♦ To hang in the balance. ♦ To seal one's fate. [see also Destiny] ♦ [v.] as though your life depended on it. It does. ♦ When the sh*t hits the fan. ♦ Your last (best) chance. ♦ Zero error factor.

Criticism

Can't you do anything right? ♦ Constructive criticism. ♦ Critic: one who puts it down on paper. – R.D. ♦ Don't knock a good thing. ♦ Don't knock it if you haven't tried it. (also, Don't knock it until you've tried it.) ♦ Never was so round a critic as Bunker was of Michael Stivik. ♦ Scratch a friend/lover and find a foe. ♦ Where love is thin, faults are thick.

Crowding
(also confined, numerous)

A big head count. ♦ A big turnout. ♦ A cast of thousands. ♦ A flash mob. ♦ A gazillion. ♦ A good/great many.

[see also Abundance] ♦ A (real) mob scene. ♦ As numerous as stars in the sky. ♦ Bumper-to-bumper traffic. ♦ Bursting at the seams. ♦ Cabin fever. ♦ Close/cramped quarters. ♦ Come in droves. ♦ Couldn't stir them with a stick. ♦ Not room enough to swing a cat. [see also Close] ♦ Packed *sshole to belly-button. ♦ Packed like sardines (in a can). ♦ Standing room only. ♦ The walls are closing in. ♦ They came out of the woodwork. ♦ They gathered like toads after the rain. ♦ They were up to the rafters. ♦ Thick as flies. ♦ Thick as ticks on a coondog/houndog. ♦ To come out of the woodwork. ♦ To come right and left. ♦ To come thick and fast. ♦ To edge in/squeeze in. ♦ To pack them in. ♦ Toe to heel. ♦ Umpteen million. ♦ Wall to wall. [see also Comprehensive] ♦ Wall-to-wall bodies.

Curiosity

(also voyeurism)

A peeping Tom. ♦ Aren't you the least bit curious? ♦ Curiosity killed the cat. (And satisfaction brought it back.) ♦ Eavesdroppers never hear anything good about themselves. ♦ Idle curiosity. ♦ Inquiring minds want to know. ♦ (Just) dying to know. ♦ (Just) out of curiosity. ♦ Morbid curiosity. ♦

Peek-a-boo; I see you. ♦ To be a curiosity seeker. ♦ To get a free show. ♦ To satisfy one's curiosity. ♦ What are you writing, a book? ♦ What gives? ♦ What, what—what are you, a light bulb? ♦ What's up with that? ♦ What's your sign? (The dollar sign!) ♦ Who, who—what are you, an owl?

Cyber-Slang

(common acronyms)

afk - (away from keyboard). ♦ aon - (all or nothing). ♦ aos - (adult over shoulder). ♦ aota - (all of the above). ♦ asap - (as soon as possible). ♦ asl - (age, sex, location). ♦ ayt - (are you there). ♦ b4n - (bye for now). ♦ bak - (back at keyboard). ♦ bbl - (be back later). ♦ biw - (boss is watching). ♦ bos - (boss over shoulder). ♦ brb - (be right back) [or, bathroom break]. ♦ btw - (by the way). ♦ cu - (see you). ♦ dl - (download). ♦ dmi - (don't mention it). ♦ f4f - (female for female). ♦ f4m - (female for male). ♦ fb - (facebook). ♦ fitb - (fill in the blanks). ♦ fyi - (for your information). ♦ *g* - (grin). ♦ g/f - (girlfriend). ♦ g2gn - (got to go now). ♦ glwt - (good luck with that). ♦ gm - (good morning). ♦ gr8 - (great). ♦ h8r - (hater). ♦ hb - (hurry back). ♦ hwth – (hate when that happens). ♦ idk - (I don't know).

ikr - (I know, right?). imho - (in my humble opinion). j/k - (just kidding). k - (ok). l8r - (see you later). lmao - (laughing my *ss off). lol - (laughing out loud). m4f - (male for female). m4m - (male for male). me2 - (me too). mos - (mom over shoulder). newbie - (new player). nota – (none of the above). np - (no problem). npi - (no pun intended). nsfw - (not safe for work). omg - (oh my God). oobl - (out of breath laughing). p@w - (parents are watching). pita - (pain in the *ss). pitr - (parent in the room). plz - (please). ppl - (people). qna - (question and answer). qt 3.14 - (cutie pie). roflmao - (rolling on the floor laughing my *ss off). rtm - (read the manual). sol - (sh*t out of luck). ttfn – (ta ta for now). ttyl - (talk to you later). tyvm - (thank you very much). udwk - (you don't want to know). waz^ - (what's up?). wb - (welcome back). wiw - (wife is watching). wolo - (we only live once). wombat - (waste of money, brains and time). woot - (woohoo). wrt - (with regard to). wtf - (what the f*ck). wtg - (way to go). wtvr - (whatever). wubu2 - (what you been up to). wysiwyg - (what you see is what you get). xfer - (transfer).

y2b - (YouTube). ybs - (you'll be sorry). ybya - (you bet your *ss). ycliu - (you could look it up). ycmtsu - (you can't make this sh*it up). yolo - (you only live once). yvw - (you're very welcome). yw - (you're welcome). zup - (what's up).

Dance

A gandy dancer. A lot of fancy footwork. An erotic/exotic dancer. Cut a rug. Dance around the Maypole. Dancing in the dark. Dinner and dancing. Do the hootchy-kootchy. Get down and boogie. If the Congress does not march at least it dances. Just because your feet are moving doesn't mean you're dancing. Killer moves. May I have (the honor of) this dance? Same old song and dance. [see also Bore] Save the last dance for me. Shake your booty/ money maker. Shall we dance? To do a jig. To diddly bop. To dipsy-doodle. To trip the light fantastic. Would you do me the honor of sharing this dance with me?

Dark

A black hole. A total blackout. As dark as a pocket. Black as coal. Black as night/pitch/sin/

soot/the ace of spades. ♦ Black on black. ♦ Can't see two feet in front of you. ♦ Can't see one's hand/nose in front of one's face. ♦ Dark as a dungeon/tomb. ♦ Darkest Africa. ♦ In total darkness. ♦ Left in the dark [see also Ignorance] ♦ Pitch black. ♦ Where were you when the lights went out?

Dearth

A dry spell. ♦ A ghost town. ♦ A lack of money coming in from everywhere. ♦ A long, dry spell. ♦ Bare as Mother Hubbard's cupboard. ♦ Bits and pieces. ♦ Dribs and drabs. ♦ Drought brings dearth. ♦ Here and there. ♦ Running on empty/fumes. ♦ Slim pickings. ♦ To scrape the bottom of the barrel. ♦ To scare up/scrape up/scrounge up. ♦ To scrounge around. ♦ You can't spend what you don't have.

Death

A death in the family. ♦ A natural death. ♦ Bang, you're dead. ♦ Better red than dead. ♦ Come to an untimely end. [see also Premature] ♦ Cut down in the prime of life. ♦ Beyond the pale. ♦ Brain dead. ♦ Breathe one's last. ♦ Carried out feet first. ♦ Cash in one's chips. ♦ Dead and buried. ♦ Dead and gone. ♦ Dead as a doornail. ♦ Dead as yesterday's news. ♦ Dead in the water. ♦ Dead men tell no tales. ♦ Dead on arrival. (DOA). ♦ Deader than a mackerel. ♦ Death and destruction/decay. ♦ Death before dishonor. ♦ Death is Nature's way of telling you to relax. ♦ Death to spies. ♦ Death, where is thy sting? ♦ Die a thousand deaths. ♦ Die a-borning. ♦ Die like a dog. ♦ Die with one's boots on. ♦ Drop dead. ♦ Dying is a part of life/living. ♦ Dying words have a halo. ♦ Enter the Pearly Gates. ♦ Give me liberty or give me death. ♦ Give up the ghost. ♦ Give one's last gasp. ♦ Go belly up. ♦ Go out feet first. ♦ Go out in a pine box. ♦ Go the way of all flesh. ♦ Go to a better world. ♦ Go to one's eternal rest. ♦ Go to one's final repose. ♦ Go to one's final resting place/reward. ♦ Go to the Great Beyond. ♦ Go to the happy hunting grounds. ♦ Go to the palace in the sky. ♦ Gone to the great beyond. ♦ Graveyard dead. ♦ He/she is in a better place. ♦ He/she passed away peacefully at home (surrounded by his/her family). ♦ In the afterlife/hereafter. ♦ In the granite garden. ♦ In the great by and by. ♦ In the marble orchard. ♦ In the midst of life we are in death. ♦ Join one's ancestors.

◆ Kick the bucket. ◆ Lay [it] to rest. ◆ Make the supreme sacrifice. ◆ Manner of death. ◆ Meet your maker. ◆ Never laugh when a hearse goes by; you may be the next to die. [see also Caution] ◆ Null and void. ◆ Only the good die young. ◆ Pass on. ◆ Pass on to the other side. ◆ Pronounced dead at the scene. ◆ Pushing up daisies. ◆ Resting in Davy Jones' locker. ◆ Rigor mortis has set in. ◆ Shuffle off this mortal coil. ◆ Six feet under. ◆ Sleep the long sleep. ◆ Stone cold dead (in the market). ◆ The Death of a Thousand Cuts. ◆ The Grim Reaper. ◆ The last roundup. ◆ The last thing on earth you want to do is die—and sure enough, that is the last thing you do! ◆ The old men know when an old man dies. ◆ The only sure things are death and taxes. ◆ Till death do us part. ◆ To be mortally wounded. ◆ To be planted in Boot Hill. ◆ To bite the big one. ◆ To buy it. ◆ To buy the farm. ◆ To come home in a body bag. ◆ To croak. ◆ To die in the saddle. ◆ To die off/out. ◆ To die the death. ◆ To die/wither on the vine. ◆ To give the last full measure of devotion. ◆ To lay down one's life. ◆ To lie in state. ◆ To make one's final arrangements. ◆ To pass away/pass on. ◆ To pay the ultimate price. ◆ To shuffle off this mortal coil. ◆ To suffer a fatal blow. ◆ To take a dirt nap. ◆ To wear a toe tag. ◆ To wither up and die. ◆ Turn in one's ticket. ◆ Turn up one's toes. ◆ We all have to go sometime. [see also Destiny] ◆ What's the most popular place in town? The cemetery: people are dying to get in!

Debt

A debt of gratitude. ◆ A negative balance. ◆ Debt before dishonor. ◆ Drowning/swimming in debt. ◆ Fortune owes many too much—but no one enough. ◆ Give me liberty or give me debt. ◆ I owe; I owe; it's off to work I go. ◆ It's better to owe than to pay. ◆ Pay one's debt to society. [see also Punishment] ◆ Speak not of my debts unless you mean to pay them. ◆ Till debt do us part. ◆ To be in hock. ◆ To be in debt/hock up to one's ears/eyeballs. ◆ To be in the hole/in the red. ◆ To have a mortgage under water. ◆ To satisfy a debt. ◆ To suffer a fate worse than debt. ◆ Up to one's ears/eyeballs in debt/hock.

Decisive

A decisive blow. ◆ A defining/pivotal moment. ◆ A lot riding on it. [see also Critical] ◆ A qualifying heat. ◆ A rubber match. ◆ A watershed moment.

♦ Case rises or falls on it. ♦ Day of reckoning. ♦ *Dies irae.* ♦ Have the final cut. ♦ Have the final say/say-so. ♦ Have the last word. ♦ Judgment Day. ♦ Ladies and gentlemen of the jury, have you reached a verdict? ♦ Now or never. ♦ Reach a turning point. ♦ The envelope, please. ♦ The moment of truth. ♦ The playoffs. ♦ This is it. ♦ To tip the balance. ♦ To tip the scales in one's favor. [see also Advantage] ♦ To turn the tide (of battle). ♦ To weigh in the balance. ♦ When the chips are down.

Deduce

By deductive reasoning. ♦ By logical inference. ♦ Connect the dots. ♦ Crunch the numbers. ♦ Do the math. ♦ Draw a conclusion. ♦ Fill in the blanks. ♦ Go figure. ♦ Process of deduction. ♦ Read between the lines. ♦ To dope out. ♦ To factor [it] in. ♦ To figure [it] out. ♦ To put two and two together. (And come up with four). ♦ To read into [it]. ♦ To read [so] like an open book. ♦ To take a fine pencil to. ♦ To work up the numbers. ♦ You can fill in the blanks for yourself. ♦ You figure it out. ♦ You take it from there.

Defeat

A cause that cannot stand defeat is not worth fighting over. ♦ A crushing blow. ♦ A crushing defeat. ♦ A signal defeat. ♦ An ignominious defeat. ♦ Be one's downfall/undoing. ♦ Cry uncle. ♦ How the mighty are fallen! ♦ Meet one's match/Waterloo. ♦ Never laid a glove on him. ♦ On the ropes. ♦ Say uncle. ♦ To admit defeat. ♦ To be licked. ♦ To clean [so]'s clock. ♦ To defeat its purpose. ♦ To fight a losing battle. ♦ To get one's *ss kicked/ whipped. ♦ To give a licking to. ♦ To go down for the count. ♦ To kayo/ get kayoed. ♦ To know when you're licked. ♦ To stoop to conquer. ♦ To take a licking/ shellacking. ♦ To take the full count. ♦ *Veni, vidi, vici* (I came, I saw, I conquered). ♦ Victory has a thousand fathers; defeat is an orphan.

Defy

Anything you dish out I can take. ♦ Bring it on. ♦ Hit me with your best shot. ♦ I can take it; I have broad shoulders. ♦ I don't see any anchor around your *ss. ♦ Lay it on me. [see also Confide] ♦ One word from me and he does as he damned well pleases. ♦ Sock it to me. ♦ To fly in the face of. ♦ To fly in the face of conventional wisdom. ♦ To fly in the face of danger.

Dejection

A bummeroo. ◆ A crying jag. ◆ A hangdog expression. ◆ A real bummer. ◆ A sad/sorry state of affairs. ◆ A slough of despond. ◆ A tearjerker. ◆ Alas and alack. ◆ Bad day at Black Rock. ◆ Blue Monday. ◆ Bummed out. ◆ Cast a pall on/over. ◆ Doom and gloom. ◆ Down in the dumps. ◆ Down in the mouth. ◆ In a vile mood. ◆ In the doldrums. ◆ In the depths of despair. ◆ In the throes of depression. ◆ Not a happy camper. ◆ On a somber note. ◆ Prophet of gloom/doom. ◆ To be a sad sack. ◆ To be in sackcloth and ashes. ◆ To be the pits. ◆ To bring/get [so] down. ◆ To bum/gross [so] out. ◆ To burst into tears. ◆ To carry the weight of the world on one's shoulders. ◆ To feel sorry for oneself. ◆ To have an albatross/millstone around one's neck. ◆ To have a long face. ◆ To have the blue devils. ◆ To shoulder the burden. ◆ Why so glum, chum? ◆ With a heavy heart. ◆ Woe is me. ◆ You look like you just lost your best friend. ◆ You look like you lost your dog.

Delay

A delayed reaction. ◆ A hang fire. ◆ A stay of execution. ◆ A traffic snarl. ◆ After while. ◆ Break stride. ◆ Delays increase desire and sometimes extinguish them. ◆ Dilly-dally. ◆ Don't put off till tomorrow what you can do today. ◆ Drag one's feet/heels. ◆ Fatootz around. ◆ Fiddle around. ◆ Fritter away the time. ◆ Good executives never put off until tomorrow what they can get somebody else to do today. ◆ He who hesitates also foxtrots. ◆ He who hesitates is lost. [see also Immediacy] ◆ Later on. ◆ Let's not be too hasty. ◆ Let's not rush into things. ◆ Prolong the agony. ◆ Rubbernecking delays. ◆ Slack off. ◆ Spring break. ◆ Take a breather. ◆ Take five. ◆ Tied up in traffic. ◆ To catch one's breath. ◆ To fart around. ◆ To fall behind. ◆ To get/give the runaround. ◆ To get pulled over. ◆ To hang fire. ◆ To have second thoughts. ◆ To hold back. ◆ To hold off. ◆ To kick the can down the road. ◆ To mark time. [see also Wait] ◆ To monkey around. ◆ To pass the time of day. ◆ To play for time. ◆ To postpone the inevitable. ◆ To put [it] off. ◆ To spin wheels. ◆ To stall for time. ◆ To string [so] along. ◆ To string [so] out. ◆ To table the issue/matter. ◆ To tread water. ◆ What's taking so long? ◆ What's the holdup?

Demeaning

A slap in the face. ◆ An affront/insult to one's intelligence. ◆ Beneath one's dignity. ◆ Beneath one's station (in life/society). ◆ Deeply offended. ◆ How could you stoop so low? ◆ How low can you get/go? ◆ *Infra dig.* ◆ I was never so insulted in (all) my life. ◆ I won't dignify that with an answer. ◆ I wouldn't lower myself. ◆ On hands and knees. ◆ The unkindest cut of all. ◆ The (very) idea! ◆ To lower oneself (to). ◆ To feel put-upon. ◆ To go slumming. ◆ To hit a new low. ◆ To lower oneself (to). ◆ To lower one's standards. ◆ To slum it. ◆ To stoop to [it]. ◆ To take offense/umbrage. ◆ To treat [so] like dirt under one's feet. ◆ To view a woman as a sex object. ◆ To wind up in the gutter.

Departure

A mass exodus. ◆ A tossed bird. ◆ All aboard! ◆ All ashore that's going ashore. ◆ And away we go ◆ Elvis has left the building. ◆ Go on one's merry way. ◆ I'm outta here. ◆ Leave in a cloud of dust. ◆ Move on to greener pastures. ◆ Off we go, into the wild blue yonder. ◆ Sally forth. ◆ Set sail. ◆ Shove off. ◆ Shuffle off to Buffalo. ◆ The train has left the station. ◆ To absent oneself. ◆ To blast off. ◆ To book. ◆ To bug out. ◆ To cut out. ◆ To duck out. ◆ To get along. ◆ To go on one's way. ◆ To hie on out of here. ◆ To hit the road. ◆ To hit the dusty trail. ◆ To pack one's bags and leave. ◆ To pull a Hank Snow. ◆ To put it (all) behind you. ◆ To ship out. ◆ To take one's leave (of). ◆ To take off (like a big ass bird). ◆ To weigh anchor. ◆ Twenty-three skidoo (and oh, you kid). ◆ We have liftoff!

Dependable

A standing order. ◆ Constant as the tides. ◆ Day in, day out. ◆ If you can't count on [n.], who *can* you count on? ◆ In fair and stormy weather. ◆ Old Faithful. ◆ Old reliable. ◆ Through thick and thin. [see also Steadfast, Thick, Thin] ◆ To be there for [so]. ◆ Tried and true. ◆ You can set your watch by it. [see also Certainty] ◆ Works first time, every time. ◆ You can trust it with your life. ◆ True to one's word.

Dereliction

A sorry excuse for a man. ◆ A sorry sack of sh*t. ◆ Actor: one who has hit the skits. ◆ Broadway: Skit Row. ◆ Dereliction of duty. ◆ Go bust. ◆ Hit rock bottom. ◆ In the gutter. ◆ No way to go but up. ◆ On the balls of one's *ss. ◆ (Scraping) the bottom of the barrel. ◆ Tapped out. ◆ The dregs of society. [see also Status] ◆ To be down and out. ♦ To be on/hit the skids. ♦ To bottom out. ♦ To touch bottom. ♦ To wind up on Skid Row.

Deserve

Assume one's rightful place. ♦ Blow up in one's own face. ♦ Earn a merit badge. ♦ Every dog has his day. [see also Dogs] ♦ Get a dose of one's own medicine. ♦ He who feeds the hen deserves the eggs. ♦ Harm watch, harm catch. ♦ Hoist by one's own petard. ♦ It serves you right. ♦ Let that be a lesson to you. ♦ No good deed goes unpunished. [ironic/sarcastic] ♦ One good turn deserves another. [see also Reciprocation] ♦ (One good term deserves another—political slogan). ♦ Poetic justice. ♦ That's what you get for [n.]. ♦ The chickens will come home to roost. ♦ To bring it on/upon oneself. ♦ To come back to bite/haunt you. ♦ To get what's coming to you. ♦ To get one's comeuppance. ♦ To get one's fair share. ♦ To get one's just deserts. ♦ To have it coming to one. ♦ To stew in one's own juices. ♦ What goes around, comes around (and when it does, you'd best be sitting down.) – R.D. [see also Slander] ♦ What've I done to deserve this? ♦ You asked for it. ♦ You get what you deserve. ♦ When you mess with the bull, you get the horns. ♦ You got

yourself into this; you get yourself out. ♦ You owe it to yourself. ♦ You'll get yours (just you wait and see). ♦ Your time will come.

Desire

A burning desire. ♦ A wannabe. ♦ Be still, my heart. ♦ Can't get enough of [it]. ♦ I never met a/an [n.] I didn't like. ♦ More than willing (to). ♦ Nobody wants that more than I. ♦ Ready, willing and able. ♦ The more you can't have it, the more you want it. ♦ To be crazy about [it]. ♦ To be drooling /dying for [it]. ♦ To be goal oriented. ♦ To be hung up (on). [see also Habit] ♦ To be in the market/mood (for). ♦ To be jonesing for. ♦ To be partial to. ♦ To be up for [it]. ♦ To be stepping on one's tongue for. ♦ To capture/ catch/tickle one's fancy. ♦ To care for [it]. ♦ To care to [v.]. ♦ To cream one's jeans (for). ♦ To eat it (right) up. ♦ To give one's eyeteeth/right arm (for). ♦ To go for [it] (in a big way). ♦ To have a craving/hankering/jonesing/yearning/yen for. [it]. ♦ To have a hang-up (for). ♦ To have a thing for. ♦ To have a weakness for. ♦ To have designs on. ♦ To have one's heart set on [it]. ♦ To have one's tongue hanging out for. ♦ To jump at the chance. ♦ To leap at the opportunity. ♦ To lick one's chops/lips (in anticipation). ♦ To lust after [it]. ♦

To want [it] in the worst way. ♦ To want [it] more than anything in the (whole wide) world. ♦ To want [it] so bad you can (almost) taste it. ♦ To want in. ♦ To your heart's desire. ♦ You always want what you can't have. ♦ You know you want it.

Destiny

A bullet with one's name on it. ♦ A strange quirk of fate. ♦ All rivers flow to the sea. ♦ By the grace of God. ♦ Everything happens for a reason. ♦ If God meant man to fly, He would have given him wings. ♦ It all works out in the end. ♦ It is what it is. [see also Reality] ♦ It'll all fall into place. ♦ It's God's will. ♦ It's (all) in God's hands. ♦ It's in the lap of the gods. ♦ It's in the stars. ♦ Let the chips fall where they may. ♦ Lightning never strikes twice in the same place. [see also Truisms] ♦ (Not) meant to be. ♦ (Not) in the cards. ♦ Que sera` sera`. (What will be will be). ♦ The cards call themselves. ♦ The die is cast. ♦ The moving finger writes, and having writ, moves on. Nor all your piety, nor tears, nor wit, can cancel out a line of it. ♦ To be captain of one's own destiny. ♦ To seal one's fate. [see also Critical] ♦ To turn/work out all right. ♦ We all have to go sometime.

[see also Death] ♦ When you gotta go, you gotta go. ♦ When your number's up, it's up. ♦ Your days are numbered.

Destroy

A demolition derby. ♦ A (complete) teardown. ♦ A scorched-earth policy. ♦ Beat to a pulp. ♦ Burn, baby, burn. ♦ Blow sky-high. ♦ Blow out of the water. ♦ Blow to bits. ♦ Blow to kingdom come. ♦ Blow to smithereens. ♦ Cut to ribbons. ♦ Drive into the dirt. ♦ Lay waste (to). ♦ Make mincemeat of. ♦ Tear limb from limb. ♦ To be toast. ♦ To go up in smoke. ♦ To hell and gone. ♦ To reduce to ashes/rubble. ♦ To tear down. ♦ To tear to tatters. ♦ To totally demolish [it]. ♦ To wipe [it] from the face of the earth. ♦ To wipe [it]/[so] out. ♦ Total carnage/destruction.

Detect

A fuzzbuster. ♦ A lie detector. ♦ Do I detect a hint/note of [n.]? ♦ A motion detector. ♦ A sensor light. ♦ Informed sources say. [see also Gossip, News] ♦ Look at it this way. ♦ On the radar. ♦ To catch/get [so]'s drift. ♦ To catch/get wind of. ♦ To have a new take on [it]. ♦ To have it on good/the highest authority. ♦ To hear tell. ♦ To pick up (on). ♦ To put [it] in/into perspective. ♦ To see another side to [so]. ♦ To see out of the corner of one's eye. ♦ To see someone/something in a new light. ♦ To see the likes of.

Deteriorate
(also offend)

A fish always rots from the head down. ♦ A nail in one's coffin. ♦ A physical wreck. ♦ A prune is a plum puckered out. ♦ A race to the bottom. ♦ A tumbledown shack. ♦ And the walls came tumbling down. ♦ Beyond repair. ♦ Down the drain/tubes. ♦ Dry rot. ♦ Erectile dysfunction. ♦ Exposed to the elements. ♦ Fish and visitors stink after three days. ♦ Good habits deteriorate over time. ♦ If/when push comes to shove. ♦ If worse comes to worse. ♦ In a bad way. [see also Discomfiture] ♦ It'll get worse before it gets better. ♦ It's all downhill from here. ♦ Just when it seemed things couldn't get any worse... ♦ Off the cliff. ♦ On the rocks. [see also Discomfiture] ♦ Out of the frying pan into the fire. ♦ Spring a leak. ♦ That's (just/exactly/ precisely) what I was afraid of. ♦ The cure is worse than the disease. ♦ The operation was a success but the patient died. ♦ The plot thickens. ♦ To resort to violence. ♦ The sun a plum does ruin into a prune. ♦ There goes the neighborhood. ♦ To

add insult to injury. ♦ To be one's own worst enemy. ♦ To be out of practice. ♦ To become an issue. ♦ To come/go to (w)rack and ruin. ♦ To compound the felony. ♦ To cut one's own throat. ♦ To dig one's own grave. ♦ To do more harm than good. ♦ To get out of shape. ♦ To give way. ♦ To go bad. ♦ To go from bad to worse. ♦ To go south. ♦ To go to pot/seed/the dogs/waste. ♦ To go into foreclosure. ♦ To heap indignity upon indignity. ♦ To hit [so] where he/she lives. ♦ To jump the shark. ♦ To kick sand in [so]'s face. ♦ To lower expectations. ♦ To lower the bar. ♦ To make matters worse. ♦ To sink into oblivion. ♦ To take a turn for the worse. ♦ To throw the baby out with the bathwater. ♦ To rob Peter to pay Paul. ♦ To rub [so]'s nose in it. ♦ To rub salt in the wounds. ♦ To spiral out of control. ♦ To take its toll. ♦ To trade down. ♦ To waste away (to nothing). ♦ To wear down. ♦ To wear out. ♦ To wear thin. ♦ When the sh*t hits the fan. ♦ Your insult may result in your injury. ♦ Your worst fears are realized. ♦ Zap, you're sterile.

Determination

A man on a mission. ♦ A man to take a letter to Garcia. ♦ Bound and determined. ♦ By cracky. ♦ By cracky, by gum. ♦ By the hair of my chinny chin chin. ♦ Come hell or high water.* ♦ Come what may. *[see also Inexorable] ♦ Dogged determination. ♦ Dogged in one's persistence. ♦ Have a good mind to. ♦ Have one's heart set on. ♦ If it's the last thing I do. ♦ Make up one's mind (to). ♦ Not if I can help it. ♦ Not on my watch. ♦ Or die trying. ♦ Or my name is mud. ♦ Or my name isn't [n.]. ♦ Pike's Peak or bust. ♦ Take it all the way to the Supreme Court. ♦ The will to live. ♦ There's always a way. ♦ Thy will be done. ♦ To be single-minded. ♦ To brook no interference/opposition. ♦ To feel like [it]. ♦ To have an iron will. ♦ To have (half) a mind to. ♦ To know one's own mind. ♦ To let nothing stand in one's way. ♦ To put/set one's mind to [it]. ♦ To psych oneself up. ♦ Where there's a will, there's a way. ♦ Will not be deterred. ♦ Will stop at nothing.

Devil

A devil-may-care attitude. ♦ And the devil take the hindmost. ♦ Better the devil you know than the devil you don't know. ♦ Between the devil and the deep blue sea. ♦ Devil take it. ♦ Give the devil his due. ♦ Go to the devil. ♦ God sends the meat and the devil sends cooks. ♦ He who sups with the devil must have a long spoon. ♦ In league with the devil. ♦ Speak of the devil and he appears. [see also Coincidence, Gossip] ♦ Tears in the devil's eyes. ♦ The devil incarnate/personified. ♦ The devil is in the details. ♦ The devil wears many disguises. ♦ The mark of the beast. ♦ To have hell/the devil to pay. ♦ To hold a candle for the devil. ♦ To play the devil's advocate. ♦ To sell one's soul to the devil. ♦ When the devil embraces you, he wants your soul. ♦ When the devil is blind. [never] ♦ Who talks of himself talks to the devil.

Difference

A world of difference. ♦ It makes all the difference in the world. ♦ The difference between clouds and mud. ♦ The difference between a man and a boy is the price of his toys. ♦ The difference between day and night. ♦ The difference between stupidity and genius is that genius has its limits. — Albert Einstein [see also Genius] ♦ The difference between the almost right word and the right word is the difference between the lightning bug and the lightning. – Mark Twain ♦ *Vive le difference.* ♦ What's the difference between a girls' track team and a tribe of pygmies? The pygmies are a bunch of cunning little runts. ♦ What's the difference between a rodeo rider and a lawyer? The rodeo rider makes a living by having the bull throw him. — R.D.

Different

A change of pace. [see also Change, Varied] ✦ A change of plans. ✦ A change of venue. ✦ A far cry from. ✦ A game-changer. ✦ A glaring inconsistency. ✦ A horse of a different color. ✦ A new regime. ✦ A radical departure. ✦ A whole 'nother animal/matter/story. ✦ A (whole) new ball of wax/ballgame. ✦ Different as a back half from a halfback. ✦ Different as a ballet dancer from a belly dancer. ✦ Different as a black boot from a bootblack. ✦ Different as a brick of gold from a goldbrick. ✦ Different as a bum steer from a steer's bum. ✦ Different as a cowpoke from a pokey cow. ✦ Different as a guitar from a target. ✦ Different as a hot dog from a dog in heat. ✦ Different as a labor force from forced labor. ✦ Different as a hiccup from a tea cup. ✦ Different as a land baron from barren land. ✦ Different as a pack rat from a rat pack. ✦ Different as a polka from a polka dot. ✦ Different as a shotgun from a gunshot. ✦ Different as a tic, from a tac, from your toe. ✦ Different as a wee key from a Kiwi. ✦ Different as an overhang from a hangover. ✦ Different as an upset from a setup. ✦ Different as an upstart from a start-up. ✦ Different as chalk from cheese. ✦ Different as Coulee dam from a damned coolie. ✦ Different as day and night. ✦ Different as night and day. ✦ Different as Passover from an overpass. ✦ Different as the back of a quarter from a quarterback. ✦ Different as your left from your right. ✦ Different strokes for different folks. ✦ It's the same—only different. ✦ No two grains of sand are alike. ✦ Polar opposites. ✦ Something else again. ✦ That's a horse of another color. [see also Horse] ✦ The gender gap. ✦ There's a new sheriff in town. ✦ To bear little resemblance (to). ✦ To be [adj.] than usual. ✦ To change the dynamic. ✦ To change the ground rules. ✦ To change the subject. [see also Irrelevant] ✦ To shift gears. ✦ To start a new thread. ✦ Under new management. ✦ Why is tonight different from all other nights? ✦ You'll never look at [n.]/[p.] the same way again.

Difficulty

A ballbuster. ✦ A backbreaking/daunting task. ✦ A Gordian knot. ✦ A Herculean task. ✦ A steep learning curve. ♦ A sticky wicket. ♦ A tall order. ♦ A tough nut to crack. ♦ A tough row to hoe. ♦ An uphill battle. ♦ Easier said than done. ♦ Go against the odds. ♦ Hard as pulling fly dung out of pepper. ♦ Hard labor. ♦ Hell's half acre. ♦ Insurmountable obstacles. ♦ It's no picnic. ♦ Like a salmon swimming upstream. ♦ It'll take an act of Congress (to). ♦ It's a dog-eat-dog world. ♦ It's a jungle out there. ♦ It's a tough world out there. ♦ It's hard to say/tell. ♦ Like giving birth to a porcupine—backwards. ♦ Like looking for a needle in a haystack. ♦ Like pulling teeth. ♦ Like pulling teeth—through the armpit. ♦ Like threading a needle with boxing gloves on. ♦ Like trying to nail Jello to the wall. ♦ Like trying to stuff a wet noodle up a wildcat's *ss. ♦ No easy task. ♦ No mean feat. ♦ Running to stay in place. ♦ Say not the struggle naught availeth. ♦ That'll take some doing. ♦ The difficult we do right away; the impossible will take a little longer. ♦ The world is too much with us. ♦ Things are tough all over. ♦ To be hard-pressed (to). ♦ To be hard put (to). ♦ To be the underdog. ♦ To be up against/overcome insurmountable odds. ♦ To do [it] the hard way. ♦ To have the deck stacked against you. ♦ To struggle against all odds. ♦ To swim against the current/stream/tide. ♦ Tough sledding.

Dilapidated

A bucket of bolts. ♦ A fixer-upper. ♦ A flivver. ♦ A handyman's special. ♦ A heap. ♦ A sad/sorry state of affairs. ♦ A shadow of one's former self. ♦ A shambles of a man. ♦ A tin Lizzie. ♦ Coming apart at the seams. ♦ Dog-eared. ♦ Dying on the vine. ♦ Get a horse! ♦ Gone to seed. ♦ Had its day. ♦ Many good tools and men rust out instead of wearing out. ♦ Over the hill. ♦ Put out to pasture. ♦ Ragged/rough around the edges. ♦ Run down at the heels. ♦ Seen better days (but not many). ♦ Shot in the *ss. ♦ Shot to hell. ♦ Shows wear and tear. ♦ Sorry state of affairs. ♦ The old grey mare she ain't what she used to be. ♦ Time has taken its toll ♦ To come to (w)rack and ruin. ♦ To fall into disrepair/disuse. ♦ To go all to hell. ♦ To run [it] into the ground. ♦ Wasted away to nothing. ♦ Yellowed with age.

Dilemma

A Catch-22. ♦ A conflict of interests. ♦ A Hobson's choice. ♦ A man on the horns of a dilemma may be easily swayed by a line of bull. - R.D. ♦ A moral dilemma. ♦ A no-win situation.

♦ A squeeze play. ♦ A thorny problem. ♦ Between a rock and a hard place. ♦ Between the devil and the deep blue sea. ♦ In a bind. ♦ In a jam. ♦ In a peck of trouble. ♦ In a pickle. ♦ In a (real) fix. ♦ In a tight spot. ♦ In deep doo-doo/sh*t. ♦ In Dutch. ♦ In hot water. ♦ In over one's head. ♦ In the soup. ♦ In (big) trouble. ♦ On the horns of a dilemma. ♦ Over a barrel. ♦ To be backed into a corner. ♦ To be hard pressed. ♦ To be in for it. ♦ To be torn between two [n.]. ♦ To be up against it. ♦ To be up against the wall. ♦ To choose between the lesser of two evils. ♦ To feel the pinch. ♦ To have a tiger by the tail. ♦ To have [so] coming and going. ♦ To have one's back against/to the wall. ♦ To have one's tit in a wringer. ♦ To have the bull by the horns. ♦ To have the wolf by the ear. ♦ To paint oneself into a corner. ♦ To wrestle with one's demons. ♦ Up a tree. ♦ Up the creek. ♦ Up sh*t creek/sh*t's creek (without a paddle). ♦ You're damned if you do and damned if you don't.

Disagree

A moot point. ♦ A difference of opinion. ♦ A point of contention. ♦ Agree to disagree. [see also Agree] ♦ Bah, humbug. ♦ Far from it. ♦ I beg to differ. ♦ I object, your honor! ♦ I resent that remark. ♦ I wouldn't (go as far as to) say that. ♦ In dispute. ♦ It's anything but. ♦ Move to strike (it from the record). ♦ No way (in hell). ♦ Not at all. ♦ Not in my backyard. ♦ Not in my book. ♦ Not in my neighborhood. ♦ Not in the least/slightest. ♦ Not on my watch. ♦ Objection overruled. ♦ Reasonable men may differ. ♦ Take exception (to). ♦ Take issue (with). ♦ That's debatable. ♦ To disabuse [so] of the idea/notion. [see also Clarification] ♦ To respectfully disagree.

Disappear

Do a disappearing/vanishing act. ♦ Going . . . going . . . gone! ♦ Gone with the wind. ♦ Missing in action. ♦ Now you see it, now you don't. ♦ Sleight of hand. ♦ To drop/fall off the face of the earth. ♦ To drop out of sight. ♦ To fall through the cracks. ♦ To go into hiding. ♦ To go missing. ♦ To go south. ♦ To leave no forwarding address. ♦ To make oneself scarce. ♦ To strike [it] from the record. ♦ To take off for parts unknown. ♦ To vanish into thin air/without a trace.

Disappointment

A big comedown/letdown. ♦ A buzzkill. ♦ A killjoy. ♦ A party pooper. [see also Bore] ♦ Can't get no satisfaction. ♦ I hate to burst your bubble, but . . . ♦ Killjoy motto: We're not happy till you're not happy. ♦ Not all it's cracked up to be. ♦ Leaves a lot to be desired. ♦ None too pleased. ♦ To burst [so]'s bubble. ♦ To cast a pall on. ♦ To curb one's enthusiasm. ♦ To dash [so]'s hopes. ♦ To dampen [so]'s spirits. ♦ To have a sobering effect (on). ♦ To let [so] down. ♦ To pour/throw cold water on. ♦ To rain on [so]'s parade. ♦ To take the wind out of [so]'s sails. ♦ You (above all people) should know better (than that). ♦ You can't/don't always get what you want.

Disapprove

Before I'm through with you, you'll regret it. ♦ Hisses and boos. ♦ It doesn't grab me. ♦ It's not my speed. ♦ Not my cup of tea. ♦ On a scale of one to 10, I give it a 144—gross. ♦ The very idea. ♦ To an *sshole, everything looks like sh*t. - R.D. ♦ To not sit well (with). ♦ To squash like a bug. ♦ To throw cold water on. ♦ To express righteous indignation. ♦ To frown on. ♦ To get/give the Bronx cheer. ♦ To get/give the kiss of death. ♦ To get/give the raspberry. ♦ To get/give thumbs down. ♦ To lodge a protest. ♦ To look askance (at). ♦ To not take

kindly to. ♦ To put the kibosh on. ♦ To rain on [so]'s parade. ♦ To strike down. ♦ To take exception (to). ♦ To take issue (with). ♦ Won't hold still for [it].

Discomfiture

(also uncomfortable, unsatisfying) A bad taste in one's mouth. ♦ A charley horse. ♦ A coughing fit/jag. ♦ A ringing in one's ears. ♦ An ice-cream headache. ♦ Beyond recognition ♦ Dry as a bone. ♦ Eaten up alive by mosquitoes. ♦ Hunger pangs. ♦ Hurtin' for certain. ♦ I feel faint. ♦ I have to p*ss so bad my teeth/tonsils are floating. ♦ In a bad way. [see also Deteriorate] ♦ In a bad/strange space. ♦ In a blue funk. ♦ In excruciating agony/pain. ♦ Indisposed at the moment. ♦ Like taking a bath with your socks on. ♦ Like trying to scratch an itchy foot through the shoe. ♦ *Mal de mer.* ♦ Motion sickness. ♦ My mouth feels like cotton. ♦ My mouth feels like the bottom of a bird cage. ♦ Muffled cats catch no mice. ♦ My [n.] is/are killing me. ♦ Not a hundred percent. ♦ Not firing/ hitting on all cylinders. ♦ Not oneself. ♦ Not up to snuff. [see also Inferior] ♦ Off kilter. ♦ On the rocks. [see also Deteriorate] ♦ Out of sorts. ♦ Post-traumatic stress syndrome. ♦ Slightly indisposed. ♦ The morning after the night before. ♦ To be seasick. ♦ To feel blah. ♦ To have a bad trip. ♦ To have a hangover. ♦ To have to p*ss like a racehorse. ♦ To have the blahs. ♦ To have withdrawal symptoms. ♦ To not feel so hot. ♦ To see spots before one's eyes. ♦ To see stars. ♦ Under the weather. [see also Drunk]

Discovery

A discovery is an accident meeting a prepared mind. ♦ Discover a well before you are thirsty. ♦ Eureka!—I've got it! ♦ Hidden fires are discovered by their smoke. ♦ Lo and behold. ♦ Look what I found. ♦ Lookie, lookie, here comes Cookie. [see also Arrival] ♦ (My, my/well, well,) what have we here? ♦ Science discovers—art creates. ♦ Ship ahoy! ♦ Tha'r she blows! ♦ To break new ground. ♦ To come to light. ♦ To come to the surface. ♦ To come up with. ♦ To dream up/think up. ♦ To find a way. ♦ To find (true) love. ♦ To find one's way. ♦ To stumble upon. (see also Accident]

Dishonest
(also underhanded)

A con artist. ♦ A confidence game. ♦ A den of thieves. ♦ A gyp joint.

♦ A hidden agenda. ♦ A low blow. ♦ A ripoff. ♦ A second-story man. ♦ A shell game. ♦ A shot below the belt. ♦ Crooked as a barrel of snakes. ♦ Not dealing with a full deck. ♦ So crooked, he could hide behind a corkscrew. ♦ So crooked, he has to screw on his socks. ♦ So crooked, they'll have to screw him into the ground when he dies. ♦ Some carve out a career, others chisel them. ♦ The money went south. ♦ Throw a sucker punch. ♦ To be light-fingered. ♦ To coldcock [so]. ♦ To deal from the bottom of the deck. ♦ To do dirt to. ♦ To do [so] dirt. ♦ To do a (great) disservice (to). ♦ To have long fingers. ♦ To be underhanded. ♦ To get a five-finger discount. ♦ To have larceny in one's heart. ♦ To have light/sticky fingers. ♦ To have one's hand in the till. ♦ To keep a double set of books. ♦ To meet with foul play. ♦ To pad the bill. ♦ To play dirty (pool)/(tricks). ♦ To rip [it]/[so] off. ♦ To skim from the till. ♦ To stack the deck. ♦ To use a crib sheet. ♦ To use a marked/shaved/stacked deck. ♦ To use loaded dice. ♦ To use marked cards. ♦ To use questionable tactics/underhanded methods. ♦ Would rob the eyes out of a blind man. ♦ Would steal anything that isn't nailed down.

Dismay

Aw, phooey. ◆ Ay, chihuahua. ◆ Boy, oh, boy. ◆ Fiddlesticks. ◆ For cripe's sake. ◆ For crying out loud. [see also Astonishment] ◆ Lordy, lordy, my china cups. ◆ My heart sank. ◆ Oh, boy. ◆ Oh, brother. ◆ Oh, me, oh, my. ◆ Oh, rats! ◆ Sufferin' succotash. ◆ To feel like the bottom fell out. ◆ To have a sinking feeling. ◆ To have a knot in the pit of one's stomach. ◆ What's this world coming to? ◆ Wouldn't you know (it)?

Disrupt

A displaced person. ◆ Coitus interruptus. ◆ Point of order. ◆ Shook to its (very) foundations. ◆ To be out of sequence/ step/synch. ◆ To blow the deal. ◆ To blow things sky high. ◆ To blow a fuse. ◆ To break [so]'s concentration/focus. ◆ To break ranks. ◆ To break stride. ◆ To call time. ◆ To call (a) time out. ◆ To cramp [so]'s style. ◆ To foil the plot. ◆ To go out of turn. ◆ To go (out) on strike. ◆ To gum up the works. ◆ To hit a rough patch. ◆ To hit a snag. ◆ To make waves. ◆ To pull the rug out from under [so]. ◆ To put [sb] out. ◆ To queer the deal. ◆ To rattle [so]. ◆ To set [so]/the [n.]/ on [p.] ear. ◆ To shake [so] up. ◆ To short-circuit. ◆ To rock the boat. ◆ To stop payment. ◆ To stop the clock. ◆ To stunt one's growth. ◆ To throw a monkey wrench into (the works). ◆ To throw everything out of whack. ◆ To throw [so] off his/her game. ◆ To throw [so] off the track. ◆ To trip [so] up. ◆ To turn [it] upside down. ◆ To upset the applecart. ◆ To upset the balance of Nature. ◆ To upset the established order of things. ◆ Tossed like a rag doll.

Distance

A hike and a half away. ◆ A hoot and a holler from here. ◆ A hop, skip and a jump. ◆ A little further down the line. ◆ A right smart piece. ◆ A stone's throw away. ◆ Across the Great Divide. ◆ Across the pond. ◆ Are we there yet? ◆ As far as the eye can see. ◆ As the crow flies. ◆ Border to border. ◆ Coast to coast. ◆ Dead ahead. ◆ Down the road a piece. ◆ East is east and west is west. ◆ From Dan to Beersheba. ◆ From here to Timbuktu. ◆ From river to river [Manhattan]. ◆ From sea to shining sea. ◆ From the halls of Montezuma to the shores of Tripoli. ◆ Hang a Louie. ◆ In the Continental U.S.A. ◆ In these parts. ◆ Just around the corner. ◆ Round yonder bend. ◆ South of the border. ◆ The shortest distance between two points is a straight line. ♦ This neck of the woods. ♦ Within shouting/ spitting/striking distance. [see also Close] ♦ Within earshot. ♦ You can't get there from here. ♦ "X" marks the spot. ♦ You can't miss it.

Divide

A [n.]-way split. ♦ Across the Great Divide. ♦ Divide and conquer. ♦ Divvy up the loot/spoils. ♦ Go halvesies (alt. halfsies). ♦ Like Gaul, divided into three parts. ♦ [n.] for me and [n.] for you. ♦ One nation, indivisible. ♦ (Right) down the middle. ♦ (Right) smack dab in the middle. ♦ Say the magic word and divide a hundred dollars between you. ♦ To divide 'em up, you first have to count 'em. ♦ To go fifty-fifty. ♦ To split, [n.] for one.

Dogs

A barking dog never bites. ♦ A seeing eye dog. ♦ Beware of the dog. ♦ Dog days. ♦ Dog is man's best friend. ♦ Doggone. ♦ Every dog has his day. [see also Deserve] ♦ Every year of a dog's life equals seven of human years. ♦ Let sleeping dogs lie. ♦ Love me, love my dog. ♦ Make your dog a companion, but clutch a stick. ♦ Never kick a fresh dog turd around on a hot day. [Harry Truman's philosophy of life] ♦ To be in the doghouse. ♦ To be top dog. ♦ To dog [so]'s footsteps. ♦ To go to the dogs. ♦ To keep a dog and bark yourself. [see also Pointless] ♦ To lead a dog's life. ♦ To put on the dog. ♦ To work like a dog.

Dominate
(also bully, control, discipline)

A control freak. ♦ A hostile takeover. ♦ A reign of terror. ♦ A slave driver. ♦ As long as you're living under my/our roof you'll do as I/we say. ♦ Because I say so. ♦ Behind the wheel. ♦ Boss [sb] around. ♦ Crack the whip. ♦ Doctor's orders. ♦ Down, boy, down! ♦ Eminent domain. ♦ He who pays the piper calls the tune. ♦ I live by the golden rule: he who has the gold, makes the rules. ♦ I'm not asking you; I'm telling you. ♦ In check. ♦ Kicking *ss(es) and taking names. ♦ Lord it over. ♦ Now I've got you where I want you. ♦ On autopilot/cruise control. ♦ Rule the roost. ♦ Rule with an iron hand. ♦ The 800-pound gorilla (in the room). ♦ The party in power. ♦ The ruling class. ♦ To batter [so] into submission. [see also Assault] ♦ To be a harsh taskmaster. ♦ To be in the driver's seat. ♦ To bulldoze [so] ♦ To call the shots. ♦ To come to power. ♦ To deal from a position of strength. ♦ To employ commando tactics. ♦

To force feed. ♦ To f*ck over [sb]. ♦ To have everything under control. ♦ To have [sb] in one's clutches. ♦ To have [sb] in tow. ♦ To have [sb] on a short leash. ♦ To have [sb] under one's thumb. ♦ To have the say-so. ♦ To have the situation (well) in hand. ♦ To keep a tight rein on [so]. ♦ To lead [so] around by the nose. ♦ To make a power play. ♦ To play God. ♦ To pull [so]'s strings. ♦ To pull rank (on). ♦ To ram/shove [it] down [so]'s throat. ♦ To show [so] who's boss. ♦ To throw one's weight around. ♦ To ride roughshod over. [see also Rough] ♦ To strongarm [sb] (into). ♦ To take over. ♦ To treat [sb] like dirt (under one's feet). ♦ To use brute force. ♦ To use strong-arm tactics. ♦ To walk all over [sb]. ♦ To wear the pants (in the family). [see also Boss] ♦ Who's your daddy? ♦ (You'll) do as I say or bear/suffer the consequences.

Doomed

A dead duck. ♦ A dying dog. ♦ A marked man. ♦ A terminal illness. ♦ And may God have mercy on your soul. ♦ At death's door. ♦ Days are numbered. ♦ Dead man walking. ♦ Go down for the third time. ♦ Had the cock. ♦ Had the course. ♦ Have you any last requests? ♦ In critical condition. ♦ It's curtains (for). ♦ It's history. ♦ Like a lamb to the slaughter. ♦ Living on borrowed time. ♦ Not long for this world. ♦ On death row. ♦ On his/her way out. ♦ On its last legs. ♦ On one's deathbed. ♦ On the chopping block. ♦ On the critical list. ♦ Over the brink. ♦ Prepare to meet thy Maker. ♦ The kiss of death. ♦ To be a goner. ♦ To be done for. ♦ To cook one's goose. ♦ To have had it. ♦ To have one foot in the grave (and the other on a banana peel). ♦ Too far gone. ♦ You're dead meat. ♦ Your goose is cooked.

Double Cliches
(also original mixed metaphors by R.D.)

Before you decide that something is on the up and up, be sure to get the lowdown. ♦ By the time you win an uphill battle, you might be over the hill. ♦ If you can pull the wool over their eyes you'll have them eating out of the palm of your hand. ♦ If you have an inside track you have an outside chance. ♦ If you want to get off on the right foot, put your best foot forward. ♦ If you want them eating out of your hand, you may have to grease their palm. ♦ It'll be a cold day in hell before those chickens come home to roost. ♦ Many a man trying to move in the right circles winds up chasing his own tail. ♦ Sometime, before you can make a stitch in time, you have to find a needle in a haystack. ♦ The best way to put your best foot forward may be to put your foot down. ♦ The difference between a hero and a coward is whether he will stand fast or run fast. ♦ To have peace of mind you may have to give [so] a piece of your mind. ♦ When you go for broke, you run the risk of going broke. ♦ When you jump on somebody else's bandwagon, take care not to upset your own applecart. ♦ When you shake a man down, you will also shake him up. ♦ When [so] says, "a penny for your thoughts" it's a good time to put your two cents in.

Drenched

Davy Jones' locker. ♦ In the drink. ♦ In the pouring rain. ♦ In the swim. ♦ It's raining, it's pouring, the old man is snoring. ♦ Singin' in the rain. ♦ Soaked to the skin. ♦ Soaking wet. ♦ Sopping wet. ♦ To doggy paddle. ♦ To look like a drowned rat. ♦ Wringing wet.

Drink

A beer joint. ♦ A bit of the bubbly. ♦ A couple of shooters. ♦ A drink after work. ♦ A few brews/ brewskies/cool ones/frosty ones. ♦ A (good) stiff drink. ♦ A liquid lunch. ♦ A quick pick-me-up. ♦ A short snort. ♦ A shot and (a) beer joint. ♦ A social drinker. ♦ Belly up to the bar. ♦ Bend an elbow. ♦ Candy is dandy but liquor is quicker. ♦ Cocktail lounges are half-lit to match the clientele. ♦ Demon rum. ♦ Drink has been the ruin of many a good man. ♦ Drink like a fish. ♦ Drink [sb] under the table. ♦ Drink to me only with thine eyes. ♦ Drown one's sorrows. ♦ Firewater. ♦ Get one's courage from a bottle. ♦ Giggle juice. ♦ Go on a bender. ♦ Go on a toot. ♦ Have another dab of the brush. ♦ Have one for the road. ♦ Have the DT's. ♦ I'd rather have a bottle in front of me than a frontal lobotomy. ♦ I'll have another. ♦ I'll have my usual. ♦ Irish courage. ♦ It's the liquor talking. ♦ I've been known to (take a sip or two). ♦ Kickapoo Joy Juice. ♦ Knock a few back/knock back a few. ♦ Last call for alcohol. ♦ Loudmouth juice. ♦ Make it a double. ♦ Ninety-nine bottles of beer on the wall, ninety-nine bottles of beer . . . take one down, pass it around . . . ninety-eight bottles of beer on the wall. ♦ Malt does more than Milton can to justify God's ways to man. ♦

Rum runner. ♦ Say when. [see also Enough] ♦ Slip [so] a Mickey (Finn). ♦ Sneaky Pete. ♦ Take a bit of the hair of the dog that bit you. ♦ Tea or whiskey, Pat? ♦ Tell me when to stop. ♦ To be on the sauce. ♦ To chugalug. ♦ To crack a bottle. ♦ To drive [so] to drink. ♦ To go pub crawling. ♦ To have a hollow leg. [see also Eat] ♦ To hit the sauce. ♦ To nurse a drink. ♦ To ply [so] with liquor. ♦ To spike a drink. ♦ Wet one's whistle. ♦ What's a wino's favorite street? Fifth Avenue! ♦ White lightning. ♦ Work is the curse of the drinking man. ♦ Yo ho ho and a bottle of rum.

Drunk

(All) liquored up. ♦ As drunk as Cooter Brown. ♦ Binge drinking. ♦ Blind out of one's mind. ♦ Drunk and disorderly. ♦ Drunk as a skunk. ♦ Drunken days all have their to-morrows. ♦ Falling down drunk. ♦ Had one too many. ♦ Have the D.T.'s. ♦ Have a snootful. ♦ High as a kite. ♦ Knee-walking, belly crawl-ing, snot-nosed drunk. ♦ Rip-roaring, rip-snorting drunk. ♦ Seeing pink elephants. ♦ The drunken driver has the right of way. ♦ Three sheets to the wind. ♦ Tight as a tick. ♦ To be in one's cups. ♦ To be/get bombed/f*cked up/ hammered/high/looped/on the sauce/ ossified/pie-eyed/p*ssed/plastered/ potted/sh*t-faced/sloshed/smashed/ sotted/squiffed/stoned/tanked up/tra-shed/wasted. ♦ To go on a bender/ binge/tear/toot. ♦ To have a jag on. ♦ To have half a bag on. ♦ To take a little nip. ♦ To hang/tie one on. ♦ To hit the bottle/sauce. ♦ To hold on to the bed to keep the ceiling from spin-ning. ♦ To hold on to the grass to keep from falling off the lawn. ♦ Under the alfluence of incohol. ♦ Under the influence (of alcohol). ♦ Under the weather. [see also Discomfiture] ♦ Whacked out. ♦ What you do while drunk you must pay for sober. ♦ Zig-Zag.

Dupe

A con artist. ♦ A Trojan horse. ♦ A wolf in sheep's clothing. [see Animals, Imitation] ♦ Bait and switch. ♦ Looks are/can be deceiv-ing. [see also Appearance] ♦ The head is always the dupe of the heart. ♦ To do a snow job on [so]. ♦ To fake [so] out. ♦ To fleece [so]. ♦ To flim-flam. ♦ To fob off/foist off on [so]. ♦ To get/give a hosing. ♦ To hornswog-gle. ♦ To lead [so] down the primrose path. ♦ To lead the lamb to slaughter. ♦ To lead one to believe. ♦ To palm off (on). ♦ To pass [it] off (as). ♦ To play a dirty trick. ♦ To play [so] false. ♦ To play [so] for a fool. ♦ To pull a Brodie. ♦ To pull a fast one. ♦ To pull a switch. ♦ To pull something on [so]. ♦ To pull the old switcheroo. ♦ To pull the wool over [so]'s eyes. ♦ To put one over on [so]. ♦ To put [so] on. ♦ To rope [so] in. ♦ To take [so] for a ride. ♦ To take (unfair) advantage of [so]. ♦ To throw [so] off the track. ♦ To trip [so] up. ♦ To use a stacked deck. ♦ To use loaded dice. ♦ To sell [so] a bill of goods. ♦ To send out a stalking horse. ♦ To snow [so]. ♦ Under false pretenses. ♦ Under the guise of. ♦ You may fool all the people some of the time; you can even fool some of the people all the time; but you can't fool all of the people all the time.

Duty

A good captain always goes down with his ship. ♦ A man must do what a man must do. ♦ Dig we must. ♦ Duty beckons/calls. ♦ Feet, do your duty. ♦ I don't make the rules; my job is to enforce them. ♦ I was only following orders. ♦ In the line of duty. ♦ Ours is not to reason why, ours is just to do or die. ♦ To answer the call of duty. ♦ To do what needs doing. ♦

When you itch you've got to scratch. ♦ When you've got to go, you've got to go. ♦ You gotta do what you gotta do.

Early

Ahead of schedule/time. ♦ An early riser. ♦ At daybreak. ♦ At (the) break of day. ♦ At the crack of dawn. ♦ Bright and early. ♦ Be pleasant until ten o'clock in the morning and the rest of the day will take care of itself. ♦ Bright and early Monday morning. ♦ By dawn's early light. ♦ Early on (in the game). ♦ Early ripe, early rotten. ♦ Early to bed, early to rise, makes a man healthy, wealthy and wise. ♦ First thing in the morning. ♦ In advance. ♦ Rise and shine. ♦ Shop early, avoid the rush. ♦ The early bird gets the worm. ♦ The morning hours have gold in their hands. ♦ To get up with the chickens. ♦ To give advance notice. ♦ To put in a p*ss call/an early call. ♦ You have to get up pretty early in the morning to fool me.

Earn

A 9-to-5 job. ♦ A quick dime is better than a slow dollar. ♦ A quick dollar is better than a slow dime. ♦ An honest day's work for an honest day's pay. ♦ An honest day's pay. ♦ Be the breadwinner. ♦ Bread and board. ♦ Bring home the bacon. ♦ Do [it] for a living. ♦ Earn/make an honest living. ♦ Earn one's keep/salt/stripes/wings. ♦ Eke out a (precarious) living. ♦ Gainful employment. ♦ He who marries for money earns it. ♦ It pays the bills/rent. ♦ It puts food on the table. ♦ It's a dirty job, but somebody's got to do it. ♦ It's a living. ♦ Make a quick buck. ♦ Make one's bones. ♦ Minimum/prevailing wage. ♦ Our daily bread. ♦ Sing for one's supper. ♦ The more you earn the more taxing life is. ♦ The head earns and the heart spends. ♦ To be in it for the money. ♦ To be worth one's salt. ♦ To get back pay. ♦ To keep body and soul together. ♦ To keep the wolf from the door. ♦ To hustle/make a buck. ♦ To knock down a big salary/big bucks. ♦ To make a living. ♦ To make ends meet. ♦ To make it worth one's while. ♦ To reap the rewards of one's labor. ♦ To turn pro/professional.

Easy

(also expedient, practical)

A cakewalk. ♦ A cushy job. ♦ A lead-pipe cinch. ♦ A piece of cake. ♦ A snap (of the fingers). ♦ A turkey shoot. ♦ A walk in the park. ♦ Easy as ABC. ♦ Easy as (blueberry) pie. ♦ Easy as duck soup. ♦ Easy as falling off a log. ♦ Easy as one, two three. ♦ Easy as taking candy from a baby. ♦ Easy come, easy go. ♦ Easy does it. ♦ Easy is as easy does. ♦ Easy on the eyes. ♦ Easy/smooth sledding. ♦ Elementary, my dear Watson. ♦ Fingers were made before forks. ♦ I can do it blind-folded/standing on my head/with my eyes closed. ♦ It is better to feed one cat than many mice. ♦ In the interests of expediency. ♦ It's easy when you know how. ♦ It's cheaper to just pay it. ♦ It's downhill all the way. ♦ It's just as easy to fall in love with somebody rich. ♦ It's not brain surgery/rocket science. ♦ Kid stuff. ♦ Like shooting fish in a barrel. ♦ (Mere) child's play. ♦ [n.]101. ♦ [n.] for dummies. ♦ [n.] made simple. ♦ Nice and easy. ♦ No contest. ♦ No muss, no fuss, no bother. ♦ No sweat. ♦ Nothing could be simpler. ♦ On Easy Street. ♦ Only what works. ♦ Over easy. ♦ So easy/simple, a child could do it. ♦ Take to [it]. ♦ Take to it like a duck (takes) to water. ♦ The Big Easy. ♦ The shortest distance between two points is a straight line. ♦ That's all there is to it. ♦ There's nothing to it. ♦ To pick the low-hanging fruit. ♦ To go easy on [so]. ♦ To take the easy way out. ♦ To take the path of least resistance. ♦ Wealth is not his who makes it, but his who enjoys it. ♦ What's so hard about that? ♦ Why do things the hard way? ♦ With just a twist of the wrist. ♦ You don't have to lift a finger. ♦You make it look so easy.

Eat

A blue-plate special. ♦ A feeding frenzy. ♦ A healthy appetite. ♦ A home-cooked meal. ♦ A hungry stomach has no ears. ♦ A meal fit for a king. ♦ A meal in itself. ♦ A moment's pleasure on the lips; a lifetime on the hips. ♦ A square meal. ♦ An army travels on its stomach. ♦ Be a brown bagger. ♦ Break bread with. ♦ But for the stomach, the back would wear gold. ♦ C-rations. [military] ♦ Come and get it (or I'll eat it myself). ♦ Dig in. ♦ Dinner is served. ♦ Don't snack before dinner; it will spoil your appetite. ♦ Eat the best and sell the rest. ♦ Eat [it], it will make your hair curl. ♦ Eat, drink, think of nothing. ♦ Eat like a horse. ♦ Eat to live; do not live to eat. ♦ Eat up. ♦ Eat up all the profits. ♦ Feed your face. ♦ Finish your dinner; it's a sin to throw food away when children in Africa are starving. ♦ Get a bite to eat. ♦ Go out to eat. ♦ He who remains at home gets eaten. He who ventures out into the world eats! ♦

Hungry as a horse. ♦ I'm trying to cut down on my calories. ♦ It's all going to the same place. ♦ Junk food. ♦ Just like mom's home cooking. ♦ Just like mama used to make. ♦ Meals on wheels. ♦ Of course carrots are good for the eyes: did you ever see a rabbit wearing glasses? ♦ Partake of a repast. ♦ Scarf it up. ♦ Take all you want, but eat all you take. ♦ The way to a man's heart is through his stomach. ♦ The whiter the bread the sooner you're dead. ♦ Three hots and a cot. ♦ Three squares a day. ♦ To be so hungry you could eat a horse. ♦ To be so hungry your stomach thinks that your throat has been cut. ♦ To brown-bag it. ♦ To chow down. ♦ To eat at the Greasy Spoon. ♦ To eat like a bird. ♦ To eat [so] out of house and home. ♦ To have a hollow leg. [see also Drink] ♦ To feed/stuff your face. ♦ To grab a bite. ♦ To have a nosh. ♦ To have a sweet tooth. ♦ To have the munchies. ♦ To pack/tuck it away. ♦ To polish it off. ♦ To put/tie on the feedbag. ♦ To rustle up some grub. ♦ To scarf it up. ♦ To sink one's teeth into. ♦ To toss down. ♦ To hit the chuck wagon. ♦ To wolf [it] down. ♦ To work up an appetite. ♦ Well fed, well bred. ♦ Where the elite meet to eat. ♦ Wine them and dine them. ♦ Work not, eat not. ♦ You are what you eat. ♦ You'll eat a ton of dirt before you die. ♦ You've gotta eat.

Egotism
(also conceit, vanity)

A legend in his own mind. ♦ A man's accusations of himself are always believed; his praises of self, never. ♦ A man wrapped up in himself makes a small package. ♦ A little humility is a good thing. ♦ An exaggerated sense of self-importance. ♦ Delusions of grandeur. ♦ Don't break your arm patting yourself on the back. ♦ Egotism is the art of seeing in yourself qualities that no one else can. ♦ Holier than thou. ♦ Humility is not thinking less of yourself, but thinking of yourself less. ♦ I wouldn't lower myself/stoop so low. ♦ Mirror, mirror on the wall; who's the fairest of them all? ♦ No great man ever thought himself so. ♦ On a head trip. ♦ People on ego trips often trip over their own feats. ♦ Self opinion is the only opinion. ♦ Self-praise stinks. ♦ There's no conceit in his/her family— he's/she's got it all. ♦ They ought to make a movie of my life. ♦ Thinking you're better than everybody comes out of your snub-conscious mind. ♦ To be above it all. ♦ To be on an ego trip. ♦ To remain above the fray. ♦ To be stuck on oneself. ♦ To talk down to [so]. ♦ To think you're hot sh*t/ hot stuff. ♦ To think you're "it." ♦ To think your sh*t doesn't stink. (But your farts give you away). ♦ Vanity, Thy Name is Woman. ♦ Vanity of vanities. ♦ Vanity, vanity, all is vanity. ♦ We must be doing something right. ♦ Who talks of himself talks to the devil. ♦ With all due modesty.

Embarrassment

A blow to one's ego. ♦ A hangdog expression. ♦ A hop in the pants. ♦ A humbling experience. ♦ A kick in the *ss/behind/butt/cojones/crumpets/pants/teeth. ♦ A put-down. ♦ Ashamed to admit [it]. ♦ Better to let it out and bear the shame than to hold it in and bear the pain. ♦ Black sheep of the family. ♦ Eat crow. ♦ Eat humble pie. ♦ Eat one's hat. ♦ Eat/swallow/ choke on one's words. ♦ Feel like two cents. ♦ Hang one's head in shame. ♦ Have you no shame? ♦ I can't take you anywhere. ♦ I felt like crawling under a rug. ♦ Live it up all you want, but never do anything you can't live down. – R.D. ♦ Nothing to be ashamed of. ♦ Now look what you've done. ♦ Now look what you've made me do. ♦ On life's menu, there are ample dishes of humble pie and crow. ♦ Red as a beet/lobster. ♦ Shame on you. ♦ Shamey-shame. ♦ Sing another tune. ♦ The joke's on me. ♦ There's something on your teeth. ♦ To be caught in one's tidy whities. ♦ To be cringeworthy. ♦ To be the butt of a joke. ♦ To blush down to the roots of one's hair. ♦ To eat crow. ♦ To eat humble pie. ♦ To have egg on one's face. ♦ To laugh out of the other side of one's mouth. ♦ To live in infamy. ♦ To lose face. ♦ To make one a/the laughing stock (of). ♦ To make [so] look sick. ♦ To put [so] in his/her place. ♦ To put [so] to shame. ♦ To show [so] up. ♦ To sing a different tune. ♦ To swallow one's pride. ♦ To wag a finger at. ♦ With one's tail between one's legs. ♦ You of all people. ♦ You ought to/should be ashamed (of yourself). ♦ You'll never live it down. ♦ Your fly is open. ♦ Your slip is showing.

Emergency

A code blue. ♦ A national emergency. ♦ A red alert. ♦ A twelve-alarm fire. ♦ A yellow alert. ♦ Any port in a storm. ♦ Break glass in case of emergency. ♦ Bring up the reserves. ♦ Call in the cavalry. ♦ Call out the militia. ♦ Call out the National Guard. ♦ Emergency measures. ♦ Hey, Rube! ♦ In one's hour of need. ♦ Martial law. ♦ Mayday, Mayday! ♦ Nine one, one—what is your emergency? ♦ Rushed to the hospital. ♦ S.O.S. (Save our ship). ♦ Send in the scrub team. ♦ Somebody do something! ♦ To call for backup. ♦ To hit/push the panic button. ♦ To press into service. ♦ To send in reinforcements. ♦ When tragedy strikes. ♦ Where are the police when you need them?

Emotion

A flood/rush of emotion. ♦ A gut reaction. [see also Guess] ♦ All choked up with emotion. ♦ A warm and fuzzy feeling. ♦ A real tearjerker. ♦ An emotional rollercoaster. ♦ Gut-wrenching. ♦ Heart-rending. ♦ Hearts and flowers. ♦ Her bladder was right between her eyes. ♦ It hits you where you live. ♦ Kind of chokes you up a little bit, (doesn't it?) ♦ Kinda gets you right here, (doesn't it?) ♦ Not a dry eye in the house. ♦ To be (deeply) moved (by). ♦ To be touched (by). ♦ To betray no emotion. [see also Cool] ♦ To choke back tears. ♦ To get all touchy-feely. ♦ To give vent to. ♦ To have mixed emotions. ♦ To play on/stir one's emotions. ♦ To tug at one's heartstrings.

Enamored

An affair of the heart. ♦ An old flame. ♦ Be enamored of. ♦ Be smitten/taken with [sb] . ♦ Fall for [sb]. ♦ Have a crush on. ♦ Have a thing for. ♦ I only have eyes for you. ♦ Mooning (about) like a lovesick calf. ♦ To be/go gaga over. ♦ To be soft/sweet on [sb]. ♦ To carry a/the torch for [sb]. ♦ To flip over [sb]. ♦ To have eyes for [sb]. ♦ To have one's heart in one's hand/eyes. ♦ To hold a flame for [sb]. ♦ To make one's heart go pitter-patter. ♦ To make one's heart skip a beat. ♦ To turn one's insides to mush. ♦ To wear one's heart on one's sleeve.

Encore

A curtain call. ♦ A daisy chain. ♦ A repeat performance. ♦ A round-robin. ♦ A spinoff. ♦ An encore presentation. ♦ Back by popular demand. ♦ Back to school. ♦ Back to the salt mines. ♦ Come again? ♦ Come back, Little Sheba. ♦ Here we go again. ♦ How's that again? ♦ If I had it to do all over again. (I'd do it all over you!) ♦ Not a day goes by that ____. ♦ Oh no, not again. ♦ Once again into the breach. ♦ Once more, with feeling. ♦ One more once. ♦ One more time. ♦ Play it

again, Sam. ♦ Repeat that, please, for the West Coast. ♦ Run that by me again. ♦ Say again, please. ♦ Stay tuned, folks! ♦ Take it from there. ♦ The Phantom strikes again. ♦ The Second Coming. ♦ There you go again. ♦ Time and time again. ♦ To be continued. ♦ To come back for more. ♦ To have another go at it. ♦ To redound to the greater glory (of God). ♦ To re-up. ♦ To ship over. ♦ What did you say? ♦ What was that you (just) said? ♦ When the swallows come back to Capistrano. ♦ What do you do for an encore? ♦ Would you mind repeating that?

End

A dead issue. ♦ A deal-breaker. ♦ A *fait accompli.* ♦ A positive outcome. ♦ A storybook ending. ♦ (And) that's that. [see also Finality] ♦ After all. ♦ After the fall. ♦ After all is said and done. ♦ After all is said and done, a lot more is said than done. ♦ After/once/when the dust settles. ♦ After the ball is over. ♦ At the end of the day. ♦ All good things must (come to an) end. ♦ All washed up. ♦ All's well that ends well. ♦ And a good time was had by all. ♦ And they lived happily ever after. [see also Romance]

◆ At the end of a rainbow is a pot of gold. ◆ Dass is dat. ◆ Dassis allus. ◆ Dead in the water. ◆ Done for. ◆ Down the drain/tubes. ◆ Enough is enough. * ◆ Enough of this stuff. ◆ Enough said (already). *[see also Enough] ◆ Exit strategy. ◆ Fade to black. ◆ Game over. ◆ In the aftermath. ◆ In the final analysis. ◆ It all falls into place. ◆ It all works out in the end. ◆ It's a done deal. ◆ It's a long lane that has no turning. ◆ It's all for the best. ◆ It's all over but the shouting. ◆ It's curtains for [n.]. ◆ In the aftermath. ◆ In the wake of. ◆ Last but not least. ◆ Now you've gone and done it. ◆ Out of business. ◆ Over and done with. [see also Finality, Forgive] ◆ So much for that. [see also Enough, Finality] ◆ That settles that. ◆ That ship has sailed. ◆ That winds it up. ◆ That'll be all. ◆ That's the end of that. ◆ The end is nigh. ◆ The end of the world (as we know it). ◆ The end of an era. ◆ The honeymoon/party is over. ◆ The war to end all wars. ◆ This sh*t must cease. ◆ To be all through. ◆ To be done with it. ◆ To blow over. ◆ To come to an end. ◆ To get [it] out of the way. ◆ To play out. ◆ To put [it] to bed. ◆ To put the final nail(s) in one's coffin. ◆ To ride off into the sunset. ◆ To ring down the final curtain. ◆ To run out of gas/steam. ◆ To see the last of [it]. ◆ To the bitter end. To use up. ◆ To wind [it] up. ◆ Wake me (up) when it's over. ◆ When all is said and done. ◆ When it comes/you get (right) down to it. ◆ Who ends an argument wins an argument.

Endearments

Angel face. ◆ Angel puss. ◆ Baby doll. ◆ Babykins. ◆ Butterball. ◆ *Cara mia.* ◆ Cookie. ◆ Cutie Patootie. ◆ Cutie Pie. ◆ Darling dearest. ◆ Darling one. ◆ Dearie. ◆ Doll face. ◆ Dreamboat. ◆ G.U.R.A.Q.T.I.N.V.U. [Gee, you are a cutie; I envy you.] ◆ Honey. ◆ Honeybunch. ◆ Lamb chop. ◆ Lambikins. ◆ Love/Lover/Lovey. ◆ *Ma Cherie.* ◆ *Mon Amour.* ◆ My darling dearest. ◆ My little Angel. ◆ My little Munchkin. ◆ My little turtledove. ◆ My precious. ◆ Oh, my darling, Clementine. ◆ Roses are red, violets are blue, sugar is sweet and so are you. ◆ S.W.A.K. [Sealed with a kiss.] ◆ S.W.A.B.K. [Sealed with a big kiss.] ◆ S.W.A.B.W.K. [Sealed with a big, wet kiss.] ◆ Sweetie (Pie). ◆ Sweet talker. ◆ Sweetmeats. ◆ To whisper sweet nothings. ◆ Tootsie Wootsie. ◆ You are my sunshine.

Endurance

A person can only take so much. ♦ Bite the bullet.

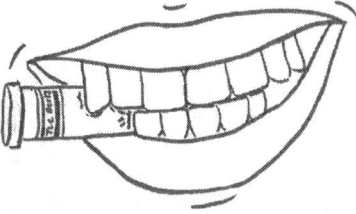

♦ Built to last. ♦ Every man has his breaking point. ♦ For as long as it takes. ♦ For however long it takes. ♦ Go the distance. ♦ God gives burdens; he also gives shoulders. ♦ Grin and bear it. ♦ Grit one's teeth. ♦ Hang in there. ♦ In for the duration. [see also Permanance] ♦ In for the long haul. ♦ It's more than a body can stand. ♦ Lord, give me the ability to change the things I can change, the strength to endure the things I cannot change and the wisdom to know the difference. —The Serenity Prayer ♦ Never admit defeat. ♦ None the worse for [n.]. ♦ Oh, God, give me the guidance to know when to hold on and when to let go. The grace to make the right decision at the right time, in the right way with dignity. ♦ Take it like a man. ♦ Take one's medicine (like a man). ♦ The evil that men do lives after them.

♦ To bear up under the strain. ♦ To do/go without. ♦ To have a long shelf life. ♦ To have legs. ♦ To have staying power. ♦ To ride out/weather the storm. [see also Weather] ♦ To ride it out/tough it out. ♦ To stand the test of time. ♦ To subject oneself to [it]. ♦ To take the heat. ♦ To wear well. ♦ What can't be cured must be endured. ♦ When you are going through hell, keep going.

Enjoyment

An all-day sucker. ♦ And a good time was had by all. ♦ Get a charge out of. ♦ Get one's jollies/kicks. ♦ Go for [it] in a big way. ♦ Have a gay old time. ♦ I'll give you a half hour to stop that. ♦ Stop it; I like it. ♦ To be on it like a duck on a June bug. ♦ To do the Party Circuit. ♦ To eat it (right) up. ♦ To get off (on) [it]. ♦ To glom it. ♦ To have a field day. ♦ To lap/snap it up. ♦ To take it in one's hot little hands.

Enlightenment

A eureka moment. ♦ A moment of clarity. ♦ Ah, so, deska. ♦ All of a sudden it dawned on me. ♦ An aha moment. ♦ An understanding ovation. ♦ Acutely aware. ♦ By George, I think she's got it. ♦ Clue me in.

♦ Come to find out . . . ♦ Come to one's senses. [see also Sensibility] ♦ Comes the dawn. ♦ Dawn breaks on Marblehead. ♦ (Finally) [it] sinks in. ♦ Got it. ♦ Gotcha. ♦ I see, said the blind carpenter to his deaf wife—as he picked up his hammer and saw. ♦ I'm beginning to see the light. ♦ It's all coming back to me (now). ♦ It hit me like a ton of bricks. ♦ Oh, now I get it. ♦ Oh, why didn't you say so? ♦ Shed a little light on the subject. ♦ That's good to know. ♦ That's what I've been trying to tell you (all along). ♦ That's when it (all) sank in. ♦ The lights go on at Wrigley Field. ♦ To catch wise. ♦ To come slowly into focus. ♦ To get it through one's head. ♦ To pick up on. ♦ To see the error of one's ways. ♦ To see the light. ♦ To see the light of day. [see also Reveal] ♦ To see things in a different light. ♦ To wise up (to). ♦ We're not in Kansas anymore, Toto. ♦ Would you mind telling me what this is all about? ♦ You dig? ♦ You had me going there.

Enough

A safe word. ♦ And damned be him that first cries, "Hold, enough!" ♦ As if that weren't enough. ♦ Don't get me going. ♦ Don't get me started. ♦ Enough is as good as a feast. ♦ Enough is enough. * ♦ Enough said (already). *[see also End] ♦ Enough to make a grown man cry. ♦ Enough to make a grown man groan. ♦ Enough to make one's blood boil. ♦ Enough to p*ss off a priest/the Pope. ♦ Enough to choke a horse/sink a battleship. ♦ Fair enough. ♦ Get over it. ♦ Give it a rest. ♦ Good enough for me. [see also Acceptance] ♦ Hold it right there; I've heard enough. ♦ I don't know what else to tell you. ♦ I have nothing more to say (on the subject). ♦ Leave the rest to me. ♦ Let's leave it/let it go at that. ♦ More than that I can't say. ♦ Need I/we say more? ♦ Once a king, always a king but once a knight is enough. ♦ Once is never enough. ♦ Say when. [see also Drink] ♦ So much for that. [see also End, Finality] ♦ Sometimes good enough isn't good enough. ♦ Suffice it to say. ♦ Tell me when to stop. ♦ That says it all. ♦ That will do/suffice. ♦ (That's) enough already. ♦ There are limits to everything. ♦ There's no need to go any further. ♦ There's nothing more to be said. ♦ This has gone far enough. ♦ To get/have one's fill. ♦ What do you want, blood? ♦ What do you want, egg in your beer? ♦ What do you want from me? ♦ What do you want out of my life? ♦ What else can I say? ♦ What more is there to say? ♦ You can only take so much.

Envy
Eat your heart out (Baby). ♦ Green with envy. ♦ How does *he/she* rate? ♦ I.N.V.U. [I envy you.] ♦ I should be so lucky. ♦ Jealousy rears its ugly head. ♦ Jealousy, the green-eyed monster. ♦ Penis envy. ♦ The grass is always greener on the other side (of the fence). [riposte: "If the grass looks greener, it's time to water your own grass."] ♦ To cast an envious eye (on). ♦ What's he/she got that I haven't got?

Err
A breach of etiquette/protocol. ♦ A case of mistaken identity. ♦ A clerical error. ♦ A comedy of errors. ♦ A false alarm. ♦ A fatal error. ♦ A glaring inaccuracy. ♦ A lapse in judgment. ♦ A minor indiscretion. ♦ A slight miscalculation. ♦ All fouled up/messed up/ screwed up like Hogan's Goat. ♦ An honest mistake. (That's the only kind there is! — R.G.D.) ♦ Barking up the wrong tree. ♦ Bungle the job. ♦ Drop the ball. ♦ Everything that could go wrong did go wrong. (alt., everything went wrong that could go wrong. ♦

For all the wrong reasons. ♦ FUBAR (Fouled/f*cked up beyond all recognition). ♦ FUMTU (Fouled/f*cked up more than usual). ♦ Grind me a pound. ♦ Human error. ♦ It is a good horse that never stumbles. ♦ It's (just) a typo. ♦ In error. ♦ Labor under a misapprehension. ♦ Learn from the mistakes of others; you can never live long enough to make them all yourself. ♦ Miss the point. ♦ Muck it up. ♦ Muff it. ♦ Murphy's Law: Anything that can go wrong, will go wrong. ♦ My bad/error/goof/ mistake. ♦ Pilot error. ♦ Radically wrong. ♦ SAPFU (Surpassing all previous foul ups/f*ck ups). ♦ SNAFU (Situation normal: all fouled/f*cked up). ♦ Premature ejaculation. ♦ Somebody goofed. ♦ That was a five/ten/twenty I gave you. ♦ Things go wrong. ♦ There must be some mistake. ♦ To be all wet. ♦ To be sadly/sorely mistaken. ♦ To blow it. ♦ To botch the job. ♦ To commit a breach of etiquette. ♦ To do it *ss-backwards. ♦ To do it bassackwards. ♦ To err is human, to forgive divine. ♦ To err on the side of caution. ♦ To fall into the wrong hands. ♦ To f*ck [it] up. ♦ To f*ck up (royally). ♦ To flub the dub. ♦ To fumfer [it]. ♦ To get off on the wrong foot. ♦ To go about it (all) wrong. ♦ To go/wander astray. ♦

To go off topic. ♦ To hit a sour note. ♦ To lose one's place in line. ♦ To make a mess. ♦ To make the same mistake twice. ♦ To mess [it] up. ♦ To miss [it] by a mile. ♦ To miss the mark. ♦ To pull a blooper. ♦ To screw the pooch. ♦ To see the error of one's ways. ♦ To slip through one's fingers. ♦ To stand corrected. ♦ To trip up. ♦ We all make mistakes (that's why they put erasers on pencils). [see also Alibi] ♦ What's wrong with this picture? ♦ Where did I go wrong? ♦ Whups, slipsies! ♦ Wide of the mark. ♦ Will blunders never cease? ♦ Wrong way Corrigan. ♦ Wrong side out.

Erroneous

(also misleading)

A bad call. ♦ A bum steer. ♦ A distortion of the facts. ♦ Come across the wrong way. ♦ Doesn't even come close. ♦ Doesn't hold water. ♦ Fuzzy thinking. ♦ It's wrong on so many levels. ♦ Sure could've fooled me. ♦ That's not what it looked like to me. ♦ To be in the wrong. ♦ To be way off base. ♦ To get/give the wrong impression. ♦ To get [it]/[so] wrong. ♦ To go off course. ♦ To have one's facts wrong. ♦ To miss by a (country) mile. ♦ To take [it] amiss/the wrong way. ♦ To take [it] out of context. ♦ Wander far afield. ♦ You're all wet. ♦ You're not as dumb as you look. [riposte: You don't look as dumb as you are.] – Richard J. Noyes. [see also Left-Handed Compliments]

Escape

Give [so] the slip. ♦ He never laid a finger/glove on me. ♦ Save face. ♦ Save one's *ss. ♦ There's always a way out. ♦ To be home free. ♦ To be well out of [it]. ♦ To beat the rap. ♦ To bust out. ♦ To get away. ♦ To get away with [it]. ♦ To get away with murder. ♦ To get off/go scot free. ♦ To be/get off the hook. ♦ To be/get out from under (the rock). ♦ To elude capture. ♦ To go out for the proverbial pack of cigarettes. ♦ To have an out. ♦ To hightail it. ♦ To make a (clean) getaway. ♦ To run away and join the circus/the French Foreign Legion. ♦ To worm one's way out of [it]. ♦ With complete impunity.

Etcetera

A little bit of this and a little bit of that. ♦ And a partridge in a pear tree. ♦ And all that good stuff. ♦ And all that happy horsesh*t. ♦ And all that jazz. ♦ And all the incidentals. ♦ And everything else you could name/think of. ♦ And like that. ♦ And the like. ♦ And so it goes. ♦ And so forth (and so on). ♦ And what have you. [see also Varied] ♦ And whatnot. ♦ And who knows what? ♦ And, you know. ♦ Etcetera, etcetera, etcetera. ♦ Or whatever. ♦ This and that. ♦ Yadda, yadda.

Eternal

A diamond is forever. (I didn't believe it till I started to make the payments. — R.D.) ♦ Diamonds are forever. ♦ For all time. ♦ For keeps. ♦ Forever after. ♦ Forever and a day. ♦ From everlasting to everlasting. ♦ From now till doomsday. ♦ From now to kingdom come. ♦ Heaven and earth will pass away, but my words will not pass away. ♦ No end in sight. ♦ Now and forever. ♦ *Sine die.* ♦ The eternal verities. ♦ Till death do us part. ♦ Till hell freezes over. ♦ Till hell won't/wouldn't have it. ♦ To the end of time. ♦ World without end.

Euphemisms

A call of nature/nature call. ♦ A fart sack. ♦ A snot rag. ♦ Bleed one's liver. ♦ Break wind. ♦ Cut the cheese. ♦ Do number one. ♦ Do number two. ♦ Excuse me while I go take a euphemism. ♦ Go to see a man about a horse. ♦ Go to powder one's nose. ♦ Hit the porcelain. ♦ Montezuma's revenge. * ♦ The Aztec two-step. *[see also Discomfiture] ♦ Pass gas/water. ♦ Pinch a loaf. ♦ Take a leak. ♦ Tap a kidney. ♦ To go to the bathroom. ♦ To hit the head. ♦ To relieve oneself. ♦ To tinkle. ♦ To use the can/euphemism/ facilities/ growler/head/john/lav/loo. ♦ Use the little boys'/little girls' room. ♦ Water the daisies/flowers/ lilies.

Eventually

After the holidays. ♦ As it turns out. [see also Happen] ♦ At length. ♦ At some point in time. ♦ By and by. ♦ In due course. ♦ In (due) time. ♦ In one's lifetime. ♦ In the fullness of time. ♦ In the long run.* ♦ In the long run, we're all dead. *[see also Future] ♦ In the meantime. ♦ In the near future. ♦ It's (just/only) a matter of time. ♦ One of these days. ♦ One of these days is none of these days. ♦ One of these years. ♦ Procrastination is the thief of time. ♦ Sooner or later. ♦ To everything there is a season. ♦ When I get around to it. ♦ When the spirit moves you.

Everyone

Anyone and everyone. ♦ Butcher, baker, candlestick maker. ♦ Each and every one. ♦ Every able-bodied citizen/man. ♦ Every last soul (on earth). ♦ Every living soul. ♦ Every man Jack. ♦ Every man, woman and child. ♦ Every mother's son. ♦ Every Tom, Dick and Harry. ♦ Everybody and his brother. ♦ Everybody in creation. ♦ Everybody who's anybody. ♦ From all walks of life. ♦ Hail, hail, the gang's all here. ♦ One and all. ♦ Rich man, poor man, beggar man, thief. ♦ Soldier, sailor, tinker, tailor. ♦ The world at large.

Everywhere

All across this great land of ours. ♦ All over the place. ♦ All over the world. ♦ All quarters of the globe. ♦ Anywhere and everywhere. ♦ Eight ways to Sunday. ♦ Every which way. ♦ Far and wide. ♦ Here, there and everywhere. ♦ Hither and thither. ♦ Hither (thither) and yon. ♦ In the good old U.S. of A. ♦ In the whole wide world. ♦ Right on down the line. ♦ Scattered to the four winds. ♦ The world over. ♦ To the four corners of the earth.

Exaggeration
(also farfetched)

A (bit of a) stretch. ♦ A cockama-mie story. ♦ A crackpot scheme. ♦ A credibility gap. ♦ A drama queen. ♦ A fish story. ♦ A harebrained scheme.

♦ A tall tale. ♦ A tempest in a teapot. ♦ A whale of a tale. ♦ Blow [it] up out of (all) proportion. ♦ Carried to its most absurd conclusion. ♦ Doesn't live up to its hype. ♦ Larger than life. ♦ Much ado about nothing. ♦ No job is too small. [translation: We'll make a big deal out of anything! – R.D.] ♦ Not all that it's cracked up to be. ♦ Not by a long shot. [see also Oppose]. ♦ Novelist: one who makes a short story long. ♦ On trumped-up charges. ♦ Propaganda: baloney repackaged as food for thought. – R.D. ♦ *Reductio ad absurdum.* ♦ So they would have you believe/think. ♦ That's a stretch. ♦ To b.s./bullsh*t [sb]. ♦ To be a bullsh*t artist. ♦ To be a windbag. ♦ To bend/stretch the truth. [see also Lie] ♦ To bump (it) up. ♦ To gild the lily. ♦ To go as far as to say. ♦ To go to ridiculous extremes. [see also Extremes] ♦ To bend/ embellish/stretch the truth. [see also Lie] ♦ To bump (it) up. ♦ To gild the lily. ♦ To go as far as to say. ♦ To carry [it] to/go to (ridiculous) extremes. [see also Extremes] ♦ To let the tail wag the dog. ♦ To make a big deal (of). ♦ To make a big to-do. ♦ To make a mountain out of a molehill. ♦ To play/punch (it) up. ♦ To pole vault over a mouse turd. ♦ To spin a yarn. ♦ To stretch a/the point. ♦ To talk through one's hat. ♦ To tell tall tales. ♦ To throw the bull. ♦ You should've seen the one that got away.

Exasperation

(And) on top of everything else. ♦ As if that weren't enough. ♦ At the end of one's rope/tether. ♦ At one's wit's end. ♦ Call me Custer because that's the last I will stand. ♦ Don't let it get to you. [see also Forbearance] ♦ Had it up to here (with [it]). ♦ It gets to you (after a while). ♦ It'll be the death of me. ♦ Mounting frustration. ♦ The straw that broke the camel's back. ♦ The tail wagging the dog. ♦ (This is) the last straw. ♦ To be fed up. ♦ To be/have it up to one's eyeballs with [it]. ♦ To be worn to a frazzle. ♦ To have a bellyful. ♦ To have it up to here. ♦ To have one's patience exhausted/wearing thin. ♦ To hit the wall. ♦ To reach one's boiling/ breaking point. ♦ To want out.

Excel

A personal best. ♦ At the top of one's game. [see also Best] ♦ Batting a thousand. ♦ Can do no wrong. ♦ Firing/hitting on all cylinders. ♦ Get one's mojo working. ♦ In tiptop/top form. ♦ In the zone. ♦ Make all the right moves. ♦ Man at his best. ♦ Off the charts. ♦ On a scale of one to ten—a ten. ♦ Play one's cards right. ♦ *Summa cum laude.* ♦ The magic touch. ♦ This time you've (really) outdone yourself. ♦ To bat a thousand. ♦ To be a crackerjack [n.]. ♦ To break/set a record. ♦ To get straight A's. ♦ To put everything/everyone else to shame. ♦ To run like a top. ♦ To run like a well-oiled machine. ♦ To walk on water.

Exceptions

All is not grist that comes to the mill. ♦ If we made an exception for you, we'd have to make one for everyone else. ♦ It is the exception that proves the rule. [see also Rules] ♦ Present company excepted. ♦ Some fish fly and other birds swim. ♦ The lunatic fringe. ♦ There's always that 10%. ♦ There's always that 10% who never get the word. ♦ There's an exception to every rule. [see also Rules] ♦ There's one in every crowd. ♦ To make an exception.

Excess

A bit much. ♦ A blivit: ten pounds of sh*t in a five-pound bag/sack. ♦

Anything/everything over a mouthful is wasted. ♦ Doesn't know when to quit. ♦ Enough to sink a battleship. ♦ Excess baggage. ♦ I'll be seeing [n.] in my sleep. ♦ If you shake it more than twice, you're playing with it. ♦ Information/sensory overload. ♦ More than one can handle. ♦ More than you need to know. ♦ Nothing exceeds like excess. ♦ One time too many. ♦ Over and above. ♦ Over the top. ♦ Starving in the midst of plenty. ♦ There's such a thing as being too right. ♦ There is such a thing as too much of a good thing. ♦ TMI (too much information). ♦ To be [adj.] to a fault. ♦ To be a fat slob. ♦ To be top-heavy. ♦ To carry things too far. ♦ To cross the line. ♦ To exceed expectations. ♦ To go begging. ♦ To go off the deep end. [see also Crazy] ♦ To go overboard. ♦ To flood the market. ♦ To go out of one's way [for]. ♦ To go over the edge/line. ♦ To make a special trip. ♦ To make waves. ♦ To rock the boat. ♦ To smoke like a chimney.* ♦ To smoke like a fiend. *[see also Cigar/ Cigarette] ♦ Too [adj.] for one's own good. ♦ Too much of a good thing. ♦ Too much of a good thing spoils it. ♦ Too much, too soon. ♦ Too much is as bad as too little. ♦ Water, water everywhere but not a drop to drink. ♦ You have to know when to stop.

Excitement

A black tie affair. ♦ A cheap thrill. ♦ A contact high. ♦ A happening spot. ♦ A heady experience. ♦ A thrill-seeker. ♦ A milestone occasion. ♦ A red-letter day. ♦ Cause for celebration. ♦ An adrenaline junkie.* ♦ An adrenaline rush. *[see also Risk] ♦ Geez, Louise! ♦ Great day for the Irish. ♦ Happy days are here again. [see also Happiness, Rejuvenation] ♦ Hot damn, Sam! ♦ Hot diggity (dog)! ♦ In full swing. ♦ In the merry, merry month of May. ♦ Is that your wallet, big boy—or are you just happy to see me? ♦ Never a dull moment. ♦ On this auspicious/momentous occasion. ♦ One thing after the other. ♦ Something special in the air. ♦ The fans are on their feet. ♦ The joint is jumping. ♦ There'll be a hot time in the old town tonight. ♦ Thrills and spills. ♦ To get/give high fives. ♦ To high five [so].

Exemplary

A piece of work. ♦ A work of art. ♦ In fine fettle. ♦ In fine form. ♦ In mint condition. ♦ In the flower of youth. ♦ In the prime of life. ♦ In tip-top condition/ shape. ♦ Man at his best. ♦ One in a million. ♦ The best years of one's life. ♦ The most [adj.] thing I've ever heard of. ♦ To be in rare form. ♦ To be in one's prime. ♦ To cut a fine/good figure. ♦ Very cherry.

Expectation

Don't expect miracles. ♦ Expect the unexpected. ♦ Expect the worst and you'll never be disappointed. ♦ From those to whom much is given, much is expected. ♦ Great expectations. ♦ I expect big things from you. ♦ If you drop a fork, expect male company, a spoon, female company. [see also Truisms] ♦ The standard of living. ♦ To exceed all expectation. ♦ To have unrealistic expectations. ♦ To set the bar high. ♦ Who did you expect, Harry Truman?

Expense

A big-ticket/high-ticket item. ♦ A down payment. ♦ A nominal charge. ♦ A pound of flesh. ♦ A tax write-off. ♦ A tidy sum. ♦ (All) for one low price. ♦ Big bananas. ♦ Check, please. ♦ Cost a pretty penny/an arm and a leg. ♦ Costrophobia—the fear of high bills. ♦ Come across with [it]. ♦ Cough [it] up. ♦ Despite the high cost of living, it's still quite popular. ♦ Dig down into one's pocket. ♦ Discretionary spending. ♦ Disposable income. ♦ Earnest money. ♦ Foot the bill. ♦ For a few dollars more. ♦ Fork/hand it over. ♦ Going once, going twice . . . sold! (to the highest bidder). ♦ If you have to ask what it costs you probably can't afford it. ♦ It'll set you back [n.] dollars. ♦ It's deductible. ♦ Name your price. ♦ Out-of-pocket expenses. ♦ Pay a premium. ♦ Pay the freight. ♦ Pay the going rate. ♦ Shop till you drop. ♦ Slush fund. ♦ Sold to the highest bidder. ♦ Swallow hard and dig down deep. ♦ The cost of doing business. ♦ The cost of living. ♦ The meter is running. ♦ This little piggy went to market. ♦ To be in the market for. ♦ To be on the clock/meter. ♦ To be/pay out of pocket. ♦ To come across (with). ♦ To cost one dearly. ♦ To cut/draft a check. ♦ To fork [it] over. ♦ To front the money. ♦ To go for one's lungs. ♦ To keep a running tab. ♦ To market, to market (to buy a fat pig). [see also Home] ♦ To nickel and dime one to death. ♦ To part with [it]. ♦ To pay one's dues. ♦ To pay the freight. ♦ To pay the going rate. ♦ To pay the piper. ♦ To pay through the nose. ♦ To pay top dollar. ♦ To pay up front. ♦ To pick up the tab. ♦ To pony up. ♦ To price [it] out of the market. ♦ To run up a bill. ♦ To set one back [n.] dollars. ♦ To shell out. ♦ Too rich for my blood. ♦ Very pricey. ♦ What do I/we owe you? ♦ What the traffic will bear. [see also Relativity] ♦ What's the damage? ♦ Worth every cent/penny.

Experience

A battle-hardened/seasoned veteran. ♦ A burnt child stays away from the fire. ♦ (A few) notches on one's belt. ♦ A life lesson. ♦ A practiced hand. ♦ A real trouper. ♦ A thoroughgoing professional. ♦ An elder statesman. ♦ An old hand (at). ♦ An old salt. ♦ An old war horse. ♦ A stumble may prevent a fall. ♦ A walking encyclopedia. ♦ Been around the block a few times. ♦ Chalk it up to experience. ♦ Experience is a tough teacher; it gives you the test first and the lesson afterwards. ♦ Experience is a wonderful thing; it enables you to recognize a mistake when you make it again. ♦ Experience is the best teacher. ♦ Experience is the comb that nature gives us when we are bald. ♦ Fool me once, shame on you; fool me twice, shame on me. ♦ Good judgment comes from experience; experience comes from bad judgment. ♦ If I knew then what I know now. ♦ Knowing what I know. ♦ Live and learn. ♦ Older but wiser. ♦ Once bitten/burned, twice shy. ♦ Sadder but wiser. ♦ The school of hard knocks. ♦ (The school of hard knocks awards no diplomas but may give bruises or scars. - R.D.) ♦ The voice of experience. ♦ To be a better man for it. ♦ To get/have it down pat. ♦ To get/have it down to a science/system. ♦ To get/have it under one's belt. ♦ To have the scars to prove it. ♦ To have seniority/tenure/time in grade. ♦ To know all the answers. ♦ To know one's way around (the block). ♦ Tricks of the trade. ♦ We get too soon oldt and too late schmardt. ♦ What doesn't kill you makes you stronger.

Extemporaneous

A drive-by shooting. ♦ A hastily improvised speech. ♦ An irresistible impulse. ♦ Come as you are. ♦ I never know what I'm going to do until I do it. ♦ Just for kicks/the hell of it. ♦ Make it up as you go along. ♦ On the fly. ♦ On a lark. ♦ On a wing and a prayer. ♦ On the spur of the moment. ♦ To feel one's way (along). ♦ To fly by the seat of one's pants. ♦ To pick it out of the air. ♦ To speak off the cuff. ♦ To speak off the top of one's head. ♦ To wing it.

Extravagant

(also spend)

A big spender. ♦ A fool and his money are soon parted. ♦ A high roller. ♦ Last of the big-time spenders. ♦ Money burns a hole in one's pocket. ♦ Money is no object. ♦ She can throw it out the window faster with a spoon than he can bring it in through the door with a shovel. ♦ To fork (it) over. ♦ To have deep pockets. ♦ To live above/beyond one's means. ♦ To overextend oneself. ♦ To p*ss [it] away. ♦ To spend money hand over fist. ♦ To spend money like a drunken sailor. ♦ To spend money like water.

Extremes

Body and soul. ♦ Day of deposit to day of withdrawal. ♦ Desperate times demand desperate measures. ♦ Don't mess with Mr. in-between. ♦ East is east and west is west and never the twain shall meet. ♦ Extremism in pursuit of virtue is no vice. ♦ Fore and aft. ♦ From A to Z. ♦ From *sshole to belly button. ♦ From bow to prow. ♦ From head to toe. ♦ From near and far. ♦ From one extreme to the other. ♦ From the ground up. ♦ From port to starboard. ♦ From pillar to post. ♦ From sole to crown. ♦ Not because you're pretty, not because you're sweet;

Just because you kissed the girl behind the magazine. ♦ From soup to nuts. ♦ From stem to stern. ♦ From the ridiculous to the sublime. ♦ In either extreme. ♦ In the extreme. ♦ It's either feast or famine. ♦ Jack Sprat could eat no fat; his wife could eat no lean. ♦ To carry [it] to/go to (ridiculous) extremes. [see also Exaggeration]

Extroverted

A people person. ♦ A (real) live wire. ♦ A social butterfly/lion. ♦ A take-charge guy/gal. ♦ A 'Type A' personality. ♦ An outty. ♦ Class clown. ♦ Hail-fellow-well-met. ♦ He/she lit up the room when she walked in. ♦ Is everybody happy? ♦ Life of the party. ♦ You've got a real live one there.

Failure

A belly flop (landing). ♦ A belly whopper. ♦ A crash landing. ♦ A dismal failure. ♦ A wipeout. ♦ An abysmal failure. ♦ An epic fail. ♦ At lowest ebb. ♦ Bombed in Boston. ♦ Despite one's best efforts. ♦ Down the tubes. ♦ Failure is temporary; giving up is permanent. ♦ Failure is the one thing that can be achieved without effort. ♦ Failure is not an option. [rejoinder: It's a guarantee! — R.D.] ♦ Failure isn't in falling down; it's in failing to get back up. ♦ He who is not handsome at twenty, nor strong at thirty, nor rich at forty, nor wise at fifty, will never be handsome, strong, rich, nor wise. ♦ Lack of planning on your part does not constitute an emergency on my part. ♦ Lions [n.], Christians, zero. ♦ Missed the boat. ♦ People do not plan to fail, they fail to plan. ♦ Tag—you're it/out. ♦ The deal fell through. ♦ Three strikes and you're out. ♦ To bagel. ♦ To come to naught. ♦ To come up with a goose egg. ♦ To crash and burn. ♦ To fail miserably. ♦ To fall flat on one's *ss/face. ♦ To fall through. ♦ To fan out/strike out. ♦ To go belly up/bust. ♦ To go broke. ♦ To go to the wall. ♦ To go under. ♦ To lay an egg. ♦ To score a goose egg/ Maggie's drawers. ♦ To shoot oneself in the foot. ♦ To wash out/zero out. ♦ To tank.

Faith

An article of faith ♦ Buy a pig in a poke. ♦ Everyone needs something to believe in. ♦ Faith, hope and charity. ♦ Faith can move mountains. ♦ He who lacks faith will be unable to command faith from others. ♦ If Clay says a mosquito can pull a plow, don't ask how, hitch him up! ♦ Keep the faith. ♦ No questions asked. ♦ Sight unseen.

♦ Some things you just have to accept on faith. ♦ The laying on of hands. ♦ To have blind faith. ♦ To take it on faith. [see also Acceptance] ♦ With faith/God, all things are possible.

Fall

A sheer/precipitous drop. ♦ Fall in! [military command] ♦ Fall like a sack of potatoes. ♦ Go asskefiddly. ♦ Go *ss over elbows. ♦ Go *ss over teakettle. ♦ Happy landings! ♦ Have a nice trip? ♦ In free fall. ♦ Keel over. ♦ Pick yourself up, dust yourself off and start all over again. ♦ Sorry you fell. Come over here and I'll pick you up. ♦ Pride goeth before a fall. ♦ The bigger they are the harder they fall. ♦ To drop like a rock/stone. ♦ To fall flat on one's face. ♦ To fall for [so]. ♦ To fall (head over heels) in love. ♦ To fall out of favor (with). ♦ To go head over heels. ♦ To go into free fall. ♦ To hit the deck/dirt. ♦ To plummet to earth. ♦ To take a dive/nosedive. ♦ To take a (nasty) fall. ♦ To take a spill.

Familiarity

A friend of a friend. ♦ A prophet is without honor in his own land. ♦ All the old, familiar faces. ♦ Cuddle up a little closer. ♦ Do/don't I know you from somewhere? ♦ Familiarity breeds contempt.

♦ Familiarity breeds contentment. ♦ Haven't I seen you somewhere before? ♦ Haven't we met somewhere before? ♦ It rings a bell. ♦ My old stomping grounds. ♦ On speaking terms. ♦ On a first-name basis. ♦ To be thoroughly versed/well-versed (in). ♦ To break the ice. ♦ To have a familiar ring. ♦ To know [so]'s face. ♦ Where do I know you from? ♦ You look vaguely familiar. ♦ Your face looks (very) familiar.

Familiarize

Carry across the threshold. ♦ Cut one's (eye) teeth. ♦ Get a feel for [it]. ♦ Get a fix on. ♦ Get a handle on. ♦ Get an angle on. ♦ Get the hang of [it]. ♦ Get the lay of the land. ♦ Get to know each other/one another. ♦ Get up to speed. ♦ Rub elbows/shoulders with. ♦ To make [so]'s acquaintance. ♦ Wrap one's brain/mind around [it].

Family

A blended family. ♦ All one big, happy family. ♦ Am I my brother's keeper? ♦ Blood brothers. ♦ Blood is thicker than water. [see also Thick] ♦ In a family way. ♦ In-laws are not the opposite of outlaws. ♦ It's a family affair. ♦ Next of kin. ♦ The family business. ♦ The family coat of arms/crest. ♦ The family who prays together stays together. ♦ The immediate family. ♦ The only time we ever see one another is at weddings and funerals. ♦ The whole fam damily. ♦ To keep it in the family. ♦ You can pick your nose, but you cannot pick your family. ♦ You choose your friends; your family is thrust upon you. ♦ One's own flesh and blood. ♦ Who was not born in your house does not belong in your house. – Marcantonio Serritella

Fanfare

A big whoop-de-doo. ♦ A three-ring circus. ♦ Bells and whistles. ♦ Get the key to the city. ♦ Hail to the chief. ♦ Pomp and circumstance. ♦ Ruffles and flourishes. ♦ To get/give the red-carpet treatment. ♦ To get/give the royal treatment. ♦ To roll out the red carpet. ♦ With trumpets and coronets.

Fantasize

(also fictitious)

A figment of the imagination. ♦ A flight of fancy/ fantasy. ♦ A left-handed monkey wrench/screwdriver/ toothbrush. ♦ A pipe dream. ♦ A skyhook. ♦ A Walter Mitty type. ♦ And then I wrote . . . ♦ An overactive imagination. ♦ Build castles in the air. ♦ Cut/made out of whole cloth. ♦ I can only imagine. ♦ I can see it all now. ♦ In a brown study. ♦ In a perfect world. ♦ It's all in your mind. ♦ Lost in reverie. ♦ Not to be believed. ♦ Out of touch with reality. [see also Crazy] ♦ So I took the fifty thousand . . . ♦ There's no such animal/thing. ♦ To conjure up a picture in one's mind. ♦ To get that faraway look (in one's eyes). ♦ To give reign to one's wildest fantasies. ♦ To have a fertile/vivid imagination. ♦ To let your imagination run away with you. ♦ To live in an ivory tower. ♦ To see in the mind's eye. ♦ To stargaze. ♦ To woolgather. ♦ Visions of sugarplums. ♦ Whistling Dixie.

Far-reaching

A bottomless pit. ♦ And thereby hangs a tale. ♦ Doesn't even come close. ♦ Far-reaching consequences/implications/significance. ♦ If you only knew. ♦ More than meets the eye. ♦ More to come. ♦ Neverending possibilities. ♦ No end in sight. ♦ No end to it. ♦ No end to the possibilities. ♦ Only the tip of the iceberg. ♦ Still waters run deep. ♦ That's not the half of it. ♦ That's only the half of it. ♦ The thin edge of the wedge. ♦ Therein lies a tale. ♦ Unlimited potential. ♦ You ain't seen nothing yet.

Farewells

A Dear John letter. ♦ Adios, motherf*cker. ♦ Be throwin' rocks at ya. ♦ Catch you later. ♦ Catch/see you on the flip side. ♦ *Ciao, bambino.* ♦ Class is dismissed. ♦ Don't be a stranger. ♦ Don't bother to get up; I'll see myself out. ♦ Don't take any wooden nickels. [I wouldn' – R.D.]. ♦ Give my regards to Broadway. ♦ Go by the board. ♦ Go (our/their/your) separate ways. ♦ Hasta laredo/luego/lumbago. [humorous] ♦ Have a good one. ♦ Have a happy. ♦ Have a nice day. ♦ (I'll) be seeing you. ♦ I'm outta here. ♦ It's been nice knowing you. ♦ It's been real, (folks). ♦ I've got to be going now. ♦ I've got to be on my way. ♦ I must be running along. ♦ Later. ♦ (Let's) keep in touch. ♦ Hasta la vista, baby. ♦ Keep those cards and letters coming in. ♦ Kiss [it] goodbye. ♦ Over and out. ♦ Parting is such sweet sorrow. ♦ Please keep this place in your mind, a better place is hard to find. ♦ *Sayonara.* ♦ See you around [ripostes: Like a donut! or Not if I see you first!]. ♦ See you around the campus. ♦ See you in church/in court. ♦ See you later, alligator. [riposte: After while, crocodile!] [further riposte: That don't rhyme, Frankenstein]. ♦ See you next week, same time, same station. ♦ See you on the rebound. ♦ So long. ♦ So long, it's been good to know you. ♦ Sweet dreams. ♦ Take care of yourself. ♦ Take (good) care. ♦ Take 'er/ it easy. ♦ [riposte: I'll take it any way I can get it!] ♦ Ta ta (for now). ♦ Ten four, good buddy. ♦ This is where I/ we came in. ♦ Till we meet again. ♦ To come to a parting of the ways. ♦ To ease on down the road. ♦ To go/wave bye-bye. ♦ To leave in a huff. ♦ To part company. ♦ To see [so] off. ♦ To sign off/out. ♦ To take one's leave. ♦ Until next time. ♦ Write when you get work. ♦ Y'all come back (and see us sometime), heah? ♦ You take the high road and I'll take the low road, and I'll be in Scotland afore ye.

Fat

A baby blimp. ♦ A beer belly/gut. ♦ A fat tub of lard. ♦ A fat cat. ♦ A fat pig. ♦ A few extra pounds. ♦ A gut. ♦ A jowly good fellow. ♦ A lard*ss. ♦ A tub of guts. ♦ A (real) porker. ♦ A spare tire. ♦ Chubby-wubby. ♦ Cottage-cheese thighs. ♦ Could stand to use a few pounds. ♦ Fat as a hog/pig/walrus. ♦ Fat and sassy. ♦ Fat, dumb and happy. ♦ Full-figured. ♦ Got more chins than a Chinese phone book. ♦ I'm not fat, I'm pleasingly plump. ♦ It's not over till the fat lady sings. [see also Premature]

♦ Junk in the trunk. ♦ Loaf-of-bread arms. ♦ Looks like two clowns fighting under a blanket. ♦ Love handles. ♦ Middle-age spread. ♦ Morbidly obese. ♦ Mr. Five by Five. ♦ Of ample girth/ proportions. ♦ Porkass. ♦ Porky pig. ♦ Roly-poly. ♦ She has an airline figure: wide body. – R.D. ♦ Short, fat and squatty—all *ss and no body. ♦ The fat's in the fire. ♦ Thick around the middle. ♦ To live off the fat of the land. ♦ To put on weight. ♦ To tip the scales (at). ♦ Two-ton Tony.

Fear

A fear monger. ♦ Afraid of one's own shadow. [see also Cowardice] ♦ Be afraid . . . be very afraid. ♦ Fear not and be just. ♦ Fear of the dark. ♦ Fear of the unknown. ♦ He who has gold has fear, who has none has sorrow. ♦ He who lives wickedly always lives in fear. ♦ Ignorance is the feedbag of fear. ♦ That's what I am afraid of. ♦ The fear of the Lord is the beginning of wisdom. ♦ The only thing we have to fear is fear itself. ♦ To be deathly afraid (of). ♦ To chicken out. ♦ To feed into one's fears. ♦ To have one's heart in one's mouth/ stomach. ♦ To have one's knees knocking. ♦ To hit/ push the panic button. ♦ To put the fear (of God) into.* ♦ To quake/shake in one's boots *[see also Scare]. ♦ Who has nothing fears nothing.

Finagle

Beg, borrow or steal. ♦ By all means (fair or foul). ♦ By all/any means necessary. ♦ By any and all means (necessary). ♦ By hook or by crook. ♦ Finesse it. ♦ Juggle the books. ♦ Keep two sets of books. ♦ One way or another. ♦ To finagle the bagel. ♦ To have a foot in both camps. ♦ To rob Peter to pay Paul. ♦ To work both sides of the street.

Finality

(also discard)

A done deal. ♦ (And) that's that. [see also End] ♦ And then there were none. ♦ At the end of the trail. ♦ At the end of one's rope. ♦ Case dismissed. ♦ Cast [it] aside, like an old shoe. ♦ It all boils down/comes down to this. ♦ It's the last thing in the world I need. ♦ In the end stages. ♦ *La comedie e finis.* ♦ Last known address/whereabouts. ♦ No further questions, Your Honor. ♦ Out the window. ♦ Over and done with. [see also End, Forgive] ♦ Played out. ♦ School's out. ♦ So much for that. [see also End, Enough] ♦ That (about) wraps it up. ♦ That does it. ♦ That takes care of that. ♦ That'll do it (for me). ♦ That's all she wrote. ♦ That's all she wrote; there ain't no more. ♦ That's it in a nutshell. ♦ That's it for now. ♦ The buck stops here. ♦ The damage is already done. ♦ The Dead Letter Office. ♦ The deed is done. ♦ The Final Solution. ♦ The gig is over. ♦ The grand finale. ♦ The gig/jig is up. ♦ The last hurrah. ♦ The party's over. ♦ The swan song. ♦ The tail end. ♦ The witness may step down. ♦ Th-th-that's all, folks! ♦ There's no coming back from that. ♦ Time's up. ♦ To be out of time. ♦ To run out of time. ♦ To button it up. ♦ To circular file [it]. ♦ To close the deal. ♦ To come to a head. ♦ To curb [it]. ♦ To cut the cord. ♦ To deep six [it]. ♦ To get/give the deep six. ♦ To dispose of the body. ♦ To eighty-six [it]. ♦ To empty the garbage/trash. ♦ To give [it] the old heave-ho. ♦ To go down fighting. ♦ To go down swinging. ♦ To go out. ♦ To go out in a blaze of glory. ♦ To go out in style. ♦ To go out not with a bang but with a whimper. ♦ To go out with a bang. ♦ To go this far and no further. ♦ To max [it] out. ♦ To pitch [it]. ♦ To reach a logical conclusion. ♦ To reach the end of the line/trail. ♦ To scuttle [it]. ♦ To send [it] to the glue factory. ♦ To sh*tcan [it]. ♦ To sound the death knell. ♦ To p*ss [it] away. ♦ To swing from the canvas.

♦ To take out the trash. ♦ To throw/ toss [it] away/out. ♦ To toss [it] into the circular file. ♦ To toss [it] on the scrap heap. ♦ To trash [it]. ♦ To wind up. ♦ What it all boils down/comes down to. ♦ What's the last thing that goes through a bug's mind when it hits your windshield? Its *sshole. ♦ When in doubt, throw it out. ♦ Your number/ time is up.

First

Be not the first by whom the new are tried, nor yet the last to lay the old aside. ♦ First and foremost. ♦ First come, first served. ♦ First order of business. ♦ First order of the day. ♦ First things first. ♦ First time out of the box. ♦ George Washington: first commander-in-chief; first president; first in the hearts of his countrymen . . . and he married a widow. ♦ Get there "fustest with the mostest." ♦ In first place. ♦ Somebody has to go first. ♦ The first go-around. ♦ The first shall be last and the last shall be first. ♦ There's a first time for everything. ♦ To begin with. ♦ To come in first. ♦ To get first crack (at). ♦ When it comes (right) down to it. ♦ Women and children first. ♦ You heard it here first. ♦ Your first thought is usually the best.

Flat

A flat denial. ♦ Flat as a board. ♦ Flat as a pancake. ♦ Flat as a schnitzel. ♦ Flat broke. ♦ Flat out. ♦ Flatter than a dysentery turd struck with a club. ♦ Flatter than p*ss on a platter. ♦ On the balls of one's feet. ♦ On the flat of one's back. ♦ The flat of one's hand. ♦ To be caught flat-footed. ♦ To be flat-footed. ♦ To fall flat on one's face. ♦ To flat-out [v.].

Flattery

All sweetness and light. ♦ Butter wouldn't melt in her/his mouth. ♦ Charm the pants off. ♦ Cozy up to. ♦ Flattery will get you everywhere. ♦ Flattery will get you nowhere. ♦ I'll bet you say that to all the girls. [rejoinder: Only the pretty ones]. ♦ It's you (to a "T.") ♦ On you it looks good. ♦ Praise to the face is open disgrace. ♦ So thick, you could spread it with a trowel. ♦ Take the sugary sweet person with a grain of salt. ♦ To be in [so]'s good graces. ♦ To buck for a promotion/raise. ♦ To butter [so] up. ♦ To cater to one's tastes. ♦ To charm the socks off [so]. ♦ To curry favor. ♦ To get in good with [so]. ♦ To get on [so]'s good side. ♦ To fall all over [so]. ♦ To ingratiate oneself with [so]. ♦ To kiss *ss. ♦ To lay it on thick. ♦ To make a fuss over. ♦ To make [so] look good. ♦ To massage [so]'s ego. ♦ To play up to [so]. ♦ To pour on the charm. ♦ To schmooze. ♦ To score brownie points. ♦ To soft soap [so]. ♦ To sweet talk [so]. ♦ To turn on the charm. ♦ To worm one's way into [so]'s heart. ♦ Treachery lurks in honeyed words. ♦ Yes sir, no sir, three bags full.

Flee

Amscray. ♦ Beat a hasty retreat. ♦ Blow town. ♦ Blow this joint. ♦ Cut and run. ♦ Feet, do your duty! ♦ Fly the coop. ♦ Get out of Dodge. ♦ Go over the hill. ♦ Head for the hills. ♦ Make a run for (it). ♦ On the lam. ♦ On the run. ♦ Pull up stakes. ♦ Run away with one's tail between one's legs. ♦ Run for one's life. ♦ Run like a thief. ♦ Run like a scared rabbit. ♦ Skedaddle. ♦ Skip town. ♦ Splitsville. ♦ Take a powder. ♦ Take it on the run. ♦ Take off like a big*ss bird. ♦ Take off for parts unknown. ♦ To be at large. ♦ To be on the lam/loose. ♦ To book. ♦ To cut out. ♦ To get away from it all. ♦ To head for higher ground. ♦ To hie on out (of). ♦ To hightail it. ♦ To jump bail. ♦ To make a break. ♦ To make an escape. ♦ To run for cover. ♦ To show the white feather. ♦ To take evasive action. ♦ To take to one's heels. ♦ To take to the hills. ♦ To split. ♦ To steal away like a thief in the night. ♦ To turn tail. ♦ To vamoose. ♦ We gotta get out of this place. ♦ You can run but you can't hide.

Flexibility

A floppy disk. ♦ Accept the status quo. ♦ Adapt to one's surroundings. ♦ Bend or break. ♦ Consistency is the hobgoblin of little minds. ♦ Don't let it throw you. ♦ Go with the flow. ♦ Hang loose. ♦ He's very flexible: like a snake. ♦ Just live one day at a time. ♦ Keep one's options open. ♦ People can get used to anything. ♦ Other than that, Mrs. Lincoln, how did you enjoy the play? ♦ Ride with the tide. ♦ Roll with the punches. ♦ Take it (all) in stride. ♦ Take it as it comes. ♦ To be a good sport. ♦ To resign oneself (to one's condition/fate). ♦ To take it in good part. ♦ To take it in the spirit in which it was intended. ♦ You never know where a path will lead.

Flirt
(also seduction)

A (big) come-on. ♦ A come-hither look. ♦ Bat one's eyelashes. ♦ Come away with me to the casbah. ♦ Come on to. ♦ Did anyone ever tell you that you have beautiful eyes? ♦ If I told you that you have a nice body would you hold it against me? ♦ Lead [so] on. ♦ Let me take you away from all this. ♦ Like what you see? ♦ Make a play for [so]. ♦ Men don't make passes at girls who wear glasses. [N.B. If men don't make passes at girls who wear glasses, then . . . girls who wear glasses must make passes at men!] ♦ Step into my parlor, said the spider to the fly. ♦ The casting couch. ♦ To "come onto" [so]. ♦ To give a tumble (to). ♦ To give [so] a tumble. To give [so] the eye. ♦ To give [so] the hairy eyeball. [see also Skepticism] ♦ To have bedroom eyes. ♦ To hit on [so]. ♦ To make a pass (at). ♦ To make eyes at [so]. ♦ To make goo goo eyes. ♦ To make time. ♦ To proposition [so]. ♦ To put the moves on [so]. ♦ Your place or mine?

Flourishing

(also successful)

A bed of roses. ♦ A fat cat. ♦ An odds-on favorite. ♦ An overnight sensation. ♦ Be fruitful and multiply. ♦ Cooking on the front burner. ♦ Expanding/ growing/ increasing exponentially/ geometrically. ♦ Growing like a weed. ♦ Have a good thing going. ♦ Have a lot going (for one). ♦ Have a pat hand. ♦ Have it knocked (up) ♦ Have it in the bag. ♦ Have it made (in the shade). ♦ Have it wired. ♦ Have one's ship come in. ♦ Have the world on a string.

♦ Have the world by the *ss/tail. ♦ How sweet it is! ♦ In like Flynn. ♦ In line for the throne. ♦ It was a very good year. ♦ It's the good life. ♦ *La dolce vita.* ♦ Never had it so good. ♦ Nice work if you can get it. ♦ On a roll. ♦ On Easy Street. ♦ On the gravy train. ♦ On the short list (for promotion). ♦ Riding high. ♦ Rolling in clover. ♦ Set oneself in a tub of butter. ♦ Sh*tting in high cotton. ♦ (Sitting) in the catbird seat. ♦ (Sitting) on top of the world. ♦ Sitting pretty. ♦ (Sure) beats working for a living. ♦ The bed is called rose; if you don't sleep, you repose. — Angela Maria Delia ♦ The favorite son. ♦ The Number One son. ♦ The world is your oyster. ♦ The world is my oyster, said the girl/Said the pearl: the oyster is my world! — R.D. ♦

To be golden. ♦ To be in Fat City. ♦ To be the fair-haired boy. ♦ To be the heir apparent. ♦ To be well-to-do. ♦ To have arrived. ♦ To have the world at one's feet. ♦ To kick it. ♦ To lead/ live the life of Reilly/Riley. ♦ To live high on the hog. ♦ To live a life of luxury. ♦ To live in the lap of luxury. ♦ To live it up. ♦ To live like a king. ♦ To make something of oneself. ♦ To take off. ♦ What a racket! ♦ What a way to go.

Fly

Come fly with me. ♦ Flying high. ♦ Goony birds can't fly. ♦ Ladybug, la-dybug, fly away. ♦ Not everything that has wings flies and not everything that flies has wings. ♦ On gossamer wing. ♦ Spread one's wings and fly. ♦ Straighten up and fly right. ♦ To do it on the fly. ♦ To fly in the face of conventional wisdom. ♦ To fly in the face of danger. ♦ To fly off the handle. ♦ To soar to new heights. ♦ Up, up and away!

Fool

A fool's paradise. ♦ A fool's pie has a lot of crust—but no filling. ♦ Answer a fool according to his folly. ♦ Don't p*ss on my head and tell me it's raining. ♦ Everybody's somebody's fool. ♦ Fools laugh at what they do not understand. ♦ Fools may be used as tools. ♦ Fools rush in where angels fear to tread. ♦ Fools' names, like fools' faces, always seen in public places. ♦ He that deals with fools is a fool. ♦ He who serves as his own lawyer has a fool for a client. ♦ If a mule's *ss was a camera, his picture would be all over the United States. ♦ If all fools wore white caps we would look like a flock of geese. ♦ If every fool wore a crown, we should all be kings. ♦ Many a man's own tongue gives evidence against his own understanding. ♦ My parents raised two fools but they were my brother and sister. ♦ Only a fool does not look both ways crossing a one-way street. ♦ No one can make a fool of you without your help. ♦ Only a fool makes his doctor his heir. ♦ Shallow wits censure everything that is beyond their depth. ♦ Some are wise and some are otherwise. ♦ The village idiot. ♦ There's no fool like an old fool. ♦ To make a fool (out) of [so]. ♦ To make an *ss/fool of oneself. ♦ To play dumb. ♦ To play the fool. ♦ What fools these mortals be. ♦ What kind of fool do you take me for? ♦ What were they thinking? ♦ Wise men learn more from fools than fools from wise men. ♦ Wise men will speak folly sooner than fools will speak wisdom. ♦ Without fools, no wise men.

♦ You can fool all of the people some of the time, and some of the people all the time but you can't fool all the people all the time. ♦ You can't fool Father Time. ♦ You can't fool Mother Nature.

Forbearance

A love-hate relationship. ♦ A mixed blessing. ♦ A necessary evil. ♦ All in a day's work. ♦ All in one lifetime. ♦ Another day, another dollar. ♦ As the world turns. ♦ Call me anything but don't call me late for dinner.* ♦ Call me anything you like but call me. *[see also Names, Slander] ♦ *C'est la guerre.* ♦ *C'est la vie.* ♦ Don't let it get to you. [see also Exasperation] ♦ Every rose has its thorn. ♦ If it's not one thing, it's another. ♦ If you ain't a-doin' this you're a-doin' somethin' else. -[Uncle Dudley] ♦ Into each life a little rain must fall. ♦ It was (all) for the best. ♦ It's always something. ♦ It's just one of those things. ♦ Life is a series of approvals and denials. ♦ *Que será será.* ♦ Sh*t happens. ♦ So it goes. ♦ Sometimes you bite the bear; sometimes the bear bites you. ♦ That's how it is. ♦ That's life. ♦ That's life in the big city. ♦ That's the way it goes. ♦ That's the way she goes, amigos. ♦ That's the way the ball bounces/cookie crumbles/world turns. ♦ The more you cry, the less you have to piss. ♦ Them's the breaks. ♦ Them's the breaks of naval air— sometimes called air breaks. ♦ This too shall pass. [see also Temporary] ♦ To learn to live with it. ♦ To let it roll off your back. ♦ To suck it up. ♦ What can you do? ♦ What're you gonna do? ♦ Win some, lose some. ♦ You can't win 'em all. [see also Win] ♦ You have to take the bad with the good. ♦ You have to take the bitter with the sweet. ♦ You'll eat a peck/pound of dirt before you die.

Forget

A blonde moment. ♦ A brain f*rt. ♦ A doo-dad/doo-hickey. ♦ A lapse of memory. ♦ A mental block. ♦ A noombob. ♦ A senior moment. ♦ A short attention span. ♦ A thingama-bob. ♦ A thingamajig/thingmajig. ♦ A whatchamacallit. ♦ A whoozy-whatsis. ♦ Attention deficit disorder. ♦ Brain freeze. ♦ Forget me not. ♦ How quickly they forget! ♦ I could've sworn that I told you. ♦ I forgot what I was going to say: (it must have been a lie). ♦ I meant to tell you. ♦ I never forget a face. ♦ I forgot all about it. ♦ I thought I told you. ♦ I'll never forget old what's-his-name. ♦ I've forgotten more than you'll ever know (about [n.]). ♦ If it was important you would have remembered it. ♦ It eludes/escapes me at the moment. ♦ It's right on the tip of my tongue. ♦ Keep a tickler file. ♦ Like riding a bicycle: you never forget how. ♦ Like the absent-minded professor. ♦ Lose one's train of thought. ♦ Lose track (of). ♦ Mind suddenly went blank. ♦ Now what was I just saying? ♦ Of all sad words of tongue of pen, the saddest are these: "I should've written it when." ♦ The attention span of a gnat. ♦ Tie a string around one's finger. ♦ To draw a blank. ♦ To go up on one's lines. ♦ To have selective memory. [see also Relativity] ♦ To lose track of time. ♦ To put it in your rear view mirror. ♦ To put it out of mind. ♦ To slip one's mind. ♦ What's-his-face. ♦ You'd forget your *ss if it wasn't attached. ♦ You'd forget your head if it wasn't screwed on.

Forgive

As we forgive those who trespass against us. ♦ Better to ask for forgiveness than to ask for permission. ♦ Bury the hatchet. ♦ Can you (ever) find it in your heart to forgive me? ♦ Come home, all is forgiven. ♦ Done and gone. ♦ Even a condemned man has a right to explain himself. — Dominick P. Delia ♦ Every dog is entitled to one bite. ♦ Forgive and forget. ♦ Forgiveness is forgetfulness. (But don't forget to forgive! — R.D.) ♦ Forgiveness is the fragrance of the violet that lingers on the heel that crushed it. ♦ Get beyond it. ♦ Get past it. ♦ He who forgives little, loves little. ♦ It's all in the past. ♦ It's over and done with. [see also End, Finality] ♦ Let bygones be bygones. ♦ Let go of it. ♦ Let it ride/slide. ♦ Let sleeping dogs lie. ♦ Live and let live. ♦ Men forget, but never forgive; women forgive, but never forget. ♦ No hard feelings. ♦ No harm, no foul. ♦ That's water over the dam/ under the bridge. ♦ To bear no ill will. ♦ To drop (all) the charges. ♦ To extend an olive branch. ♦ To forgive is to forget. ♦ To get over it. ♦ To get past it. ♦ To kiss and make up. ♦ To know all is to forgive all. ♦ To mend (one's) fences. ♦ To put it (all) behind you. ♦ To put it in one's rear-view mirror. ♦ To turn the other cheek. ♦ What's done is done.

Fours

A four-in-hand-knot. ♦ A four-lane highway. ♦ Four and twenty blackbirds baked in a pie. ♦ Four is a sacred number to Masons. ♦ Four on the floor. ♦ Fourscore and seven years ago. ♦ On all fours. ♦ The Fab Four. ♦ The four corners of the earth. ♦ The Four Freedoms. ♦ The Four Freshmen. ♦ The Four Horsemen of the Apocalypse. ♦ The Four Noble Truths. ♦ The four seasons/winds. ♦ The four walls. ♦ Three, four, open the door. ♦ To face life foursquare. ♦ When angry, count to four; when very angry, swear. ♦ When you point a finger at someone else, remember that four of your fingers are pointing at you.

Frail

A 97-lb. weakling. ♦ A bag of bones. ♦ A good gust of wind would blow him away/over. ♦ A walking skeleton. ♦ Light as a feather. ♦ Nothing but skin and bones. ♦ The closer the bone, the sweeter the meat. ♦ Thin as a rail. ♦ Weak as a kitten.

Free

At no charge. ♦ At no cost (to you). ♦ Compliments of a friend. ♦ Compliments of the chef. ♦ Doesn't cost one thin dime. ♦ Free and clear/easy. ♦ Free as a bird. ♦ Free as the breeze/the wind. ♦ Free of charge. ♦ Help yourself. ♦ My compliments. No purchase necessary. ♦ No strings attached. ♦ Nobody gives you nothing. ♦ On the house. ♦ *Pro bono.* ♦ Shipping and handling not included. ♦ The best things in life are free. ♦ There is no such thing as a free lunch. ♦ This one's on me. ♦ To get a freebie. ♦ You don't get something for nothing. ♦ Your money's no good (around) here.

Fresh

(also neat)

A breath of fresh air. ♦ A fresh start. ♦ Farm fresh. ♦ Fresh as a daisy. ♦ Fresh as a dewdrop. ♦ Fresh as a flower/rose. ♦ Fresh as a spring breeze. ♦ Fresh as a new-minted penny. ♦ Fresh as hell. ♦ Fresh as paint. ♦ Neat as a pin. ♦ Not a hair out of place. ♦ To freshen up. ♦ To look as if one just stepped out of a bandbox. ♦ To take a fresh approach/look/direction.

Friend

A fair-weather friend. ♦ A friend in need is a friend indeed. ♦ A friend of a friend. ♦ A friend of mine. ♦ A friend of the court. ♦ A friend of the family. ♦ A long-lost friend. ♦ A shoulder to cry on. ♦ Any friend of [n.]'s is a friend of mine. ♦ A boon companion. ♦ Better an open enemy than a false friend. ♦ Choose your friends; don't let your friends choose you. ◆ Circle of friends. ◆ Diamonds are a girl's best friend. ◆ Evil companions corrupt good morals. ◆ Fast friends. ◆ Friend or *faux*? ◆ Friend or foe? ◆ Friends are like fiddle strings: they mustn't be screwed too tight. ◆ Friendship is a two-way street. ◆ Old friends are the best friends, after all. ◆ Our fine feathered friends. ◆ Show me your friends and I will show you who you are. ◆ Take a friend to lunch. ◆ The best mirror is an old friend. ◆ There are two things a man must do alone. God will not help. He must find friend and teacher. ◆ To be chummy-wummy/palsy-walsy. ◆ True friends, like real diamonds are precious and rare; false ones, like autumn leaves, can be found everywhere. ◆ We go way back. ◆ With friends like this, who needs enemies? [see also Ingratitude]

Fugitive

A fugitive from justice. ◆ A menace to society. ◆ A wanted man. ◆ An escaped convict. ◆ An outlaw. ◆ America's Most Wanted. ◆ On the lam/loose/run. ◆ Rogue's Gallery. ◆ The FBI's 10 Most Wanted list. ◆ They'll never take me alive. ◆ To be one step ahead of the law/sheriff. ◆ To be under the radar. [see also Inconspicuous] ◆ To have a bounty/price on one's head. ◆ To keep a low profile. ◆ To lay/lie low. ◆ To take to the mattresses. ◆ Wanted: Dead or Alive.

Fun

All in (good, clean) fun. ◆ Blondes have more fun. ◆ Fun and games. ◆ Fun in the sun. ◆ Have a ball. ◆ I was just funning you. ◆ Just for the fun of it. ◆ More fun than a barrel of monkeys. ◆ More fun than a tornado in a trailer park. ◆ The last time I looked, fun was not one of the Seven Deadly Sins. – R.D. ◆ Time flies when you're having fun. ◆ To do it (just) for fun. ◆ To have fun. ◆ Today was good. Today was fun. Tomorrow is another one.

Futility

For all the good/lotta good that'll do ya. ◆ Like dropping a BB into the ocean and expecting to see ripples. – R.D. ◆ Like dropping a flower petal into the Grand Canyon and waiting for the echo. – R.D. ◆ Like fishing in trees. ◆ No matter how you struggle and strive, you'll never get out of this world alive. ◆ Nothing to show for it. ◆ Once the bell is rung, it cannot be un-rung. ◆ P*ssing in the wind. ◆

P*ssing up a rope. ♦ To beg of the miser is to dig a trench in the sea. ♦ To come up/leave empty-handed. ♦ To go against the tide. ♦ To tilt at windmills. ♦ To shovel sand/sh*t against the tide. ♦ To square the circle. ♦ You can't dip clear water from a muddy stream. ♦ You can't get blood from a stone/turnip. ♦ You can't get chop suey out of chopsticks. ♦ You can't get ham out of a hamster. ♦ You can't get honey from a honeydew. ♦ You can't get pea soup from peanuts. ♦ You might as well bail out the ocean with a Dixie Cup.

Future

A man without thought for the future must soon have present sorrow. ♦ Children yet unborn. ♦ File it away, for future reference. ♦ Future generations. ♦ In a (little) bit/while. ♦ In the end, everybody dies. ♦ In the foreseeable future. ♦ In the long run. * ♦ In the long run, we're all dead. *[see also Eventually] ♦ In the pipeline. [see also Potential] ♦ Nobody can see into the future. ♦ Nobody has a crystal ball. ♦ Nobody knows tomorrow. ♦ Over the long haul. ♦ Shallow men: past. Wise: present. Fools: future. ♦ Study the past if you would define the future. ♦ The future is not ours to see. ♦ The next big thing. [see also Trendy] ♦ The next generation. ♦ The wave of the future. ♦ What's coming down the pike.

Gambling

A card shark/sharp. ♦ A game of chance. ♦ A one-armed bandit. ♦ Aces and eights, the dead man's hand. ♦ Against all odds. ♦ An outside chance. ♦ Baby needs a new pair of shoes. ♦ Call and raise. ♦ Coffee housing (also, speech play). ♦ Come seven, come eleven. ♦ Come to papa. ♦ Deuces never loses. ♦ Eight ball in the side pocket. ♦ Eighter from Decatur. ♦ I call you and raise you. ♦ I'd be willing to bet. ♦ I'm willing to bet. ♦ Niner from Carolina. ♦ Pot's right. ♦ Rack 'em up. ♦ Rattle/roll them bones. ♦ Read 'em and weep. ♦ 7 come 11. ♦ Sweeten the pot. ♦ The joker is wild. ♦ The price of poker just went up. ♦ To buy the pot. ♦ To crap out. ♦ To draw lots/straws. ♦ To feed the ponies. ♦ To have a Chinese straight. ♦ To have a poker face. ♦ To keep [it] as a kicker. ♦ To lay even money (on). ♦ To leave it to chance. ♦ To raise the stakes. ♦ To roll the dice. ♦ To take a chance. ♦ To take potluck. ♦ To up the ante. ♦ Wanna lay some money on it? ♦ What are the odds?

Gardening

As ye sow, so shall ye reap. ♦ Gardeners don't get old, they go to pot. ♦ Gardening—just another day at the plant. ♦ Gardening is a work of heart. ♦ Mary, Mary, quite contrary, How does your garden grow?/ With silver bells, and cockle shells, And pretty maids all in a row. ♦ Save a tree. Eat a beaver. ♦ This rule in gardening never forget: To sow dry and set wet. ♦ To have a green thumb. ♦ To till the soil. ♦ You reap what you sow. ♦ "Your feet are killing me," says the Earth.

Generalizations

Above all. ♦ All generalizations are false, including this one. ♦ All in all. ♦ All other things/all else being equal. ♦ (All) that being said. ♦ All that notwithstanding. ♦ All things considered. ♦ Among other things. ♦ And another thing. ♦ And I use the term loosely. ♦ Apropos of that/which. ♦ As a (general) rule. ♦ As a practical matter. ♦ As a whole. ♦ As far as that goes. ♦ As it were. ♦ As never before. ♦ As the case may be. ♦ At any rate. ♦ Be that as it may. ♦ By and large. ♦ By any standard. ♦ By any stretch of the imagination. ♦ If I may say so. ♦ For/ to all intents and purposes. ♦ For all practical purposes. ♦ For argument's sake. ♦ For that matter. ♦ For the life of me. ♦ For the sake of argument. ♦ Generally, it never pays to generalize. ♦ Generally speaking. ♦ Given all that. ♦ In a manner of speaking. ♦ In and of itself. [see also Solitary] ♦ In any case. ♦ In any event. ♦ In effect. ♦ In essence. ♦ In large measure. ♦ In light of (that). ♦ In terms of. ♦ In that case. ♦ In the broadest sense. ♦ In the event that (that happens). ♦ In the grand scheme of things. ♦ In the strictest sense of the word. ♦ In view of. ♦ Let alone. ♦ Let me say this about that. ♦ Let's just say: ♦ Loosely speaking. ♦ Not to mention. ♦ Not to speak of. ♦ Now more than ever. ♦ Now that you bring it up. ♦ Now that you mention it. ♦ On a [adj.] note. ♦ On the [adj.] side. ♦ On the whole. ♦ Seeing as (how). ♦ Shall we say. ♦ Since you brought the subject up. ♦ So to say/speak. ♦ Speaking of which. ♦ Still and all. ♦ Strange as it may seem. ♦ Strictly speaking. ♦ That being the case. ♦ To say nothing of. ♦ To whom it may concern. [see also Indeterminate] ♦ Which reminds me. ♦ While we're on the subject. ♦ With all due respect. ♦ With reference/regard/respect to. ♦ With that as a given.

Generosity

(also charity)

A big spender. ♦ A golden parachute. [see also Venality] ♦ A heart as big as Texas. ♦ A heart of gold. ♦ A mercy f*ck. ♦ A noble gesture. ♦ A non-profit organization. ♦ A patron of the arts. ♦ A sugar daddy. ♦ A soft touch. ♦ Charity begins at home. ♦ For a good/worthy cause. ♦ Give till it hurts. ♦ God bless the cheerful giver. ♦ Have a heart. ♦ He'd give you the shirt off his back. ♦ It is more blessed to give than to receive. ♦ Nothing's too good for you. ♦ Spread the wealth. [see also Reciprocation] ♦ That's sporting of [n.]/[p.]. ♦ The Lord giveth; the Lord taketh away. ♦ The milk of human kindness. ♦ To be all heart. ♦ To be in a generous mood. ♦ To do [so] a favor/ a solid. ♦ To give away the store. ♦ To give selflessly of oneself. ♦ To grace [so] with her/his/their/your presence. ♦ To pass the hat (for). ♦ To raise money (for charity). ♦ To spring for [it]. ♦ To take up a collection. ♦ You've got to give to get. ♦ Your generosity is exceeded only by your good looks.

Genius

A cluttered desk is the mark of genius. ♦ A stroke of genius. ♦ Genius is the capacity for infinite detail. ♦ Genius is 1% inspiration and 99% perspiration. ♦ Talent is a gift from God, but genius is God. ♦ The difference between stupidity and genius is that genius has its limits. — Albert Einstein [see also Difference] The fault of genius is that it knows too much. ♦ There's a fine line between genius and madness. ♦ Wisdom in youth is genius.

Glare

A withering stare. ♦ Don't look at me in that tone of voice. ♦ If looks could kill (I'd be dead). ♦ To get/give a dirty look. ♦ To get/give a (funny) look from [so]. ♦ To get/give the fisheye from [so]. ♦ To make/pull a face. ♦ To make faces. ♦ To roll one's eyes. ♦ To stare daggers at [so]. ♦ To stare [so] down.

Glory

A place in the sun. ♦ Glory be. Glory be and hallelujah. ♦ Glory, glory hallelujah/teacher hit me with the ruler/now she's sitting in the cooler/while I go marching on. ♦ In all its [adj] glory. ♦ 'Morning, glory, what's your story? ♦ Mine eyes have seen the glory of the coming of the Lord. ♦ No guts, no glory. [see also Courage] ♦

The crowning glory. ✦ The desire of glory is the torch of the mind. ✦ The glory hole. ✦ To have one's moment in the sun.

Gluttony
(also greed)

A chow hound. ✦ A gold digger. ✦ A man may dig his grave with his teeth. ✦ A road hog. ✦ Feed sparingly and starve the doctor. ✦ Give them an inch and they'll take a mile. ✦ Glutton for punishment. ✦ If one is good, two have to be better. ✦ Insatiable appetite/desire/lust. ✦ That secret thief, the table, sends its master to the hospital. ✦ The best exercise is pushing yourself away from the table. ✦ The more you get, the more you want. ✦ To bite off more than you can chew. [see also Shortsighted] ✦ To eat you out of house and home. ✦ To lengthen your life, lessen your meals. ✦ To pig out. ✦ To smoke like a fiend/chimney. ✦ Your eyes are bigger than your stomach.

Good

A force for (the) good. ✦ As good as the day is long. ✦ For one's own good. ✦ For the greater good. ✦ Good things come in small packages. ✦ Good things come in threes. ✦ Have a good thing going. ✦ If it seems too good to be true it probably is. ✦ It'll do you a world of good. ✦ It's good for what ails you. ✦ It's good for you. ✦ No good deed goes unnoticed. ✦ No good deed goes unpunished. [ironic/sarcastic] ✦ Onto a good thing. ✦ Received in good order. ✦ The stuff dreams are made of. ✦ Too good to be true.

Gossip

A little bird told me. ✦ An idle tongue is soon wagging. ✦ And he says to me . . . ✦ As full of rumors as a boarding house. ✦ By all accounts. ✦ (Dame) rumor has it. ✦ Dish the dirt. ✦ Have I got one for you. ✦ Heard it through the grapevine. ✦ I heard one say so is half a lie. ✦ Informed sources say. [see also Detect, News] ✦ It's just hearsay. ✦ Just so you know. ✦ Like an old washerwoman. ✦ Never talk to your aunt about your mother. ✦ Pass it along/take it for what it's worth. ✦ Pass it on. ✦ People will talk. ✦ Please don't talk about me when I'm gone. ✦ So I says to him . . . ✦ So they say. ✦ Speak of the devil (and he appears). [see also Coincidence, Devil] ✦ The husband is always the last to know. ✦ The rumor mill. ✦ The scuttlebutt. ✦ The talk of the town. ✦ The word on the street. ✦ To be nosey. ✦ To carry tales. ✦ To dig the dirt. ✦ To get/hear it second hand.

♦ To know one's comings and goings. ♦ To set tongues wagging. ♦ Were your ears ringing? (We were just talking about you.) ♦ What will the neighbors think? ♦ Word of mouth. ♦ You didn't hear it/this from me.

Gratitude

A God-given gift. ♦ A lot to be thankful for. ♦ All contributions/donations graciously and gratefully accepted. ♦ Be thankful for what you've got. ♦ Better that I should owe you than I should stick you. ♦ Better one's minnow to fillet than to cry about the one that got away! ♦ Count your blessings. ♦ Don't bite the hand that feeds you. ♦ Don't look a gift horse in the mouth. ♦ Don't thump a free melon. ♦ Give thanks for small blessings. ♦ How can I/we ever make it up to you? ♦ How can I/we ever repay/thank you? ♦ I complained because I had no shoes till I met a man who had no feet. ♦ I/we owe you (big time). ♦ I/we owes ya. ♦ It could have been worse. ♦ It means the world to me. ♦ It's the thought that counts. ♦ Let us give thanks. ♦ Make the most of what comes and the least of what goes. ♦ Much obliged. ♦ Put a snake to your bosom and it will sting when it is warm. ♦ Someday you'll thank me for this. ♦ Thank God. ♦

Thank God for small favors. ♦ Thank goodness/ heaven. ♦ Thanks a million. ♦ Thanks, I needed that. ♦ Thank you/ thanks (ever) so much. ♦ Thanks to. ♦ The gayest laughter doesn't always come from stately mansions. ♦ There but for the grace of God go I. ♦ There's always somebody worse off than you. ♦ To be eternally grateful. ♦ To give thanks. ♦ To have make-up sex. ♦ To pay it forward. ♦ To say grace. ♦ To thank one in advance. ♦ To thank one's lucky stars. ♦ You have a funny way of showing it. ♦ You'd do the same for me, wouldn't you? ♦ You'd've done the same (thing) for me.

Grooming

Are my seams straight? ♦ Does this dress make me look fat? ♦ I met a pretty girl with a pretty curl right in the middle of her forehead. ♦ Just take a little off the top. ♦ Primping and prissing. ♦ Put on your face. ♦ Shave and a haircut, two bits. ♦ To get one's ears lowered. ♦ To pat down a cowlick. ♦ To tuck [it] in. ♦ Tuck in your shirt.

Grudge

A grudge match. ♦ It requires weakness, not strength, to carry a grudge. ♦ To be down on [so]. ♦ To be gunning for [so]. ♦ To have a grievance against [so]. ♦ To harbor ill feelings. ♦ To have a bone/crow to pick with [so]. ♦ To have it in for [so]. ♦ To hold it against [so]. ♦ To bear/carry/harbor/nurture a grudge.

To talk in round numbers. ♦ To venture to say. ♦ Unless I miss my guess. ♦ Use Kentucky windage. ♦ You've gotta wonder. ♦ You're looking at x to y dollars. ♦ Your guess is as good as mine.

Guess

A ballpark figure. ♦ A conservative estimate. ♦ A guesstimate. ♦ A gut reaction. [see also Emotion] ♦ A lucky guess. ♦ A rough idea. ♦ An outside guess. ♦ As near as I can reckon. ♦ By dead reckoning. ♦ Correct me if I'm wrong. ♦ Do it by guess and by gosh. ♦ Dr. Livingston, I presume? ♦ God/Lord only knows. ♦ I daresay that . . . ♦ I'll give you three guesses. ♦ It's anybody's guess. ♦ Keep 'em guessing. ♦ Make a snap decision. ♦ Make an educated guess. ♦ Not to put too fine a point on it. ♦ Pick things out of the air. ♦ Take a guess; if you guess right, you won't forget it; if you guess wrong, you won't forget that either. ♦ Take a wild stab at [it]. ♦ There's no telling what. ♦ To ballpark it. ♦ To hazard/venture a guess. ♦ To hazard/venture an opinion. ♦ To jump to conclusions. ♦ To read [so]'s mind. ♦ To rush to judgment. ♦ To second-guess [sb]. ♦ To take a shot in the dark. ♦ To take a (wild) guess. ♦

Guilt

A guilty conscience needs no accuser. ♦ Guilt by association. ♦ Guilty as charged. ♦ Guilty as sin. ♦ Guilt is regret for what we've done; regret is guilt for what we didn't do. [see also Regret] ♦ Guilty pleasures. ♦ Had something to do with it. ♦ On a guilt trip. ♦ The guilty party. ♦ The guilty think all talk is of themselves. ♦ To be stricken with remorse. ♦ To enter a plea of guilty. ♦ To gnaw at one's conscience. ♦ To have a guilty conscience. ♦ To have buyer's remorse. ♦ To have complicity in the matter. ♦ To have guilty knowledge. ♦ To lay the blame at/on [so]'s doorstep. ♦ To plead guilty (to a lesser charge). ♦ To weigh (heavily) on one's conscience. ♦ Was somehow involved.

Gullibility

An easy mark. ♦ Believe that and I'll tell you another one. ♦ Buy a white elephant. ♦ Fall for/swallow it hook, line and sinker. ♦ Fall for it (like a ton of bricks). ◆ If you go for the bait you get stuck with the freight. ◆ Play (right) into [so]'s hands. ◆ Rise to the bait. ◆ That's the oldest trick in the book. ◆ They saw you coming. ◆ To be bamboozled/flummoxed/horn-swoggled. ◆ To soak [so]. ◆ To take [so] to the cleaners. ◆ To take [so] for a ride.

Guns

A hired gun. ◆ A Saturday night special. ◆ A six-shooter. ◆ Guns don't kill people; people kill people. ◆ Guns or butter. ◆ I didn't know the gun was loaded. [see also Alibi] ◆ I'll give you my gun when you pry it from my cold, dead hand. ◆ If guns are outlawed, only outlaws will have guns. ◆ It is always the empty gun that kills. ◆ This is my rifle, this is my gun; one is for fighting, the other's for fun. [military] ◆ To go gunning for.

Habit

A conditioned reflex. ◆ A creature of habit. ◆ A way of life. ◆ Bad habits are easy to make but hard to break. ◆ Bad habits grow wild, but the good ones must be cultivated. ◆ Force of habit. ◆ Old habits are hard to break. ◆ Old habits/ways die hard. [see also Imitation] ◆ To be up to one's old

tricks. ◆ To be/get hung up (on). [see also Desire] ◆ To be/get used to [it]. ◆ To break the habit. ◆ To get into the habit. ◆ To grow accustomed to. ◆ To make a habit/practice of [it].

Hackneyed

(also passé)

An old chestnut. ◆ An old saw. ◆ A passing fancy. ◆ Don't scorn corn. [It can make a big pop — R.D.] ◆ Everything's already been thought of. ◆ Gone the way of the dodo/horse and buggy/8-track tape/floppy disk. [see also Relic] ◆ I haven't heard that one in a long while. ◆ I haven't heard that one since last time. ◆ If I had a nickel for every time I've heard that, I'd be a millionaire. ◆ It's been done before. ◆ It's been done to death. ◆ It's old hat. ◆ If I've heard that once I've heard it a thousand times. ◆ In time one gets tired even of *kreplach*. ◆ Nothing can bring back the moment of splendor in the grass, of glory in the flower. ◆ Old hat. ◆ Past its/one's prime. ◆ Pop corn: when dad makes a bad pun. ◆ Planned obsolescence. ◆ That is so last millennium. ◆ That was funny the first time I heard it. ◆ That went out with boom boxes and Walkmans. ◆ That went out with buggy whips and high-button shoes. ◆ That's so yesterday. ◆ The bloom is off the rose. ◆ The honeymoon is over. ◆ The novelty wears off. ◆ There is nothing new under the sun. ◆ To go out of fashion/style.

Handicapped

A disabled vehicle. ◆ A glass ceiling. ◆ Blind in one eye, can't see out of the other.* ◆ Color blind. ◆ Deaf, dumb and blind. *[see also Oblivious] ◆ Deaf in one ear, can't hear out of the other. ◆ Disabled does not mean unable. ◆ Hard of hearing. ◆ Hopalong Cassidy. ◆ Physically challenged. ◆ Stone deaf. ◆ Tone deaf. ◆ The lame, the halt and the blind. ◆ To be tongue-tied. ◆ To have four eyes. ◆ To have a tin ear. ◆ To walk with a gimp.

Happen

As it turns out. [see also Eventually] ◆ Come into being/existence. ◆ Come off. ◆ Come to be. ◆ Come to pass. ◆ Come true. ◆ It just so happens. ◆ Pan out. ◆ Take place. ◆ Things happen in threes. ◆ This too shall come to pass. [see also Prediction] ◆ To bear fruit. ◆ To become a reality. ◆ To chance upon. ◆ To come about. ◆ To come across [it]. ◆ To come alive. ◆ To come one's way. ◆ To come to fruition. ◆ To crop up. ◆ To cross paths. ◆ To happen upon. ◆ To just happen along. ◆ To kick in. ◆ To rear its ugly head. [see also Arrival] ◆ To see the light of day. ◆ What happened? ◆ What's happening?

Happiness

(also delicious, delight, joy, smug)
A garden of earthly delights. ◆ A happy ending. ◆ A happy camper. ◆ A joy to behold. ◆ A mouth-watering delight. ◆ A wave of euphoria. ◆ Another satisfied customer. ◆ As accidents will happen, so will happiness. ◆ Bowls you over. ◆ Contented as a cow/kitten. ◆ Drives you wild. ◆ Don't you just love it? ◆ Fat, dumb and happy. ◆ Finger-licking good. ◆ Flying is the second greatest happiness known to man . . . landing is the first! ◆ Goody goody gumdrop. ◆ Grin from ear to ear. ◆ Happier than a fee lark. ◆ Happiness adds and multiplies as we divide it with others. (And subtracts from one's worries). ◆ Happiness doesn't come in great big batches; it comes in little snatches! ◆ Happiness forgets the hours; sorrow counts the minutes. ◆ Happiness is a place somewhere between too much and too little. ◆ Happiness is a warm puppy. ◆ Happiness is like jam: you

can't spread it without getting a little on you. ◆ Happiness is like potato salad: share it and you have a picnic. ◆ Happiness is walking barefoot in the grass. ◆ Happiness is where you find it. ◆ Happiness isn't having what you want; it's wanting what you have. ◆ Happiness lies in your own back yard. ◆ Happy as a camel on Wednesday. ◆ Happy as a clam (at high tide). ◆ Happy as a duck in Arizona. [ironic/sarcastic] ◆ Happy as a hummingbird. ◆ Happy as a June bug. ◆ Happy as a kitty with a ball of yarn. ◆ Happy as a lark. ◆ Happy as a pig in sh*t/slop. ◆ Happy as a skunk in a whirlwind. ◆ Happy as a tornado in a trailer park. ◆ Happy as a witch in a broom factory. ◆ Happy as a woodpecker in a lumber yard. ◆ Happy as all get-out. ◆ Happy days are here again. [see also Excitement, Rejuvenation] ◆ Head in the clouds. ◆ High on life. ◆ I like to have died. ◆ I thought I'd died and gone to heaven. ◆ I was never so happy in (all) my life. ◆ In doggie/hog heaven. ◆ In Seventh Heaven. ◆ In the throes of ecstasy. ◆ It does one's heart good. ◆ Joy to the world. ◆ Joy when it is shared, its pleasure doubles; and sorrow, loses half its troubles. ◆ Like a dog in a bone yard. ◆ Like a kid in a candy store. ◆ Like a kid with a new toy. ◆ Like the cat that ate/swallowed the canary. ◆ Merry as

the month of May. ◆ Money can't buy happiness. (but it can get you pretty close) ◆ My heart skipped a beat. ◆ On cloud nine. ◆ *Ooo, la, la!* ◆ Pleased as Punch. ◆ Quicken the pulse. ◆ Sets you on your ear. ◆ Some cause happiness wherever they go. Others whenever they go. ◆ Squealing with delight. ◆ The thrill of a lifetime. ◆ There is no way to happiness; happiness is the way. ◆ This has a "more-ish" taste. — Hugh Paulk ◆ This tastes like more. ◆ Tickled down to your toes. ◆ Tickled pink. ◆ Tickled to death. ◆ To blow you away. ◆ To be in a good/happy space. ◆ To cream your jeans. ◆ To do cartwheels. ◆ To feel good about oneself. ◆ To feel ten feet tall. ◆ To floor [so]. ◆ To get a bang/charge/kick out of [it]. ◆ To gladden the heart. ◆ To have a good feeling about [it]. ◆ To have good vibes/vibrations about [it]. ◆ To jump for joy. ◆ To knock one's socks off. ◆ To ring one's chimes. ◆ To shed tears of joy. ◆ To sweep you off your feet. ◆ To take your breath away. ◆ To one's (little) heart's content/desire. [see also Unrestrained] ◆ To walk on air/a cloud. ◆ Warms the cockles of one's heart.

Harmless

A toothless tiger. ◆ He won't bother you if you don't bother him. ◆ He's just a big kid at heart. ◆ He's just a great big teddy-bear. ◆ His bark is worse than his bite. ◆ Underneath it all, he's just a big pussycat. ◆ Wouldn't harm/hurt a fly. ◆ Wouldn't harm a hair on anyone's head.

Haste

Go off half-cocked. ◆ Good and quickly seldom meet. ◆ Haste makes waste. ◆ He who hurries stumbles. ◆ Shoot first, ask questions later. ◆ Short pleasures, long laments. ◆ Speed kills. ◆ To be shot on sight. ◆ To come running. ◆ To get ahead of oneself. [see also Premature] ◆ To jump the gun.

Hate

Hate is a bottomless cup. ◆ Hate mail. ◆ Hate the sin, not the sinner. ◆ I hate to be the one to tell you this, but . . . ◆ I hate when that happens. ◆ Love and hate are horns on the same bull. ◆ Love openly—hate quietly. ◆ Mortal/sworn enemies. ◆ Small men hate, great men pity. ◆ The [n.] you love to hate. ◆ The only good [n.] is a dead [n.]. ◆ To hate [so]'s guts. ◆ To have bad blood between them. ◆ What has been torn by hate must be mended with understanding.

Health

A healthy mind in a healthy body. ◆ Able to sit up and take nourishment. ◆ Alive and kicking/well. ◆ All better (now). ◆ Brown as a berry. ◆ Down to one's fighting weight. ◆ Fit as a fiddle. ◆ Hale and hardy/hearty. ◆ He who has good health is a rich man and does not know it. ◆ He who has good health is young, and he is rich who has no debts. ◆ Health is wealth. ◆ Healthy as a horse. ◆ If you have your health you have everything. ◆ In the flesh. ◆ Never been sick a day in her/his/my life. ◆ Never felt better in my life. ◆ Of sound mind and body. ◆ Rosy cheeks. ◆ Sound as a dollar. ◆ Tanned and rested. ◆ That's all that counts. ◆ To be a whole person. ◆ To be in top form. ◆ To be the picture of health. ◆ To be/feel in the pink. ◆ To feel like a million bucks/dollars. ◆ To get a clean bill of health.

Heaviness
(also burden)

A heavy date. ◆ Dead weight. ◆ Heavy as lead. ◆ He ain't heavy; he's my brother. ◆ It weighs a ton. ◆ Pound for pound. ◆ To weigh x pounds, soaking wet. Stone is heavy and sand a burden, but aggravation by a fool is heavier than both. ♦ To have the weight of the world on one's shoulders. ♦ To tip the scales at [n.] pounds. ♦ Two-ton Tony. ♦ With a heavy heart. ♦ Worry makes a man's heart heavy. But a kind word cheers him up.

Hedonism

Carpe diem. (Seize the day)! ♦ Don't let life pass you by. ♦ Enjoy what is, before it isn't! ♦ Enjoy yourself, it's later than you think. ♦ Gather ye rosebuds while ye may. ♦ Have (yourself) a good time. ♦ If you can't eat it, drink it or smoke it . . . f*ck it. ♦ Let the good times roll. ♦ Life in the fast lane. [see also Risk] ♦ Life is (too) short. [rejoinder: False! It's the longest thing you will ever do.] ♦ Live each day as though it is your last. (One of these days you'll be right!) ♦ Live fast, love hard, die young—and leave a beautiful memory. ♦ Live for/in the moment. ♦ Live life to the fullest. ♦ The Jet Set. ♦ To live in the now. ♦ While the cat's away, the mice will play. ♦ You have but one life to live. ♦ You only live once. ♦ You're a long time dead. ♦ You're a long time in the tomb; so while you're alive, zoom, zoom, zoom!

Hell

A sorry day in hell. ♦ All hell broke loose. ♦ Come hell or high water. ♦ Going to hell if I don't change my ways. ♦ Hell no; we won't go. ♦ Hell on wheels. ♦ Hell's bells! ♦ Hell's half acre. ♦ Hellfire and damnation. ♦ Hell hath no fury like a woman scorned. ♦ Hotter than hell. ♦ Hounds of hell. ♦ How in/the hell? ♦ It'll be a lot hotter in hell. ♦ It'll be hell on you. ♦ Just for the hell of it. ♦ Like hell. ♦ No way in hell. ♦ One hell of a [n.]. ♦ People in hell want ice water. ♦ Till hell wouldn't have it. ♦ To go to hell in a handbasket. ♦ To have hell/the devil to pay. ♦ To raise hell. ♦ To shoot to hell. ♦ War is hell. ♦ What (in) the hell.

Henpecked

An Oedipus complex. ♦ He who marries a widow will often have a dead man's head thrown in his dish. ♦ Hit with the rolling pin. ♦ In the dog house. ♦ To have him wrapped around her little finger. ♦ The best way to fight with a woman is with your hat: take it and leave. ♦ The successful husband always has the last word: "Yes, dear." ♦ Tied to his wife's apron strings. ♦ To be pussy-whipped. ♦ Who beats his wife hits the whole house.

Hero

A hero is a man who is afraid to run away. ♦ A central/key role. ♦ A hero today, a bum tomorrow. ♦ A leading man. ♦ A national hero. ♦ Every hero becomes a bore at last. ♦ Hail to the conquering hero. ♦ Knight in shining armor. ♦ Knight on a white charger. ♦ My hero! ♦ My main man. ♦ No man is a hero to his valet. ♦ Our hapless hero. ♦ The anointed one. ♦ The difference between a coward and a hero is whether he will run fast or stand fast. − R.D. ♦ The fair-haired boy. ♦ The golden boy. ♦ The man of the hour. ♦ The man to beat. ♦ Those who place you on a pedestal today may call you marblehead tomorrow. − R.D. ♦ You da man.

Hint

(also suggestion)

A leading question. ♦ A rough/thumbnail sketch. ♦ Are they/you trying to tell me something? ♦ Body language. ♦ Can/can't you take a hint? ♦ Drop a hint. ♦ Fishing for compliments. ♦ If you get my drift. ♦ In a roundabout way. ♦ It's just/only a suggestion. ♦ Open to suggestion. ♦ Power of suggestion. ♦ Say (it) in so many words. ♦ Something tells me. ♦ Take a cue (from). ♦ The suggestion box. ♦ To beg the question. ♦ To hint at [it]. ♦ To let on. ♦ To take a hint. ♦ You're getting warmer.

History

A backward glance. ♦ A bygone era. ♦ A distant memory. ♦ A long time ago in a land far away. ♦ A matter of record. ♦ A period piece. ♦ A rap sheet. ♦ A while/some time ago. ♦ A while back. ♦ A year and a day. ♦ A year to the day. ♦ And the rest is history. ♦ Back in the day. ♦ Days of yore. ♦ From then until now. ♦ From way back. ♦ Handed down through the ages. ♦ Has long since ceased to be. ♦ Historian: a past master. ♦ History in the making. ♦ History is made every minute. ♦ History is what gets reported. ♦ History is written by the winners. ♦ History makes us some amends for the shortness of life. ♦ History repeats itself. ♦ If history is any guide . . . ♦ If history teaches us anything . . . ♦ History teaches nothing but punishes those who don't learn its lessons. ♦ In days gone by. ♦ In days of old, when knights were bold. ♦ In recent memory. ♦ In the annals of history. ♦ In those days. ♦ (Just) the other day. ♦ Long ago and far away. ♦ Nothing improves the 'good old days' like memory. ♦ On file. ♦ Return with us now to those thrilling days of yesteryear. ♦ Seems like it was just yesterday. ♦ Since time immemorial/out of mind. ♦ That was then, this is now. ♦ That's ancient history. ♦ The day after tomorrow. ♦ The day before yesterday. ♦ The days of yore. ♦ The dead hand of the past. ♦ The good old days. ♦ The night before last. ♦ The past is prologue. ♦ The way it was. ♦ The week/year that was. ♦ Those days are gone forever. ♦ Those glorious days of yesteryear. ♦ Those were the days. ♦ Those who cannot remember the past are condemned to repeat its mistakes. ♦ Time was. ♦ To alter the course of history. ♦ To date. ♦ To dwell on the past. ♦ To go back in time. ♦ To go down in history. ♦ To the present (day). ♦ To think back. ♦ To this (very) day. ♦ To turn back the hands of time. ♦ Turn of the century. ♦ Up till/to now. ♦ Way back when. ♦ What's done is done. ♦ When you were just a gleam/twinkle in your old man's eye. ♦ With the passage of time. ♦ Yesterday's gone.

Home

A house is not a home. ♦ A man's home is his castle. ♦ A place to hang one's hat. ♦ A place to stay. ♦ A roof over one's head. ♦ All the comforts of home. ♦ Base of operations. ♦ Be it ever so humble there's no place like home. ♦ Born and bred/reared/raised [in]. ♦ East, west, home's best. ♦ Give me a home where the buffalo roam. ♦ God bless our home. ♦ God bless this home and all who enter. ♦ Home away from home. ♦ Home court/ground/turf. ♦ Home is where the heart is. ♦ (Home is where the hearth is. — R.D.) ♦ Home base. ♦ Home for the holidays. ♦ Home plate. ♦ Home is where, when you have to go there, they have to take you in. ♦ Home is where you hang your hat. ♦ Home, James. ♦ Home on the range. ♦ Home sweet home. ♦ Hometown hero. ♦ Humble abode. ♦ In new digs. ♦ It ain't much, but it's home. ♦ It takes a heap/lot of living to make a house a home. ♦ Make oneself at home/comfortable. ♦ On one's own turf. ♦ One's crib/digs/nest/pad. ♦ Our fair city/metropolis. ♦ The Ponderosa. ♦ These hallowed halls. ♦ To head (for) home. ♦ To market, to market, to buy a fat pig. Home again, home again, jiggity-jig. [see also Expense] ♦ To stay/stick close to home. ♦ Where do you think you are, at home or some other dirty place?

Homosexuality
(also bisexuality, gender identity)
A bull dyke. ♦ A butch. ♦ A closet queen. [see also Secret] ♦ AC/DC. ♦ A dyke. ♦ A (flaming) faggot. ♦ A

gender bender. ♦ A latent homosexual. ♦ A rug muncher. ♦ A swinger. ♦ A switch-hitter. [see also Versatile] ♦ A queer. ♦ Don't bend over in the shower (for the soap). ♦ Gay and lesbian pride. ♦ Goes/swings both ways. ♦ Light in the loafers. ♦ Light on his feet/heels/toes. ♦ Limp-wristed. ♦ On the down low. [see also Secret] ♦ Same-sex marriage. ♦ To come out of the closet. [see also Reveal] ♦ To get in touch with one's feminine/masculine side. ♦ To travel with two tribes. ♦ To turn gay/queer. ♦ We're here and we're queer.

Honesty
(also fairness)

A stand-up guy. ♦ A straight shooter. ♦ An arm's-length transaction. ♦ An honest face is life's best currency. ♦ An honest John. ♦ An honest man is the noblest work of God. ♦ An upstanding citizen. ♦ As honest as the day is long. ♦ By (all) rights. ♦ Good fences make good neighbors. ♦ He who locks his door will be blessed with honest neighbors. ♦ Honesty is the best policy. ♦ I have to be honest with you. ♦ It's only fair/right. ♦ In all candor/fairness/honesty. ♦ Level with me. ♦ Locks are not meant to keep thieves out but to keep honest people honest.

♦ On the level. ♦ On the up and up. ♦ Straight as an arrow. ♦ The Fairness Doctrine. ♦ To be (brutally) frank/honest. ♦ To be (perfectly) candid/frank/honest. ♦ To face (the) facts. ♦ To get/give a fair deal/hearing/ trial/ shake. ♦ To give [so] an even break. ♦ To lay (all) one's cards on the table. ♦ To level with [so]. ♦ To make (a) full disclosure. ♦ To play it straight. [see also Seriousness] ♦ To speak straight from the heart. ♦ To take the high road. ♦ To tell the truth. ♦ To walk the straight and narrow. ♦ True to one's word. ♦ Up and above board. ♦ What's fair is fair. ♦ What's right is right. ♦ When you meet an honest man, he'll have hair in the palm of his hand. ♦ You have an honest face.

Honor

A deal's a deal. ♦ A gentlemen's agreement. ♦ A man of his word. ♦ Congressional Medal of Honor. ♦ Give/have a sporting chance. ♦ High-minded. ♦ My word is my bond. ♦ Never kick a man when he's down. ♦ On one's word of honor. ♦ On the honor system. ♦ Scout's honor. ♦ The (right) honorable judge [n.] presiding. ♦ There is honor among thieves. ♦ To act in good faith. ♦ To be as good as one's word. ♦ To be honor bound (to).

♦ To defend a lady's honor. ♦ To do business on a handshake. ♦ To have honorable intentions. ♦ To keep a promise. ♦ To keep/make good on one's word. To play by the rules. ♦ To take the high ground. ♦ To what do I owe this honor? ♦ Vast concepts like honor are as oversized socks: ill-fitted to cover the spindly feet of everyday situations. ♦ You have my word on it. ♦ You're only as good as your word.

Hope

A beacon of hope. ♦ A glimmer/ray of hope. ♦ A Hail Mary pass. ♦ Anything is possible. ♦ Beware the light at the end of the tunnel is not a train. ♦ Cross one's fingers. ♦ Everything will be/ come out/ turn out alright/ OK. ♦ False hopes. ♦ Here's hoping. ♦ Hope and pray. ♦ Hope for the best but prepare for the worst. — Angela Maria Delia ♦ Hope is a good breakfast but a bad supper. ♦ Hope springs eternal in the human breast. ♦ If it's any consolation. ♦ It'll all be fine. ♦ Lost and found. ♦ Never say never. ♦ Pie in the sky. ♦ Seed of hope. ♦ The Great White Hope. ♦ The South will rise again. [see also Rejuvenation] ♦ There's always a chance. ♦ There's always tomorrow. ♦ There's hope for you yet. ♦ There's still hope for you.

♦ 'Tis a consummation devoutly to be wished. ♦ To get one's hopes up. ♦ To have high expectations/hopes. ♦ To hold out/offer hope. ♦ To hope against hope. ♦ To see daylight/light at the end of the tunnel. ♦ To see the light of day. ♦ To show (a great deal of) promise. ♦ Where there's life there's hope.

Hopeless
(also never, unlikely)

A hopeless case. ♦ A lose-lose situation. ♦ A lost cause. ♦ A lost soul. ♦ A remote possibility. ♦ About as much chance as the man in the moon. ♦ An exercise in futility. ♦ Another knockout from the mouth. ♦ At about never-thirty. ♦ Bailing out the Atlantic with a Dixie cup/sieve/ teaspoon. ♦ Beyond redemption/repair. ♦ Champion of lost causes. ♦ Doesn't have a prayer. ♦ Doesn't have the chance of a snowball in hell. ♦ Doesn't stand a chance. ♦ Don't hold your breath. [see also Skepticism] ♦ Don't sew buttons on balloons. ♦ Everything went wrong that could go wrong. ♦ Fat chance. ♦ Given up for dead. ♦ In the unlikely event. ♦ It doesn't have a prayer. ♦ It won't wash. ♦ It'll be a cold day in hell/in July. ♦ It'll never fly. ♦ It'll never get off the ground. ♦ It'll never see the light of day. ♦ It's no use. ♦ Lot of good that will do you. ♦ Never happen. ♦ No more [n.] than the Man in the Moon. ♦ No way in hell. ♦ No way, shape or form. ♦ Not a Chinaman's chance. ♦ Not a ghost of a chance. ♦ Not a hope in hell. ♦ Not by a long shot. ♦ Not (even) a remote possibility. ♦ Not in this lifetime. ♦ On the off chance. ♦ Save your breath. ♦ Someday never comes. ♦ That'll be the day. ♦ That's easy for you to say! ♦ The day after the Pope. [In response to, "When are you getting married?"] ♦ To beat a dead horse. ♦ To defeat the purpose. ♦ To no avail. ♦ To waste one's breath. ♦ To what end? ♦ To whistle for [it]. ♦ What's the point/use? ♦ When all seems hopeless, throw the cat another goldfish. ♦ Why bother? ♦ Worst of the worst. ♦ Worst-case scenario. ♦ You cannot weave a net to catch the wind. ♦ You have two chances: slim and none. ♦ You should live so long. [ironic/sarcastic] [see also Oppose] ♦ You'd sooner grow hair on a billiard ball. ♦ You'll see a white blackbird before that happens. ♦ Your solution will help about as much as medicine will help a corpse. ♦ When pigs fly.

Horse

Better an ass that carries you than a horse that throws you. ♦ Don't change/switch horses in midstream. [see also Change] ♦ Don't lock the barn door after the horse runs away. [Unless you have an expensive bridle and saddle. — R.D.] ♦ Don't look a gift horse in the mouth. ♦ Don't put the cart before the horse. ♦ Don't spare the horses. ♦ For want of a nail, the shoe was lost, for want of a shoe the horse was lost, for want of a horse, the battle was lost, for want of a victory, the kingdom was lost. ♦ Horse sense doesn't win horse races. ♦ If an ass goes traveling it will not come home a horse. ♦ Like paying for a dead horse. ♦ My kingdom for a horse! ♦ No sense/use beating a dead horse. ♦ Seabiscuit and War Admiral are neck-and-neck in the homestretch. Suddenly, War Admiral falls down and Seabiscuit shoots over the finish line. Alas, War Admiral has broken his neck and is dead. Who wins the race? No, not Seabiscuit—War Admiral! Why? You can't beat a dead horse! ♦ Spur not a willing horse. ♦ That's a horse of another color. [see also Different] ♦ The lean horse runs the long race. ♦ To horse around. ♦ Under the master's eye, the horse grows fat. ♦ Wild horses couldn't drag me away. ♦ You can lead a horse to water but you can't make it drink. ♦ You can't shoe a running horse.

Hospitality

A guest room. ♦ A smile is the universal welcome. ♦ Beauty is everywhere a welcome guest. ♦ She/he can park her/his shoes under my bed anytime. ♦ He: can you put me up for one night? She: I'm not sure I can put up with you for one night. ♦ If I knew you were coming, I'd've baked a cake. ♦ Make yourself (right) at home. ♦ My house is your house. ♦ Said one frog to the other: your pad or mine? ♦ The hostess with the mostest. ♦ (To extend) a warm reception/welcome. ♦ To put [so] up.

Hot

A heat wave. ♦ A hot potato. ♦ Are you hot or are you not? ♦ Beastly hot. ♦ Boiling/scalding hot. ♦ Hot as a firecracker/pistol. ♦ Hot as hell. ♦ Hotter than hades/hell. ♦ Hot enough for you? ♦ Hotter than a whore on Saturday night. ♦ Is it hot in here or is it just me? ♦ Piping hot. ♦ Red hot. ♦ Red hot mama. ♦ Scalding hot. ♦ So hot you could fry an egg on it. ♦ Sweating bullets. ♦ Too hot to handle.

♦ When you're hot you're hot (and when you're not you're not). ♦ White hot.

Humanity

A common effect of the human condition is that it produces a conditioned human. - R.D. ♦ A human being. ♦ Common sense is the genius of humanity. ♦ I love humanity; it's every Tom, Dick and Harry I can't stand. ♦ Man is a party animal. ♦ Oh, the humanity! ♦ One small step for man; one giant leap for mankind. [see also Progress] ♦ The human condition. ♦ The more I know people, the more I love my dog. ♦ The proper study of mankind is man. ♦ The urge to save humanity is almost always a false front for the urge to rule.

Humiliation

Show [so] a thing or two. ♦ Take the wind out of [so]'s sails. ♦ That's one on me. ♦ To bring [so] to his/her knees. ♦ To clip [so]'s wings. ♦ To cut [so] down to size. ♦ To have the last laugh. ♦ To make [so] eat his/her words. ♦ To rub [so]'s nose in it. ♦ To take [so] down a notch/peg (or two). ♦ To take [so] down a few pegs. ♦ To talk down to. ♦ You got me good.

Humorous

A dumb blonde joke. ♦ A funny thing happened on my way to the office. ♦ A gas. ♦ A humdinger. ♦ A knock-knock joke. ♦ A laugh a minute. ♦ A Laurel and Hardy routine. ♦ A p*sseroo. ♦ A private joke. ♦ A rapier wit. ♦ A real p*sser/doozy/lalapalooza. ♦ A sick joke. ♦ A running/ standing joke. An inside joke. ♦ Anything for a laugh. ♦ Black comedy. ♦ Can't you take a joke? ♦ Comedian: grin reaper. ♦ Comic relief. ♦ Did you hear the one about [n.]? ♦ Funny as a crutch. ♦ Gallows humor. ♦ Good for a laugh ♦ Guy walks into a bar. ♦ Har de har har. ♦ He who jests at scars never felt a wound. ♦ In stitches. ♦ Side-splitting. ♦ That's a (real) dilly. ♦ That's a (real) humdinger. ♦ To bust a gut. ♦ To come out with a (real) lulu. ♦ To crack a joke. ♦ To crack [so] up. ♦ To have a good laugh. ♦ To have them rolling in the aisles. ♦ To laugh one's *ss/ (fool) head off. ♦ To laugh till the tears roll down one's cheeks. ♦ To play a practical joke. ♦ To p*ss one's pants. ♦ To short-sheet [so]. ♦ To split one's sides. ♦ To yuk it up. ♦ Tongue in cheek. ♦ Uproarious laughter.

Hunch

A gut feeling. ♦ By dead reckoning. ♦ Can't quite put my finger on it. ♦ On a wing and a prayer. ♦ Something tells me. ♦ To act on/follow a hunch. ♦ To fly blind. ♦ To fly by the seat of one's pants. ♦ To feel it in one's bones. ♦ To feel one's way along. ♦ To have a gut feeling. ♦ To play a hunch. ♦ To play it by ear. ♦ To shoot from the hip. ♦ To wing it. ♦ Woman's intuition.

Hurry

A mile a minute. ♦ A rolling stone gathers no moss. ♦ A whirlwind romance. [see also Love] ♦ As soon as possible (ASAP). ♦ As Speedy Gonzalez said, "It won't hurt—did it?" ♦ At a good clip. ♦ At breakneck speed. ♦ At one's earliest convenience. ♦ Balls to the wall. ♦ Can't you move any faster than that? ♦ Chop chop. ♦ Damn the torpedoes, full speed ahead. [see also Unrestrained] ♦ Don't let any grass grow under your feet. ♦ Drag ass. ♦ Eat and run. ♦ Fast as your (little) legs will carry [you]. ♦ Full speed/steam ahead. ♦ Get a move on. ♦ Get cracking/moving/rolling. ♦ Get 'er done. ♦ Get on with it. ♦ Get the lead out (of one's *ss/feet). ♦ Get to the punch line. ♦ Going great guns. ♦ Grass doesn't grow on a busy street. ♦ Haul *ss. ♦ Have the throttle wide open. ♦ Hell-bent. ♦ Hell-bent for election. ♦ Hell-bent for leather. ♦ Hop to it. [see also Motion] ♦ Hurry up. ♦ Hurry up and wait. ♦ Hurry up, I haven't got all day. ◆ Hustle and bustle. ◆ I don't have all day. ◆ In a hurry. ◆ In a hurry to go nowhere. ◆ In a time bind/crunch. ◆ Jiggity-jig. ◆ Just do it! (already). ◆ Kick it/shift into overdrive. ◆ Last one in is a rotten egg/an old stick in the mud. [see also Invitation] ◆ Leave in a cloud of dust. ◆ Like a bat out of hell. ◆ Like a shot out of hell. ◆ Likkity-split. ◆ Look alive. ◆ Make it snappy. ◆ Make tracks. ◆ Mush, you huskies! ◆ On the double. ◆ PDQ (Pretty damn quick). ◆ Post-haste. ◆ Pour on the steam. ◆ Put on a burst of speed. ◆ Put the pedal to the metal. ◆ Run around like a chicken with its head cut off. ◆ Shake a leg. ◆ Shake your *ss. ◆ Speed demon. ◆ Step lively. ◆ Step on it. ◆ Take off like a ruptured duck. ◆ Take off like a scalded dog. ◆ The ink was not even dry. ◆ The sooner the better. ◆ To barrel *ss. ◆ To be pressed for time. ◆ To beat/race the clock. ◆ To floor it. ◆ To get it over with. ◆ To get one's rear in gear. ◆ To give it the gun. ◆ To go balls out. ◆ To go flat out. ◆ To go full blast. ◆ To go full bore/full tilt. ◆ To go like a house afire. ◆ To go like hell. ◆ To go like sixty. ◆ To gun it. ◆ To gun the engine. ◆ To haul *ss. ◆ To have a lead foot. ◆ To heigh on down (to). ◆ To hit on all 8 cylinders. ◆ To hotfoot it. ◆ To make a beeline for. ◆ To make a mad dash/ rush (for). ◆ To make good time. ◆ To make up for lost time. ◆ To peel rubber. ◆ To shag *ss/tear *ss. ◆ To take off like a big ass bird. ◆ To tear off. ◆ To whip something up. ◆ What's taking (you) so long? ◆ What's your hurry? ◆ What's your rush? ◆ Where's the fire? ◆ Where's the fire, (buddy/pal)? ◆ With all deliberate speed. ◆ You can't speed on a winding road.

Hush

A closed mouth gathers no feet. ◆ Can it. ◆ Down in front. ◆ Hark, I hear a pistol shot. ◆ Hark, the lark. ◆ Hold one's tongue. ◆ Hush now, the deacon is speakin'. ◆ Hush your mouth. ◆ I don't want to hear a peep out of you. ◆ I t'ot I heard/taw a puddy tat. ◆ Keep it down to a dull roar. ◆ May I have your (undivided) attention, please. ◆ Order in the court. ◆ Pipe down. ◆ Put a cork/sock in it. ◆ Settle/simmer down. ◆ Shut (the f*ck) up. ◆ Shut your pie hole. ◆ Shut your yap. ◆ Take it down a notch. ◆ To die down. ◆ To not say boo/peep. [see also Silence] ◆ To speak in hushed tones. ◆ Tone it down. ◆ Zip your lip.

Hypocrisy

(also equivocate)

Beat around the bush. ◆ Dodge the issue/question. ◆ Don't condemn the criminal by committing a crime. ♦ Do as I say, not as I do. ♦ Every stick has two ends. ♦ First you say you do and then you don't, then you say you will and then you won't. ♦ Hem and haw. ♦ It is a poor cook who cannot lick his fingers. ♦ Let he who is without sin among you cast the first stone. ♦ People who live in glass houses shouldn't throw stones. ♦ People who live in grass houses shouldn't play with matches. — R.D. ♦ Send out mixed signals. ♦ Shilly-shally. ♦ Skirt the issue. ♦ Speak with forked tongue. ♦ Straddling the fence is a half-*ssed position. ♦ The frying pan/pot calling the kettle black. ♦ There are skeletons in every closet. ♦ There are two sides to every story (and then there's the truth). ♦ Tiptoe around the subject. ♦ To couch one's words carefully. ♦ To shed crocodile tears. ♦ To have a foot in both camps. ♦ To say one thing and do/mean another. ♦ To straddle the fence. ♦ To talk around the point. ♦ To talk out of both sides of one's mouth.

Idea

A bright idea. ♦ A crackerjack idea. ♦ A gem of an idea. ♦ A whale of an idea. ♦ A good idea in theory, but what about in practice? ♦ A viable concept. ♦ An idea whose time has come. ♦ One of the great ideas of the twenty-first century. ♦ One of the great ideas of western man. ♦ Sometimes the exchange of ideas is not free. ♦ That's the general idea. ♦ The big idea. ♦ The germ of an idea. ♦ The very idea. ♦ There are many more warmed-over ideas than hot ones. ♦ There is no force on earth as powerful as an idea whose time has come. ♦ What's the (big) idea? [see also Scold] ♦ Whose idea was this anyway?

Idle

An idle mind is the devil's workshop. ♦ Don't let your stream of consciousness become a cesspool. ♦ Idle hands are the devil's tools. ♦ If the brain sows not corn it plants thistles. ♦ Mind unemployed is mind unenjoyed. ♦ The devil makes work for idle hands. ♦ The unexamined life is not worth living. ♦ To bum around/goldbrick/hang around/loaf. ♦ To fritter one's time away. ♦ To have (too much) time on one's hands.

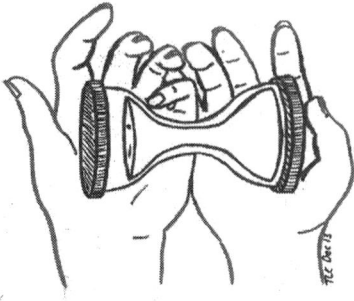

♦ To sit around with one's thumb up one's *ss. ♦ To sit on one's hands. ♦ To twiddle one's thumbs. ♦ To waste time.

If

Danny Boy went to war with the Africans; if it wasn't for his crooked legs they'd have captured him. –Vito Serritella ♦ If and when. ♦ If all goes according to plan. ♦ If all goes well. ♦ If and when that happens. [see also Premature] ♦ If frogs had wings they wouldn't bump their butts when they jump. ♦ If I may be permitted to say . . . ♦ If I were you . . . [see also Advice] ♦ If is a little word but it means a lot. ♦ If it looks like a duck and swims like a duck and quacks like a duck, it is probably a duck. ♦ If it please the court/Your Honor. ♦ If Jack the Ripper were French, he'd be *Jacques le Rippaire*. ♦ If my aunt had balls she'd be my uncle. ♦ If pigs had wings they could fly. ♦ If that be the case. ♦ If

the hound dog hadn't stopped to sh*t, he'd've caught the rabbit. ♦ If the rich could hire people to die for them, the poor could make a wonderful living. ♦ If and when the time comes. ♦ If things take their natural course. ♦ To be iffy. ♦ What if.

Ignorance

A BB brain. ♦ A bear of very little brain. ♦ A blithering idiot. ♦ A blockhead. ♦ A brain like a sieve. (Is that an open mind?) ♦ A brain the size of a pea. ♦ A coffee-can brain: vacuum-packed. ♦ A ding-a-ling. ♦ A dingbat. ♦ A dipsh*t. ♦ A ditz. ♦ A dumb bunny/ox. ♦ A dunderhead. ♦ A knuckle dragger. ♦ An airhead. ♦ An *sshat. ♦ Beauty fades; dumb is forever. ♦ Bone head. ♦ Butt head. ♦ Can't fathom [it]. ♦ Completely in the dark. ♦ Couldn't pour p*ss out of a boot if directions were printed on the heel. ♦ Dead from the neck up. ♦ Denny Dimwit. ♦ Doesn't have both oars in the water. ♦ Doesn't have the brains that God gave geese. ♦ Don't have the slightest idea. ♦ Don't know a black boot from a bootblack. ♦ Don't know a blind duck from a duck blind. ♦ Don't know a farm animal from an animal farm. ♦ Don't know a gunshot from a shotgun. ♦ Don't know a housecat from a cathouse. ♦ Don't know a house fire from a firehouse. ♦ Don't know a racehorse from a horse race. ♦ Don't know a rear admiral from an admiral's rear. ♦ Don't know a showhorse from a horse show. ♦ Don't know a stool pigeon from a pigeon stool. ♦ Don't know a stopped bus from a bus stop. ♦ Don't know a well wisher from a wishing well. ♦ Don't know a whole ass from an *sshole. ♦ Don't know from nothing. ♦ Don't know nothing from nothing. ♦ Don't know one's *ss from one's belly button/elbow. ♦ Don't know which end is up. ♦ Dumb and dumber. ♦ Dumb as a bag of doorknobs. ♦ Dumb as a stump. ♦ Dumb cluck. ♦ *Dummkopf!* ♦ Dumber than a bag/sack of hammers. ♦ Elevator doesn't go to the top floor. ♦ God must love stupid people. He made so many. ♦ Has to take shoes off to count to eleven. ♦ He/she doesn't have the brains he/she was born with. ♦ If he/she had a brain, he/she would be dangerous. ♦ If you put his brain on the edge of a razor, it would look like a BB rolling down a 4-lane highway. ♦ Ignorance is bliss. ♦ Ignoranus: a dumb *sshole. ♦ In the dark. ♦ Knuckle head. ♦ Left in the dark [see also Dark] ♦ Little did [n.]/[p.] know. ♦ Meathead. ♦

[n.] born and [n.] bred, strong in the arm and weak in the head. ♦ None the wiser. ♦ Never attribute to malice that which can adequately be explained by incompetence/stupidity. ♦ Not dealing/playing with a full deck. ♦ Not enough sense to come in out of the rain. ♦ Not that I know (of). ♦ Not the sharpest knife in the drawer/tool in the shed. ♦ Not to my knowledge. ♦ Not too swift. ♦ Peckerhead. ♦ Scatterbrain. ♦ Sh*t for brains. ♦ Slap-happy. ♦ So dumb he signs with an "X." ♦ So dumb he thinks Cheerios are donut seeds. ♦ So dumb he thinks oral sex is talking about it. ♦ The day they handed out brains he was hiding behind the door. ♦ The left hand doesn't know what the right hand is doing. ♦ The lights are on but there's nobody home. ♦ The right hand doesn't know what the left hand is doing. ♦ Thick between the ears. ♦ To be a lamebrain. ♦ To be in the dark. ♦ To know nothing from nothing. ♦ To not know beans. ♦ To not know diddly-squat/diddly-sh*t. ♦ To not know Jack/Jack sh*t. ♦ To not know sh*t from Shinola. ♦ To not know the first thing about [it]. ♦ To not know one's *ss from a hole in the ground. ♦ (To not know one's *ss from a hole in one's face. — R.D.). ♦ To not know zoo. ◆ To plead ignorance. ◆ Unbeknownst to [n.]/[p.]. ◆ What [n.]/[p.] doesn't/don't know about it would fill a book. ◆ When ignorance is bliss, 'tis folly to be wise. ◆ Who knows nothing has confidence in everything. ◆ You don't know what you don't know. ◆ He/she wouldn't know a good thing if it bit him/her on the *ss. ◆ He/she wouldn't know a good thing if he/she tripped over it.

Ignore

(also spurn)

A viper is immune to its own venom. ◆ Can't we just be friends? ◆ Didn't think twice about it. ◆ Dismiss as the rantings of a lunatic. ◆ Don't give it a second thought. ◆ Don't mind me. ◆ Don't say hello. ◆ Don't think twice about it. ◆ Don't take it personally. ◆ Don't worry; be happy. ◆ Don't worry your pretty little head (about it). ◆ I need more space. ◆ I want to see other people. ◆ I'm not interested in you in 'that way.' ◆ In one ear and out the other. ◆ Ignore your teeth and they'll go away. [dentist's maxim] ◆ Laugh/shrug it off. ◆ Let it slide. ◆ Like water off a duck's back. ◆ One word from you and they do as they (damn well) please. ◆ Pay no mind. ◆ Pay not the slightest bit of attention. ◆ Pretend it's not there—maybe it'll go away. ◆ Shrug it off. ◆ Talk to the hand (because the ears ain't listening). ◆ To act like nothing ever happened. ◆ To avert one's eyes. ◆ To close one's eyes to. ◆ To fall on deaf ears. ◆ To fall through the cracks. ◆ To get/give the cold shoulder. ◆ To get/give the silent treatment. ◆ To get/send a Dear John letter. ◆ To get a glazed look in one's eyes. ◆ To go into zombie mode. ◆ To have a thick skin. ◆ To let it go. ◆ To look right through [so]. ◆ To look the other way. ◆ To pay no attention/mind (to). ◆ To pay no never-mind. ◆ To proceed, against/despite one's better judgment. ◆ To put [so] on iggy. ◆ To shrug it off. ◆ To take no notice (of). ◆ To tune [it] out. ◆ To turn a blind eye/deaf ear (to). ◆ To zone out. ◆ You don't wanna/want to know. ◆ You haven't heard a word I've said.

Illegal

A back-alley deal. ◆ A lady of the evening. ◆ A moving violation. ◆ A shaved/stacked deck. ◆ Against the law. ◆ An extramarital affair. ◆ Breaking and entering. ◆ Criminal trespass. ◆ Contributing to the delinquency of a minor. ◆ Disorderly conduct. ◆ Do you have any idea how fast you were driving/going, sir? ◆

Driving under the influence. (DUI) ♦ Driving while intoxicated. (DWI) ♦ Grounds for divorce. ♦ Identity theft. ♦ Illicit intercourse breeds divorce. ♦ Insider trading. ♦ Jack a deer. ♦ Jailbait. ♦ Jury tampering. ♦ Off the books. ♦ On the black market. ♦ On the wrong side of the law. ♦ Out of wedlock. ♦ To be in the rackets. ♦ To bend the rules. ♦ To break the law. ♦ To chase the dragon. ♦ To do business under the table. ♦ To kite a check. ♦ To roll/smoke a joint. ♦ To run afoul of the law. ♦ To spike the ball. ♦ To turn tricks. ♦ To work off the books/under the table. ♦ To write a rubber check.

Illness

A frog in the throat. ♦ A little touch of (the) arthritis. ♦ A hoarse voice. ♦ A long, lingering illness. ♦ A nasty cold. ♦ A runny nose. ♦ A sick cat. ♦ A sick puppy. ♦ A sore throat. ♦ A splitting headache. ♦ A trick knee. ♦ Aches and pains. ♦ All illness is caused by one or both of two things: constriction and excess. ♦ Carpal tunnel syndrome. ♦ Catch (a) cold. ♦ Get ill/sick. ♦ Heartburn. ♦ I must be coming down with something. ♦ I think I'm coming down with something. ♦ Laid up. ♦ Montezuma's revenge. ♦ Out on sick leave. ♦ Sick as a dog. ♦ Sick in bed. ♦ Tennis elbow. ♦ The Aztec two-step. ♦ The big C. ♦ The runs. ♦ The screamin' mimis. ♦ The sh*ts. ♦ The trots. ♦ To be ailing. ♦ To be deathly/violently ill. ♦ To break out in a cold sweat. ♦ To call in sick. ♦ To catch one's death of cold. ♦ To come down with. ♦ To fall ill. ♦ To run a fever/temperature. ♦ To take a sick day. ♦ To take sick. ♦ Walking pneumonia. ♦ Writer's block/cramp.

Illusion

A dead cat bounce. ♦ A false positive. ♦ A figment of the imagination. ♦ A paper bag millionaire. ♦ A shadow government. ♦ All are not soldiers that go to the wars. ♦ All that glitters is not gold. ♦ [So too, all gold does not glitter. — R.D.] ♦ Any sufficiently advanced technology is indistinguishable from magic. ♦ Being poked in the eye with a doorknob does not make an eavesdropper or a voyeur. ♦ Buck teeth do not make a rat. ♦ Dazzle you with footwork. ♦ Do my eyes deceive me? ♦ Fine feathers do not make fine birds. ♦ It looks good on paper. ♦ It's all done with mirrors. ♦ It's all smoke and mirrors. ♦ It's not what it looks like. ♦ It's really a cry for help. ♦ Just because a dog likes it doesn't make it a bone. ♦ Just because you sing in the bathtub doesn't make you Caruso. ♦ Just because you smell of ape sh*t doesn't mean you're Tarzan. ♦ Just because you're movin' your feet don't mean you've got the beat. ♦ Just because your mother calls you Sonny doesn't make you bright. ♦ My eyes are playing tricks on me. ♦ Not all that clicks/ticks is a clock. ♦ Not all with wings are angels. ♦ Not every bird which is black is a blackbird. ♦ Not everything that goes around is a ferris wheel. ♦ One robin does not spring make. ♦ Or so it seems. ♦ Stone walls do not a prison make, nor iron bars a cage. ♦ Stripes do not the tiger make. ♦ The cowl does not make the monk. ♦ Things are not always what they seem. ♦ To be seeing things. ♦ To give the outward appearance (of). ♦ To put on one's game face.

Imitation

(also custom, impersonation)

A bleach(ed) blonde. ♦ A blessing in disguise. ♦ A body/stunt double. ♦ A cherished tradition. ♦ A craven image/false idol/tin god. ♦ A crossdresser. ♦ A drag queen. ♦ A family tradition. ♦ A female impersonator. ♦ A good likeness. ♦ A knockoff. ♦ A local custom. ♦ A poor imitation. ♦ A pretender to the throne. ♦ A pseudo-intellectual. ♦ A reasonable facsimile thereof. [see also Alike] ♦ A stand-in. ♦ A wolf in sheep's clothing. [see Animals, Dupe] ♦ Along the same lines. ♦ Along those lines. ♦ Any resemblance to persons living or dead is purely coincidental. ♦ Beware of cheap imitations. ♦ Borrowed interest. ♦ Cut and paste. ♦ Canned laughter. ♦ Dressed in drag. ♦ Follow suit. ♦ Follow the leader. ♦ Her hair has come from a bottle, which nobody can deny. ♦ I'll have what he's/she's having. ♦ If all your friends jumped off a cliff, would you do it too? ♦ If it was good enough for grandpa, it's good enough for me. ♦ Imitation is the sincerest form of flattery. ♦ Impersonating an officer. ♦ In drag. ♦ In like manner. ♦ In the same/a similar fashion. ♦ In the time-honored tradition. ♦ Keeping up with the Joneses. ♦ Life imitates art. ♦ Monkey see; monkey do. ♦ Often imitated, never duplicated. ♦ Old habits/ways die hard. [see also Habit] ♦ On the order of. ♦ Or, words to that effect. ♦ Phantom pains. ♦ Phony/queer as a three-dollar bill. ♦ Phony baloney. ♦ Polly wants a cracker. [see also Repetition] ♦ Send in the clones. ♦ The great pretender. ♦ The likes of. ♦ To act the part. ♦ To be a copycat.

◆ To carry on the tradition. ◆ To do a takeoff (on). ◆ To draw parallels to. ◆ To follow in the footsteps of. ◆ To follow in one's father's footsteps. ◆ To hold one's self out to be. ◆ To knock off. ◆ To look the part. ◆ To palm off (as). ◆ To pass for. ◆ To reverse engineer. ◆ To steal a page/take a leaf out of [so]'s book. ◆ To take after [so]. ◆ To the manner born. [var. – see Rich, "To the manor born"] ◆ Under an assumed name. ◆ Variations on a/the theme. [see also Varied] ◆ We've always done it that way. ◆ What children see, they will imitate. ◆ When in Rome, do as the Romans do. ◆ Will the real [n.] please stand up?

Immaterial
(also tie)

A borderline case. ◆ A dead heat. ◆ A flip of the coin. ◆ A split decision. ◆ Doesn't cut any ice. ◆ If it's all the same to you. ◆ It doesn't matter if you win or lose, it's how you play the game. ◆ It makes no never-mind. ◆ It's a toss-up. ◆ It's all the same to me. ◆ It's six of one, half dozen of the other. ◆ Might as well, can't dance. ◆ To finish nose to nose. ◆ To run neck and neck. ◆ Too close to call. ◆ Two sides of the same coin. ◆ While we're at it. ◆ Whatever. ◆ Whether the pitcher hits the stone or the stone hits the pitcher, it goes ill with the pitcher. ◆ Who am I/are we to judge/say? ◆ Why not?

Immediacy

A sense of urgency. ◆ Act now. ◆ At any moment. ◆ At this (very) moment. ◆ Do it now. ◆ Do or die. ◆ Don't put off till tomorrow what you can do today. ◆ Fish or cut bait. ◆ Get it while the getting is good. ◆ Got a minute? ◆ He who hesitates is lost. [see also Delay] ◆ Here and now. ◆ Is now a good time? ◆ Is you is or ain't you ain't? ◆ It's now or never. ◆ Make hay while the sun shines. ◆ Now is the time for all good men to come to the aid of their country. ◆ Now more than ever. ◆ Now's as good a time as any. ◆ On a moment's notice. ◆ On short notice. ◆ (Payable) on demand. ◆ Publish or perish. ◆ Put up or shut up. ◆ Put your money where your mouth is.

[see also Money] ♦ Root, hog, or die. ♦ Sh*t or get off the pot. ♦ Sink or swim. ♦ Speak now or forever hold your peace. ♦ Strike while the iron is hot. ♦ The matter at hand. ♦ The moment it happens. ♦ The time has come. ♦ The time has never been better. ♦ The time is right/ ripe. ♦ There comes a time. ♦ There's no time like the present. ♦ Use it or lose it. ♦ When you're up to your *ss in alligators is no time to clear the swamp. ♦ You're not getting any younger.

Impasse

A circle jerk. ♦ At loggerheads (with). ♦ Between a rock and a hard place. ♦ Bogged down. ♦ Caught in the crossfire. ♦ Stuck in the mud. ♦ This town isn't big enough for both of us. ♦ To be knee-deep (in). ♦ To be swamped. ♦ To go round and round. ♦ To bang/beat/hit one's head against the wall. ♦ To lock horns (with). [see also Conflict] ♦ To reach a Mexican standoff. ♦ To hit/reach a sticking point. ♦ To run up against a brick/ stone wall. ♦ To spin one's wheels.

Impolite

It's impolite to belch in public. ♦ It's impolite to cough/ sneeze/yawn without covering one's mouth. ♦ It's impolite to cut in line. ♦ It's impolite to leave the table without excusing oneself. ♦ It's impolite to pick one's nose in public. ♦ It's impolite to shake hands with a lady unless she offers her hand first. ♦ It's impolite to speak with one's mouth full. ♦ It's impolite to stare. ♦ It's impolite to turn your back when someone's speaking to you. ♦ The boarding house reach. ♦ To be in bad form/taste.

Impossibility

All the king's horses and all the king's men, couldn't put Humpty together again. ♦ An immovable obstacle. ♦ Damned near impossible ♦ It can't happen here. ♦ Never happen. ♦ Never in a million years. ♦ Never in your wildest dreams. ♦ No can do. ♦ No way around it. ♦ No way in hell. ♦ Not a chance (in a million). ♦ Not by any stretch of the imagination. ♦ Not for all the tea in China. ♦ Not for love nor money. ♦ Nothing is impossible (if you don't have to do it yourself). ♦ When pigs fly. ♦ When the devil is blind. ♦ You can't be in two places at once.

Imprisonment

A bird in a gilded cage. ♦ A jailbird. ♦ Bars and stripes forever. ♦ Behind bars. ♦ Chains are chains, be they made of gold or iron. ♦ Clapped in irons. ♦ Confined to quarters. ♦ Doing (hard) time. ♦ Doing one's time. ♦ Don't do the crime if you can't do the time. [see also Crime, Punishment] ♦ Everybody in here is innocent. ♦ Held without bail. ♦ In college—State pen. ♦ In jail. ♦ In solitary confinement. ♦ In the big house/brig/can/ hoosegow/pokey/ slammer. ♦ On death row. ♦ Released on one's own recognizance. ♦ Time off for good behavior. ♦ To bake a file into a cake. ♦ To be a lifer. ♦ To do a stretch. ♦ To make a citizen's arrest. ♦ To make a collar. ♦ To place [so] under arrest. ♦ To post bail. ♦ To send [so] up. ♦ To do/serve (hard) time. ♦ To serve one's sentence/time. ♦ Under house arrest. ♦ Up for/out on parole. ♦ Up the river. ♦ You're under arrest.

Improve

Build a better mousetrap and the world will beat a path to your door. ♦ Constant improvement. ♦ Extenuating circumstances. ♦ Iron out the wrinkles. ♦ Mitigating circumstances. ♦ New and improved. ♦ Pull oneself up by one's bootstraps. ♦ Some things can't be improved upon. ♦ There's got to be a better way. ♦ To improve one's lot in life. ♦ To

make the world a better place. ♦ To straighten [things] out. ♦ To take the curse off [it]. ♦ Work out the bugs.

Improvise

(also ingenuity, makeshift)

A poor substitute. ♦ A Rube Goldberg device. ♦ Better the ass that carries you than the horse that throws you. ♦ Catch as catch can. ♦ Cobble/piece/ string/throw [it] together. ♦ Do it on the fly. ♦ Held together with glue/spit and baling wire. ♦ Good old Yankee ingenuity. ♦ A hit-or-miss proposition. ♦ If life gives you lemons, make lemonade. ♦ If you don't have the things you want, want the things you have. ♦ It'll do in a pinch. ♦ Let's put it another way. ♦ Make the best of a bad bargain. ♦ Make do (with). ♦ Make the most of [it]. ♦ Play it as it lays. ♦ Play it by ear. ♦ Stopgap measures. ♦ The long way around is sometimes the shortest route home. ♦ There are horses for courses. ♦ There are ways and there are ways. ♦ There's more than one way to skin a cat. ♦ To ad-lib. ♦ To bridge the gap. ♦ To do the best you can do with the tools that you've got. ♦ To have two strings to one's bow. ♦ To make good use of. ♦ To make it up as you go (along). ♦ To piece and patch. ♦ To play it by ear. ♦ To put [it] to good use. ♦ To take another tack.

Incite

(also rouse, stimulate)

A battle cry. ♦ A call to arms. ♦ A (clarion) call to action. ♦ A pep rally. ♦ A rabble rouser. ♦ A rallying cry. ♦ Create a stir. ♦ Drum up business/support. ♦ Go, cat, go! ♦ Go, team, go! ♦ I sure bit a pig in the *ss with that one. ♦ Keep the ball rolling. ♦ Onward, Christian soldiers. ♦ Sic 'em! ♦ To add fuel to the fire/flames. ♦ To blow on/stir the embers. ♦ To boost morale. ♦ To cause an uproar. ♦ To create a disturbance. ♦ To egg [so] on. ♦ To fan/fuel the fire/flames. ♦ To fire the imagination. ♦ To get [so] going. To give a pep talk. ♦ To ignite a firestorm. ♦ To incite a riot. ♦ To keep the balls in the air. ♦ To keep/sustain the momentum. ♦ To make the fur fly. ♦ To open (up) a can of worms. ♦ To open (up) a Pandora's Box. ♦ To put [so] up to [it]. ♦ To rally the troops. ♦ To rile [so] up. ♦ To shake things up. ♦ To sic the dogs on [so]. ♦ To soup [it] up. ♦ To spur one on. ♦ To stir up a hornet's nest. ♦ To stir up sh*t. ♦ To stir the pot. ♦ To touch off. ♦ To whip up. ♦ To work up (a lather). ♦ You go, girl! ♦ You figure it out. ♦ You're asking for trouble.

Inconspicuous

A fly on the wall. ♦ A code word. ♦ Blend in with the woodwork. ♦ Burrowed into the woodwork. ♦ Can't see the forest for the trees. ♦ Face down. ♦ Hidden in plain sight. ♦ Invisible to the naked eye. ♦ Lurking in the shadows. ♦ No sign of forced entry. ♦ Not readily apparent. ♦ Not so's you'd notice. ♦ Out of sight. ♦ The fine print. ♦ To be under the radar. [see also Fugitive] ♦ To come in a plain brown wrapper. ♦ Where's Waldo? ♦ Wouldn't even know he was there.

Increase

A high rate of return. ♦ An escalation clause. ♦ An inflationary spiral. ♦ An arms buildup. ♦ An uptick. ♦ Exponential growth. ♦ On the rise. ♦ Double-digit inflation. ♦ Mission creep. ♦ Runaway inflation. ♦ To bulk up. ♦ To flesh [it] out. ♦ To gain/put on weight. ♦ To hike the price. ♦ To inch up. ♦ To put on a couple of/a few pounds. ♦ To ride up. ♦ To round [it] out. ♦ To set the clocks ahead. ♦ To sweeten the pot. ♦ Zero to sixty.

Incredulity

A sight to be seen/behold. ♦ Can you top this? ♦ I couldn't believe my (own) ears/eyes. ♦ I wouldn't believe it if I didn't see it with my own eyes. ♦ I'll go you one better. ♦ Incredible as it may seem. ♦ It defies logic. ♦ Just when you think you've heard/seen it all. ✦ No sh*t? ✦ Now I've heard/seen everything. ✦ Now I've seen it all. ✦ Say it isn't so. ✦ Stop me if you've heard this one. ✦ Surely you jest. ✦ That's one for the books. ✦ The Seven Wonders of the World. ✦ Top this if you can. ✦ Well, dip me in honey and call me sweetie. ✦ Well, I'll be. ✦ Well, I'll be dipped (in sh*t). ✦ What'll they think of next? ✦ You aren't tugging my bibs? ✦ You're not gonna believe this (in a million years). ✦ You're woofing me. ✦ You've got to be kidding. ✦ You've got to see it to believe it. ✦ You can't even begin to imagine.

Independent

A good yardstick for a man is whether he can stand on his own two feet. ✦ A rugged individualist. ✦ A self-made man. ✦ An independent cuss. ✦ Be one's own boss. [see also Boss] ✦ Be one's own man/woman. ✦ Have a mind of one's own. ✦ I'm a big boy/girl; I can take care of myself. ✦ Make up one's own mind. ✦ Marching to the beat of a different drummer. ✦ On one's own time. ✦ Pull one's own weight. ✦ Stand on one's (own) two feet. ✦ To be (out) on one's own. ✦ To come into one's own. ✦ To do for oneself. ✦ To do it your way. ✦ To do one's (own) thing. [see also Selfishness] ✦ To fend/shift for oneself. ✦ To go off on one's own. ✦ To go one's (own) way. ✦ To make one's way in the world. ✦ To pay one's way. ✦ To go/strike out on one's own. ✦ To take on a life of its own. ✦ To think for oneself.

Indeterminate

(also inconclusive, indifferent, indiscriminate)

A borderline case. ✦ A grey area. ✦ Any number of things. ✦ As good/well as can be expected (under the circumstances). ✦ Betwixt and between. ✦ *Cum si, cum sa.* ✦ Can't be bothered. ✦ Dash/hang it all. ✦ Depraved indifference. ✦ Doesn't show me much. ✦ Excuse me, but I think you mistook me for someone who gives a sh*t. ✦ Fair to middling. ✦ For whatever it's worth. ✦ Frankly, my dear, I don't give a damn. ✦ I could/ couldn't care less. ✦ I don't give two hoots and a holler. ✦ I don't give two sh*ts. ✦ I don't know, I don't care; I don't wear underwear. ✦ It's all the same to me. ✦ It's no skin off my back/nose. ✦ It's no sweat off my balls. ✦ It's something or other. ✦ Just (going) along for the ride. ✦ Makes no nevermind to me. ✦ *Mezzo e mezzo* (half and half). ✦ Neither fish (nor flesh) nor fowl. ✦ Neither here nor there.

♦ Not (half) bad. ♦ Not (in the least bit) interested. ♦ Right up/down the middle. ♦ See if I care. ♦ Six of one, half dozen of the other. ♦ So-so. ♦ So what? ♦ So what? Sew buttons! ♦ So, what the hell. ♦ Such and so. ♦ Such and such. ♦ This, that and the other thing. ♦ To be noncommittal. ♦ To be underwhelmed. ♦ To have no skin in the game. ♦ To not give a (fiddler's) f*ck. ♦ To not give a hoot. ♦ To not give a rat's *ss/patoot/rear. ♦ To not give a sh*t. ♦ To not have a dog/pony in the race. ♦ To play to the cheap seats. ♦ To whom it may concern. [see also Generalizations] ♦ What difference does it make? ♦ What's the difference? ♦ Whatever (turns you on). ♦ Whatever you want/say. ♦ Well, lah de dah. ♦ Who cares? ♦ Who knows and who cares? ♦ Wishy-washy.

Industrious

A workaholic. ♦ To bust [so]'s agates/chops/hump. ♦ To make short work (of). ♦ To work a double shift. ♦ To work like a beaver/dog/horse. ♦ To work the graveyard shift. [see also Late] ♦ To work one's *ss/balls/buns/butt/hiney/tail off. ♦ To work one's fingers to the bone. ♦ Tote that barge, lift that bale. ♦ Work around the clock.

Inept

Can't boil water. ♦ Can't walk and chew gum at the same time. ♦ Couldn't carry a tune in a bucket/bushel basket. ♦ Couldn't cut hot butter with a knife. ♦ Couldn't find his *ss with both hands. ♦ Couldn't find the navel on a navel orange. — R.D. ♦ Couldn't hit a bull in the *ss with a banjo. ♦ Couldn't hit the broad side of a barn. ♦ Couldn't get laid/make out in a women's prison (with a handful of pardons). ♦ Couldn't pour water out of a boot with directions printed on the heel. ♦ Couldn't drive a needle up his *ss with a hammer. ♦ He'd f*ck up a wet dream. ♦ He'd mess up/a ball bearing with a rubber mallet. ♦ He'd screw up a free lunch. ♦ To be an empty suit. ♦ Where'd you get your driver's license?—in a grab bag/CrackerJack box?

Inexorable

All roads lead to Rome. ♦ An irresistible force. ♦ Come hell or high water.* ♦ Come what may. *[see also Determination] ♦ Don't stop me now. ♦ Good, bad or indifferent. ♦ In fair or foul weather. ♦ Inevitable as death and taxes. ♦ It can't be helped. ♦ Life goes on. ♦ Love will find a way. [see also Love] ♦ Neither rain, nor hail, nor snow, nor gloom of night, can stay these couriers from the swift completion of their appointed rounds. ♦ No getting around it. ♦ No matter what. ♦ Nothing can be done about it. ♦ Rain or shine. ♦ The mail must go through. ♦ The show must go on. (It sho' must.) ♦ The wheels grind slow, but they grind fine. ♦ There's no stopping [p.]/[it] now. ♦ This too shall come to pass. [see also Happen] ♦ Whatever the weather. ♦ Whether it's cold or whether it's hot, we've got to have weather, whether or not. [see also Weather] ♦ Whether or not. ♦ Win, lose or draw.

Inexpensive

A bargain at twice the price. ♦ A cheap date. ♦ A steal. ♦ Bargain-basement/cut-rate prices. ♦ Cheap as dirt. (Similarly, dirt cheap). ♦ Cheap at twice the price. ♦ Cheaper by the dozen. ♦ Costs little or nothing. ♦ Down and dirty. ♦ For pennies on the dollar. ♦ For ten cents on the dollar. ♦ I can get it for you wholesale. ♦ If you pay peanuts, you get monkeys. ♦ Low maintenance. ♦ Low overhead. ♦ The cheap seats. ♦ The nosebleed section. ♦ To buy [it] for next to nothing. ♦ To buy [it] for a song/for spit/on the cheap. ♦ To cost peanuts. ♦ To work for peanuts. ♦ You want it good, or you want it cheap? I want it good and cheap.

Inferiority

(also diminutive, small)

A day late and a dollar short. ♦ A half-baked idea. ♦ A half-pint. ♦ A lemon. ♦ A little shaver. ♦ A little squirt. ♦ A p*ss-poor performance. ♦ A poor/sorry excuse for a/an [n.]. ♦ A sad commentary. ♦ A second-class citizen. ♦ A sick joke. ♦ A sorry specimen. ♦ An inferiority complex. ♦ Before they made him, they broke the mold. ♦ Below/under par. ♦ Better than nothing. ♦ Can't hold a candle to. ♦ Come from the wrong side of the tracks. ♦ Diminished capacity. ♦ Doesn't do [it] justice. ♦ Doesn't do justice to [it]. ♦ Doesn't live up to its hype. ♦ If you can't do it fast, don't do it half-fast. — R.D. [N.B. say that one aloud.] ♦ It leaves a lot/much/something to be desired. ♦ It loses something in translation. ♦ It'll never hold up in court. ♦ In bad form. ♦ In bad/poor taste. ♦ Low self-esteem. ♦ No f*cking good. ♦ Not fit for human consumption. ♦ Not so good/hot. ♦ Not up to snuff. [see also Discomfiture] ♦ The goat must browse where she is tied. ♦ Shakespeare, it ain't. ♦ Slow help is no help. ♦ (Strictly) for the birds/from hunger. ♦ The *sshole of the world. ♦ The bush league/minor league. ♦ The lesser of two evils. ♦ The runt of the litter. ♦ The Third world. ♦ The weakest link. ♦ Third-world nations. ♦ To be half-*ssed. ♦ To be no match for. ♦ To come from a broken home. ♦ To fall short/shy of the mark. ♦ Too little, too late. ♦ Vertically challenged. ♦ We live in an imperfect world. ♦ Woefully inadequate/lacking. ♦ You can only do so much.

Influence

A spin doctor. ♦ As the twig is bent, so grows the tree. ♦ Have them eating out of the palm of one's hand. ♦ Influence peddler. ♦ Putty in one's hands. ♦ Sphere of influence. ♦ Spin control. ♦ To act upon. ♦ To cast a spell (on). ♦ To do a number on. ♦ To do damage control. ♦ To drive under the influence. ♦ To have an effect (on). ♦ To have an in with [so]. ♦ To have [sb] in one's hip pocket. ♦ To have the right connections. ♦ To have [so] twisted/wrapped around one's (little) finger. ♦ To have [so]'s ear. ♦ To hold sway. ♦ To lead [so] to believe. ♦ To move the needle. ♦ To pull strings. ♦ To put a bug in [so]'s ear. ♦ To put a spin on [it]. ♦ To put English on [it]/ the ball. ♦ To put one in mind of. ♦ To put words in [so]'s mouth. ♦ To rub off on [so]. ♦ To tip the scales (in one's favor). ♦ To work on/upon [so]/[n.].

Ingratitude

A kindness too quickly repaid is a form of ingratitude. [see also Repay] ♦ A thankless job. ♦ Ain't that a real kick in the *ss? ♦ And this is (all) the thanks I get. ♦ How about that, now? ♦ Is this the thanks I get? ♦ Isn't that something? ♦ It ain't funny, McGee. ♦ No thanks to [n.]/[p.]. ♦ That's a fine how-do-you-do. ♦ That's a fine kettle of fish. ♦ That's a helluva note. ♦ What a kick in the crumpets. ♦ What a revolting development! ♦ What the hell good are you? ♦ Where were you when I needed you? ♦ Who serves everybody gets thanks from nobody. ♦ With friends like this, who needs enemies? [see also Friend] ♦ You have a funny way of showing it.

Inherit

Hand-me-downs. ♦ Heredity gives us the blueprint, environment gives us the building. ♦ It runs in the family. ♦ It's a family affair. ♦ It's all in the family. ♦ Last will and testament. ♦ To have [it] in one's blood. ♦ To keep it in the family. ♦ To remember [so] in one's will.

Inimitable

A conversation piece. ♦ A rara avis. ♦ A rare bird. ♦ Accept no substitutes. ♦

Each case is different. ♦ Has no peers. ♦ No two are alike. ♦ Nothing else will do. ♦ One of a kind. ♦ (Really) something else. ♦ The genuine article. ♦ The one and only. ♦ The only game in town. ♦ The real deal. ♦ The Real Mc Coy. ♦ To be for real. ♦ To be (really) something else. ♦ When they made him/her they broke/threw away the mold.

Initiative

A self-starter. ♦ A take-charge person. ♦ Affirmative action. [see also Action] ♦ Ask and ye shall receive; seek and ye shall find; knock, and the door shall be open. ♦ Get a zets going. ♦ God helps those who help themselves. (And God help those who get caught helping themselves! — Angela Maria Delia) ♦ Grab it and run with it. ♦ If the mountain will not come to Muhammad, then Muhammad must go to the mountain. ♦ Make one's move. ♦ Some men are like wheelbarrows, they only get going when pushed. ♦ Take matters/the law into one's own hands. ♦ The quest for the Holy Grail. ♦ To bring [it] up. ♦ To broach the subject. ♦ To get/move off the dime. ♦ To go up to bat. ♦ To grab the bull/cat by the balls. ♦ To make it on one's own. ♦ To prime the pump. ♦ To put [it] on the table. ♦ To raise the issue. ♦ To set the wheels in motion. ♦ To step up to the bat/plate. ♦ To take it on/upon oneself. ♦ To take the ball and run with it. ♦ To take the bull by the balls/horns. ♦ To take the initiative. ♦ To take the liberty of.

Injury

A nasty cut. ♦ Battered wife syndrome. ♦ Bleeding like a (stuck) pig. ♦ Blunt force trauma. ♦ Hurts like hell/the dickens. ♦ Hurtin' for certain. ♦ I forgot to duck. [see also Alibi] ♦ I ran into a lamppost. ♦ Out cold. ♦ Sporting a shiner. ♦ To get the wind knocked out of you. ♦ To have a fat lip. ♦ To lose consciousness. ♦ To pass out. ♦ To pull a muscle. ♦ To put a hurt/hurtin' on [so]. ♦ To win the Purple Heart.

Innocence

A babe in arms. ♦ A babe in the woods. ♦ A childlike innocence. ♦ A victim of circumstances. ♦ An innocent abroad. ♦ An innocent bystander. ♦ Beyond reproach. ♦ Convicted by a kangaroo court. ♦ Don't look at me. ♦ I didn't do it. ♦ I had nothing to do with it. ♦ Innocent until proven guilty. ♦ It's not my fault. ♦ Innocent fun. ♦ More sinned against than sinning. ♦ Not a shred of evidence. ♦ Not guilty (by reason of insanity). ♦ Presumption of innocence. ♦ Sorry, wrong fall guy. ♦ Take a bum rap. ♦ The salad days/years. ♦ There's no harm in looking. ♦ Through no fault of one's own. ♦ To be in the clear. ♦ To be railroaded. ♦ To maintain/protest one's innocence. ♦ To plead ignorance. ♦ To railroad [so]. ♦ Wholesome, clean-cut fun.

Inoperative

Hors de combat. ♦ Kaput. ♦ Kaputski. ♦ In war, laws are inoperative. ♦ On downtime. ♦ On the beach/ blink/ bum/fritz/shelf. ♦ Out of circulation. ♦ Out of commission. ♦ Out of kilter/whack. ♦ Out of order. [see also Misbehavior] ♦ Stripped gears. ♦ On the flat of one's back. ♦ Out of the ballgame. ♦ To be sidelined. ♦ To have a glitch. ♦ To have one's *ss in a sling.

Insecurity

An identity crisis. ♦ It's hard to walk forward while looking over your shoulder. ♦ People are never more insecure than when they become obsessed with their fears at the expense of their dreams. ♦ On shaky ground. ♦ To play it safe. ♦ Uneasy lies the head that wears the crown. ♦ Who wears the crown can go nowhere but down. ♦ You need eyes in the back of your head.

Insincere

A fair-weather friend. ♦ A half-hearted attempt. ♦ A token blessing/gesture. ♦ A mind f*cker. ♦ A phony. ♦ After a fashion. ♦ Damn by/with faint praise. ♦ For appearance's sake. ♦ In name only. [see also Names] ♦ The token [n.] of (the group). [see also Prejudice] ♦ To act in bad faith. ♦ To be just/only kidding. ♦ To be play-acting. ♦ To be two-faced. ♦ To blow smoke up one's *ss. ♦ To blow sunshine up one's skirt. ♦ To glad-hand [so]. ♦ To (just/only) go through the motions. ♦ To have multiple personalities. ♦ To kick [so] upstairs. ♦ To (just) mouth the words. ♦ To not believe one's own hype. ♦ To pat [so] on the back, looking for a place to bury the knife. ♦ To pay a backhanded/left-handed compliment. [see also Left-Handed Compliments] ♦ To pay lip service (to). ♦ To say [it] in jest. ♦ To speak tongue in cheek.

Insist

Dig one's heels in. ♦ Give strict orders. ♦ Issue an ultimatum. ♦ Lay down the ground rules. ♦ Lay down the law. ♦ On one condition. ♦ Put one's foot down. ♦ To draw the line. ♦ To stand fast. ♦ You've got to draw the line somewhere.

Insults

A pox on thee. ♦ Anyone with half a brain would know that. ♦ Argo f*ck yourself. ♦ Blow it out your *ss. ♦ Dry up and blow away. ♦ Eat sh*t and die. ♦ F*ck you. ♦ F*ck you—and the horse you rode in on. ♦ F*ck you—and your mother too. ♦ F*ck you where you sit/eat/live/breathe. ♦ Fooey on you. ♦ Go fly a kite. ♦ Go f*ck a duck. ♦ Go f*ck a rubber duck. ♦ Go f*ck yourself. ♦ Go goose a moose. ♦ Go jump in the creek/lake. ♦ Go pound salt/sand (up your *ss). ♦ Go scratch your *ss with broken glass. ♦ Go sh*t in your hat and punch it. ♦ Go soak your head. ♦ Go suck an egg. ♦ Go take a flying leap through a rolling donut. ♦ Go to blazes. ♦ Go to hell. ♦ I've got yours, swinging. ♦ Kiss my *ss. [riposte: It looks too much like your face.] ♦ May you live in interesting times!— [Chinese curse] ♦ Shove/stick it up your *ss. ♦ So's your mother. ♦ Stick it where the sun don't shine. ♦ Stuff it. ♦ Take it and shove it. ♦ The best part of you dribbled down your old man's leg. ♦ To flip the bird (at [so]). ♦ To get/give the finger from/to [so]. ♦ To give the Italian/middle-finger salute. ♦ Up your *ss. ♦ Up your gigi/hole with a ten-foot pole. ♦ Up yours. ♦ Up yours too. ♦ Where do you think you are: home or some other dirty place? ♦ You [v.] like a girl. ♦ You're on a roll – like toilet paper. ♦ Your grandmother sucks eggs.

Intensity

(also ultimate, utmost)

A(n) [n.] on steroids. ♦ A take-no-prisoners approach. [see also Merciless] ♦ Above and beyond (the call of duty). ♦ All or nothing. ♦ All-out [n.]. ♦ All the more. ♦ As [adj./adv.] as all get-out. ♦ As [adj./adv.] as can be. ♦ As [adj.] as Dick's hatband. ♦ At/to a fever pitch. ♦ Double-dyed. ♦ Even more so. ♦ Exacting standards. ♦ Good and [adj.]. ♦ Held to a higher standard. ♦ Hell-bent (for leather). ♦ In a big way. ♦ In full swing. ♦ In spades. ♦ In the dead of [n.]. ♦ Nothing short of [adj.]. ♦ On [it] like a duck on a June bug. ♦ On [it] like stink on a skunk. ♦ On [it] like white on rice. ♦ Out and out. ♦ Play hardball. ♦ Right out the window. ♦ So [adj./adv.] it's not even funny. ♦ Souped-up. ♦ Stand on one's head and spit nickels. ♦ To be caught up in [it] ♦ To bear down (on). ♦ To bear the brunt of. ♦ To bear the burden. ♦ To become an issue. ♦ To boil over. ♦ To come to a boiling point/reach a boiling point. ♦ To do it to death. ♦ To do (it) up brown. ♦ To do the heavy lifting. ♦ To do one's utmost. ♦ To double down.

◆ To dwell/harp on. ◆ To go all out. ◆ To go all the way. ◆ To go in with both guns blazing. ◆ To go out of one's way. ◆ To go the extra mile. ◆ To go the vole. ◆ To go the whole nine yards. ◆ To go to the wall. ◆ To give [it] 110 percent. ◆ To hit the high note. ◆ To hop/soup [it] up. ◆ To jump through hoops (for). ◆ To kick it up a notch. ◆ To moonlight. ◆ To outdo oneself. ◆ To pick up the pace. ◆ To push the boundaries (of good taste). ◆ To push the envelope. [see also Progress] ◆ To put one's heart into it. ◆ To put oneself out. ◆ To ramp [it] up. ◆ To reach a tipping point. ◆ To reach critical mass. ◆ To redouble one's efforts. ◆ To step up one's game. ◆ To summon (up) all one's strength. [see also Strive] ◆ To take (great) pains. ◆ To take off the gloves. ◆ To take the [n.] by storm. ◆ To the *nth* degree. ◆ To [v.] for all it's worth. ◆ To [v.] for all one is worth. ◆ To [v.] full blast/full bore/full tilt. ◆ To [v.] like a champ. ◆ To [v.] like there's no tomorrow. ◆ To [v.] one to death. ◆ To [v.] one's *ss/head/keyster off. ◆ To [v.] right and left. ◆ To [v.] right out the window. ◆ To [v.] one's brains out. ◆ To [v.] to a fare-thee-well. ◆ To [v.] to a fine turn. ◆ To [v.] to no end. ◆ To [v.] with a vengeance. ◆ (Up) to the hilt. ◆ With all one's might.

Intimacy

Better to have your enemies inside the tent p*ssing out, than outside the tent, p*ssing in. ◆ Everyone knows best where his own shoe pinches. ◆ I'll show you mine if you show me yours. ◆ Keep your friends close and your enemies closer. ◆ My good fellow/man. ◆ Nothing in between them but Vaseline. ◆ One's fellow man. ◆ P*ssing through the same quilt. ◆ Pillow talk. ◆ The troubles of the pot only the spoon that stirs it knows. ◆ To be palsy-walsy. ◆ To have a ringside seat. ◆ Up close and personal. ◆ You never really know a man until you've walked a mile in his shoes. ◆ You're only a stranger here once.

Investigate

A background check. ◆ A board of inquiry. ◆ A cavity search. ◆ A Congressional probe. ◆ A double-blind study. ◆ A dress rehearsal. ◆ A dry run. ◆ A gumshoe. ◆ A person of interest. ◆ A private eye/investigator. ◆ A Q&A session. ◆ A search warrant. ◆ A shakedown cruise. ◆ A spot check. ◆ A table read. ◆ A trial run. ◆ Attention to detail. ◆ An ongoing investigation. ◆ Before you berate, get your facts straight. ◆ By the process of elimination. ◆ Case the joint. ◆ Check it out. ◆ Do a smell check. ◆ Don't take my word for it. ◆

Find out what makes [it]/[so] tick. ◆ Get a rundown on. ◆ Get the lowdown (on). [see also Confide] ◆ Get to the bottom of [it]. ◆ Go on a "go-see." ◆ Google it. ◆ Have a look. ◆ Have a look-see. ◆ Have a looky-look. ◆ In search of. ◆ Investigate before you invest. ◆ Just the facts, ma'am. ◆ Look that up in your Funk and Wagnalls. ◆ Name, rank and serial number. ◆ On closer examination/inspection. ◆ Pending further investigation. ◆ Pore over. ◆ Run it up the flagpole and see who salutes. ◆ Run the numbers. ◆ Scope it out. ◆ See which way the wind is blowing. ◆ Seek a second opinion. ◆ Seek and ye shall find. ◆ Size it up. ◆ Take stock (of). ◆ The bear went over the mountain, to see what he could see. ◆ There had better be a good explanation for this. ◆ This call may be monitored or recorded for quality purposes. ◆ To ask/ferret/look/poke/snoop around. ◆ To card [so]. ◆ To channel surf. ◆ To comparison shop. ◆ To crack the case. ◆ To dig beneath the surface. ◆ To dig up. ◆ To do a smell/sniff test. ◆ To do due diligence. [see also Caution] ◆ To drill down (to). ◆ To examine in microscopic detail. ◆ To feel [so] out. ◆ To gather information. ◆ To get the dirt/goods on [so]. ◆ To get the inside poop/scoop. ◆ To get the particulars (on). ◆ To get the scoop. ◆ To get the (straight) skinny. ◆ To give [so] the third degree. ◆ To get/give the once-over. ◆ To go on a fishing expedition. ◆ To go over [it] with a fine-tooth comb. ◆ To go (deep) undercover. ◆ To hold up to public scrutiny. ◆ To kick the tires. ◆ To know who's doing what to whom (and when). ◆ To look/search high and low (for). ◆ To look at [it] in the cold/naked light of day. ◆ To look into [it]. ◆ To look under the hood. ◆ To make an informed decision. ◆ To pay (close) attention (to). ◆ To plumb the depths. ◆ To put a tracer on [it]. ◆ To put [it] in/into perspective. ◆ To put out feelers. ◆ To put the question to [so]. ◆ To run [it] by [so]. ◆ To scope [it] out. ◆ To see how the other half lives. ◆ To see what's up/what's what. ◆ To send up a trial balloon. ◆ To size [it] up. ◆ To surf the net. ◆ To suss [it] out. ◆ To take a fine pencil to. ◆ To take a good look. ◆ To take a cold, hard look. ◆ To take a long, hard look. ◆ To take [it] into consideration. ◆ To tap a phone. ◆ To test the water. ◆ To turn the place inside out/upside down. [see also Pursue] ◆ To vet [it]. ◆ To wear a wire. ◆ To weigh the pluses and minuses/pros and cons. ◆ Under investigation. ◆ We shall see what we shall see. ◆ What can the matter be? ◆ What is the meaning of this? ◆ What (the hell) is going on (here)? ◆ What's going on?

♦ What's happening? ♦ What's shaking? ♦ What's shakin' bakin'? ♦ What's the deal, MacNeil? ♦ What's this all about? ♦ What's up, Doc? ♦ Wired for sound. ♦ You can't tell the players without a scorecard. ♦ You could look it up.

Investment
As you sow, so shall ye reap. ♦ Before you invest, investigate. ♦ Beware the dead cat bounce. ♦ Cast one's bread upon the waters. ♦ Do not put your trust in money, put your money in trust. ♦ Garbage in, garbage out. ♦ Never stop selling. ♦ Past performance is no guarantee of future results. ♦ Take stock of your assets. ♦ You can't sell from an empty wagon. — Dominick P. Delia ♦ You've got to invest in shot glasses if you're going to sell whiskey. ♦ You have to know when to hold 'em . . . know when to fold 'em. ♦ You only get out of it what you put into it.

Invitation
(also welcome)
All ashore who's going ashore. ♦ An open invitation. ♦ As welcome as the flowers in May. ♦ Be there or be square. ♦ Call, click or visit us at [n.] dotcom. ♦ Come on down! ♦ Come on in, the water's fine. ♦ Come one,

come all. ♦ Extend an invitation. ♦ If you're in the neighborhood, drop in. ♦ Last one in is a rotten egg/an old stick in the mud. [see also Hurry] ♦ Let's do lunch. ♦ Make me/us an offer. ♦ May I have this dance? ♦ Make you an offer you can't refuse. ♦ Open locks, whoever knocks. ♦ Roll me over in the clover. ♦ Roll me over, Rover. ♦ Step right up, folks/ladies and gentlemen. ♦ Take me out to the ballgame. ♦ To leave the door open. ♦ To lay out the welcome mat. ♦ To throw open the door. ♦ To welcome with open arms. ♦ Welcome to the neighborhood. ♦ Why don't you come (on) up and see me sometime? ♦ Would you care to dance? ♦ You are cordially invited. ♦ Y'all come. ♦ Y'all come back (now), heah?

Irk
(also displeasure, irritation, nuisance)
A ballbuster. ♦ A burr under one's saddle. ♦ A guest is like rain: when he lingers on, he becomes a nuisance. ♦ A nerve-racking (or nerve-wracking) experience. ♦ A pain in the neck. ♦ A pet peeve. ♦ A (royal) pain in the *ss/tucas/tush. ♦ A sour note. ♦ A thorn in one's side. ♦ Go down the wrong way. ♦ It is inherent in the nature of

a grain of sand to irritate. ♦ Kept [n.]/[p.] awake the whole night. ♦ Know what really burns my *ss? A fire about yay high. ♦ Like chalk/fingernails on the blackboard. ♦ One's *bête noire*. ♦ Small, but not swallowed. ♦ Sour grapes. ♦ The bane of one's existence. ♦ Therein lies the rub. ♦ To be a ball-buster. ♦ To be a sourpuss. ♦ To be bummed out/grossed out. ♦ To be off-putting. ♦ To be put off [by]. ♦ To be underfoot. ♦ To crack one's knuckles. ♦ To frown upon [it]. ♦ To get a rise out of [so]. [see also Tease] ♦ To get burned up. ♦ To get in one's hair. ♦ To get on one's nerves. ♦ To get to [so]. ♦ To get under one's skin. ♦ To get one's goat. ♦ To get one's back/hackles/Irish up. ♦ To go against the grain. ♦ To grate on one's nerves. ♦ To have an aversion to. ♦ To hit a sore point/spot. ♦ To hit/touch/ strike a (raw) nerve. ♦ To hurt [so]'s feelings. ♦ To incur [so]'s wrath. ♦ To look down one's nose at/on. ♦ To make a nuisance/pest of oneself. ♦ To make one nervous. ♦ To push one's buttons. ♦ To rub one the wrong way. ♦ To ruffle one's feathers. ♦ To skeeve [it]. ♦ To sour on. ♦ To step on [so]'s toes. ♦ To stew in one's (own) juices. ♦ To stick in one's craw/maw/ throat. ♦ To take a dim view of. ♦ To p*ss/tee/tick [so] off. ♦ To try one's patience. ♦ To turn over in one's grave. ♦ To play/wreak havoc with [it].

Irrelevant

A chicken drinks water and looks at the sky. ♦ A nothing-to-win, nothing-to-lose situation. ♦ But I digress. ♦ It (really) doesn't matter (to me). ♦ It's/that's got nothing to do with anything. ♦ Just a throwaway. ♦ Size doesn't matter. ♦ It's/that's beside the point. ♦ It/that doesn't apply (here). ♦ That's neither here nor there. ♦ To be all over the lot. ♦ To change the subject. [see also Different] ♦ To cut no ice/sh*t (with). ♦ To go off on a tangent. ♦ To go off topic. ♦ To have no bearing (on). ♦ To wander from the point. ♦ What's that got to do with anything/it? ♦ What's that got to do with the price of eggs? [var. with the price of cheese/fish/meat/sausage/rice/tea in China, etc.]

Judgment
(also decisions)

A command decision. ♦ A hasty conclusion. ♦ A judgment call. ♦ A rush to judgment. ♦ As far as I can see/tell. ♦ Decisions, decisions . . . ♦ Here come de judge. ♦ Impaired judgment. ♦ Sober as a judge. ♦ To be arbitrary. ♦ To be on to [so]. ♦ To have [so]'s number. ♦ To have [so] pegged (just right). ♦ To judge each one on a case-by-case basis, solely on [p.] own merits. ♦ To make a snap decision/judgment. ♦ To make up one's mind (to). ♦ To pass judgment (on). ♦ To serve as both judge and jury. ♦ To sit in judgment. ♦ To size [so] up. ♦ To suspend judgment. ♦ To think less of. ♦ What to do, what to do? ♦ You be the judge. ♦ You can judge another and be correct—but it is never correct to prejudge another.

Kill

A cold-blooded killer. ♦ A hired gun. ♦ A hitman. ♦ A killing spree. ♦ A ritual sacrifice. ♦ Bump off. ♦ Deliver the *coupe de grace*. ♦ Do away with. ♦ Drop the hammer. ♦ First degree murder. ♦ Fit with cement shoes. ♦ Give a necktie party. ♦ He'd shoot you as soon as look at you. ♦ Hit the kill switch. ♦ Kill or be killed. ♦ Kill the umpire. ♦ Kill (all) your darlings. [see also Writing] ♦ Killer instincts. ♦ Lord high executioner. ♦ Man/officer down. ♦ Move in for the kill. ♦ Murder in the first degree. ♦ Murder most foul. ♦ Murder for hire. ♦ Negligent homicide. ♦ Premeditated murder. ♦ Put a period to. ♦ Put an end to. ♦ Put [so] out of her/his misery. ♦ Serial killer. ♦ Shoot to kill. ♦ Shot at sunrise. ♦ Shot down like a dog. ♦ Shot on sight. ♦ Summarily executed. ♦ To cap [so]. ♦ To deal a death/fatal blow. ♦ To do in. ♦ To do wet work. ♦ To kill with kindness. ♦ To knock [so] off. ♦ To liquidate [so]. ♦ To off [so]. ♦ To mortally wound. ♦ To pop a cap into [so]. ♦ To pull the plug (on). ♦ To put to death. ♦ To snuff [so] (out). ♦ To stretch [so]'s neck. ♦ To string [so] up. ♦ To take [so] out. ♦ To take [so]'s life. ♦ To take [so] off (of) life support. ♦ To use deadly/lethal force. ♦ To waste [so].

Kindness

A little kindness goes a long way. ♦ As a personal favor. ♦ Be a sport. ♦ Be kind to our web-footed friends; for a duck may be somebody's mother. ♦ Have a heart. ♦ He who plants kindness gathers love. ♦ Heart's in the right place. ♦ If you do good, forget about it; if you do bad, think about it. ♦ Kill them with kindness. ♦ Kind hearts are more than coronets. ♦ Mission of mercy. ♦ My good deed for the day. ♦ Out of the goodness of one's heart. ♦ Red Cross ship: blood vessel. ♦ The milk of human kindness. ♦ The wind is kind to the shorn lamb. ♦ To do right by [so]. ♦ To do [so] a good turn. ♦ To open your heart to [so].

Kiss

A kiss bestowed infrequently tastes sweeter. ♦ A smacker/smackeroo/smooch. ♦ A Yankee dime. ♦ Georgie Porgy puddin' pie, kissed the girls and made them cry. ♦ If your nose itches, you're going to kiss a fool. ♦ Kiss and make up. ♦ Kiss and tell ♦ Kiss [it] goodbye. ♦ K.I.S.S. – (Keep It Simple, Stupid). ♦ Kiss me quick, I'm coming. ♦ Kiss me, you fool. ♦ Kiss the boo-boo (and make it better). ♦ Kiss the ground. ♦ Kiss the hand you cannot bite. ♦ Kiss your *ss goodbye. ♦ Kissin' don't last; cookin' do. ♦ Kissing cousins. ♦ One aches to plant kisses on whom one misses. ♦ One kisses the child for the mother's sake, and the mother for the child's sake. ♦ Sweet sixteen and never been kissed. ♦ To blow a kiss. ♦ To kiss [it] goodbye. ♦ To kiss the Blarney Stone. ♦ To kiss up (to). ♦ To plant a kiss. ♦ To plant (a big, wet) one on [so]. ♦ To play kissy-face. ♦ To play Spin the Bottle. ♦ To pucker up. ♦ To purse one's lips. ♦ To swap spits (with). ♦ To suck face (with). ♦ You may kiss the bride.

Knowledge

A known issue. ♦ A little knowledge is a dangerous thing. ♦ A mile wide and an inch deep. ♦ An open secret. ♦ Common knowledge. ♦ He who understands most is other men's master. ♦ He who will not be counseled cannot be helped. ♦ It's not what you know, it's who you know. [see also Understanding] ♦ It's public knowledge. ♦ Know something about everything, and everything about something. ♦ Knowledge is power. ♦ Tell me what you know and I'll tell you who you are. ♦ To know full well/only too well/perfectly well. ♦ To the best of my knowledge. ♦ What you don't know can't hurt you. (But what you don't know can't help you. – R.D.) ♦ What you know, nobody can take away from you. ♦ You know as well as I. ♦ You know damned good and well.

Language

A/the language barrier. ♦ A catchphrase. ♦ A command of the language. ♦ A figure of speech. ♦ A play on words. ♦ A turn of the phrase.—a filmstrip on language produced by Richard A. Delia ©1973 - NY, Westinghouse Learning Press. ♦ An old saying. ♦ Buzzwords. ♦ Lost in translation. ♦ Ooday ooyay eekspay igpay atinlay? ♦

The language dodge. ♦ The [n.] have a word for it. ♦ To mix metaphors. ♦ To speak the king's English. ♦ To use the editorial "we." ♦ To use twenty-five-cent words. ♦ Witty ditties.

Late

A late bloomer. ♦ After the fact. ♦ All through the night. ♦ An ungodly hour. ♦ Better late than never. ♦ (Better never late! — R.D.) ♦ Better three hours too soon, than one minute late. ♦ Burning the midnight oil. ♦ Fashionably late. ♦ I'm late, I'm late, for a very important date. ♦ In the black/dead of night. ♦ In the middle of the night. ♦ In the midnight hour. ♦ In the still of the night. ♦ In the wee hours. ♦ Just in time to be too late. ♦ The stroke of midnight. ♦ The witching hour. ♦ To be a night-owl. ♦ To be late to one's own funeral. ♦ To pull an all-nighter. ♦ To take the redeye. ♦ To work the graveyard shift. [see also Industrious] ♦ Twelve bells and all is well. ♦ (Way) past your bed-time. ♦ When the moon comes over the mountain.

Laughter

A barrel of laughs. ♦ A laugh a min-ute. ♦ A maid who laughs is half won. ♦ Always leave them laughing. ♦ Contagious laughter. ♦ Gales/ peals of laughter. ♦ Har de har-har. ♦ He is not laughed at who laughs at himself first. ♦ He who laughs last, laughs best. ♦ He who laughs last may be slow on the uptake. ♦ I like he who laughs at all my jokes. ♦ I too would laugh if the fool were not mine. ♦ Infectious humor. ♦ It only hurts when I laugh. ♦ Laugh and the world laughs with you; cry/weep and you cry/weep alone. ♦ Laugh before breakfast, cry before night. ♦ Laugh it up. ♦ Laugh on Friday, cry on Sunday. ♦ Laughing matter. ♦ Laughing to keep from crying. [see also Pretend] ♦ Laughter is the best medicine. ♦ Never laugh when a hearse goes by; you may be the next to die. ♦ Side-splitting laugh-ter. ♦ That really cracks me up. ♦ The court jester. ♦ To break up with laughter. ♦ To break you up. ♦ To bust a gut. ♦ To crack you up. ♦ To die laughing. ♦ To double up with laughter. ♦ To have a laughing jag. ♦ To have the last laugh. ♦ To laugh all the way to the bank. ♦ To laugh until you cry. ♦ To laugh one's *ss off. ♦ To split one's sides. ♦ To hit/ tickle one's funny bone. ♦ You don't stop laughing because you grow old; you grow old because you stop laughing.

Law

A hard-and-fast rule. [see also Rules] ◆ A jury of one's peers. ◆ A run-in with the law. ◆ An arrest warrant. ◆ An officer of the law. ◆ An unwritten law. ◆ Due process of law. ◆ Law enforcement. ◆ Fond of lawsuits, little wealth; fond of doctors, little health. [see also Medical] ◆ Ignorance of the law is no defense/excuse. ◆ Justice delayed is justice denied. [see also Relativity] ◆ Justice is blind. ◆ Law and order. ◆ Law-abiding citizen. ◆ Legal mumbo-jumbo. [see also Confused] ◆ Legalese. ◆ Legally blind/dead. ◆ Make a mockery of justice. ◆ No one is above the law. ◆ Obstruction of justice. ◆ Open up in the name of the law! ◆ Police brutality. ◆ Sue the bastards! ◆ Sworn to uphold the law. ◆ The cop on the beat. ◆ The lawyer's best client is a rich man in trouble. ◆ The law is a ass. ◆ The law is clear on that point. ◆ The law is the law. ◆ The law of averages. ◆ The law of diminishing returns. ◆ The law of supply and demand. ◆ The law of the jungle. ◆ The law of the land. ◆ The letter of the law killeth. ◆ The halls of justice. ◆ The long arm of the law. ◆ The rule of law. ◆ The rules of engagement. ◆ The rules of the road. ◆ The toothless cry for laws with teeth. ◆ There oughtta be a law. ◆ There's a loophole in every law. ◆ To adopt a ruling. ◆ To bring the guilty to justice. ◆ To collar [so]. ◆ To enact legislation. ◆ To exact justice. ◆ To file a lawsuit. ◆ To file suit. ◆ To get off on a technicality. ◆ To lawyer up. ◆ To pass a law. ◆ To place [so] under arrest. ◆ To run [so] in. ◆ To slap [so] with a lawsuit. ◆ To stand trial. ◆ To take [so] to court. ◆ To the fullest extent of the law. ◆ To the letter of the law. ◆ Where there is no law there is no crime/transgression. [see also Crime] ◆ You're under arrest. ◆ Your license and registration, please.

Lazy

A couch potato. ◆ A lazy sack of sh*t. ◆ A lazy sheep thinks its wool is heavy. ◆ A slacker. ◆ Don't kill the job. ◆ Hard work doesn't scare me; I can lie down and fall asleep right next to it. ◆ He hasn't done an honest day's work in his life. ◆ I'll do it tomorrow. ◆ Lazy bones. ◆ Lazy people work the best when the sun sets in the west. —Dominick P. Delia ◆ Lie down on the job. ◆ Never stand when you can sit; never run when you can walk; never walk when you can ride. ◆ Prostitute: one who gets paid for lying down on the job. ◆ Prostitute: one who makes it a business to do pleasure. ◆ To back up to one's pay/paycheck. ◆ To bag it. ◆ To fall down/lie down on the job. ◆ To f*ck off. ◆ To featherbed. ◆ To goldbrick. ◆ To goof off. ◆ To rest on one's laurels. ◆ To sandbag. ◆ Wouldn't lift a finger.

Leadership

Ahead of the curve. ♦ Captains of industry. ♦ Follow my lead. ♦ Follow the leader. ♦ If you are not the lead dog/horse/mule the view never changes. ♦ Lay/lead on, Macduff. [see also Challelnges] ♦ Leaders are born, not made. ♦ Let me show you how it's done. ♦ Never lead with your chin. ♦ Our fearless leader. ♦ Step right this way. ♦ Take me to your leader. ♦ The leader of the pack. ♦ To be a leader of men, you must turn your back on men. ♦ To boldly go where no man has gone before. ♦ To establish/set a precedent. ♦ To lead by example. ♦ To lead [so] around by the nose. ♦ To lead the charge. ♦ To lead the way. ♦ To play follow-the-leader. ♦ To set the standard. ♦ To show the way. ♦ To talk the talk and walk the walk.

Learn

(also study)

A crash course (in). ♦ A home without books is a home without windows. ♦ A man never wakes up his second baby just to see it smile. ♦ As the twig is bent, so grows the tree. ♦ Back to school. ♦ By George, I think she's got it. ♦ Commit [it] to memory. ♦ Go to the head of the class. ♦ I never met a man so ignorant I couldn't learn something from him. ♦ In boot camp. ♦ It's never too late to learn. ♦ Learn the hard way. ♦ Learn [it] by heart. ♦ Learn to listen and listen to learn. ♦ Learning is a scepter to some, a bauble to others. ♦ Learning is like rowing upstream—not to advance is to drop back. ♦ Live and learn. ♦ Live it up and learn. ♦ Live to learn and you will learn to live. ♦ Man only learns when he refuses to repeat his mistakes. ♦ Now I know my ABC's; tell me what you think of me. ♦ Read any good books lately? ♦ That's a new one on me. ♦ The best way to learn is by doing. ♦ The halls of ivy. ♦ The school of hard knocks. ♦ The three R's (reading and writing and 'rithmetic). ♦ Those who apply themselves at the little red schoolhouse are never unread. ♦ To bone up/brush up/read up (on). ♦ To broaden one's horizons. ♦ To burn the midnight oil. ♦ To catch on. ♦ To crack the books. ♦ To cram for the exam. ♦ To get one's sheepskin. ♦ To learn about the birds and the bees.

♦ To learn by trial and error. ♦ To learn from one's mistakes. ♦ To learn the ABC's (of). ♦ To learn the facts of life. ♦ To learn one's lesson. ♦ To learn the ropes. ♦ To pay one's dues. ♦ To sit at the feet of. ♦ To sit at the master's feet. ♦ We learn from experience. ♦ You catch on fast/quick. ♦ You learn something new every day. ♦ You're never too old to learn.

Left-handed Compliments
(a.k.a. asterisms)

Beautiful name—it's my dog's name. ♦ I don't care what anyone else says about you—you're OK (in my book). ♦ He/she puts the sty in style. ♦ I like your outfit—it matches today. ♦ I love your hair—what color dye do you use? ♦ I never would have expected such a brilliant idea from you. ♦ If you keep at it, you could become pretty good one day. ♦ I'll bet that you were very handsome/beautiful when you were younger. ♦ Not that there's anything wrong with that. ♦ Others have done a lot worse. ♦ She's a pirate's dream: sunken chest. ♦ That's an amazing insight, for an uneducated person. ♦ The important thing is that you tried. ♦ You drive very well—for a woman. ♦ You look great . . . for your age. ♦ You're invincible—in your armor of ignorance. ♦ You're not as dumb as you look. [rejoinder: And you don't look as dumb as you are. — [Richard J. Noyes] [see also Ripostes] ♦ You're pretty/smart for a [n.]. ♦ You're smarter than you look. ♦ Your teeth are like the stars: they come out every night.

Lend

Always borrow money from a pessimist. He won't expect it back. ♦ Can you lend me five till my brother straightens out?—he's a hunchback. ♦ Friends, Romans, Countrymen, lend me your ears. ♦ Give a dime before you lend a dollar. ♦ He that lends, gives. ♦ In God we trust—all others must pay cash. [sign]. [see also Trust] ♦ Neither a borrower nor a lender be. ♦ Usurer: a lendlord. ♦ When you lend money to a friend, you may lose your money—and a friend. ♦ Who goes a-borrowing, goes a-sorrowing. ♦

Lengthy

A long weekend. ♦ A never-ending saga/tale. ♦ *Ad infinitum.* ♦ All the livelong day. ♦ All night long. ♦ Dawn to dusk. ♦ Days/hours/months/weeks on end. ♦ Every waking minute/moment. ♦ For the better part of a(n) [n.]. ♦ From sunrise to sunset. ♦ This could go on all day. ♦

Till hell freezes over. ♦ Till the cows come home. ♦ Till you're blue in the face. ♦ To go into extra innings/overtime.

Liberty

A free man. ♦ A free agent/spirit. ♦ A get-out-of-jail-free card. ♦ A liberated woman. ♦ All you gotta do is die and pay taxes. ♦ An emancipated slave. ♦ Come and go as you please. ♦ Do as you damn well please. ♦ Do one's (own) thing. ♦ Free and clear. ♦ Free and easy. ♦ Free as a bird/the breeze/the wind. ♦ Free, white and twenty-one. ♦ Give them enough rope and they'll hang themselves. ♦ It's a free country. ♦ Olly, olly, all free! ♦ On the loose. ♦ Out/up and about. ♦ Out on the town. ♦ Stone free. ♦ Sweet land of liberty. ♦ Talk may or may not be cheap, but freedom of speech is dear. ♦ The freedom to make (one's own) mistakes. ♦ The Great Experiment. ♦ The unexpurgated version. ♦ To act at will. ♦ To be in circulation. ♦ To be out of debt. ♦ To get out from under. ♦ To go about one's business. ♦ To have the run of (the house). ♦ To make the rounds. ♦ To see your way clear. ♦ To take full liberty. ♦ To take liberties (with). ♦ To take the liberty of [v.].

♦ Women's liberation. ♦ You're free to go.

Lie

A b.s./bullsh*t artist. ♦ A congenital/pathological liar. ♦ A feather merchant. ♦ A liar needs a good memory. ♦ A lie stands on one leg, the truth on two. ♦ A (little) white lie. ♦ A novelist is an exalted liar. ♦ A pack/web of lies. ♦ Deceive not thy physician, confessor, or lawyer. ♦ Figures don't lie; but liars use figures. ♦ I cannot tell a lie. ♦ If you cross your fingers when telling a lie, it doesn't count. ♦ If you tell one lie, you must tell ten more to cover it up. ♦ Liar, liar, pants on fire. ♦ Lies have very short legs. ♦ Look me in the eye and say that. ♦ Nothing could be further from the truth. ♦ Nothing of the kind/sort. ♦ Oh, what a tangled web we weave when first we practice to deceive. ♦ Once a liar always a liar. (A liar in all ways) ♦ Sin has many tools but a lie is the handle that fits them all. ♦ The camera doesn't lie. ♦ The credit of a lie lasts only until the truth comes by. ♦ The liar is not believed when he speaks the truth. ♦ The three greatest lies in the world: There is no Mafia. The check is in the mail. I promise not to come in your mouth. ♦ There are three kinds of lies: lies, damned lies and statistics. ◆ Thin lips may utter fat lies. ◆ To bend/stretch the truth. [see also Exaggeration] ◆ To feed/hand [so] a line. ◆ To lie left and right. ◆ To lie through one's teeth. ◆ To perpetuate a lie. ◆ To sling it. ◆ To sling the bull. ◆ To trump up. ◆ You lie like a rug.

Life

C'est la vie. ◆ It's a great life if you don't weaken. (But who wants to be strong?) ◆ It's a tough life. ◆ Life after death. ◆ Life can be beautiful. ◆ Life goes on. ◆ Life is a bitch and then you die. ◆ Life is a sunny beach. ◆ Life is but a dream. ◆ Life is but a look out the window. ◆ Life is like a cat in the bag: you never know where it will end. ◆ Life is the gift of nature; but beautiful living is the gift of wisdom. ◆ Life is (too) short. ◆ Life is what happens when you're busy making other plans. ◆ Life is what you make it. ◆ Life is worth living. ◆ Live spelled backwards is evil. ◆ Such is life (without a wife). ◆ The secret of life is not to do what you like, but to like what you do. ◆ To show signs of life. ◆ We pass this way but once. ◆ Where there's life there's hope. ◆ You only get out of life what you put into it. ◆ Your life

is a gift from God; what you do with your life is a gift to God.

Lifelong

As long as I live. ◆ For as long as you both shall live. ◆ For the rest of your (natural) life. ◆ If I live to be a hundred. ◆ In all my livelong days. ◆ Till the day you die. ◆ To live to a ripe, old age. ◆ To one's dying day. ◆ To the end of one's days.

Limited

A limited edition. ◆ A limited repertoire. ◆ A one-hit wonder. ◆ A one-trick pony. ◆ All the good ones are taken. ◆ As far as that goes. ◆ Certain restrictions may apply. ◆ For a limited time only. ◆ He/she is not without his/her faults. ◆ I don't do windows. ◆ I only have two hands. ◆ I'm only one person. ◆ I'm only human. ◆ In one sense of the word. ◆ In a way. ◆ In some (small) way. ◆ Know your limits. ◆ Life is too short. ◆ One to a customer. ◆ Not available in stores. ◆ The mouse that hath but one hole is easily caught. ◆ There are not enough hours in the day. ◆ There are only so many days in a week/hours in a day. ◆ To a certain degree/extent. ◆ To a/some degree. ◆ To an/some extent. ◆ To one degree or another. ◆ To run the gamut from A to B. ♦ To the best of one's knowledge. ♦ Up to a (certain) point. ♦ While supplies last. ♦ Within bounds/limits. ♦ Within city limits. ♦ You can't have everything.

Listen

(also hear, heed)

A boom box. ♦ Get the sh*t out of your ears. ♦ Get this through your thick skull. ♦ Give a listen (to). ♦ Hear me out. ♦ I'm all ears. [riposte: Like a jackass!] ♦ If I've told you once I've told you a thousand times. ♦ Lend a sympathetic ear. ♦ Lend an ear. ♦ Let those who have ears, hear. ♦ Listen closely. ♦ Listen here. ♦ Listen, my children, and you shall hear. ♦ Listen to reason. ♦ Listen to this. ♦ Listen up, (people). ♦ Now you listen to me. ♦ Pay attention. ♦ Read my lips. ♦ To cock an ear/your head. ♦ To give one's undivided attention. ♦ To take an interest (in). ♦ You heard me (right) the first time. ♦ (You) see here.

Long

As long as your arm. ♦ As long as you're up . . . ♦ For as long as you both shall live. ♦ For/in the longest time/while. ♦ Haven't seen you in a dog's

age. ♦ Hey, Sam, you made the pants too long. ♦ It's a long, long way to Tipperary. ♦ Long ago and far away. ♦ Long time no see. ♦ Love me little, love me long. ♦ To be long on [it]. ♦ Yay long.

Lore

Bigfoot. ♦ Johnny Appleseed. ♦ Old wives' tales. ♦ Paul Bunyan. ♦ Santa Claus. ♦ Sasquatch. ♦ The Abominable Snowman. ♦ The bogeyman/Boogie Man. ♦ The Chupacabra. ♦ The Easter Bunny. ♦ The fallen angel. ♦ The Good Fairy. ♦ The Loch Ness Monster. ♦ The Mothman. ♦ The Sandman. ♦ The Tooth Fairy. ♦ Your Guardian Angel.

Loser

A good loser is . . . a loser. ♦ A three-time loser. ♦ Behind the 8-ball. ♦ Born to lose. ♦ Curses, foiled again. ♦ (F*cked by) the fickle finger of fate. ♦ Left holding one's hands on one's *ss. ♦ On a losing streak. ♦ On the schneid. ♦ The first thing a loser is apt to lose is his temper. ♦ To be a sore loser. ♦ To be a spoil sport. ♦ To be/get skunked. ♦ To be/get stiffed. ♦ To get the green weenie. ♦ To go whistling for [it]. ♦ To lose one's eyeteeth (on). ♦ To lose one's shirt.

♦ To take a bath/loss (on). ♦ To take it on the chin/chops. ♦ To take one's lumps. ♦ To win the booby prize. ♦ Whistling in the dark/wind. ♦ You'll whistle for it.

Loss

A losing proposition. ♦ A loss leader. ♦ A staggering loss. ♦ Butterfingers! [see also Clumsy] ♦ Deficit spending. ♦ Famous lost words. ♦ Finders keepers, losers weepers. ♦ Go by the board. ♦ It's the want of it not the worth of it. ♦ Loss of capital. ♦ Lost in space. ♦ Lost in the shuffle. ♦ Missing and presumed dead. ♦ Missing in action. ♦ My bucket's got a hole in it. ♦ Not responsible for lost property. ♦ Nowhere to be found. ♦ Right out from under one's nose. ♦ Slip (right) through one's fingers/through the cracks. ♦ Slipsies! ♦ The Lost Generation. ♦ Their loss is our gain. ♦ To be aced out. ♦ To be in the hole/the red. ♦ To miss the boat. ♦ We never seek things for themselves but for the search. ♦ What's easily lost is not worth keeping. — Angela Maria Delia ♦ You can't win ('em all). ♦ You can't win for losing. ♦ You never miss the water till the well runs dry.

Love

A love triangle. ♦ A loving couple. ♦ A mother's love is blind. ♦ A teenage crush. ♦ A whirlwind romance. [see also Hurry] ♦ All the world loves a lover. ♦ Ever lovers, never friends. ♦ Follow love and it will flee; flee love and it will follow. ♦ Greater love hath no man than to lay down his life for his friends. ♦ Head over heels in love. ♦ Hopelessly, helplessly in love. ♦ Hot love soon cool. ♦ I love you (very much). ♦ In spring, a young man's fancy turns to thoughts of love. ♦ It is better to flunk your Wasserman than never to have loved at all. ♦ It is better to have loved and lost than never to have loved at all. ♦ Love and foolishness differ from one another only in name. ♦ Love at first sight. ♦ Love conquers all. ♦ Love is a feather bed and a maidenhead. ♦ Love is a four-letter word. ♦ Love is above it. ♦ Love is blind. ♦ Love is in the air. ♦ Love is just around the corner. ♦ Love is the inability to resist. ♦ Love is the joy of the good, the wonder of the wise, the amazement of the Gods. ♦ Love is where you find it. ♦ Love laughs at locksmiths. ♦ Love makes the world go round. ♦ Love me little, love me long. ♦ Love one another, as I have loved you. ♦ Love is not always in the loving cup. ♦ Love thy neighbor as thyself. ♦ Love will find a way. [see also Inexorable] ♦ Love will overlook anything—except being overlooked. ♦ Loving cup. ♦ Madly in love. ♦ Make love, not war. ♦ One's main squeeze. ♦ One's significant other. ♦ Parrot falls in love with a duck: "Polly wants a quacker." ♦ Puppy love. ♦ Purple passion. ♦ Somebody/someone special. ♦ That special someone. ♦ Tender loving care. (TLC). ♦ The course of true love never did run smooth. ♦ The love bug will get you if you don't watch out. ♦ The love of one's life. ♦ The object of one's affection. ♦ There's a thin line between love and hate. ♦ Those nearest and dearest. ♦ To be loved, be lovable. ♦ To be romantically involved. ♦ To carry the torch for [so]. ♦ To do it out of love. ♦ To fall in love. ♦ To feel the love. ♦ To know me is to love me. ♦ To love [it]/[so] to pieces. ♦ To love [it]/[so] more than life itself. ♦ To pitch woo. ♦ Two hearts beating as one. ♦ Torrid love scenes. ♦ To shower [so] with affection. ♦ Unbridled passion. ♦ Unconditional love. ♦ Will you still love me when I'm old and grey? ♦ With no bread and no wine, even love will pine. ♦ You always hurt the one you love.

Low

A lowdown cuss. ♦ As low as a spittoon in a saloon. ♦ As low as you can get. ♦ How low can you go? ♦ I wouldn't lower myself. ♦ Low as a bedbug's balls. ♦ Low as Hell. ♦ I wouldn't sink/stoop to his/her level. ♦ Lower than a snake's *sshole/belly. ♦ Lower than whalesh*t—and that's at the bottom of the ocean. ♦ Not fit to lick your boots.

Loyalty

A hired hand/gun. ♦ A hungry man cares little about the character of the person who's feeding him. ♦ Dance with the one who brung you. ♦ Don't bite the hand that feeds you. ♦ Follow the leader. ♦ Follow to the ends of the earth. ♦ No man can serve two masters. ♦ One raven will never poke another raven's eye out. ♦ *Semper fidelis.* ♦ Stand by your man. ♦ To be a lifelong/sworn [n.]. ♦ To stand by [so]. ♦ To stick with [so]. ♦ To know which side one's bread is buttered on. ♦ True blue. ♦ You've gotta believe.

Luck

(also superstition)
A four-leaf clover is good luck. ♦ A horseshoe is good luck. ♦ A lucky buck/duck/stiff. ♦ A lucky streak. ♦ A

rabbit's foot is good luck. ♦ A stroke of luck. ♦ A losing/winning streak. ♦ As luck would have it. [see also Accident] ♦ As long as one's luck holds out. ♦ Beginner's luck. ♦ Better to luck out than to be out of luck. ♦ Born under a lucky star. ♦ Break a leg. ♦ By blind luck. ♦ Don't push your luck. ♦ Dumb luck. ♦ How lucky can you get? ♦ I should be so lucky. ♦ I wish you all the luck in the world. ♦ It's in the cards. ♦ Just my luck. ♦ Keep your fingers (and toes) crossed. ♦ Fingers crossed. [see also Religion] ♦ Knock (on) wood (alt., touch wood). ♦ Lots of luck. ♦ Luck is the idol of the idle. ♦ Of all the luck! ♦ Rotsa ruck. ♦ Some are born lucky, others lucky to be born. ♦ Some people have all the luck. ♦ St. Patrick charmed all the snakes out of Ireland. ♦ The harder you work, the luckier you get. ♦ The luck of the draw. ♦ The luck of the Irish. ♦ Third time's a charm. ♦ This must be my lucky day. ♦ To be in luck. ♦ To be in the right place at the right time. ♦ To be the best thing that ever happened to [so]. ♦ To catch a (lucky) break. ♦ To come out/up smelling like a rose. [see also Rejuvenation] ♦ To count oneself lucky. ♦ To have an open *ss. ♦ To have it fall into one's lap. ♦ To have open-*ssed luck. ♦ To have things go one's way. ♦ To lead a charmed life. ♦ To luck into [it]. ♦ To luck out. ♦ To make out like a bandit. ♦ To open an umbrella indoors is bad luck. ♦ To (step in sh*t and) come out smelling like a rose. ♦ To succeed in spite of one's self. ♦ To take pot luck. ♦ To win by default. ♦ While you are waiting for luck to walk through the door, it flies in through the window. ♦ Wish me luck. ♦ With a little bit of luck. ♦ With any luck at all. ♦ You don't need intelligence to have luck but you need luck to have intelligence. ♦ You lucky dog. ♦ You make your own luck. ♦ You should be so lucky. ♦ You've got to be in it to win it.

Manners

As the ship sails the sea, I move my spoon away from me. ♦ Barroom manners. ♦ Good manners and good morals are sworn friends and fast allies. ♦ In a manner of speaking. ♦ Keep a civil tongue. ♦ Manners make the man. ♦ Manners will get you where money won't. ♦ Mind your manners. ♦ Table manners. ♦ To have a good bedside manner.

Marginal

A buzzer-beater. ♦ A close call/ shave. [see also Almost, Close] ♦ By a gnat's hair. ♦ By a hair's breadth. ♦ By a slight margin. ♦ Close enough. ♦ Get in/make it by the seat of one's pants. ♦ Get in/make it under the wire. ♦ In the nick of time. ♦ It'll do in a pinch. ♦ Just in time. ♦ (Just) squeak by. ♦ Just under the wire. ♦ Make a shoestring catch. ♦ None/not a moment too soon. ♦ None too [adj.]/[adv.]. ♦ Not by much. ♦ Shoehorn it in. ♦ Something is better than nothing. ♦ To barely make it. ♦ To beat the clock. ♦ To get by (by the skin of one's teeth). ♦ To hit (too) close to home. ♦ To just make it. ♦ To muddle through. ♦ To win on points. ♦ Too close for comfort. ♦ With not a moment/second to spare. ♦ Without so much as.

Marriage

A man is incomplete until he's married. Then he's finished. ♦ A marriage/match made in heaven. ♦ A marriage of convenience. ♦ A shotgun wedding. [see also Compel] ♦ A wedding band. ♦ Already spoken for. ♦ But would you want your daughter to marry one? ♦ Connubial bliss. ♦ Dearly beloved, we are gathered here. ♦ Don't marry a woman who you love; marry a woman who loves you. ♦ Engaged to be married. ♦ Exchange vows. ♦ First comes love, then comes marriage; then comes baby in a baby carriage! ♦ For success in marriage, treat all disasters as incidents and no incidents as disasters. ♦ How much does it cost to get married? I don't know, I'm still paying. ♦ I want a girl just like the girl who married dear old dad. ♦ It is better for a woman to marry a man who loves her than a man she loves. ♦ Joined in holy matrimony. ♦ Keep your eyes open before marriage, half shut afterwards. ♦ Life partners. ♦ Love and marriage: you can't have one without the other. ♦ Man is the head of the house; woman is the neck that turns the head. ♦ Marriage: a ceremony in which the ring goes on the girl's finger and through the man's nose. ♦ Marriage is a great institution—if you want to live in one. ♦ Marriage is love parsonified. ♦ Marriage is the process of finding out what sort of a man your wife would have preferred. ♦ Marriage licenses should first require a learner's permit. ♦ Marriage on the rocks. ♦ Marriages are made in heaven. ♦ Married men don't live longer; it just seems longer. ♦ Marry for money, my little sonny, a rich man's joke is always funny. ♦ Marry in haste, repent at leisure. ♦ Mother said I could marry anybody I pleased; trouble is, I never pleased anybody. ♦ Pop the question. ♦ Puppy love is often the start of a dog's life. ♦ Socrates, when asked, is it better to get married or remain single, replied: "Whatever you do you will regret." ♦ Take the plunge. ♦ The betrothed. ♦ The blushing bride. ♦ The marital bonds. ♦ The marrying kind. ♦ The ties that bind. ♦ Tie the knot. ♦ 'Tis better to marry than to burn. ♦ To be/get engaged. ♦ To get hitched. ♦ To give/take one's hand in marriage. ♦ To grow old together. ♦ To have and to hold, from this day forward, for better, for worse, for richer, for poorer, in sickness and in health, until death do us part. ♦ To live as husband and wife. ♦ To make an honest woman out of her. ♦ To marry into money. ♦ To marry is to halve one's rights (and double one's duties). ♦ To marry one's daughter off. ♦ To plight one's troth (with) ♦ To put the ring on her finger. ♦ To publish the banns of marriage. ♦ To put down roots. ♦ To settle down and raise a family. ♦ To set the date. ♦ To walk down the aisle. ♦ We've got to stay together for the kids' sake. ♦ Wedded and bedded. ♦ What God has joined together, let no man put asunder. ♦

What groom is brave enough to tell his bride the true reason he prays before every meal? ♦ What's marriage? Just a piece of paper. ♦ What's a wedding without a bride? ♦ When am I getting married? The day after the Pope. ♦ Why any man wants a wife is a mystery; why any man wants more than one wife is a bigamystery. ♦ Who's the lucky guy? ♦ With this ring, I thee wed.

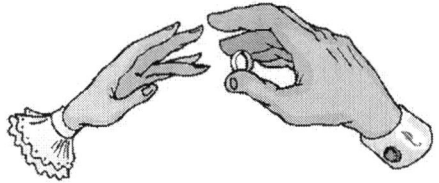

♦ You can only marry one.

Masculine

A big bruiser. ♦ A chiseled torso. ♦ A doting father/husband. ♦ A sculpted physique. ♦ A family man. ♦ A (gorgeous) hunk of man. ♦ A he-man. ♦ A gentleman's gentleman. ♦ A macho man. ♦ A (real) "hunk." ♦ A regular Charles Atlas. ♦ A stag party. ♦ An able-bodied man. ♦ Are you man enough? ♦ Every inch a man. ♦ He has muscles on top of his muscles. ♦ I don't know whether it's a Greek god or a g*ddamn Greek. ♦ In this man's army. ♦ Joe Adonis. ♦

Male chauvinist pig. ◆ Me Tarzan, you Jane. ◆ Mr. Fixit. ◆ Mr. Macho. ◆ The strong silent type. ◆ To be a man's man. ◆ To have one's mojo working.

Maybe

A definite maybe. ◆ A dicey situation. ◆ A fifty-fifty chance. ◆ A qualified yes. ◆ A distinct possibility. ◆ A remote possibility. ◆ Anything's possible. ◆ Barring unforeseen circumstances. ◆ Could (very well) be. ◆ Endless possibilities. ◆ God willin' and the creek don't rise. ◆ If need be. ◆ If/should that be the case. ◆ I'll see what I can do. ◆ If you play your cards right. ◆ In/within the realm of possibility. ◆ It could/might (just) come to that. ◆ It/that remains to be seen. ◆ It's not carved in stone/etched in granite. ◆ It's not out of the question. ◆ It's possibly impossible. ◆ Mayhaps. ◆ On the off chance. ◆ Should the need arise. ◆ Stranger things have happened. ◆ To admit the possibility. ◆ The possibilities are endless. ◆ To be or not to be, that is the question. ◆ To stand a chance. ◆ We can't guarantee/promise/say that won't happen. ◆ (Well,) yes and no.

Mean

A dog in the manger. ◆ A (mean) son of a gun. ◆ A real pr*ck. ◆ A real stinker. ◆ A son of a bitch. (SOB). ◆ A stinkeroo. ◆ An ornery cuss. ◆ Did you take nasty pills this morning? ◆ Got up on the wrong side of the bed. ◆ Have the rag on. ◆ She/he is in one of her/his moods. ◆ It must be that time of the month. ◆ I guess he/she didn't get any last night. ◆ Lean and mean. ◆ Mean as a lizard's gizzard. ◆ Meaner than a junkyard dog. ◆ Meaner than a striped snake. ◆ Meaner than a two-headed snake. ◆ Sheesh, what a grouch. ◆ To be mean-spirited. ◆ To have a mean streak. ◆ What crawled up your *ss and died? ◆ What's bugging/eating you? ◆ What's gotten into you?

Meddle

A buttinsky. ◆ Alienation of affection. ◆ Those, who in thoughts interpose, prepare to wipe a bloody nose. ◆ To barge in. ◆ To butt in. ◆ To establish a beachhead. ◆ To get a foot/toe in the door. [see also Progress] ◆ To horn in (on). ◆ To insinuate oneself (into). ◆ To keep one's finger in the pie. ◆ To listen in. ◆ To muscle in (on). ◆ To poke/stick one's nose where it doesn't belong.

[see also Nose] ◆ To wheedle/worm (one's way) into.

Medical

A medical discharge. ◆ A practicing physician. ◆ A pecker-check. ◆ A short-arm inspection. ◆ Bend over and grab your ankles. ◆ Bend over and touch your toes. ◆ Call a doctor. ◆ Doctors bury their mistakes. ◆ Fond of lawsuits, little wealth; fond of doctors, little health. [see also Law] ◆ God cures the patients but the doctors collect the fees. ◆ If the condition persists, see your doctor. ◆ Irritable bowel syndrome. ◆ Is there a doctor in the house? ◆ Open wide and say ahh. ◆ Physician, heal thyself. ◆ Socialized medicine. ◆ St. Vitus' Dance. ◆ Take only as directed. ◆ Take two aspirins and call me in the morning. ◆ The doctor will see you now. ◆ To balm /salve one's wounds. ◆ To catch a dose (of the clap). ◆ To go into cardiac arrest. ◆ To go under the knife. ◆ To have a coronary. ◆ To minister to [so]'s needs. ◆ To play Nancy Nurse. ◆ To see a shrink. ◆ To seek medical attention. ◆ Turn your head (to one side) and cough. ◆ When the patient is under the knife, the surgeon is under the gun. – R.D. ◆ You (really) should see someone about that.

Meek

A candy-ass. ◆ A shrinking violet. ◆ A Walter Mitty type. ◆ In like a lion, out like a lamb. ◆ Meek and mild. ◆ Meek as a lamb. ◆ Meekness does not equal weakness. ◆ The meek shall inherit the earth. ◆ Underneath it all, he's really a pussycat. ◆ Wouldn't harm a fly.

Menstruation

A visit from Aunt Flo. ◆ At my pill-popping stage. ◆ Checked in at the Red Roof Inn. ◆ Got/on my period. ◆ Got the Curse. ◆ Miss Scarlett's come home to Tara. ◆ Rebooting the OSS (Ovarian Operating System). ◆ Ridin' the cotton pony. ◆ Sanitary napkins. ◆ Shark Week. ◆ Taking Carrie to the prom. ◆ That time of the month. ◆ To be on the rag. ◆ To be wearing the red flag. ◆ To have your Aunt. ◆ To have your "friend." ◆ To have your aunt from Red Bank.

Merciless

A cruel twist of fate. ◆ A take-no-prisoners approach. [see also Intensity] ◆ Cold-blooded. ◆ Cold-hearted. ◆ Cruel and unusual punishment.

♦ Cruelty to animals. ♦ Draconian measures. ♦ Heart of stone. ♦ In cold blood. ♦ Man playing wolf to man. ♦ Man's inhumanity to man. ♦ Show no quarter. ♦ Stone cold. ♦ Take no prisoners. ♦ Thin-lipped. ♦ To be into S&M. ♦ To have ice water in one's veins. ♦ Tough love. ♦ You've got to be cruel to be kind.

Messy

A real sty. ♦ Abject filth. ♦ Abject squalor. ♦ At ease, disease, there's a fungus among us. ♦ Like a pig-pen. ♦ Look for dirt and you will find it. ♦ Looks like an explosion in a hayloft. ♦ The creeping crud. ♦ This place looks like a cyclone hit it. ♦ To foul one's own nest. ♦ To live in (abject) squalor. ♦ To make a mess (of). ♦ To wallow in the mire. ♦ What a dump.

Misbehavior

Acting like a bozo. ♦ Act one's age. ♦ Acting like a two-year-old child. ♦ Bad to the bone. ♦ Conduct un-befitting an officer (and a gentle-man). ♦ He's/she's a handful. ♦ Men behaving badly. ♦ Nicholas, don't be so ridiculous. ♦ Peck's bad boy. ♦ To abuse the privilege. ♦ To act out. ♦ To act up/cut up. ♦ To be out

of order. [see also Inoperative] ♦ To be/get/step out of line. ♦ To kick over the traces. ♦ To live in sin. ♦ To overstep one's bounds. ♦ To raise eyebrows. ♦ To throw a tantrum. ♦ When [n.]/[p.] was bad, [n.]/[p.] was very, very bad.

Moderation

Don't burn the barn to kill the rats. ♦ Don't crush walnuts with a sledge-hammer. ♦ Don't fix what ain't broke. (var. If it ain't broke, don't fix it). ♦ Don't make traumas of trifles; don't shoot butterflies with rifles! ♦ Don't pound at an open door. ♦ Don't preach to the choir.

♦ Don't teach your grandmother to suck eggs. ♦ Don't use a cannon for a flyswatter. ♦ Don't use an elephant gun to kill an ant. ♦ Moderation in all things. ♦ Never waste powder on a dead duck. ♦ Why use a pitchfork to drive out a frog?

Money

A buck is a buck. ♦ A C-note. ♦ A cool million. ♦ A dollar's not a dollar anymore. ♦ A double saw. ♦ A double sawbuck. ♦ A fin. ♦ A finsky. ♦ A fiver. ♦ A grand. ♦ A sawbuck. ♦ A yard. ♦ All things go on green. ♦ An itchy left palm means money will soon come to you. [see also Truisms] ♦ Another day, another dollar; squeeze a nickel 'til the buffalo hollers. * ♦ Another day, another dollar; squeeze the eagle 'til he holler. *[see also Stingy] ♦ Anything for a buck. ♦ Bought and paid for. ♦ Cash and carry. ♦ Cash in hand. ♦ Cash on the barrelhead. ♦ Coin of the realm. ♦ Cold cash. ♦ Cold, hard cash. ♦ Come up with the money. ♦ Dead presidents. ♦ Don't put your trust in money, put your money in trust. ♦ Dough ray mi. ♦ Easy money. ♦ Filthy lucre. ♦ Follow the money. ♦ For what is worth in anything, as so much in money as 'twill bring? ♦ Front money. ♦ Get a run for one's money. ♦ He who thinks money can do anything, may be suspected of doing anything for money. ♦ I don't want to be a millionaire; I just want to live like one. ♦ If I had your money, I'd burn mine. ♦ If you don't tell your money where to go, it will go everywhere. ♦ If you have a problem that money can solve, you don't have a problem. ♦ If you've got the money, honey, I've got the time. ♦ It all spends. ♦ It takes money to make money. ♦ It's all about the money. ♦ It's not the money; it's the principle of the thing. ♦ It's nothing that time and money won't cure. ♦ It's only money. ♦ Ill-gotten gains. ♦ Jingle in your pocket. ♦ Lack of money is the root of all evil. ♦ Legal tender (for all debts public and private). ♦ Liquid assets. ♦ Man does not live by bread alone. ♦ Money borrowed is money spent. ♦ Money can't buy happiness. (But it buys a pretty good facsimile!) ♦ Money changed hands. ♦ Money costs money. ♦ Money doesn't grow on trees, but every bank has branches. ♦ Money doesn't grow on trees. ♦ Money hungry. ♦ Money is a good servant but a bad master. ♦ Money is life's report card. ♦ Money is like holy water; everybody dips his fingers in. ♦ Money is no object. ♦ Money is power. ♦ Money is the root of all evil. ♦ Money is the rules of old eagles. [Uncle Baron] ♦ Money isn't everything. (But it helps)! ♦ Money makes money. ♦ Money makes the man. ♦ Money matters. ♦ Money, money, thou art so holy; I often wonder how you can go out so fast and come in so slowly. ♦ Money not wasted is called profit. ♦ Money talks. ♦ Money talks; bullsh*t walks. ♦ Never be money weak; you meet an obstacle and cannot budget. ♦ Other people's money. ♦ Put your money where your mouth is. [see also Immediacy] ♦ Ready cash. ♦ Seed money. ♦ Show me the money. ♦ Smackeroos/smackers. ♦ Some people are always against money—as long as others have it. ♦ Spending money. ♦ That kind of money. ♦ The eagle sh*ts today. ♦ The first million is the hardest. ♦ The love of money is the root of all evil. ♦ The only sure way to double your money is to fold it in two. ♦ There are some things money can't buy. ♦ Time is money. (But money is not time. — R.D.) ♦ To get more/the most bang for your buck. ♦ To get your money's worth. ♦ To have money to burn. ♦ To have more money than God. ♦ To have more money than Fort Knox. ♦ To be (out) spending money. ♦ To have spending money. ♦ To lay even money on. ♦ To make a ton of money. ♦ To make change. ♦ To make money by the bushel. ♦ To make money hand over fist. ♦ To pay/get blood money. ♦ To plunk down one's hard-earned money. ♦ Two bits. ♦ Walking around money. ♦ What do you think, I'm made of money? ♦ Whatever money can buy. ♦ When money talks, nobody pays attention to the grammar. ♦ Cash in hand. ♦ (Yankee) greenback dollar bills. ♦ You can't take it with you. ♦ You say you're not satisfied? You say you want more for your money? Tell you what I'm going to do. ♦ Your money or your life. ♦ You've got to spend money to make money.

More

All this and more. ♦ Bigger is not necessarily better. ♦ More bounce to the ounce. ♦ More for your money. ♦ More (than that) I cannot say. ♦ More [n.] than Carter has Little Liver Pills. ♦ More [n.] than Quaker has oats. ♦ More than meets the eye. ♦ More than one bargained for. ♦ More than you can shake a snake at. — R.D. ♦ More than you can shake a stick at. ♦ More to come. ♦ The more, the merrier. ♦ To a greater extent. ♦ What more do you want? ♦ What more can you ask? ♦ Who could ask for anything more?

Mother

A mother knows. ♦ A stay-at-home mom/mother. ♦ Coming, mother! ♦ Does your mother know you're out? ♦ Honor thy father and mother. ♦ I'm going home to mother. ♦ Like a mother hen. ◆ Mother Earth. ◆ Mother knows best. ◆ Mother Nature. ◆ Mother Wit. ◆ Not while you're living under my roof. ◆ *One day to honor mothers/Is really not enough/For who else ever bothers/To care for us so much?/Suitor, lover, fiancée/Teacher, counselor, spouse/None will love us constantly/The way our mother does/So God bless every mother/On this and every day/We never get another/For all eternity.* — R.D. ◆ Please, mother, I'd rather do it myself. ◆ Step on a crack and break your mother's back. ◆ The hand that rocks the cradle rules the world. ◆ The kind of girl you'd bring home to mother. ◆ The miserable daughter makes the talented mother. ◆ The motherland. ◆ Why mothers get grey! — Angela Maria Delia

Motion

A whirling dervish. ◆ And away we go. ◆ A gathering storm. ◆ A storm brewing. ◆ Batter up! ◆ Better wear out shoes than sheets. ◆ Build up a head of steam. ◆ Gather momentum. ◆ Get cracking. ◆ Get in the groove. ◆ Here we go loop de loop. ◆ Hit one's stride. ◆ Hop to it. [see also Hurry] ◆ Mirth and motion prolong life. ◆ Off and running. (Often running). ◆ On the hoof. ◆ On the way home. ◆ One hot dog to go/on wheels/rolling. ◆ Perpetual motion. ◆ Rack 'em up. ◆ Ride 'em cowboy! ◆ Ring around the rosie. ◆ Round and round and round she goes; where she stops nobody knows. ◆ Round robin. ◆ Shift into high gear. ◆ The fat's in the fire. ◆ Three moves are as bad as a fire. ◆ To build to a climax/crescendo. [see also Progress] ◆ To come full circle. ◆ To go round and round. ◆ Up and running.

Motionless

A logjam. ◆ At a virtual standstill. ◆ Bound hand and foot. ◆ Come to a dead stop. ◆ Caught in a time warp. ◆ Come to a screeching halt. ◆ Don't anybody make a move. ◆ Don't make any false moves. ◆ Don't move a muscle. ◆ Don't touch that dial! ◆ Freeze in your tracks. ◆ Frozen assets. ◆ Frozen in time. ◆ Grind to a halt. ◆ Hang fire. ◆ Hold it. ◆ Hold it (right) there/where you are. ◆ Hold that pose. ◆ In limbo. ◆ In suspended animation. ◆ Is this an audience or an oil painting? ◆ Paralysis by analysis. ◆ Rooted to the spot. ◆ Stay put. ◆ Stay (right) there. ◆ Stay (right) where you are. ◆ Stick around. ◆ Stiff as a board. ◆ Stop cold. ◆ Time in a bottle. ◆ Time stands/stood still. ◆ To grind to a halt. ◆ To hold [it] in abeyance. ✦ To seize up. ✦ To stand pat. ✦ To stand (stock) still. ✦ To stop on a dime. ✦ To stop cold/short. ✦ To stop [n.]/[p.] in [p.] tracks. [see also Quit] ✦ Watch the birdie.

Music

A gentle refrain. ✦ A haunting melody/refrain. ✦ A pretty girl is like a melody. ✦ Ah, one, and ah, two. ✦ An earworm. ✦ And the band played on. ✦ Beat me, daddy, eight to the bar. ✦ Dulcet tones. ✦ Elevator music. ✦ Every good boy deserves fudge. ✦ Every good boy does fine. ✦ Goodnight, Irene. ✦ If music be the food of love, play on. ✦ Longhair music. [see also Stodgy] ✦ Music hath charms to soothe the savage beast/breast. ✦ Music is the food of love. ✦ Music, maestro, please. ✦ Music to your ears. ✦ Name that tune. ✦ Stop the music. ✦ Strike up the band. ✦ To carry a tune. ✦ To tickle the ivories. ✦ We could make such beautiful music together.

Mystery

A murder mystery. ✦ A page-turner. ✦ A whodunnit? ✦ An air of mystery. ✦ By person or persons unknown. ✦ Cloaked/shrouded in mystery. ✦ God only knows. ✦ One of the great unsolved mysteries of all time. ✦ That's the Sixty-Four-Dollar Question. ✦ Twinkle, twinkle, little star, how I wonder what you are. ✦ To unravel the mystery. ✦ What was that all about? ✦ Who knows what evil lurks in the hearts of men? The Shadow knows. ✦ Who was that masked man? ✦ Why any man wants a wife is a mystery; why any man wants more than one wife is a bigga mystery.

Nag

A gentle reminder. ✦ A good, swift kick (in the *ss). ✦ A noodge. ✦ A tickler file. ✦ Get along, little dogie. ✦ Get off one's (dead) *ss. ✦ Give [so] a hard/rough time. ✦ Light a fire under. ✦ Jog one's memory. ✦ Refresh one's memory. ✦ To dwell/harp on. ✦ To give [so] a zinger. ✦ To rub [it] in. ✦ To rub salt into the wounds.

Naked

Au naturel. ✦ Balls-*ss naked. ✦ Buck nekkid. ✦ Full-frontal nudity. ✦ In the altogether/buff/raw. ✦ In one's birthday suit. ✦ Let's get naked. ✦ Make it naked. ✦ Naked ambition/lust. ✦ Naked as a jaybird. ✦ Naked as the day he/she was born. ✦ Not a stitch (of clothing) on. ✦ Not wearing a stitch. ✦ Stark naked/nekkid.

♦ Stripper: one who takes it from the top—and bottom! ♦ To drop trou. ♦ To go bare*ss. ♦ To go skinny-dipping. ♦ To moon [so]. ♦ Without a stitch (of clothing) on.

Names

A rose by any other name would smell as sweet. ♦ A rose is a rose is a rose. ♦ Call me anything but don't call me late for dinner.* ♦ Call me anything you like but call me. *[see also Forbearance, Slander] ♦ Empty heads are fond of long titles. ♦ I don't care what they call me as long as they mention my name. ♦ I don't care what they print about me as long as they spell my name right. ♦ In name only. [see also Insincere] ♦ Miss, Mrs. or Ms.? ♦ Sticks and stones will break my bones but names will never hurt me. ♦ Stop! In the name of the law. ♦ That/[it] is my middle name. ♦ The [n.] have a word for it. ♦ To go by the name of. ♦ What's in a name?

Nature

A breathtaking view. ♦ A call of nature. ♦ A natural born [n.]. [see also Capability] ♦ All-natural. ♦ Doing what comes naturally. ♦ Don't B sharp; don't B flat; just B natural. [see also Self] ♦ In its natural habitat. ♦ In the nature of things. ♦ It's only natural. ♦ Let Nature take its course. ♦ Mother Earth. ♦ Mother Nature. ♦ Nature abhors a vacuum. ♦ Of natural causes. ♦ Survival is the first law of nature. ♦ The great outdoors ♦ The mighty Mississippi. ♦ The nature of the beast. ♦ To be a natural. ♦ To be second nature. ♦ To have [it] in one's blood. ♦ We are all Mother Nature's children. ♦ You can't fool Mother Nature.

Nausea

A wave of nausea. ♦ An upset stomach. ♦ Barf bag. ♦ Green around the gills. ♦ It must have been something I/you ate. ♦ *Mal de mer.* ♦ Projectile vomit. ♦ Sick to one's stomach. ♦ To be grossed out. ♦ To blow chunks. ♦ To hurl. ♦ To have the dry heaves. ♦ To heave up one's guts. ♦ To lose one's lunch. ♦ To serve up a dog's breakfast. ♦ To toss one's cookies. ♦ To turn one's stomach. ♦ To throw up. ♦ To upchuck.

Necessity

A must. ♦ A must-have. ♦ A staple of one's diet. ♦ [n.]? We don't need no stinking [n.]! ♦ I need this like I need a hole in the head. [ironic/sarcastic] ♦ If you have to, you have to. ♦ Invention is the child of necessity. ♦ Is this really necessary? ♦ It ain't necessarily so. ♦ Necessity is the mother of invention. ♦ Necessity is the invention of mothers. – R.D. ♦ No [n.] is complete without [it]. ♦ No tickee, no laundry/shirtee. ♦ Not necessarily. ♦ That's all I need. [ironic/sarcastic] ♦ The end justifies the means. ♦ The *sine qua non.* ♦ To make a virtue of necessity. ♦ We don't need no education. ♦ Who needs it? ♦ You've gotta do what you've gotta do.

Negotiate

A bargaining chip. ♦ A (mere) pawn in the negotiations. ♦ A wheeler-dealer. ♦ Collective bargaining. ♦ Conflict resolution. ♦ Everything's negotiable. ♦ Hondle with care. ♦ No money down. ♦ To chew the price down. ♦ To deal from (a position of) strength. ♦ To drive a (hard) bargain. ♦ To hondle. ♦ To negotiate a turn. ♦ To negotiate from strength. ♦ To schnorr. ♦ To strike a bargain. ♦ To wheel and deal.

Nervous

(also anxiety, suspense)

A basket case. ♦ A bundle of nerves. ♦ A cliffhanger. ♦ A nail-biter. ♦ A nervous Nelly. ♦ A nervous wreck.

♦ A panic attack. ♦ A war of nerves. [see also Conflict] ♦ All keyed up. ♦ All shook up. ♦ All wound up like a two-dollar watch. ♦ An emotional wreck. ♦ Biting one's nails. ♦ Bouncing off the walls. ♦ Butterflies in one's stomach. ♦ Climbing (the) walls. ♦ Coming apart at the seams. ♦ Drum roll, please. ♦ Fiddle-footed. ♦ Going up a wall. ♦ I can't cope! ♦ Go (all) to pieces. ♦ Nervous as a bridegroom. ♦ Nervous as a long-tailed cat in a roomful of rockers. ♦ Nervous as a pregnant fox in a forest fire. ♦ Nervous as a rabbit in a cage of rattlesnakes. ♦ Nervous as a whore in church. ♦ Nervous as an old maid. ♦ Nervous in/from the service. ♦ Nervous laughter. ♦ On edge. ♦ On pins and needles. ♦ On tenterhooks. ♦ On the edge of one's seat. ♦ Shell-shocked. ♦ Skittish as a newborn calf/colt. ♦ Stage fright. ♦ Stressed out. ♦ Strung out. ♦ The envelope, please. ♦ The natives are restless tonight. ♦ The suspense is killing me. ♦ To make buttons. ♦ To make [so] nervous. ♦ Taut as a bowstring. ♦ To be (all) rattled. ♦ To be beside oneself. ♦ To be climbing the walls. ♦ To be trigger happy. ♦ To be wired. ♦ To bite one's fingernails. ♦ To come apart at the seams. ♦ To come unglued/

unstuck. ♦ To go (all) to pieces. ♦ To have a meltdown. ♦ To have a nervous breakdown. ♦ To have an itchy trigger finger. ♦ To have ants in one's pants. ♦ To have/set one's mind racing. ♦ To have the creeps/heebie-jeebies/jitters/willies. ♦ To make buttons. ♦ To pace the floor. ♦ To set one's teeth on edge. ♦ To sweat it out. ♦ Unchecked emotions. ♦ Wound tighter than an 8-day clock. ♦ You could cut the tension with a knife.

Nervy

A snot-nosed kid. ♦ Nervy little bastard, isn't he? ♦ Of all the (colossal) nerve/unmitigated gall. ♦ Sassier than a jay. ♦ That takes a lot of nerve. ♦ The balls of him to say something like that. ♦ The nerve of some people! ♦ To be ballsy/pushy. ♦ To be cheeky. ♦ To be cocksure. ♦ To be self-assured. ♦ To be sure of oneself. ♦ To have a bulldog personality. ♦ To have (a lot of) balls/cheek. ♦ To have (a lot of) *chutzpah*. ♦ To have (big) *cojones*. ♦ To have the balls/cheek/chutzpah/effrontery/gall/nerve/stones/temerity (to).

New

A babe in the woods. ♦ A Johnny-come-lately. ♦ A new angle. ♦ A new twist/wrinkle. ♦ Batteries not included. ♦ Brand-new. ♦ Brand spanking new. ♦ Factory fresh. ♦ Fresh off the boat. ♦ Hot off the press. ♦ Just off the (banana) boat. ♦ Never seen the likes of. ♦ New to these parts. ♦ Not from around here. ♦ Right out of the box. ♦ The new kid on the block. ♦ Untouched by human hands. ♦ Where have you been all my life?

News

A human interest story. ♦ All the news all the time. ♦ "All the news that's fit to print." [motto of The New York Times] ♦ An all-points bulletin. ♦ Bad news travels fast. ♦ Breaker, breaker. ♦ Breaking news. ♦ By word of mouth. ♦ Dog bites man isn't news: Man bites dog is news. ♦ Evening news is where they begin with 'Good evening', then proceed to tell you why it isn't. ♦ Extra! Extra! Read all about it! ♦ Get it straight from the horse's mouth. ♦ Glad tidings. ♦ Have I got news for you. ♦ Here's the deal/scoop. ♦ Hot off the press. ♦ I have good news and bad news. ♦ I have news for you. ♦ I regret to inform you. ♦ Informed sources say. [see also Detect, Gossip] ♦ Late-breaking news. ♦ News flash. ♦ No news is good news. ♦ Oral tradition. ♦ So what else is new? [see also Bore] ♦ That's a new one on me. ♦ That's news to me. ♦ The Peanut Gallery is heard from. ♦ There's nothing deader than yesterday's news. ♦ This just in. ♦ This just in, from the west coast. ♦ To be the bearer of bad/ good tidings. ♦ To bruit [it] about. ♦ To check in with. ♦ To clue [so] in. ♦ To fill [so] in. ♦ To get the word out. ♦ To have it on good authority. ♦ To go public (with it). ♦ To hit the wind. ♦ To keep/stay in touch (with). ♦ To let [it] be known. ♦ To let [so] know. ♦ To make [it] known. ♦ To put it out there. ♦ To put out/send out the call. ♦ To put [so] wise (to). ♦ To serve notice. ♦ To shout it from the treetops. ♦ To spam. ♦ To spread the word. ♦ To talk [it] up. ♦ To touch base (with). ♦ To update [so]. ♦ Up-to-the-minute report. ♦ Verily I say unto you. ♦ What gets reported is history. ♦ What's black and white and read all over? A newspaper. ♦ What's new, gnu? ♦ What's new, pussycat? ♦ You'll be the first to know.

No

Absolutely not. ♦ By no means. ♦ By no stretch of the imagination. ♦ Naysayer: a "no" it all. — R.D. ♦ Negatory on that. ♦ No answer is also an answer. ♦ No answer is often an answer of no. ♦ No is no. ♦ No means no. ♦ No, no; a thousand times no. ♦ Out of the question. ♦ The right of first refusal. [see also Right] ♦ They always see all the negatives first. ♦ To say "nay" is not necessarily to show horse sense. ♦ Until you ask, the answer is always no. ♦ When I say no I mean no. ♦ Yes, we have no bananas.

None

And then there were none. ♦ Breathes there the man with soul so dead . . . ♦ Down to zero/zilch/zip. ♦ Nary a one/ soul. ♦ Nobody but nobody. ♦ None, at all, period. ♦ None whatsoever. ♦ Nary/not a soul. ♦ Not a soul around (for miles) (and miles). ♦ There ain't no such animal/thing.

Nose

A honker. ♦ A nose for news. ♦ A nose job. ♦ A runny nose. ♦ Eek, what a beak—is it a nose or a hose? ♦ It's as plain as the nose on your face. ♦ The old schnozzola. ♦ To brown-nose [so]. ♦ To count noses. ♦ To go wherever your nose leads you. ♦ To hit it right on the nose. ♦ To keep one's nose clean/to the grindstone. ♦ To nose around. ♦ To nose out. ♦ To poke/stick one's nose where it doesn't belong. [see also Meddle] ♦ To take a nosedive. ♦ To win by a nose.

Notoriety

It takes a very short time to lose a good reputation but a long, long time to regain it. ♦ Murderer's Row. ♦ Notoriety is short-lived; fame is lasting. ♦ Public Enemy Number One. ♦ Rogue's Gallery. ♦ The whipping boy. ♦ To have the dubious distinction [see also Uncertainty] ♦ Trust departs on horseback but returns on foot.

Now

Along/ right about now. ♦ As it (now) stands. ♦ As of now. ♦ As of this moment. ♦ At present. ♦ At the present moment/time. ♦ At this juncture/point. ♦ At this moment/point (in time). ♦ At this (particular) time. ♦ At this stage of the game. ♦ At this writing. ♦ By today's standards. ♦ Do it now. ♦ Effective immediately. ♦ (Even) as we speak. ♦ For the moment. ♦ Immediately, if not sooner. ♦ In medias res.* ♦ In the thick of (it).* ♦ In the throes of. *[see also Action] ♦ In this day and age. ♦ Living in the moment. ♦ Now is the time for all good men to come to the aid of their country. ♦ Now playing in a theater near you. ♦ Now this instant. ♦ Right away. ♦ (Right) here and now. ♦ Right now. ♦ The time is always now. ♦ This magic moment. ♦ To this (very) day. ♦ While we're on the subject. ♦ We need it yesterday.

Obedience

As long as you're living under my/our roof, you'll do as I/we say. ♦ Balls, said the queen: if I had to I'd be king. The king laughed, not because he wanted to but because he had two! ♦ By obeying we learn to rule. ♦ I was only following orders. ♦ Sh*t said the king, and a thousand *ssholes strained at the royal throne. ♦ To follow the chain of command.

Objectivity

A third party. ♦ A friend of the court. ♦ An impartial opinion. ♦ Keep an open mind. (Like a sieve? — R.D.) ♦ Never be so open-minded as to have holes in your logic. ♦ To be an impartial judge. ♦ To get/give a fair hearing. ♦ To keep one's options open. ♦ To listen to both sides of the story. ♦ To play (the) Devil's advocate. ♦ To suspend judgment.

Oblivious

Asleep at the switch/wheel. ♦ Blind as a bat. ♦ Blind in one eye and can't see out of the other. * ♦ Can't see past (the end of) one's nose. ♦ Can't see the forest for the trees. ♦ Completely in the dark. ♦ Deaf, dumb and blind. *[see also Handicapped] ♦ Doesn't have a clue/the slightest idea. ♦ In denial. ♦ In full/total denial. ♦ In for a rude awakening. ♦ Out of it. ♦ Out to lunch. ♦ Riding for a fall. ♦ There is none so blind as he who will not see. ♦ To be blindsided. ♦ To be clueless. ♦ To be lulled into a false sense of security. ♦ To be in for a big letdown/shock/surprise. ♦ To bury one's head in the sand. ♦ To have no idea. ♦ To have one's head up one's *ss.

Obsequies

And may her/his soul rest in peace. ♦ Ashes to ashes; dust to dust. ♦ He/she always had a kind word for everybody. ♦ He belongs to the ages now. ♦ He/she had everything to live for. ♦ He/she led a good life. ♦ He/she looks so natural. ♦ I want to remember her/him the way she/he was. ♦ Last remains. ♦ May he/she find eternal rest. ♦ Our dear departed brethren. ♦ They've done such a good job on her/him. ♦ To be in/go into mourning. ♦ To fly the flag at half mast. ♦ To go to one's final resting place/reward. ♦ To mourn the loss (of). ♦ To pay one's last respects.

Obvious

A crane standing amid a flock of chickens. ♦ A dead giveaway. ♦ A distinguishing feature. ♦ A no-brainer. ♦ A public display of affection. ♦ A swan among geese. ♦ An open-and-shut case. ♦ As anyone can see. ♦ As everybody knows. ♦ As clear/plain as black and white. ♦ As plain as day/daylight. ♦ As plain as the nose on your face. ♦ Can see [it] with half an eye. ♦ Could it be any clearer/plainer? ♦ Do I have to draw you a diagram/map/picture? ♦ Face up. ♦ For all the world to see. ♦ God gave you eyes to look. ♦ If it had teeth/was a snake, it would have bitten you. ♦ If it quacks like a duck and walks like a duck, it must be a duck. ♦ In broad daylight. ♦ In full view. ♦ In plain sight/view. ♦ It might as well be in blinking neon. ♦ It speaks for itself. ♦ It speaks volumes. ♦ It's [adj.] on its face. ♦ It's an open book. ♦ It's written all over your face. ♦ In-your-face. ♦ Just follow your nose; you can't miss it. ♦ Leaves little/nothing to the imagination. ♦ Let those who have eyes to see, see . . . ♦ Lipstick on your dipstick. ♦ Needless to say. ♦ Needs no introduction. ♦ No hiding the fact. ♦ Oh, say can you see. ♦ Open and notorious. ♦ Out in the open for all to see. ♦ Patently obvious.

♦ Plain as day/daylight. ♦ Readily apparent. ♦ Right before one's very eyes. ♦ Right under one's nose. ♦ Self explanatory. ♦ Sometimes the obvious is the most difficult thing to see. ♦ Staring one (right) in the face. ♦ Some things you can tell just by looking. ♦ Telltale signs. ♦ That says a lot about [n.]/[p.] ♦ That's a bad/good sign. ♦ That's gotta be telling you something. ♦ The eyes say as much as the tongue. ♦ The facts speak for themselves. ♦ The handwriting's on the wall. ♦ There for all the world to see. ♦ There is no need to explain the obvious. ♦ There's no mistaking [it]. ♦ This can mean only one thing. ♦ To glow in the dark. ♦ To have all the earmarks (of). ♦ To have [adj./n.] written all over it. ♦ To have X-ray vision. ♦ To hit you over the head. ♦ To jump (right) out at you. ♦ To lay it out in lavender. ♦ To read the tea leaves. ♦ To see (right) through [it]/[sb]. ♦ To show signs of. ♦ To speak volumes. ♦ To stand out from the crowd/in a crowd. ♦ To state the obvious. ♦ To stick out like a sore thumb. ♦ Visible to the naked eye. ♦ We hold these truths to be self-evident. [see also Reality] ♦ You are here. ♦ You can see/spot it a mile away. ♦ You can tell the good guys: they always wear the white hats. ♦ You've got eyes, haven't you? ♦ X marks the spot.

Oddball

A freak of nature. ♦ A queer duck. ♦ A slightly warped sense of humor. ♦ A space cadet. ♦ A space shot. ♦ An out-of-body experience. ♦ In a strange space. ♦ In a world of one's own. ♦ It's a strange, strange world we live in. ♦ Padiddle. ♦ Odds bodkins. -[archaic] ♦ To be a freak/geek. ♦ To be out of character. ♦ To be spacey. ♦ To depart/deviate from the norm.

Official

Affairs of state. ♦ Duly recorded. ♦ For the record. ♦ I dub thee Knight. ♦ Fully bonded, licensed and insured. ♦ Just a formality. ♦ Let the record show. ♦ On the books. ♦ Signed, sealed and delivered. ♦ That makes it official. ♦ To be duly elected. ♦ To be under oath. ♦ To go on record (as saying). ♦ To hold (public) office. ♦ To run for office. ♦ (To state) for the record. ♦ To swear out a warrant. ♦ To swear [so] in. ♦ To take the oath of office.

Ogle
(also notice, see)

A spectator sport. ♦ Cast your baby blues/peepers on. ♦ Check the fuzz on that. ♦ Eyes bugged out. ♦ Feast your eyes on (this). ♦ Get a load of (this). ♦ Hey, bobba-reeba. ♦ Hot diggity. ♦ Hubba-hubba. ♦ Hubba-hubba, ding-ding; she's got everything. ♦ Let's have a look. ♦ Let's have a look-see. ♦ Sneak a peek. ♦ To catch sight of. ♦ To clap/lay eyes on. ♦ To get a good look (at). ♦ To get an eyeful. ♦ To give the once-over (-lightly). ♦ To eyeball. ♦ To get/give the eye. ♦ To engage in a staring contest. ♦ To lock eyes. ♦ To look [sb] up and down. ♦ To make eye contact. ♦ To rubberneck. ♦ To stare [sb] down. ♦ To take a gander at. ♦ To take it all in. ♦ To take note/notice (of).

Open

An open marriage/relationship. ♦ An open question. ♦ An open secret. ♦ I'll try anything once. ♦ Keep your eyes open. ♦ My life is an open book. ♦ Open and above board. ♦ Open house. ♦ Open season. [see also Unrestrained] ♦ Open, Sesame. ♦ Open the door, Richard. ♦ Open to all comers. ♦ Open to suggestions. ♦ Open 24/7/365. ♦ Open up—police! ♦ Open up in the name of the law. ♦ Open your mouth and close your eyes. ♦ Opening night. ♦ Opening remarks. ♦ Out in the open. ♦ To keep an open mind. ♦ Wide open.

Opinion

A matter of opinion. ♦ A preconceived notion. ♦ A sounding board. ♦ An unbiased opinion. ♦ Another country heard from. ♦ As far as I'm concerned. ♦ Are you thinking what I'm thinking? [see also Ally] ♦ As I see it. ♦ Everyone's entitled to her/his opinion. ♦ From where I sit. ♦ How does that grab you? ♦ I, for one. ♦ If you ask me . . . ♦ If you think that, you've got another think coming. ♦ In my book. ♦ In my considered judgment/opinion. ♦ In my (humble) opinion. ♦ In the eyes of [n.]. ♦ It seems to me. ♦ One man's opinion. ♦ Opinion is formed by feeling, not intellect. ♦ Opinions are like *ssholes: everybody's got one. ♦ Point of view. ♦ Run it up the flagpole and see who salutes. ♦ Say/think what you will. ♦ So I said to myself—'self,' I said. ♦ That's what you think. ♦ To be of the opinion (that). ♦ To be under the impression (that). ♦ To bounce an idea off [so]. ♦ To get positive feedback. ♦ To my mind/way of thinking. ♦ To take the pulse of. ♦ To voice an opinion. ♦ What did/do you have in mind? ♦ What do you make of it? ♦

What do you think? ♦ When three people call you an ass, put on a bridle. ♦ Wouldn't you say? ♦ Ya think? ♦ You can say/think what you want to say/think.

Opportunity

A golden opportunity. ♦ A photo op. ♦ A window of opportunity. ♦ A once-in-a-lifetime opportunity. ♦ Get it while it's hot. ♦ Get in on the ground floor. ♦ Get it while the getting is good. ♦ God closes one door, and opens another. ♦ Have one's day in court. ♦ If/when the opportunity presents itself. ♦ It's never too late. ♦ Make haste/hay while the sun shines. (So when the moon shines, you can lay in it). ♦ Make hay with. ♦ Now hiring. ♦ Opportunity knocks but once. ♦ The chance/ opportunity of a lifetime. ♦ The world is one's oyster. ♦ To avail oneself of the opportunity. ♦ To get first crack (at). ♦ To have dibs on. ♦ To have every opportunity. ♦ To have occasion (to). ♦ To put [it] to good use. ♦ To seize/take the opportunity. ♦ To take advantage of [it]. ♦ To take it and run with it. ♦ When one door shuts, another opens. ♦ When the cotton bolls get rotten, you can't pick very much cotton. ♦ When you are the anvil, bear; when you are the hammer, strike. ♦ When you open the door wide to opportunity, it may fly in the window.

Oppose

(also decline, demur, obstruct)
Ain't/not gonna happen. ♦ All those opposed to [n.], say "nay." ♦ Beg off. ♦ Block that kick! ♦ By me. ♦ Can't stand [it]. ♦ Certainly not. [see also Certainty] ♦ Count me out. ♦ Dead set against. ♦ Don't bring that up. ♦ Don't do me any favors. ♦ Don't go there. ♦ Don't tell me what to do. ♦ Due to previous commitments, I must respectfully decline. ♦ Far be it from me (to). ♦ Get off my back. ♦ Here's where I get off. ♦ I pass. ♦ I remain to be convinced. [see also Skepticism] ♦ I think not. ♦ I won't have it. ♦ I won't hear of it. ♦ I would prefer not to. ♦ I wouldn't be caught dead in/doing that. ♦ I wouldn't do it on a bet. ♦ I wouldn't hold still for that. ♦ I'll sit this one out. ♦ In your dreams. ♦ Include me out. ♦ Let this cup pass from me. ♦ Let's not and say we did. ♦ Like fun! ♦ Like hell! ♦ Much as I'd like to, no. ♦ No dice/soap. ♦ No go. ♦ No thanks; I'm driving. ♦ No way, Jose. ♦ No way on God's greet earth. ♦ None for me, thank you. ♦ Not by a long shot. [see

also Exaggeration] ♦ Not about to [v.]. ♦ Not for all the tea in China. ♦ Not for all the world. ♦ Not for any amount of money. ♦ Not for anyone or anything. ♦ Not for anything in the world/on earth. ♦ Not for the life of me. ♦ Not if I have anything to say about it. ♦ Not if I have my way. ♦ Not on your life! ♦ Nothing doing. ♦ Out of the question. ♦ Over my dead body. ♦ Please don't go through all that trouble just for me. ♦ Stick it where the sun don't shine. ♦ Thanks all/just the same. ♦ Thanks anyway. ♦ Thanks but no thanks. ♦ The nays have it. [see also Vote] ♦ To be/get in the way. ♦ To blow [it] off. ♦ To buck the system. ♦ To contest the will. ♦ To cop an attitude. [see also Attitude] ♦ To flatly refuse. ♦ To have no part of it. ♦ To have none of it. ♦ To have something against [it]. ♦ To issue a flat denial. ♦ To lodge strenuous objections. ♦ To put in the way of. ♦ To put up a roadblock. ♦ To raise an objection. ♦ To respectfully decline. ♦ To shy away from. [see also Avoid] ♦ To stand in the way of progress. ♦ To take exception (to). ♦ To take a pass (on). ♦ What've you got against [it]? ♦ Will not stand for [it]. ♦ Wouldn't be caught dead doing [it]. ♦ Wouldn't dream of [it]. ♦

You know what you can do with it. ♦ You should live so long. [ironic/sarcastic] [see also Hopeless]

Optimism

A cockeyed optimist. ♦ A spring in one's step. ♦ Accentuate the positive. ♦ After the rain, the rainbow. ♦ All is right with the world. ♦ An optimist builds a castle in the air, the pessimist a dungeon in the sand. ♦ An optimist is someone who tells you to cheer up when things are going his way. ♦ As it should be. ♦ April showers bring May flowers. (April showers may bring flowers.) – R.D.) ♦ Be of good cheer. ♦ Birds have bills too, but they keep on singing. ♦ Cheer up; things could be worse. ♦ Every cloud must have a silver lining. ♦ Every day is like a Friday. [see also Zeal] ♦ Everything always happens for the best. ♦ Everything is copacetic. ♦ Everything is hunky-dory/hotsy-totsy. ♦ Everything's coming up roses. ♦ Find the pony. ♦ Is the glass half empty or half full? (beats me—but fill 'er up! – R.D.) ♦ Get your chin (up) off the floor. ♦ Isn't life grand. ♦ It's all for the best. ♦ It's all good. ♦ It's always darkest before the dawn. ♦ It's an ill wind that blows nobody/no one any good. ♦ It's better to try and fail than to fail to try. ♦ Keep your sunny side up. ♦ Life can be so sweet on the sunny side of the street. ♦ Life is getting better all the time. ♦ Life is just a bowl of cherries. ♦ Look on the bright side. ♦ My cup is not half empty, it's half full. ♦ No darker than midnight can it get.— Angela Maria Delia ♦ Nowhere to go but up. ♦ Right side out/up. ♦ See the world through rose-colored glasses. ♦ Sunny side up. ♦ The best is yet to come. ♦ The best of all possible worlds. ♦ The eternal optimist. ♦ There are better days ahead. ♦ There is good in the world (after all). ♦ There's always next year. ♦ There's no cause for alarm. ♦ Things have never been better. ♦ Things are looking up. ♦ Think positive. ♦ To have a positive outlook. ♦ To paint a rosy picture. ♦ Today is the first day of the rest of your life. ♦ What's the worst (thing) that can happen? ♦ Whatever is, is right. ♦ Where seldom is heard a discouraging word. ♦ Wildly enthusiastic/optimistic. ♦ You cannot prevent the birds of sorrow from flying over your head; but you can prevent them from building nests in your hair.

Ordeal

A holy terror. ♦ A horror show. ♦ A living hell. ♦ A scene of unspeakable horror. ♦ Been through the mill/wringer. ♦ Hell on earth. ♦ House of horrors. ♦ Nightmare alley. ♦ Suffer a fate worse than death. ♦ To fall prey (to). ♦ To go/be put through hell/the mill/the wringer. ♦ To rake [so] over the coals. [see also Scold] ♦ To run the gauntlet. ♦ To suffer the slings and arrows. ♦ To suffer the torment of the damned. ♦ Trials and tribulations. ♦ Your worst nightmare.

Organize

A place for everything and everything in its place. ♦ (All) squared away. ♦ Bag and tag. ♦ Get/set one's affairs/house in order. ♦ Get one's ducks in a row. ♦ Get one's act/sh*t together. ♦ In apple-pie order. [see also Apple] ♦ Like goes with like. ♦ Not everything that can be counted counts, and not everything that counts can be counted. ♦ Next week I've got to get organized. ♦ Pull oneself together. ♦ To establish some semblance of order. ♦ To establish/set one's priorities. ♦ To get everything shipshape. ♦ To have everything just-so. ♦ To hold it all together. ♦ To make reservations. ♦ To right all wrongs. [see also Revenge] ♦ To set the stage. ♦

To straighten things out. ◆ To tie up (all the) loose ends.

Ostracism

(also dismiss, oust)

A social leper. ◆ Amscray. ◆ Amscray umchay. ◆ Away with you. ◆ Back off, Jack. ◆ Back off, J*ckoff. ◆ Beat it. ◆ Booted out. ◆ Buzz off. ◆ Don't call us; we'll call you. ◆ Don't go away mad.— Just go away. [diner sign] ◆ Don't let the door hit ya where the Good Lord split ya. ◆ Don't let the door hit you in the *ss on the way out. ◆ Everybody out of the pool. ◆ Fired on the spot. ◆ F*ck off. ◆ Get away from me. ◆ Get lost. ◆ Get out and stay out. ◆ Get outta here. ◆ Get outta my face. ◆ Get one's marching orders. ◆ Give a lover the gate. ◆ Give [so] the old heave-ho. ◆ Go peddle your papers elsewhere. ◆ Good riddance to bad garbage. ◆ Goodbye and good riddance. ◆ Hit the road, Jack. ◆ Leave me alone. ◆ Make like a frog and croak. ◆ Make like a tree and leave. ◆ Never darken my door again. ◆ Out of favor. ◆ Out, damned spot. ◆ Out of my sight. ◆ Send you on your merry way. ◆ Take a hike. ◆ Take a long walk off a short pier. ◆ The outside world. ◆ Throw the bum out. ◆ Thrown out on one's ear. ◆ To be an outsider. ◆ To be in the doghouse. ◆ To be kicked upstairs. ◆ To be on the outs (with). ◆ To be on the outside looking in. ◆ To be on [so]'s sh*t list. ◆ To be *persona non grata*. ◆ To be tarred and feathered. ◆ To be the hatchet man. ◆ To blackball [so]. ◆ To cut [so] out. ◆ To drum [so] out of the corps. ◆ To fall from grace. ◆ To force [so] to walk the plank. ◆ To get/give a letter of dismissal. ◆ To get/give a pink slip. ◆ To get canned. ◆ To get one's walking papers. ◆ To get/give the boot/bum's rush/(old) heave-ho. ◆ To give [so] the air/axe/brush/gate. ◆ To relieve [so] of command. ◆ To run [so] out of town (on a rail). ◆ To see [so] out. ◆ To send [so] about her/his business. ◆ To send [so] on her/his way. ◆ To send [so] packing. ◆ To show [so] the door. ◆ To slam the door in [so]'s face. ◆ Typhoid Mary. [see also Personalities] ◆ Yankee go home. ◆ You can't fire me; I quit. ◆ You're fired. ◆ Your services are no longer required.

Outcry

(also noisy)

Loud enough to wake the dead. ◆ Holler like a stuck pig. ◆ Howl like a banshee. ◆ Let out a blood-curdling scream. ◆ Noisier than two skeletons screwing on a tin roof. ◆ So loud/noisy I can't hear myself think. ◆ To make a racket. ♦ Yell your (fool) head off. ♦ Yell at the top of one's lungs. ♦ Yell bloody murder.

Outspoken
(also candid)

A few well-chosen words. ♦ An open quarrel is better than hidden resentment. ♦ Another country heard from. ♦ As a matter of fact. ♦ Blow off steam. ♦ Chime in. ♦ Does not suffer fools gladly. ♦ Does not pull any punches. ♦ Does not take any guff. ♦ Excuse/pardon my French. ♦ Get it out in the open. ♦ He/she has quite a mouth on him/her. ♦ He who outshouts stands out. ♦ I call(s) 'em as I see(s) 'em. ♦ I was angry with my friend; I told my wrath, my wrath did end/I was angry with my foe, I told it not, my wrath did grow. ♦ In point of fact. ♦ Lay it on the line. [see also Straightforward] ♦ Make no bones about it. ♦ Mince no words. ♦ Not to put too fine a point on it. ♦ No-bull prize. ♦ Pipe up. ♦ Put [so] in her/his place. ♦ Put the mouth on. ♦ Put one's two cents in. ♦ Sass [so] back. ♦ Say what you mean and mean what you say. ♦ Say what's on your mind even though someone may mind what you say. ♦ Shoot one's mouth off. ♦ Sound off. ♦ Speak one's mind/piece. ♦ Spoken like a true [n.]. ♦ Stand up and be counted. ♦ State one's case. ♦ Tell it like it is. ♦ Tell [so] where to get off. ♦ Tell [so] off. ♦ Tell you flat out. ♦ Tell you point blank. ♦ The leaky faucet doesn't get fixed till it gets noisy. ♦ The squeaky wheel gets the (most) grease. ♦ (The squeaky wheel gets replaced. – R.D.) ♦ To be (quite) matter-of-fact. ♦ To be forthcoming. ♦ To be thinking out loud. ♦ To be upfront about [it]. ♦ To be upfront (with). ♦ To call a spade a spade. ♦ To come right out and say it. ♦ To come/get (right/straight) to the point. ♦ To express oneself. ♦ To get through to [so]. ♦ To get one's idea/message/point across. ♦ To give [sb] lip. ♦ To give [so] a piece of one's mind. ♦ To give [so] an earful. ♦ To have a say (in the matter). ♦ To have one's say. ♦ To make one's point. ♦ To make so bold as to say. ♦ To mouth off. ♦ To not beat around the bush. ♦ To not mince/waste words. ♦ To put it bluntly. ♦ To raise one's voice. ♦ To rant and rave. ♦ To rattle/reel off. ♦ To send a message. ♦ To shoot off one's mouth. ♦ To sound off (loud and clear). ♦ To speak out/up. ♦ To speak out of line. ♦ To speak straight from the shoulder. ♦ To talk out of turn. [see also Blab] ♦ To talk turkey. ♦ To tell you straight (out). ♦

To vent. ◆ To weigh in (on the subject). ◆ To whisper an aside. ◆ What am I, chopped liver?

Outwit

Ace [so] out. ◆ Beat [so] at his own game. ◆ Beat [so] to it. ◆ Beat [so] to the draw/punch. ◆ Make a monkey out of [so]. ◆ Nose [so] out. ◆ Not to be outdone. ◆ Out-Herod Herod. ◆ Steal [so]'s thunder. ◆ To beat [so]'s time. ◆ To fake [so] out. ◆ To get a leg up on. ◆ To get the best of [so]. ◆ To get the draw/drop/jump on [so]. ◆ To have 'em where you want 'em. ◆ To one-up [so]. ◆ To outfox [so]. [see also Animals] ◆ To poke holes in an argument. ◆ To psych [so] out. ◆ To put something over on [so]. ◆ To show [so] up. ◆ To steal a march on. ◆ To take advantage of. ◆ To turn the tables (on). ◆ To use one-upsmanship. ◆ To use reverse psychology.

Overseas

Across the pond. ◆ Beyond the blue horizon. ◆ Far, far away. ◆ In a strange land. ◆ Foreign ports of call. ◆ Hands across the sea. ◆ In a land faraway. ◆ In the old country. ◆ Innocents abroad. ◆ Over there. ◆ The Third world. ◆ Third world nations.

Oversee

Big Brother is watching you. ◆ Invasion of privacy. ◆ Keep an eye on. ◆ Roll call. ◆ Run a tight ship. ◆ The all-seeing eye. ◆ The revolution will be televised. ◆ To be/get on [so]'s case. ◆ To breathe down [so]'s neck. ◆ To count noses. ◆ To do a head count. ◆ To keep a running tab. ◆ To keep tabs (on). ◆ To keep track (of). ◆ To keep/place under surveillance. ◆ To look after. ◆ To ride herd (on). ◆ To see to [it]. ◆ To take attendance. ◆ Under close scrutiny. ◆ Under the watchful eye (of).

Paltry
(also inconsequential, minimal, worthless)

A/the bare minimum. ◆ A bit part. ◆ A borderline case. ◆ A break-even. ◆ A candle in the wind. ◆ A case of flaucinaucinihilipilification. ◆ A drop in the bucket/ ocean. ◆ A fart in a hailstorm/whirlwind. ◆ A flash in the pan. ◆ A little thing like that. ◆ A mere formality. ◆ A no-account. ◆ A paltry sum. ◆ A pinch of (salt) ◆ A pop fly. ◆ A skeleton crew. ◆ A sparrow fart in a typhoon. ◆ A teeny-weeny bit. ◆ A token gesture/ presence. ◆ A trifing matter. ◆ A two-bit [n.]. ◆ A walk-on part. ◆ A wash. ♦ All it was was a ring dang doo. ♦ An eensy-weensy bit. ♦ An itsy-bitsy amount. ♦ Are you going to let a little thing like that bother you? ♦ At best. ♦ At (the very) least. ♦ At most. ♦ At the outside. ♦ Bare bones. ♦ Bread and water. ♦ Big deal.* ♦ Big help that is/you are. * ♦ Big whoop. *[ironic/sarcastic] ♦ Chicken feed. ♦ Chicken scratch. ♦ Chump change. ♦ Doesn't amount to a bird turd on bacon. ♦ Doesn't amount to a hill of beans. ♦ Doesn't amount to a pimple on a gnat's *ss. ♦ Doesn't do it for me. ♦ Doesn't even scratch the surface. ♦ Doesn't make a dent in [it]. ♦ Doesn't ring my chimes. ♦ Don't lose any sleep over it. ♦ Don't spend it all in one place. [ironic/sarcastic] ♦ Don't sweat the petty sh*t. ♦ Don't sweat the petty stuff (or pet the sweaty stuff). ♦ Doesn't count. ♦ Doesn't make the slightest bit of difference. ♦ Don't fret/worry your pretty little head about it. ♦ For two cents, I'd . . . ♦ Here and there. ♦ I didn't feel a thing. ♦ I have bigger fish to fry. ♦ I've got more important things to do. ♦ Inadmissible evidence. ♦ It's a nonstarter. ♦ It's not the end of the world. ♦ It's nowhere. ♦ It's the (very) least one could do. ♦ Last of the big spenders. ♦ Like nothing ever happened. ♦ Meaningless variation. ♦ More bother/trouble than it's worth. ♦ Minimum requirements. ♦ No big deal/thing/ whoop. ♦ No biggie. ♦ No great loss. ♦ No sweat. ♦ Not (even) worth mentioning. ♦ Not in the least/ slightest. ♦ Not that big a deal. ♦ Not to worry. ♦ Nothing to be concerned/worry about. ♦ Nothing to speak of. ♦ Nothing to write home (to mother) about. ♦ Not worth a bucket of warm p*ss/spit. ♦ Not worth a pimple on a mosquito's *ss. ♦ Not worth a plugged nickel. ♦ Not worth a rap. ♦ Not worth (a) sh*t. ♦ Not worth a tinker's dam. ♦ Not worth all that/the trouble. ♦ Not worth diddly-sh*t/diddly-squat. ♦ Not worth the paper it's written on/powder to blow it (all) to hell. ♦ Nothing to speak of. ♦ Of little (or no) value. ♦ Of no consequence. ♦ Of no evidentiary value. ♦ Penny-ante (stuff). ♦ Pin money. ♦ Sh*t for the birds. ♦ Small change. ♦ Small fry. ♦ Small beer/potatoes. ♦ Smaller than a tick turd. ♦ So, what's the big deal? ♦ (Strictly) from hunger. ♦ Spit in the ocean. ♦ (Strictly) for the birds. ♦ That and a nickel won't get you a cup of coffee. ♦ That's the least of my headaches/worries. ♦ The bare essentials/minimum/necessities. ♦

The break-even point. ♦ The game is not worth the candle. ♦ The least little thing. ♦ There are a lot more fish in the ocean. ♦ There are more things in heaven and earth. ♦ There are plenty of (other) fish in the sea/pebbles on the beach. ♦ There is nothing to apologize for. ♦ To break even. ♦ To say the least. ♦ Trace amounts. ♦ Worth *bupkis* [goat sh*t]. ♦ Worth peanuts. ♦ You don't have anything to feel sorry about. ♦ You don't have to feel sorry about a thing. ♦ You paid money for this? ♦ Worth *borscht*.

Participate

A vested interest. [see also Profit] ♦ Chip in. ♦ Count me in. ♦ Do one's bit/duty/part. ♦ Do the honors. ♦ Exercise one's rights. ♦ Get in (on) the act. ♦ Go to it. ♦ Kick in. ♦ Pitch in. ♦ Play one's part. ♦ Pull one's weight. ♦ Roll up one's sleeves. ♦ Take up the slack. ♦ To be hands-on. ♦ To be in the arena/ring. ♦ To bring to the table. ♦ To get in/into the act. ♦ To get in on [it]. ♦ To give it a go. ♦ To give it a whack. ♦ To have/take a hand in [it]. ♦ To have a seat at the table. ♦ To have a stake in [it]. ♦ To join in (the fun). ♦ To play a role (in). ♦ To sign on/sign up. ♦ To take a crack/whack at [it]. ♦

To take a hit on [it]. ♦ To take part (in). ♦ To take the field. ♦ To toss [it] into the mix/hopper. ♦ To try one's hand at [it].

Patience
(also restraint)

All good things come to him who waits. ♦ All good things take time. ♦ All (things) in good time. ♦ An acquired taste. ♦ Bear and forbear. ♦ Bear with me. ♦ Don't fire till you see the whites of their eyes. ♦ For it's a long, long time from May to December. ♦ Hold your water. ♦ If I wanted to wait, I'd be a waiter. ♦ It takes (some) getting used to. ♦ Keep your pants/shirt on. ♦ Kindly wait your turn. ♦ Nobody can eat an elephant in one dinner. ♦ Pain is built into patience. ♦ Patience and fortitude. ♦ Patience is a virtue, possess it if you can; it's seldom found in women, but never in a man. — Angela Maria Delia ♦ Patience will be rewarded. ♦ Rome wasn't built in a day. ♦ Rome wasn't burned in a day. ♦ Sit tight. ♦ Some things can't be rushed. ♦ Some things take forever. ♦ The harvest comes not every day though it comes every year. ♦ The key to everything is patience. ♦ There's always a next time. ♦ There's always next year. ♦ There's always tomorrow. ♦ To bear with [so]. ♦ To bide one's time. ♦ To find the pot of gold at the end of the rainbow, you must wait out the rain. ♦ To have the patience of a saint. ♦ To have the patience of Job. ♦ You get the chicken by hatching the egg—not by smashing it. ♦ You have to endure caterpillars if you want to see butterflies.

Patriotic

All-American. ♦ A red-blooded American (boy/girl). ♦ A wholesome, clean-cut American (boy/girl). ♦ America the beautiful. ♦ America: love it or leave it. ♦ As American as mom and apple pie. ♦ Ask not what your country can do for you; ask what you can do for your country. ♦ For God and country. ♦ God bless America. ♦ In America, the streets are paved with gold. ♦ Land of the free, home of the brave. ♦ Let freedom ring. ♦ Life, liberty and the pursuit of happiness. ♦ My country, right or wrong. ♦ My fellow Americans. ♦ Oh, the monkey wrapped his tail around the flagpole. ♦ Only in America. ♦ Patriotism is the last refuge of the scoundrel. ♦ Stars and stripes forever. ♦ Such is life in these United States. ♦ The American Dream. ♦ The (good ol') U.S. of A. ♦ The land of milk and honey. ♦ The land of opportunity. ♦ Three cheers for the red, white and blue. ♦ To rally round the flag. ♦ Uncle Sam wants YOU.

♦ Yankee Doodle Dandy. ♦ You're a grand old flag.

Peace

A Just Peace. ♦ [Just Peace. — R.D.] ♦ A lasting peace. ♦ A peace offering. ♦ Fighting for peace is like screwing for virginity. [see also Pointless] ♦ God's in His heaven; all's right with the world. ♦ Halcyon days. ♦ In the home there is no peace when the crow and the rooster are quiet. ♦ Peace and quiet. ♦ Peace be with you. ♦ Peace is more than the absence of war. ♦ Peace of mind. ♦ Peace on earth, goodwill to men. ♦ Peace on you. ♦ Smoke the peace pipe. ♦ Sometimes, to have peace of mind, you have to give somebody a piece of your mind. — R.D. ♦ To cease hostilities. ♦ To extend an olive branch. ♦ What do we want? Peace! When do we want it? Now! ♦ Why can't we all just get along? — Rodney King ♦ World Peace through world trade.

Penny

A penny for your thoughts. ♦ A penny saved is . . . a penny. ♦ A penny saved is a penny earned. ♦ Always turns up, like a bad penny. ♦ Everyone has a penny to spend at a new alehouse. ♦ Finding a penny with heads up is good luck. ♦ If you could get just one penny from everyone in the country you'd be rich. ♦ Not one red cent. ♦ Pennies from heaven. ♦ Penny ante. ♦ Penny wise, dollar/pound foolish. ♦ To pinch pennies. ♦ To pitch pennies. ♦ Worth a pretty penny.

Penultimate

(also desperate)

A last-ditch effort. ♦ A photo finish. ♦ At the last minute. ♦ Desperation Row. ♦ Down for the count. ♦ Down to the short strokes. ♦ Down to the wire. ♦ Get the last word in. ♦ Get one's last licks in. ♦ Going down for the third time. ♦ Going out of business (sale). ♦ Grasping at straws. ♦ Have a final fling. ♦ Heading for the last roundup. ♦ In a downward spiral. ♦ In dire straits. ♦ In the eleventh hour. ♦ In the final/latter/last stages (of). ♦ In the homestretch. ♦ In the last quarter. ♦ In the midnight hour. ♦ In the top of the ninth. ♦ It's late in the day. ♦ Just about done/over. ♦ Last but not least. ♦ Last leg of the journey. ♦ Last of the Mohicans. ♦ Next to (the) last. ♦ On final approach. ♦ On the wane. ♦ On the way out. ♦ Right down to the wire. ♦ Rounding the clubhouse turn. ♦ Rounding the far turn. ♦ Save the best for last. ♦ Slightly burned out, but still smokin'. ♦ That's about it. ♦ The beginning of the end. ♦ The bucket list. ♦ The court of ultimate appeals. ♦ The end days. ♦ The end is in sight/near. ♦ The end of the world is approaching/is near/is nigh. ♦ The endgame. ♦ The last resort. ♦ There's a buck-thirty left in regulation. ♦ Time is running out. ♦ To balance the books. ♦ To come in for a landing. ♦ To draw to a close. ♦ To fine tune [it]. ♦ To have two strikes against you. ♦ To make final adjustments. ♦ To round the horn. ♦ To round up the strays. ♦ To smooth out the rough edges. ♦ To tie up the loose ends. ♦ To trim one's sails. ♦ To tune up.

Perfection

A fussbudget. ♦ A perfect/spotless record. ♦ A stickler for perfection. ♦ An unblemished record. ◆ Don't make the best the enemy of the good. ◆ If it weren't for the piles, you'd be a perfect *sshole. ◆ It makes perfect sense. ◆ It's not too hot, not too cold, it's just right. ◆ Letter perfect. ◆ Picture perfect. ◆ Practice makes perfect. ◆ Progress, not perfection. ◆ Trifles make up perfection but perfection is no trifle.

Permanence

A lasting impression. ◆ A lifer. ◆ Ain't going nowhere. An unquenchable thirst. ◆ An unscratchable itch. ◆ ◆ Carved in granite. ◆ Cast in bronze. ◆ Etched in stone. ◆ For good. ◆ For the rest of one's (natural) life. ◆ Forever and a day. ◆ From here on in/out. ◆ From here to eternity. ◆ From here to kingdom come. ◆ From now on. ◆ From now till/to Doomsday. ◆ From this day forth/forward. ◆ In for the duration. [see also Endurance] ◆ In perpetuity. ◆ Inalienable rights. ◆ Inexhaustible supply. ◆ Life has no rewind button. ◆ Looks fade, but dumb is forever. ◆ Once and for all. ◆ Once the bell is rung, it can not be unrung. ◆ Past the point of no return. ◆ So long as you both shall live. ◆ There's no turning back (the clock). ◆ There's no undoing what is done. ◆ What's done is done. ◆ You can't put the genie back in the bottle. ◆ You can't put the toothpaste back in the tube.

Perquisites

A cat may look at a king. ◆ Ability comes from responsibility. ◆ Beyond the Alps lies Italy. ◆ Fringe benefits. ◆ If the gorilla wants to eat the banana with the skin on, you have to let the gorilla eat the banana with the skin on. [see also Powerless] ◆ It's lonely at the top. ◆ *Jus primae noctis.* ◆ Lion's skin is never cheap. ◆ No pain, no gain. ◆ RHIP (Rank has its privileges). ◆ *Noblesse oblige.* ◆ Success has its burdens. ◆ The general must be allowed his private thoughts. ◆ The goose is heavy as the road is long. ◆ The job has its perks. ◆ The Rabbi is allowed. ◆ To be privy to. ◆ Where the Pope is, there is the church. ◆ With big jumps come big headaches.

Perseverance

A big shot is a little shot who kept shooting. ◆ Don't give up so easily. ◆ Don't give up the ship. ◆ Don't (stop to) look back; someone may be catching up. ◆ Don't take no for an answer. ◆ Dripping water will eat through a stone. ◆ Every little bit, added to what you've got, makes just a little bit more. ♦ Grain by grain, you will deplete a heap of wheat. ♦ Hang in there. ♦ Hanging in, like an old pair of nuts. ♦ He who would eat the fruit must climb the tree. ♦ He who would eat the kernel must crack the nut. ♦ He who would have the eggs must endure the cackling of hens. ♦ If at first you don't succeed, try and try again. [see also Try] ♦ If you throw enough sh*t at the wall, eventually something's gotta stick. ♦ Keep at it. ♦ Keep it up. ♦ Keep on adding one bean and you will have a full sack. ♦ Keep on keeping on. ♦ Keep on trucking. ♦ Keep plugging away. ♦ Keep the pace. ♦ Keep one's nose to the grindstone. ♦ Little strokes fell great oaks. ♦ Miracles do happen. ♦ Never say die/never. ♦ No bees, no honey; no work, no money. ♦ Persistence pays. ♦ Pick yourself up, dust yourself off, and start all over again. ♦ Plug away at. ♦ Pray to God but continue to row to the shore. ♦ Ride it out. ♦ Shoemaker, stick to thy last. ♦ Slow and steady wins the race. ♦ Something's gotta click. ♦ Stay the course. ♦ Stick it out. ♦ Take another shot at it. ♦ The man who rows the boat generally doesn't have time to rock it. ♦ The only way you can fail is to stop trying. ♦ The pig that keeps its head down grubs the deepest root. ♦ The third time's the charm. ♦ To be dogged in one's persistence. ♦ To believe a thing is impossible is to make it so. ♦ To go on with the show. ♦ To have stick-to-it-iveness. ♦ To hold down a job. ♦ To knuckle down. ♦ To let nothing stand in one's way. ♦ To make an omelette, you have to break some eggs. ♦ To pick up the pieces (and go on). ♦ To see [it] through (to its logical conclusion). ♦ To soldier on. ♦ To stick to/with it. ♦ To wear down one's resistance. ♦ Yard by yard, it's hard; but inch by inch, it's a cinch. — Angela Maria Delia ♦ When the going gets tough, the tough get going. [see also Adversity] ♦ You can't keep a good man down. ♦ You never know how strong you are until being strong is your only option.

Personalities

Alexander the Great. ♦ Alibi Ike. ♦ Attila the Hun. ♦ Bill Nye the Science Guy. ♦ Billy the Kid. ♦ Bloody Mary. ♦ Broadway Joe. ♦ Casper the Friendly Ghost. ♦ Charlie the Tuna. ♦ Conan the Barbarian. ♦ Crazy Horse. ♦ Dirty Harry. ♦ Diamond Jim. ♦ Dora the Explorer. ♦ Dudley Do-Right. ♦ Edward the Confessor. ♦ Fearless Fosdick. ♦ Gentleman Jim. ♦ Gorgeous George.

♦ Gravel Gertie. ♦ Henry the Eighth. ♦ Honest Abe. ♦ Ivan the Terrible. ♦ Jack the Giant Killer. ♦ Jack the Ripper. ♦ Jake the Snake. ♦ Jersey Joe. ♦ Jimmy the Greek. ♦ Johnny Appleseed. ♦ Jojo from Kokomo. ♦ Joltin' Joe. ♦ Jude the Obscure. ♦ Kermit the Frog. ♦ Kermit the Hermit. ♦ Louie the Lip. ♦ Mack the Knife. ♦ Mandrake the Magician. ♦ Marrying Sam. ♦ Merlin the Magician. ♦ Murray the K. ♦ Nutsy Fagin. ♦ Omar the Tentmaker. ♦ Peter the Great. ♦ Pliny the Elder. ♦ Pliny the Younger. ♦ Quick draw McGraw. ♦ Richard the Lionhearted. ♦ Saint John the Divine. ♦ Sinbad the Sailor. ♦ Sitting Bull. ♦ Speedy Gonzalez. ♦ Stan the man. ♦ Stonewall Jackson. ♦ Suzy Q. ♦ Stormin' Norman. ♦ The Brown Bomber. ♦ The Cincinnati Kid. ♦ The Unsinkable Molly Brown. ♦ Typhoid Mary. [see also Ostracism] ♦ Tokyo Rose. ♦ Tom Thumb. ♦ Tony the Tiger. ♦ Tricky Dick. ♦ Vlad the Impaler. ♦ William the Conquerer. ♦ Winnie the Pooh.

Persuasion

A command of the language. ♦ A pickup artist. ♦ A sales pitch. ♦ A way with words. ♦ An elevator pitch. ♦ By force of argument. ♦ Could charm the birds (right) out of the trees. ♦ Could talk a dog off a meat wagon. ♦ Could con a peacock out of its tailfeathers. ♦ Make you an offer you can't refuse. ♦ Talk a good ballgame. ♦ To have a silver tongue. ♦ To have the gift of gab. ♦ To lead you to believe. ♦ To level an argument. ♦ To make a believer of [so]. ♦ To make a cogent argument. ♦ To make a (good) case for/against [it]. ♦ To make [so] see things your way. ♦ To sell [so] on [it]. ♦ To soft soap [so]. ♦ To talk [so] into/out of [it]. ♦ To talk (some) sense into [so]. ♦ To win [so] over by logic. ♦ You silver-tongued devil, you. ♦ You're an old smoothie.

Pessimism

(also cynic)

A grade A grey day. ♦ Bad day at Black Rock. ♦ I should have stayed in bed. ♦ In one's darkest hour. ♦ It's going to be one of those days/nights. ♦ Mother told me there'd be days like this. ♦ Pessimist: one who sees the world through woes-colored glasses. ♦ The cynic is one who knows the price of everything and the value of nothing. ♦ The cynic route. ♦ The kitchen cynic. (Restaurant reviewer.) ♦ The worst-case scenario. ♦ They said smile, things could be worse. So I smiled and sure enough, things got worse.

Pictures

A mug shot. ♦ Can't you just picture it? ♦ Do I have to draw you a picture? ♦ Do you belong in this picture? ♦ Every picture tells a story. ♦ One picture is worth a thousand words. [But sometimes the right words can be worth a thousand pictures. — R.D.] ♦ Picture perfect. ♦ Picture this. ♦ The big picture. ♦ The camera does not lie. (But liars use cameras). ♦ The camera loves her. ♦ To be out of the picture. ♦ To get the picture. ♦ What's wrong with this picture? ♦ Where's Waldo?

Placate

A go-between. ♦ Blow smoke up [so]'s *ss. ♦ Break it gently. ♦ Give an ego massage. ♦ Pour oil on troubled waters. ♦ Smooth [so]'s feathers. ♦ String [so] along. ♦ To stroke [so]. ♦ Tell them what they want to hear. ♦ To cushion the blow. ♦ To ease the pain. ♦ To have a calmative effect. ♦ To humor [so] along. ♦ To play along with [so]. ♦ To settle one's stomach. ♦ To throw/toss [so] a bone/crumb.

Pleading

(also request)

A plea bargain. ♦ Be a good scout, and … ♦ Be a real pussycat, would you, and … ♦ By your leave, Sir/ Ma'am. ♦ Cut me some slack. ♦ Do me a favor. ♦ Gimme a break, willya? ♦ I beg your pardon. ♦ If it please the Court. ♦ If it's alright/OK with you. ♦ If it's all the same to/with you. ♦ If it's not too much trouble. ♦ If you don't mind. ♦ May I trouble you for a(n) [n.]? ♦ Plead ignorance. ♦ Plead the fifth. ♦ Plead one's case. ♦ Pretty please (with sugar on it). ♦ To ask on bended knee. ♦ To beg [so]'s indulgence/pardon. ♦ To call upon. ♦ To cop/enter a plea. ♦ To lodge a (formal) request. ♦ To petition the court. ♦ To plead for one's life. ♦ To request permission. ♦ To trouble [so] for. ♦ Would you be so kind as to.

Poetry

All words lead to rhyme. — R.D. ♦ Nursery rhymes. ♦ Ode to a twee, by Percy Dovetonsils. ♦ Pocket full of poesy. ♦ Poetry in motion. ♦ Poets are born but orators made. ♦ Take poetic license. ♦ Sir, I admit your rule/That every poet is a fool/But you yourself may show it/That not every fool is a poet. ♦ The bird is on the wing.

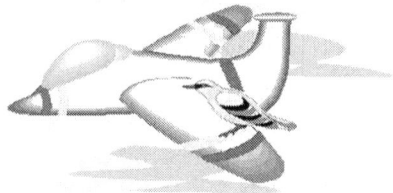

(But that's absurd: the wing is on the bird!) ♦ The world is my oyster, said the girl./Said the pearl: the oyster is my world. – R.D. ♦ To wax poetic. ♦ You're a poet and you don't even know it. [riposte: That don't rhyme, Frankenstein.]

Pointless

A hollow victory. ♦ A loop-de-loop. ♦ A (total) waste of time. ♦ All for naught. ♦ Apropos of nothing. ♦ Art for art's sake. ♦ Carrying coals to Newcastle. ♦ Economics can be very useful as a profession for employing economists. ♦ Fighting for peace is like screwing for virginity. [see also Peace] ♦ For no apparent reason. ♦ For no earthly/good reason. ♦ Going (around) in circles. [see also Setback] ♦ Getting/going nowhere fast. ♦ It won't do (you) any good. ♦ Like a dog chasing its tail. ♦ No one ever started a revolution by talking in circles. ♦ The gods send nuts to those who have no teeth. ♦ Throwing money down a rathole. ♦ To [v.] for the sake of [n.]. ♦ To chase one's (own) tail. ♦ To go on a fool's errand. ♦ To keep a dog and bark yourself. [see also Dogs] ♦ To little (or no) purpose. ♦ To no avail does the dog chase its tail. ♦ To serve no purpose. ♦ To throw good money after bad. ♦ Why bring a ham sandwich to a banquet? ♦ Without rhyme or reason.

Politics

A bleeding-heart liberal. ♦ A public servant. ♦ Any taxpayer knows there's no such thing as a cheap politician. ♦ Guardian of the public trust. ♦ Keeper of the keys. ♦ Keeper of the flame. ♦ Mainstream politics. ♦ Party politics. ♦ Politics makes strange bedfellows. ♦ Politically motivated. ♦ The body politic. ♦ The G.O.P. (Grand Old Party). ♦ To be politically correct. [see also Correct] ♦ To kiss babies and shake hands. ♦ To glad-hand [so]. ♦ To make a presidential run. ♦ To play politics. ♦ To press the flesh. ♦ To reach across the aisle. ♦ To seek elective office. ♦ Unless good citizens hold office, bad citizens will.

Popularity

A chart-topper. ♦ A happening spot. ♦ A runaway bestseller. ♦ And the crowd goes wild! ♦ A popular girl is like a cliché: heavily dated. ♦ A popularity contest. ♦ At the top of the charts. ♦ (Back) by popular demand. ♦ Big box office. ♦ Critics' choice. ♦ Fan mail. ♦ Flying off the shelves. ♦ In (great) demand. ♦ Knock 'em dead. ♦ Lay them in the aisles. ♦ Mr./Miss Popularity. ♦

(Much) sought after. ♦ Oohs and aahs. ♦ Open to rave reviews. ♦ Popularity is like glass—when it breaks it cannot be repaired. ♦ Selling like hotcakes. ♦ Standing room only. ♦ Talk of the town. ♦ The Hit Parade. ♦ The phone is ringing off the hook. ♦ To be [n.] Central. ♦ To be society's darling. ♦ To blow them away. ♦ To bowl 'em over. ♦ To bring down the house/bring the house down. ♦ To go down a bomb/storm with [so]. ♦ To go over big. ♦ To have to beat 'em off with a stick. ♦ To set the world on its ear. ♦ To steal the show. ♦ To take the town/world by storm. ♦ To turn out in force. ♦ To turn out in record numbers. ♦ To win an/the Oscar. ♦ To win popular support. ♦ Where the action is.

Position

A position of power. ♦ An untenable position. ♦ Assume the position. ♦ Caught in a compromising position. ♦ Get into striking position. ♦ In a position to say. ♦ In an enviable position. ♦ In no position to argue. ♦ Jockey for position. ♦ Position is everything in life. ♦ The missionary position.

Possession

(All one's) earthly possessions. ♦ All rights reserved. ♦ Already spoken for. ♦ Gain clear title. ♦ In one's name/possession. ♦ Joint possession. ♦ Lay claim to. ♦ Mine all mine. ♦ Personal effects. ♦ Possession is nine points/nine-tenths of the law. ♦ Stake a claim. ♦ Stake out one's territory. ♦ Take title to. ♦ The door belongs to who's opening it. ♦ To be possessed (by a demon/the devil). ♦ To get it in one's hot little hand. ♦ To get one's hooks into. ♦ To mark one's territory/turf. ♦ To one's name. ♦ To own [it] outright. ♦ Yours alone.

Postpone

A pleasure postponed is a pleasure lost. ♦ Hang fire. ♦ Hold off. ♦ Hold that thought. ♦ In a holding pattern. ♦ In cold storage. ♦ In dry dock. ♦ Keep [it] in the back of one's mind. ♦ Let's come back to that. ♦ Put a hold on [it]. ♦ Put [it] in mothballs. ♦ Put [it] on the back burner. ♦ Rained out. ♦ Table the issue. ♦ Take a rain check. ♦ To buy time. ♦ To procrastinate. ♦ To shelve.

Potential

A dark horse. ♦ A diamond in the rough. ♦ A fertile field. ♦ A real sleeper. ♦ A ways off. ♦ A would-be [n.]. ♦ As the twig is bent, so grows the tree. ♦ Coming down the pike.

♦ Every little fish would become a whale. ♦ In contention. ♦ In store. ♦ In the offing. ♦ In the pipeline. [see also Future] ♦ In the running. ♦ In the wind. ♦ It's got possibilities. ♦ Mighty oaks from little acorns grow. ♦ On tap. ♦ On the brink/cusp/verge of. ♦ Patent pending. ♦ Thar's gold in them thar hills. ♦ To be about to [v.]. ♦ To have a fighting chance. ♦ To live up to one's (full) potential. ♦ Under consideration.

Poverty

(also depleted, empty)

A money crunch. ♦ Abject poverty. ♦ At the subsistence level. ♦ Blessed be nothing. ♦ Bone dry. ♦ Broke as the Ten Commandments. ♦ Can't afford to pay attention. ♦ Caviar tastes with a tuna budget. ♦ Champagne tastes but a beer budget. ♦ Don't know where one's next meal is coming from. ♦ Dirt poor. ♦ Down and out. ♦ Flat broke. ♦ Fresh out. ♦ In the breadline. ♦ [see also Unemployed] ♦ Insufficient funds. ♦ Low-income families. ♦ Money talks: poverty pinches. ♦ No visible means of support. ♦ Nobody knows you when you're down and out. ♦ Not a pot to p*ss in (or a window to throw it out of). ♦ On one's uppers. ♦ On the balls of one's *ss. ♦ Out of stock. ♦ Poor as a churchmouse. ♦ Poor as corn. ♦ Poverty in the door drives love out the window. ♦ Poverty Row. Stone broke. ♦ Strapped (for cash). ♦ Tap City. ♦ Tapped out. ♦ Tapsville. ♦ The cupboard is bare. ♦ (The lack of) money is the root of all evil. -R.D. ♦ The pinch of poverty ♦ The poor man is not he who has least but he who needs most. ♦ The poor you always have with you. ♦ Those less fortunate than ourselves ♦ To be financially embarrassed. ♦ To be hard up. ♦ To be collecting unemployment/in the breadline/on food stamps. ♦ To be property poor. ♦ To cry poverty. ♦ To go (into) Chapter 11. ♦ To have a cash flow interruption problem. ♦ To have a negative cash flow. ♦ To live (from) hand to mouth. ♦ To live (from) paycheck to paycheck. ♦ To not have two nickels to rub together. ♦ To not know where your next meal is coming from. ♦ To take a vow of poverty. ♦ Verbosity is poverty. ♦ What you don't have, you don't miss. ♦ What you don't have, you can't spend. ♦ Who has nothing knows nothing; and who knows nothing is nobody. ♦ You'll never get rich by digging a ditch (you're in the Army now!) [see also Rich]

Power

By the power vested in me. ♦ Drunk with power. ♦ Flower power. ♦ Karate: the power behind the thrown. ♦ More power to you. ♦ Never underestimate the power of stupid people in large numbers. ♦ Never underestimate your opponent. ♦ Nothing is more powerful than an idea whose time has come. ♦ Power corrupts; absolute power corrupts absolutely. ♦ Power to the people. ♦ The balance of power. ♦ The big fish eat the little fish. ♦ The full force and effect. ♦ The power behind the throne. ♦ The power grid. ♦ The power of positive thinking. ♦ The powers that be. ♦ To be power hungry/mad. ♦ To carry weight. ♦ To do everything in one's power. ♦ WASP power.

Powerless

Bound and gagged. ♦ I only have two hands. ♦ I'm only one person. ♦ If the gorilla wants to eat the banana with the skin on, you have to let the gorilla eat the banana with the skin on. [see also Perquisites] ♦ If you can't beat 'em, join 'em. [see also Cooperation] ♦ It's out of my/your hands. ♦ My hands are tied. ♦ Not my department. ♦ Not much you can do. ♦ There's only so much you can do. ♦ To be locked into [it]. ♦ To have no say (in the matter). ♦ To have one's hands tied (behind one's back). ♦ You can't buck the system. ♦ You can't fight City Hall. ♦ You can't fight what you can't see.

Praise

An A-plus rating. ♦ Can't say enough good things about [it]/[so]. ♦ [n.], [n.], he's our man; if he can't do it, no one can! ♦ Praise a fool to use as a tool. ♦ Praise makes good people better and bad people worse. ♦ Praise the Lord. ♦ Praise the Lord and pass the ammunition. ♦ Put in a good word (for). ♦ Praise to high heaven. ♦ Self-praise is half scandal. ♦ Self-praise is no praise. ♦ Self-praise stinks. ♦ The best way to get praise is to die. ♦ To be over the moon for. ♦ To be wild about. ♦ To describe in glowing terms. ♦ To give a 5-star rating (to). ♦ To get/give rave reviews. ♦ To get/give the red-carpet treatment. ♦ To heartily/highly recommend. ♦ To make a fuss over [so]. ♦ To make glowing remarks about [it]/[so]. ♦ To pay [so] a compliment. ♦ To put in a good word (for). ♦ To rave about. ♦ To root for. ♦ To talk [it] up. ♦ To throw bouquets. ♦ You don't know what you're missing. ♦ You're good . . . really good.

Preach

A Bible thumper. ♦ A man can preach no better than he prays. ♦ On the stump. ♦ Practice what you preach. ♦ Thus spake Zarathustra. ♦ To get (up) on a soap box. ♦ To hold forth. ♦ To preach fire and brimstone. ♦ To pronounce from on high. ♦ You can preach a better sermon with your life than with your lips.

Precaution

A hedge against inflation. ♦ A prenup. ♦ A prenuptial agreement. ♦ A stitch in time saves nine. ♦ A suit of armor/mail. ♦ Always drink upstream from the herd. ♦ An ounce of prevention is worth a pound of cure. ♦ Batten down the hatches. ♦ Be on one's guard. ♦ Better ask twice than lose your way once. ♦ Better to be redundant than remiss. ♦ Bunker mentality. ♦ Child-resistant cap. ♦ Check and double-check. ♦ Checks and balances. ♦ Couldn't hurt. ♦ C.Y.A. (cover your *ss). ♦ Cover your back. ♦ Dental floss prevents dental flaws. — R.D. ♦ Don't give the skin when you can buy with the wool. ♦ Don't let the camel's nose under the tent. (or the rest of the camel will soon follow.) ♦ Don't squat with your spurs on. ♦ Fasten your seatbelts and observe the no-smoking sign. ♦ (Fragile) handle with care. ♦ Hang on for dear life. ♦ Hang on to your hat. ♦ Hedge one's bets. ♦ Hold on tight. ♦ Holding out on us, eh? ♦ Hunker down. ♦ If anything (ever) happens to me. ♦ Just in case. ♦ Keep in with the bad body because the good body won't do you any harm. ♦ Keep out of the reach of children. ♦ Keep your powder dry. ♦ Love thine enemies. ♦ Locks don't keep dishonest people out; they keep honest people honest. ♦ Measure twice, cut once.—[carpenter's maxim]. ♦ Never drink downstream from the piggery. ♦ Never play cards with a man called Doc. ♦ Never eat at a place called Mom's. ♦ Never sleep with a woman whose troubles are worse than your own. ♦ On suicide watch. ♦ Only you can prevent forest fires. ♦ Paint costs nothing. ♦ Preventive maintenance. ♦ Pull one's horns in. ♦ Siege mentality. ♦ Something to fall back on. ♦ The best armor is to keep out of range. ♦ The best defense is a good offense. ♦ The best offense is a good defense. ♦ The first line of defense. ♦ To assume the fetal position. ♦ To bell the cat. ♦ To circle the wagons. ♦ To curl into a ball. ♦ To hold/keep at bay. ♦ To make doubly sure. ♦ To secure the area. ♦ To shore things up. ♦ To take cover. ♦ To take elaborate precautions. ♦ To take every precaution. ♦ To ward off. ♦ Watch out for the other guy. ♦ Watch your back/step. ♦ You watch my back and I'll watch yours. [see also Reciprocation]

Predictable

A boilerplate statement. ♦ A conditioned reflex. ♦ A distinct possibility. ♦ A foregone conclusion. ♦ A pre-existing condition. ♦ A stock answer/reply. ♦ As/per usual. [N.B. "as" and "per" are separate. "As per" is losing favor as acceptable English]. ♦ As likely as not. ♦ Didn't I tell you? ♦ Every single time. ♦ For the most part. ♦ I could have told you as much/that. ♦ I am not (in the least) surprised. ♦ I hate to say I told you so—but I told you so. ♦ I told you so. ♦ I wouldn't be (a bit) surprised. ♦ In all likelihood/probability. ♦ Isn't that just like (a) [n.]/[p.]. ♦ It comes as no surprise. ♦ It doesn't/wouldn't surprise me (one bit). ♦ It figures. ♦ It happens every time. ♦ It happens in the best (of) circles. ♦ It happens to the best of us. ♦ It makes (good) sense. ♦ It never fails. ♦ It should come as no surprise. ♦ It stands to reason. ♦ It was ever thus. ♦ It won't/wouldn't be the first time (that's happened) (and it won't be the last). [see also Repetition]

♦ It's grandfathered in. ♦ It's happened before; it can happen again. ♦ It's only logical. ♦ It's (just/only) a matter of time. ♦ It's to be expected. ♦ It's what makes the world go round. ♦ Look in the dictionary under [adj.]/[n.] and you'll find his/her picture. ♦ More likely than not. ♦ More often than not. ♦ Most likely to succeed. [see also Success] ♦ Nine times out of ten. ♦ On a regular basis. ♦ On planet Earth, anything's possible. ♦ Once a [n.], always a [n.]. ♦ Perfect timing. ♦ Pretty much. ♦ (Right) on cue. ♦ See? You never listen to me. ♦ Some things never change. ♦ That's just like [n.]/[p.]. ♦ That's [n.] for you. ♦ That's the story of my life. ♦ The die is cast. ♦ They'll do it every time. ♦ To be a given. ♦ True to form. ♦ What did I tell you? ♦ What else could/did you expect (from a [n.])? ♦ Wouldn't you know it?

Prediction

A self-fulfilling prophesy. ♦ A shaggy dog will pass among you. ♦ Give a dog a bad name and he'll deserve it. [see also Reputation] ♦ I have a dream. ♦ Mark my words. ♦ [Mock my words. – R.D] ♦ This too shall come to pass. ♦ To augur ill/well. ♦ To be psychic. ♦ To foretell/see into the future. ♦ To have a vision. ♦ To prophesy upon velvet. ♦ To read it in the tea leaves. ♦ To read the (hand) writing on the wall. ♦ To see it in the cards. ♦ To tell [so]'s fortune. ♦ You will meet a tall, dark (and handsome) stranger.

Preference

As you wish. ♦ Different strokes for different folks. ♦ Everyone to his own fashion. ♦ Gentlemen prefer blondes. ♦ If I had my 'druthers. ♦ If we all liked the same things, we'd all be married to the same person. ♦ Know your audience. ♦ One man's meat is another man's poison. ♦ One man's trash is another man's treasure. ♦ That's what makes a horse race. ♦ That's what makes baseball! ♦ There is no accounting for tastes. ♦ There is no disputing taste. (De gustibus non est disputandum.) ♦ To each his own. ♦ To each his peach. ♦ To have a different take (on). ♦ Whatever floats your boat. ♦ Whatever turns you on. ♦ Whatever you say (boss).

Pregnant

An expectant mother. ♦ Barefoot and pregnant. ♦ Eating for two. ♦ Expecting a visit from the stork. ♦ How far along are you? ♦ How far along is she? ♦ I don't care what it is, as long as it's healthy. ♦ In a family way. ♦ In a hatching jacket. ♦ She swallowed a watermelon seed. ♦ There is no such thing as being half pregnant. ♦ To be expecting. ♦ To be knocked up/preggers/up the stump. ♦ To have a bun in the oven. ♦ To be showing a baby bump. ♦ To be with child. ♦ What's your due date? ♦ When are you expecting?

Prejudice

A racial slur. ♦ An Uncle Tom. ♦ But would you want your daughter/sister to marry one? ♦ I don't care what color your skin is, as long as the color of your money is green. ♦ If you're white you're alright; if you're brown you can hang around; if you're black, stand back! ♦ Jim Crow. ♦ Not in my back yard. ♦ Some of my best friends are [n.]/[adj.]. ♦ The only good [n.] is a dead [n.]. ♦ The token [n.] of (the group).[see also Insincere] ♦ To play the race card.

Premature

A long way from home. ♦ A long way to go. ♦ Come to an untimely end. [see also Death] ♦ Don't count your chickens before they hatch. ♦ Don't put the cart before the horse. ♦ Don't sell the bearskin before you've killed the bear. ♦ Don't say it has a hump till you see its back. ♦ Don't shoot the firecrackers before the parade. ♦ Don't speak too soon. ♦ Don't take your buns from the oven until they're done. ♦ Don't taunt the alligator until you've crossed the creek. ♦ Famous last words. ♦ I have nothing to wear. ♦ If and when that happens. [see also If] ♦ I'm getting ahead of myself. ♦ I'm not prepared to take that final step. ♦ It ain't over till it's over. ♦ It's just getting good. ♦ It's not over till it's over. ♦ It's not over till the fat lady sings. [see also Fat] ♦ Just because she gives you a tumble does not guarantee a roll in the hay. – R.D. ♦ Let's cross that bridge when we come to it. ♦ Let's deal with that when and if it happens. ♦ Light years away. ♦ Man plans, God laughs. ♦ Man proposes, God disposes. ♦ Never praise the day before midnight. ♦ Not so fast. ♦ So near, yet so far. ("*Tan prope. Tan proculque.*") ♦ Spoke too soon. ♦ Take it easy, Greasy, you've got a long way to slide. ♦ The best laid plans of mice and men often go awry. ♦ There's many a slip 'twixt the cup and the lip. ♦ To be ahead of one's time. ♦ To get ahead of oneself. [see also Haste] ♦ To go off half-cocked. ♦ To grow old before one's time. ♦ To rob the cradle. ♦ To tip one's hand. ♦ Too early/soon to tell/say. ♦ Unfinished business. ♦ We'll (just) see about that. ♦ When and if. ♦ Who counts without his host counts twice. ♦ Whoa, Hoss. ♦ You can't eat the calf in the cow's belly. ♦ You don't have a problem until it becomes a problem. ♦ You're getting ahead of yourself. ♦ You're not out of the woods yet.

Preparation

A plan of action. ♦ A plan of attack. ♦ A rain date/day. ♦ Be prepared. [The Boy Scout motto] ♦ Beef up. ♦ Being prepared is half the battle. ♦ In times of peace, prepare for war. ♦ Lock and load. ♦ Plan your work and work your plan. ♦ Rack 'em up. ♦ The best laid plans of mice and men. ♦ The best time to prepare for a sunny day is when it's raining. ♦ The seven P's: Proper Prior Planning Prevents P*ss-Poor Performance. ♦ Save the date. ♦ Thou preparest the table before me. ♦ To allow (sufficient) lead time. ♦ To be fixin' to [v.]. ♦ To blaze a trail. ♦ To clear the way. ♦ To cover (all) one's bases. ♦ To dim the lights. ♦ To do one's homework. ♦ To fan out/spread out. ♦ To fatten [it] up for the kill. ♦ To gird one's loins. ♦ To haul off. ♦ To have all good/the best of intentions. ♦ To lay the groundwork. ♦ To limber up. ♦ To make an appointment. ♦ To make ready. ♦ To make the bed. ♦ To pave the way. ♦ To psych up (for). ♦ To saddle up. ♦ To set the scene/stage. ♦ To set the table. ♦ To slice and dice. ♦ To suit up (for). ♦ To tool up. ♦ To turn the lights down low. ♦ To whip it up. ♦ (Warming up) in the bullpen. ♦ We can secure peace only by preparing for war.

Pressured

A man who says he's under pressure may be full of hot air. ♦ A squeeze play. ♦ Backed into a corner. ♦ In the clutch. ♦ If you can't stand the heat, get out/stay out of the kitchen.

♦ In the crucible. ♦ In the hot seat. ♦ In the line of fire. ♦ In the thick of [it]. ♦ Now look/see what you've done. ♦ Now you did it. ♦ Now you done dood it. ♦ Now you're in for it. ♦ On the firing line. ♦ Peer pressure. ♦ Put the squeeze on. ♦ Sitting in the hot seat.

♦ So many [n.], so little time. ♦ Tag—you're it! ♦ The heat is on. ♦ To be on the spot. ♦ To be under the gun. ♦ To be under the gun is better than to be in front of it. - R.D. ♦ To bear the brunt (of). ♦ To bring [it] to a head. ♦ To field questions. ♦ To force the issue. [see also Compel] ♦ To have one's back against/to the wall. ♦ To have one's mind racing. ♦ To hold a gun to [so]'s head. ♦ To hold [so] accountable. ♦ To hold [so]'s feet to the fire/flames. ♦ To hold [so] to a promise. ♦ To put the screws to [so]. ♦ To put the squeeze on. ♦ To ram/shove [it] down [so]'s throat. ♦ To shake [so] down. ♦ To take the heat. ♦ To turn up the heat on. ♦ When the chips are down. ♦ Where the action is. ♦ When the patient is under the knife, the surgeon is under the gun. — R.D. ♦ Where the rubber meets the road. ♦ Working against the clock. ♦ You're (really) going to get it. ♦ You're in for a real shellacking. ♦ You're (really) in for it (now).

Pretend

A dress rehearsal. ♦ A dry run. ♦ A fire drill. ♦ A love tap. ♦ Crying with a loaf of bread under each arm. ♦ Fake it till you make it. ♦ Fake [sb] out. ♦ False alarm. ♦ Laughing on the outside, crying on the inside. ♦

Laughing to keep from crying. [see also Laughter] ♦ Make believe. ♦ Never howl until you're hit. ♦ Play possum. ♦ Put on a front. ♦ Put on an act. ♦ Put up a good front. ♦ Roll over and play dead. ♦ To cry all the way to the bank. ♦ To cry wolf. ♦ To fake it. ♦ To feign interest. ♦ To fudge it. ♦ To hang [so] in effigy. ♦ To make as if/as though/like. ♦ To play dumb. ♦ To play house. ♦ To play on one's sympathy. ♦ To play the fool. ♦ To smile through the tears. ♦ To turn in a false alarm. ♦ To wear a rug. ♦ To wear falsies.

Pride

Bursting with pride. ♦ Every crow thinks its little crow is the blackest. ♦ He/she thinks he's/she's all that. ♦ I wouldn't give her/him/them/you the satisfaction. ♦ I've got my pride. ♦ My pride and joy. ♦ Pride goeth before a fall. (And after a good, swift kick). ♦ Pride is a flower in Satan's garden. ♦ Pride is at the bottom of all great mistakes. ♦ Pride of authorship/ownership. ♦ Proud as a peacock. ♦ The apple of one's eye. ♦ The few, the proud, the Marines. ♦ The proud papa. ♦ To be full of oneself. ♦ To be highfalutin. ♦ To do it up proud. ♦ To do oneself proud. ♦ To draw oneself up to one's full height. ♦ To get up-pity. ♦ To go to one's head. ♦ To have a swell head. ♦ To hold one's head (up) high. ♦ To pop one's buttons. ♦ To pride oneself (on) ♦ To swallow one's pride. ♦ To take pride in. ♦ To walk tall. ♦ To walk with one's head held high.

Problem

A problem child. ♦ Houston, we have a problem. ♦ If you're not part of the solution you're part of the problem. ♦ No problem. ♦ Problem solved. ♦ Problems are cowards: confront them and they'll run away. ♦ The further away you get from your problems, the smaller they seem. ♦ To have a hang-up. ♦ To have issues. ♦ To pose/present a problem. ♦ You don't have a problem until it becomes a problem.

Profanity

A dirty old man. ♦ A potty mouth. ♦ Adult language. ♦ Do you kiss your mother with that mouth? ♦ Foul/vile language. ♦ Go wash your mouth out with soap. ♦ Gutter talk. ♦ Language that would curl your hair. ♦ Off-color humor/jokes/remarks/stories. ♦ Talk dirty to me. ♦ The F-bomb. ♦ To have a foul mouth. ♦ To have one's mind in the gutter. ♦ To say the F-word. ♦ To swear like a trooper. ♦ To spew/unleash/utter a volley of epithets/oaths. ♦ To take God's name in vain. ♦ To talk dirty. ♦ To use four-letter words. ♦ To use salty language. ♦ Watch your language/mouth. ♦ Watch your language please, there are ladies present.

Profit

A bull market. ♦ A cash cow. ♦ A paying proposition. ♦ A positive balance. ♦ A positive cash flow. ♦ A vested interest. [see also Participate] ♦ Ahead of the game. ♦ An all-time high. ♦ Get a piece of the action. ♦ It's all gravy. ♦ Live off the fat of the land. ♦ Make it worth one's while. ♦ Profitability Through Social Responsibility. – Harry Reingold [motto of Projects for Peace, Inc.] ♦ Surefire secret of stock market success: buy low, sell high. ♦ There is no incongruity in doing well and doing good. ♦ To be in the black. ♦ To bring in/earn the big bucks. ♦ To cash in (on) [it]. ♦ To corner the market. ♦ To do well by doing good. ♦ To feather one's nest. ♦ To fill one's coffers/war chest. ♦ To have something to show for it. ♦ To line one's pockets. ♦ To make a killing (in the market). ♦ To make a mint. ♦ To make it worth one's while. ♦ To make/realize/show/turn a profit. ♦ To pocket the difference. ♦

To profit by. ♦ To rake in the money. ♦ To trade on. ♦ What profit a man if he shall gain the whole world, and shall lose his own soul? ♦ What's in it for me? ♦ What's it worth to you?

Progress

A developing country. ♦ A paradigm shift. [see also Change] ♦ A quantum leap ahead/forward. ♦ A step in the right direction. [see also Correct] ♦ A stepping stone (to). ♦ A turtle makes progress when it sticks its neck out. ♦ A work in progress. ♦ Bit by bit. ♦ Coming (right) along. ♦ Don't look back. ♦ Forge ahead. ♦ Go as/so far as to [v.]. ♦ Go/move on to bigger and better things. ♦ Growing pains. ♦ It's on back order. ♦ If you're not moving ahead you're falling behind. ♦ In progress. ♦ In session. ♦ In the works. ♦ Little by little. ♦ Moving right along. ♦ Now we're getting somewhere. ♦ On the way. ♦ One down, [n.] to go. ♦ One small step for man; one giant leap for mankind. [see also Humanity] ♦ One thing after another. ♦ One thing after the next. ♦ One thing at a time. ♦ One word led to another. ♦ Onward, Christian soldiers. ♦ Onward and upward. ♦ Pay as you go. ♦ Progress, not perfection. ♦ Rites of passage. ♦ Slowly but surely. ♦ So far, so good. ♦ Step by step. ♦ Take off the training wheels. ♦ That's half the battle. ♦ The more the marble wastes, the more the statue grows, said Michelangelo. ♦ To advance the ball. ♦ To answer to/heed a higher calling. ♦ To begin a new chapter. ♦ To build to a climax/ crescendo. [see also Motion] ♦ To chip away at. ♦ To come up/rise through the ranks. ♦ To get over the hump. ♦ To get to first base (with). ♦ To go a long way toward. ♦ To go so far as (to). ♦ To kick it up a notch. ♦ To make a dent in [it]. ♦ To make great strides. ♦ To make headway/yardage. ♦ To move on (to greener pastures). ♦ To move the ball forward. ♦ To narrow the gap. ♦ To overcome that hurdle. ♦ To phase [it] in/out. ♦ To push the envelope. [see also Intensity] ♦ To put a toe into the water. ♦ To put [it] behind you. ♦ To run its course. ♦ To shake the dust from one's feet. ♦ To start from the top and work down. ♦ To step up one's game. ♦ To take a flight of stairs. ♦ To take it one step further. ♦ To take it to a whole new level. ♦ To take it to the next level. ♦ To take the next step. ♦ To think outside the box. ♦ To turn the corner/page. ♦ To work one's way up (the ladder). ♦ To work (one's way) up to [it]. ♦ We're getting there. ♦ Years in the making. ♦ You've come a long way (baby).

Promise

A broken promise and a broken heart go hand in hand. ♦ A deal is a deal. ♦ A money-back guarantee. ♦ A promise is a promise. ♦ Cross my heart (and hope to die). ♦ Don't make promises you can't keep. ♦ Eggs and vows are easily broken. ♦ Empty promises. ♦ He loses his thanks who promises and delayeth. ♦ I swear on my mother. ♦ I swear to God. ♦ Is that a threat or a promise? ♦ Oh, promise me. ♦ On my word of honor. ♦ Promise little, do much. ♦ Promises are easier made than kept. ♦ Promises, promises, all I ever get are promises. ♦ So help me (God). ♦ To break a promise. ♦ To deliver/make good on one's promise. ♦ To keep one's promise. ♦ To promise the moon. ♦ To swear by all that is holy. ♦ To swear up and down. ♦ Vows made in storms are forgotten in calms. ♦ You can't eat promises. ♦ You have my (solemn) word.

Proof

A preponderance of the evidence. ♦ A proving ground. ♦ Baptism/trial by fire. ♦ Cut the mustard. ♦ If that's not [adj.]/[adv.]/[n.] I don't know what is. ♦

Just/only goes to show (you). ♦ Make the cut. ♦ Make the grade. ♦ Measure up. ♦ Pass muster. ♦ Pass the acid test/litmus test. ♦ Proof positive. ♦ Prove beyond a reasonable doubt. ♦ See for yourself. ♦ Seeing is believing. ♦ Stand the test of time. ♦ The clincher. ♦ The proof of the pudding is in the eating. (often shortened to: The proof is in the pudding.) ♦ The smoking gun. ♦ To catch [so] in a lie. [see also Catch] ♦ To have the motive, means and opportunity. ♦ To hold up in court. ♦ To admit/introduce [it] into evidence. ♦ To introduce into evidence. ♦ To make a liar out of [so]. ♦ To make (absolutely) certain. ♦ To make one's bones. ♦ To make (doubly) sure. [see also Certainty, Precaution] ♦ To poke holes in [so]'s argument/story. ♦ To prove a point. ♦ To prove one's point. ♦ To prove oneself. ♦ To prove beyond a reasonable doubt. ♦ To put [p.] through [p.] paces. ♦ To put [p.] to the test. ♦ To put the lie to. ♦ To run the numbers. ♦ To show cause. ♦ To test one's mettle. ♦ To try [it] on/out. ♦ What more proof do you need/want? ♦ Worthy of consideration. ♦ Up to snuff.

Protection

A security blanket. ♦ A stage mother. ♦ A ward of the court/state. ♦ As closely guarded as Fort Knox. ♦ Bar the door. ♦ Born in a barrel, fed through the spout. ♦ Bringing up baby. ♦ Guard [it] with one's life. ♦ In protective custody. ♦ Place [it] for safekeeping. ♦ Shelter from the storm. ♦ The care and feeding of [n.] ♦ The witness protection program. ♦ To bring up/raise/rear a child. ♦ To fatten [it]/[so] up for the kill. ♦ To get/have a restraining order. ♦ To have [so]'s back. ♦ To hold/man the fort. ♦ To keep the home fires burning. ♦ To lead a sheltered life. ♦ To look after. ♦ To mind the store. ♦ To nurse [so] back to health. ♦ To play nursemaid (to). ♦ To run interference (for). ♦ To seek (political) asylum. ♦ To take shelter. ♦ To take under one's wing. ♦ To tend to. ♦ To watch over. ♦ Under lock and key. ♦ Under the aegis/auspices of. [see also Ally] ♦ I've/we've got you covered. ♦ I've/we've got your back.

Proverbs

A proverb is much matter decocted into (a) few words. ♦ A proverb is no proverb till your life has illustrated it. ♦ A proverb is one man's wit and all men's wisdom. ♦ An old saw may have sharp teeth. ♦ Good sayings are like pearls strung together. ♦ Many a monument was built with an old saw. ♦ Maxims are the condensed good sense of nations. ♦ Proverbs are, for the most part, rules of moral, or still more properly, of prudential conduct. ♦ Proverbs are the children of experience. ♦ Proverbs are the wisdom of the ages. ♦ Proverbs bear age, and he who would do well may view himself in them as a mirror. ♦ The genius, wit, and spirit of a nation are discovered in its proverbs. ♦ The greatest of sayings are those which remind us of other great sayings. ♦ The proverb is a short sentence from long experience. ♦ The proverb is the literature of the illiterate. ♦ The proverb serves when the sermon fails. ♦ The proverb sheds much light in one flash.

Public

A public nuisance. ♦ Adoring public. ♦ Contrary to popular belief/opinion. [see also Clarification] ♦ Give public notice. ♦ In the public domain. ♦ John Doe. ♦ John Q. Public. ♦ Just a poor, bill-paying slob. ♦ Main Street, U.S.A. ♦ Middle America. ♦ Nobody ever went broke underestimating the intelligence of the American public. ♦ Public opinion is what people think other people think. ♦ The court of public opinion. ♦ The general public.

♦ The great unwashed. ♦ The hoi polloi. ♦ The man in the street. ♦ The little old lady in Peoria. ♦ The poor slob. ♦ The public be damned. ♦ The Moral Majority. ♦ The Silent Majority. ♦ There's a sucker born every minute. ♦ To go public. ♦ What will my public think? ♦ Your average Joe (Schmo).

Pun

A play on words. ♦ A pun is a pistol shot off at the ear, not a feather to tickle the intellect. ♦ A pun is the lowest form of wit. ♦ A witty bit true. ♦ Compunations. ♦ He who would make a pun would pick a pocket. ♦ No pun intended. ♦ Once a pun a time. ♦ Pun City. ♦ Pun Lovers. ♦ Punache. ♦ Pun-ographic. ♦ Pun-ography. ♦ Pun-tificate. ♦ Pun-upsmanship. ♦ The pun is mightier than the word. ♦ To corn a phrase.

Puns

A collection of puns: compundium. ♦ A farce of Nature. ♦ A farce to be reckoned with. ♦ A frayed knot. ♦ A Mercedes bends. ♦ A merry-thon. ♦ A mocked man. ♦ A money-ac. ♦ A tour de farce. ♦ A weekend worrier. ♦ A weakened warrior. ♦ A whore's voice. ♦ Absinthe makes the heart grow fonder. ♦ Actor: one who has hit the skits. ♦ Alcoholics unanimous. ♦ All choked up with emulsion. ♦ All choking aside. ♦ All pregnant and accounted for. ♦ All thinks considered. ♦ An active God. ♦ An optical delusion. ♦ Are you friend or *faux*? ♦ As I live and breed. ♦ Between Iraq and a hard place. ♦ Born to luge. ♦ Brassiere: a booby trap. ♦ Britannia waives the rules. ♦ Broadway: Skit Row. ♦ Charles of the Rich. ♦ Clothed Encounters of the Thread Kind. ♦ Composure self. ♦ Contested will: splitting heirs. ♦ Curve appeal. ♦ Denial is not a river in Egypt. ♦ Did you hear about the prostitute who became a poet? She went from bed to verse. — R.D. ♦ Dolly Parton: Rack to Riches. ♦ Donald Duck is not all he's quacked up to be. ♦ Eat, drink and be merry, for tomorrow we diet. ♦ Ex-screamly horrifying. ♦ Fit to be tried. ♦ For he's a jowly good fellow. ♦ Fort Knocks. ♦ Genessee *quoi*. ♦ Genre-lly speaking. ♦ Hip, hip, puree. ♦ Hair today, gone tomorrow. ♦ He's just a flash in the pants. ♦ Home is where the hearth is. ♦ Homing bird /humming pigeon. ♦ How do they make holy water? They boil the hell out of it! ♦ Hypocrite: a holy tearer. ♦ I resemble that remark. ♦ I'm beginning to see delight. ♦ Indiana father: Hoosier daddy. ♦ Internally grateful. ♦ Itch and every one. ♦ It's anybody's guest. ♦ Join the Navy and seed the world. ♦ Jose, can you see. ♦ Lashed but not leashed. ♦ London britches falling down. ♦ London derriere. ♦ Lug it or leave it. ♦ Lying ghost: a boo-sh*tter. - R.D. ♦ Messy *beaucoup*. ♦ Money is at the root of all egos. ♦ More bank for your buck. ♦ My wordy opponent. ♦ No-bull prize. ♦ No eye dear. ♦ Off to a frying start. ♦ One small step for man; one giant schlep for mankind. - R.D. ♦ One nation, indefensible. ♦ Penis: a guided muscle. ♦ Pickpocket: one who has the gift of grab. ♦ Pock Avenue. ♦ Post-Dramatic Dress Syndrome. ♦ Present company accepted. ♦ Pun-upmanship. ♦ Rice to the occasion. ♦ Risque business. ♦ Role call. ♦ Selfie: a picture taken with myself phone. - R.D. ♦ Shifts happen. ♦ Sight effects. ♦ Site effects. ♦ Smellbound. ♦ Soulful security. ♦ Spurt of the moment. ♦ Stars and strife forever. ♦ Star-craving mad. ♦ Status-faction. ♦ The best thinks in life are free. - R.D. ♦ The champion of breakfasts. ♦ The cream of the crap. ♦ The cynic route. ♦ The Kink of all Media. ♦

The kitchen cynic. (Restaurant reviewer.) ♦ The Linked-In Memorial. ♦ The oaf of office. ♦ The pen is smitier than the sword. ♦ The plot sickens. ♦ The Prince of Wails. ♦ The realm of the coin. ♦ The sweat smell of success. ♦ The taste that launched a thousand sips. – R.D. ♦ The thighs that bind. ♦ The ties that blind. ♦ The troops will set you free. ♦ This guy's the limit. ♦ Thistle dew. ♦ To bodily go where no man has gone before. [see also Leadership] ♦ To get away with merger. ♦ To go for the jocular. ♦ To pun amok. ♦ Too clothed for comfort. ♦ Too true to be good. ♦ Trite and true. ♦ Trojan whores. ♦ Turn out in full farce. ♦ Wanted: debtor alive. ♦ Win or take all. ♦ Writer: a line tamer.

Punishment

A pound of flesh. ♦ A suspended sentence. ♦ Capital punishment. ♦ Crime and punishment. ♦ Death to spies. ♦ Do hard time. ♦ Don't do the crime if you can't do the time. [see also Crime, Imprisonment] ♦ Dock [so]'s pay. ♦ Drawn and quartered. ♦ Fifty lashes (with a wet noodle). ♦ Hanging's too good for him. ♦ Heads will roll. ♦ I don't know why he hates me so, I never did him a good turn. ♦ Just as virtue is its own reward, so is vice its own punishment. ♦ Keel haul. ♦ Let the punishment fit the crime. ♦ Life without the possibility (of parole). ♦ Make an example of [so]. ♦ Man punishes acts; God, thoughts. ♦ No good deed goes unpunished. ♦ Off with his head! ♦ Pay one's debt to society. [see also Debt] ♦ Racked and pilloried. ♦ Send [so] off to Siberia. ♦ Send [so] off to the salt mines. ♦ Serve [so]'s head upon a platter. ♦ Service without reward is punishment. ♦ Spare the rod and spoil the child. ♦ Stoned in the square. ♦ The death of a thousand cuts. ♦ Thirty dollars or thirty days. ♦ This is going to hurt me more than it hurts you. ♦ To be boiled in oil. ♦ To be grounded. ♦ To be disbarred. ♦ To be tarred and feathered. ♦ To exact a pound of flesh. ♦ To fan [so]'s bottom. ♦ To garnish [so]'s wages. ♦ To get/give a slap on the wrist. ♦ To get the chair. ♦ To get/have a time out. ♦ To hold [so] in contempt (of court). ♦ To lock the door and throw away the key. ♦ To send [so] to bed with no supper. ♦ To serve (hard) time. ♦ To slap [so] around/silly. ♦ To stay after school. ♦ To suffer the consequences. ♦ To take [so] out behind/to the woodshed. ♦ To teach [so] a lesson. ♦ To throw the book at [so]. ♦ Tough love. ◆ Whom the Lord loveth, He chasteneth. ◆ You've been naughty; go stand in the corner.

Pure
(also inexperienced, untried)

A 90-day wonder. ◆ A clean/clear conscience (is a soft pillow). ◆ A newbie. ◆ A rank amateur. ◆ A rookie. ◆ A shavetail. ◆ A *tabula rasa*. ◆ Contains no additives (or preservatives). ◆ Green/wet behind the ears. ◆ Greener than a gourd. ◆ Honest-to-goodness goodness. ◆ In a state of grace. ◆ Innocent as a newborn babe. ◆ Just got off the (banana) boat. ◆ Lily white. ◆ Maiden voyage. ◆ 99 & 44/100% pure—it floats! ◆ Not bad for an amateur. ◆ Plain/pure and simple. ◆ Pure as the driven snow. ◆ *Tabula rasa*. ◆ To have a lot to learn. ◆ To the pure all things are pure. ◆ Uncharted waters. ◆ Unmapped terrain. ◆ Virgin territory.

Purpose

A man with a mission. ◆ A reason to get up in the morning. ◆ A thing created is loved, before it exists, in the mind of the creator. ◆ An end in itself. ◆ Battle doesn't need a purpose; the battle is its own purpose. ◆ In order to achieve any goal, you must first set it. ◆ Singularity of purpose. ◆ The name of the game. ◆ To do [it] on purpose. ◆ To have imagination without learning is to have wings with no feet. ◆ To [v.] for the sake of [n.]. ◆ To speak just to hear oneself talk. ◆ What the mind can conceive, man may achieve.

Pursue

A man chases a girl until she catches him. ◆ A wild goose chase. ◆ A witch hunt. ◆ Breathing down [so]'s neck. ◆ Don't look now but I think we're being followed. ◆ Fox hunting: the unspeakable in pursuit of the inedible. ◆ Head 'em off at the pass! ◆ Hot on the heels/tail/trail (of). ◆ In (hot) pursuit (of). ◆ On the prowl. ◆ Search the world over. ◆ The chase is on. ◆ They went thataway. ◆ To be closing in (on). ◆ To be hard/hot on [so]'s heels. ◆ To beat the bushes. ◆ To bird-dog. ◆ To close in (on). ◆ To follow to the ends of the earth. ◆ To give chase. ◆ To lead on a merry chase. ◆ To take it all the way (up) to the Supreme Court. ◆ To throw oneself at [so]. ◆ To track down. ◆ To turn the place inside out/upside down. [see also Investigate]

Quality

A golden key opens every lock (except to Heaven). ◆ A silver key can open an iron lock. ◆ Do not care how many but whom you please. ◆ It's quality not quantity that counts. ◆ Large trees give more shade than fruit. ◆ Made of good wood. ◆ Quality second to none. ◆ Top of the line. ◆ Top shelf. ◆ You get what you pay for.

Question

A loaded question. ◆ A pop quiz. ◆ Anybody home? ◆ Ask a foolish question and you'll get a foolish answer. ◆ Ask a good question and you'll get a good answer. ◆ Ask and you shall receive. ◆ Ask me no questions, I'll tell you no lies. ◆ Ask no questions, hear no lies. ◆ Don't ask! ◆ Don't ask, don't tell. ◆ How come? ◆ How do you get to Carnegie Hall? Practice, practice, practice! ◆ How many angels can dance on the head of a pin? ◆ How many fingers do I have up? ◆ How/what about [it]? ◆ How/what/when/where/who/in creation/in the world/on (God's green) earth? ◆ I get asked that all the time. ◆ If you don't ask, you don't get. ◆ Is it animal, vegetable or mineral? ◆ Is it bigger than a bread box? [see also Big] ◆ Is this seat taken? ◆ Is there anyone (sitting) in this seat? ◆ Knock, knock. Who's there? ◆ May I ask you a personal question? ◆ May I ask you a question? [Riposte: Yes, that's one.] ◆ Or what? [see also Choices] ◆ Pop the question. ◆ There's no such thing as a dumb question. [is this T or F?] ◆ To answer a question with a question. ◆ To beg the question. ◆ To raise more questions than it answers. ◆ What in God's name? ◆ What, pray tell? ◆ Whatever happened to [n.]? ◆ Wherefore art thou, Romeo? ◆ Who's buried in Grant's tomb? ◆ Who's on first? ◆ You don't wanna know.

Quickly

(also immediate, unhesitating)
A flash flood. ◆ A flash mob. ◆ A fleeting moment. ◆ A knee-jerk reaction. ◆ A quick fix. ◆ A quick spritz. ◆ A reflex action. ◆ Alley-oop! ◆ At the drop of a hat. ◆ At the speed of light. ◆ At warp speed. ◆ Bada bing, bada boom. ◆ Bam, just like that. ◆ Before you can bat an eye. ◆ Before you know it. ◆ Before you know what hit you. ◆ Break the sound barrier. ◆ By leaps and bounds. ◆ Catlike reflexes. ◆ Don't give it a second thought. ◆ Didn't think twice about it. ◆ Fast and

furious. ◆ Fast as greased lightning. ◆ Fast as lightning. ◆ Faster than a speeding bullet. ◆ Faster than the speed of sound. ◆ Faster than you can say Jack Robinson. ◆ In a heartbeat. ◆ In a jiffy. ◆ In a New York Minute. ◆ In a trice. ◆ In a twink. ◆ In jig time. ◆ In less than no time. ◆ In no time (at all). ◆ In no time flat. ◆ In rapid fire. ◆ In record time. ◆ In short order. ◆ In the bat of an eye/eyelash. ◆ In the blink/twinkling of an eye. ◆ In two shakes (of a lamb's tail). ◆ Instant gratification. ◆ It all happened so fast. ◆ It'll only take a minute/second. ◆ Lightning fast. ◆ Like a finger through the flame. ◆ Like sh*t through a tin horn. ◆ More haste, less speed. ◆ Multiply like rabbits. ◆ Next thing you know. ◆ On a fast track. ◆ Quick as a bunny/flash/wink. ◆ Quick as a cat can wink her eye. ◆ Quick like a bunny. ◆ Quick draw McGraw. ◆ No sooner done than said. [radio news program's motto] ◆ No sooner said than done. ◆ Quick on the draw/uptake. ◆ (Right) then and there. ◆ So fast it'll make your head spin/your eyeballs snap. ◆ The five-second rule. ◆ To be fleet of foot. ◆ To beat all get-out. ◆ To break the sound barrier. ◆ To come thick and fast. ◆ To go viral. ◆ To have split-second timing. ◆ To make short work of. ◆ To spread like wildfire. ◆ Wham, bam, thank you, ma'am. ◆ With blinding/lightning speed. ◆ With the speed of light. ◆ Without batting an eye/eyelash. [see also Cool] ◆ Without (giving it) a second thought. ◆ Without missing a beat. ◆ Without thinking twice about it.

Quiet

All quiet on the western front. ◆ Hush, puppy! ◆ Quiet as a mouse. ◆ Quiet down. ◆ So quiet you can hear the grass grow. ◆ So quiet you can hear yourself think. ◆ So quiet you could hear a mosquito/mouse p*ssing on cotton all the way from Georgia. ◆ So quiet you could hear a pin drop. ◆ The calm before the storm. ◆ The natives are quiet tonight. . . . Too quiet. ◆ To lower one's voice.

Quit

And another one bites the dust. ◆ Break it up. ◆ Call off the dogs. ◆ Cease and desist. ◆ Cut it out. ◆ Give it a rest. ◆ In at the death. ◆ I rest my case. ◆ Knock it off. ◆ Quit cold turkey. ◆ Quit it! ◆ Quit the sh*t. ◆ Quit while you're ahead. ◆ Quitting time. ◆ Roger, over and out. ◆ Take one's marbles and go home. ♦ Take the rest of the day off. ♦ Tender one's resignation. ♦ That's a wrap! ♦ To ankle. ♦ To bag it. ♦ To bail (out). ♦ To bite the dust. ♦ To bow out (gracefully). ♦ To button it/things up. ♦ To call a halt (to). ♦ To call it a day/night. ♦ To call [it] off. ♦ To call it quits. ♦ To conk out/crap out. ♦ To cut [so] short. ♦ To drop from sheer exhaustion. ♦ To drop like flies. ♦ To drop out. ♦ To drop the hammer. ♦ To fall by the wayside. ♦ To flake out. ♦ To fold/throw in one's hand. ♦ To fold (up) one's tent (and steal away into the night). ♦ To give (one's 2-week) notice. ♦ To hang up one's gloves/jock/jockstrap/spurs/ sword. ♦ To hit/slam on the brakes. ♦ To hit the silk. ♦ To knock it off. ♦ To make a clean break. ♦ To pack it in. ♦ To pack up and go home. ♦ To pass the torch. ♦ To put a stop to. ♦ To put an end to. ♦ To put the brakes on. ♦ To put [it] to bed. ♦ To sever all ties. ♦ To step down. ♦ To stop short. ♦ To stop [n.]/[p.] in [p.] tracks. [see also Motionless] ♦ To tender one's resignation. ♦ To throw in the sponge/towel. ♦ You can't fire me—I quit. ♦ You have to know when to hold 'em, know when to fold 'em. ♦ You have to know when to quit.

Quote

All I can say/have to say is . . . ♦ And you may quote me (on that). ♦ As Cleopatra said, "Up your asp!" ♦ As David said to Goliath, "You have rocks in your head." ♦ As the accountant said, "that about sums it up." ♦ As the doctor said, "Lord, give me patients!" ♦ As the ironing board said, "I am pressed." ♦ As the pitcher said, "I'll bet my right arm on it." ♦ As the psychic said, "that's the spirit!" ♦ As the tailor said, "suit yourself." ♦ In the immortal words of . . . ♦ Quote, unquote. ♦ Quoth the raven, nevermore. ♦ Sez who?—sez me, that's who. ♦ Those who seldom quote are rarely quoted. ♦ To quote, chapter and verse. ♦ To steal a page from [so]'s book.

Rarely

A rainy day special. ♦ A special occasion. ♦ A sometime thing. ♦ (Every) now and again/now and then. ♦ (Every) once in a while. ♦ Every so often. ♦ Few and far between. [see also Scarce] ♦ From time to time. ♦ In a coon's age/dog's age. ♦ It's not every day you see something like [it]. ♦ Little-known facts. ♦ Never in (all) my born days/in my life. ♦ Not your average [n.]. ♦ On occasion. ♦ Once in a blue moon. ♦ Once in a (great) while. ♦

Once in a lifetime. ♦ Once in a month of Sundays. ♦ Out of the ordinary. ♦ Several years of rainy Wednesdays.

Readiness

All set. ♦ All signals/systems (are) go. ♦ Are you ready, Freddy? ♦ As good as done. ♦ At hand. ♦ At the first sign of trouble. ♦ At the ready. ♦ Available for duty. ♦ Drop your socks and grab your c*cks. ♦ Fire when ready, Gridley. ♦ Fire at will. (Who's Will?) ♦ Geared up. ♦ Get ready to roll. ♦ Good to go. ♦ Hot to trot. [see also Amorous] ♦ I'm on it. ♦ Johnny-on-the-spot. ♦ Just say the word. ♦ Not till I'm damned good and ready. ♦ On call. ♦ On duty. ♦ On full/high alert. ♦ On hand. ♦ On the count of three: One, two . . . ♦ On your mark, get set, go! ♦ One man's ready—everybody should be ready. [military] ♦ Only too [adj.] (to). ♦ Plug and play. ♦ Psyched up for. ♦ Raring to go. ♦ Ready as I'll ever be. ♦ Ready for prime time. ♦ Ready on the right, ready on the left, all ready on the firing line. ♦ Ready or not, here I come. ♦ Ready, set, go! ♦ Ready to wear. ♦ Ready when you are, C.B. ♦ Ripe and ready. ♦ Rough and ready. ♦ The duty roster. ♦ To be all set. ♦ To be fully prepared. ♦ To be game (for). ♦ To be in a state of preparedness /readiness.

♦ To be ready for one's closeup. ♦ To be there with bells on. ♦ To be up for anything. ♦ To come to a boil/head. ♦ To get right on it. ♦ To reach the point (of). ♦ You don't have to ask me twice. ♦ You have but to ask. ♦ You have only to ask.

Reality

A reality check. ♦ Actual unretouched photo. ♦ And that's the way it is today. ♦ As a matter of fact. ♦ As is. ♦ At face value. ♦ At heart. ♦ Cut and dried. ♦ Get real. ♦ Facts and figures. ♦ His bite is worse than his bark. ♦ I am what I am (and that's all that I am). ♦ In point of fact. ♦ In real life. ♦ In the cold light of day. ♦ It is what it is. [see also Destiny] ♦ It makes eminent sense. ♦ Keep it real. ♦ No more, no less. ♦ Nothing more, nothing less. ♦ Sometimes a straight line is not the shortest distance between two points. ♦ The facts speak for themselves. ♦ The material world. ♦ This is not a drill. ♦ To face facts. ♦ To get down to reality. ♦ We hold these truths to be self evident. [see also Obvious] ♦ Welcome to the Big Leagues. ♦ Welcome to the real world. ♦ Whatever is, is. ♦ Whatever is, is right. ♦ What you see is what you get. ♦ Whizzywig (WYSIWYG). ♦ You can't make this sh*t/stuff up.

♦ Your head may be in the clouds but keep your feet planted firmly on the ground.

Rebukes

Beat it. ♦ Butt out. ♦ Buzz off. ♦ Call off the dogs. ♦ Don't you understand English? ♦ F*ck off! ♦ Feel lucky today? ♦ Forget I asked. ♦ Get off my back/case. ♦ Get outta my face. ♦ Hands off. ♦ Have you no decency, man? ♦ How could you? ♦ How dare you? ♦ Keep your cotton-picking hands off. ♦ Lay off. ♦ Let my people go. ♦ Look, but don't touch. ♦ Lookie but no touchie. ♦ Mind your (own) business. ♦ Never (you/you just) mind. ♦ None of your beeswax. ♦ None of your business. ♦ Not that it's any of your business. ♦ Of all the nerve! ♦ Pick on somebody your own size. ♦ Shoemaker, stick to thy last. ♦ Stay out of my hair. ♦ Stay the hell out of this. ♦ Take a hike. ♦ What are you trying to prove? ♦ What of it? ♦ What's it to you? ♦ When I want your opinion, I'll ask for it. ♦ What are you, deaf? ♦ What part of "no" do you not understand? ♦ Where do you get off doing/saying that? ♦ Who asked you, anyway? ♦ Who (the hell) do you think you are (anyhow)? ♦ Wipe that (silly) grin/smile/smirk off your face. ♦ Wipe that sh*t-eating grin off your face. ♦ You haven't heard the last of this. ♦ You heard me (right) the first time. ♦ You heard what I said. ♦ You keep your nose out of this. ♦ You stay out of this. ♦ You'll hear from my lawyers. ♦ You've got a lot of nerve. ♦ You've got some/your nerve.

Reciprocation
(also share)

A double-edged sword. ♦ A trade-off. ♦ A two-way street. ♦ A zero-sum game. ♦ An even exchange. ♦ Do unto others as you would have them do unto you. [see also Consideration] ♦ Don't dish it out if you can't take it. ♦ Even-Steven. ♦ For every action there is an equal and opposite reaction. ♦ Give and take. ♦ In turn. ♦ It's a wash. ♦ It cuts both ways. ♦ On balance. ♦ One good turn deserves another. [see also Deserve] ♦ One hand washes the other (and together they both scratch your head/wash your face). ♦ Point, counterpoint. ♦ Put yourself in my place. ♦ *Quid pro quo.* ♦ Repay/reward in kind. [see also Repay] ♦ RSVP *Repondez s'il vous plait* (Please reply). ♦ Separate but equal. ♦ Share and share alike. ♦ Split it right up the middle. ♦ Spread the wealth. [see also Generosity] ♦ Strike and counter-strike. ♦ The barter system. ♦ The brother-in-law effect. ♦ The risk-reward factor. ♦ Thrust and parry. ♦ Tit for tat. ♦ To call in one's favors. ♦ To get/give a piece of the action. ♦ To give as good as you get. ♦ To go fifty-fifty. ♦ To go halfsies/halvesies. ♦ To parry the thrust. [see also Ripostes] ♦ To play ball with [so]. ♦ To repay [so] in kind. ♦ To return the compliment. ♦ To return the favor. ♦ To strike back. ♦ To take it out in trade. ♦ To take turns. ♦ To uphold one's end of the bargain. ♦ Was it good for you? [see also Sex] ♦ What [n.]/[p.] lacks in [n.] . . . [p.] makes up for in [n.]. ♦ What's good for the goose is good/sauce for the gander. ♦ You can't judge a person until you've walked a mile in her/his shoes. ♦ You never know a person until you've shared a pound of salt. ♦ You scratch my back and I'll scratch yours. ♦ You watch my back and I'll watch yours. [see also Precaution] ♦ You show me yours and I'll show you mine. ♦ Your turn in the barrel/tank.

Reckless

Come on, you sons of bitches, do you want to live forever? ♦ He who will avenge every affront means not to live long. ♦ If I had revenged every wrong, I had not worn my shirt so long. ♦ Leaping dogs never look. ♦ Reckless youth. ♦ The reckless man never has a gray beard. ♦ Throw caution to the winds. ♦ To be freewheeling. ♦ To cut loose. ♦ To fly into the teeth of the storm. ♦ To have more guts than brains. ♦ To go (hog) wild. ♦ To play fast and loose. ♦ With wild abandon. ♦ You can only die once.

Recuperation

In rehab. ♦ Let the healing begin. ♦ Lick one's wounds. ♦ Nurse a wound. ♦ Nurse back to health. ♦ On the disabled list. ♦ On the mend. ♦ On the (rocky) road to recovery. ♦ Only an open mind can be healed. ♦ R and R (rest and recovery/recuperation/relaxation). ♦ Salve one's wounds. ♦ To make a full recovery. ♦ To take (some much-needed) time off.

Reduce
(also compress, trivialize)

A market correction. ♦ Boil [it] down. ♦ Find the least common denominator. ♦ On a smaller scale. ♦ On the wane. ♦ Pare [it] down. ♦ Reduce to lowest terms. ♦ Starvation diet. ♦ Take a little off the top. ♦ Take one's belt in a notch. ♦ To cut back (on). ♦ To do without. ♦ To downplay [it]. ♦ To downsize. ♦ To ease up (on). ♦ To go on a diet. ♦ To institute an austerity plan. ♦ To limit one's intake. ♦ To make a molehill out of a mountain. ♦ To narrow the field. ♦ To phase [it] out. ♦ To pull in/tighten the reins. ♦ To reduce [it] to its lowest terms. ♦ To reduce to rubble. [see also Destroy] ♦ To scale/play [it] down. ♦ To snug [it] up. ♦ To staunch the flow. ♦ To stem the tide. ♦ To take [it] lightly. ♦ To take [it] off. ♦ To take the sting out of. ♦ To taper off. ♦ To think nothing of [it]. ♦ To tighten one's belt. ♦ To trade down. ♦ To trim the fat. ♦ To undercut the competition. ♦ To water [it] down. ♦ To wear off. ♦ To weed out. ♦ To whittle [it] down (to size). ♦ To wind down.

Refinement

A city slicker. ♦ A perfect gentleman (is just a patient wolf). ♦ A touch of class. ♦ An appreciation for the finer things (in life). ♦ Chivalry is not dead. ♦ How you gonna keep 'em down on the farm after they've seen *Paree*? ♦ Sophistication is the absence of vulgarity. ♦ The height of good taste. ♦ The man who has music in his soul will be most in love with the loveliest.

♦ Within the bounds of decorum/good taste/propriety.

Regret

A lifetime of regret. ♦ Don't cry over spilt milk. ♦ Guilt is regret for what we've done; regret is guilt for what we didn't do. [see also Guilt] ♦ I regret that I have but one life to give for my country. ♦ If I'd known I was going to live this long, I'd have taken better care of myself. ♦ It seemed like (such) a good idea at the time. ♦ Not a day goes by that I don't regret it. ♦ Of all sad words of tongue or pen, the saddest are these: "It might have been." ♦ Regrets only. ♦ Rue the day you were born. ♦ The life of every man is a diary in which he means to write one story, but instead writes another. And his saddest hour is when he compares the volume as it is with what he vowed to make it. ♦ To kick oneself in the *ss. ♦ To one's (ever)lasting regret. ♦ To rue the day. ♦ Woulda, shoulda, coulda. ♦ You can't miss what you never had. ♦ You'll be sorry. ♦ You'll live to regret that.

Rejection

Give me/I want my money back. ♦ Include me out. ♦ Reject [it] out of hand. ♦ Return to sender. ♦ Rule out the possibility. ♦ Sticks nix hick pix. [see also Rustication] ♦ The hell/to hell with [it]/[so]. ♦ To blow [it] off. ♦ To blow [it] out of the water. ♦ To fart [it]/[so] off. ♦ To get/give the brush-off. ♦ To get shot down/shoot down (in flames). ♦ To get/give (the) thumbs down. ♦ To have a low opinion of [it]/[so]. ♦ To have no use for. ♦ To have nothing to do with. ♦ To not think much of [it]/[so]. ♦ To opt out. ♦ To pass up. ♦ To reject [it] categorically/out of hand. ♦ To slam the door in [so]'s face. ♦ To take a pass (on). ♦ To think little of [it]/[so]. ♦ To thumb one's nose/turn one's nose up/turn up one's nose (at). ♦ To turn [it]/[so] away/down. ♦ To turn one's back on. ♦ To want out. ♦ To wash one's hands of.

Rejoinders

And that goes double for you! ♦ Are you a wise guy—or otherwise? ♦ Are you talking to me? [see also Clarification] ♦ Are you queer for my gear, boy? ♦ Chew on that for a while. ♦ Deal with it. ♦ 'Deed I do! ♦ Do tell.! ♦ Funny you should ask. ♦ I should hope so! ♦ I should say so. ♦ If brains were dynamite, you couldn't blow your nose. ♦ If I wanted to hear from an *sshole, I'd fart! ♦ If it weren't for us pr*cks, you c*cksuckers would be out of business. ♦ If that's what you think, you've got another think coming. ♦ Imagine that! ♦ Is that a fact? ♦ Is that so? ♦ It takes one to know one. ♦ Now see here. ♦ Now you listen to me. ♦ Pray tell. ♦ Put that in your bong and blow it. ♦ Put that in your pipe and smoke it. ♦ Really. ♦ Same to you, (Bub/Buddy/Pal). ♦ So there! ♦ So's your old man! ♦ That's the understatement of the year. ♦ Them's fighting words, pardner. ♦ Well, I have news for you. ♦ Who do you think you are? Anyhow? ♦ Who (the hell) do you think you are anyhow? ♦ You and what/whose army? ♦ You better grab a pick. ♦ You don't say. ♦ Your father's moustache. ♦ Your mother wears army/ combat boots. ♦ Your sister's *ss. ♦ You're cruisin' for a bruise/bruisin'. ♦ You're cruisin' for a bruisin' and achin' for a breakin'.

Rejuvenation
(also recycle, re-use)

A born-again Christian. ♦ A burst of energy. ♦ A complete overhaul. ♦ A new day is dawning. ♦ A new lease on life. ♦ A shot in the arm. ♦ All over again. ♦ As good as new. ♦ As I was saying. ♦ Back from the dead. ♦ Back in harness. ♦ Blow off/clear the cobwebs. ◆ Changing of the guard. ◆ Dumpster diving. ◆ Everything old is new again. ◆ Get back to nature. ◆ Hand-me-downs. ◆ Happy days are here again. [see also Excitement, Happiness] ◆ I feel like a new man/woman. ◆ Hit the rewind button. ◆ In a former/ past life. ◆ It gives new meaning to the term/word. ◆ It'll get worse before it gets better. ◆ It's better the second time around. ◆ It's *déjà vu* all over again. ◆ It's hard to make a comeback when you haven't been anywhere. ◆ Make a clean break with the past. ◆ Make a fresh start. ◆ Make an honest woman of. ◆ Mend one's ways. ◆ Old wine in new bottles. ◆ On the comeback trail. ◆ On the rebound. ◆ On the upswing. ◆ Open a new chapter. ◆ Out with the old, in with the new. ◆ Regroup one's forces. ◆ Ring out the old; ring in the new. ◆ Same horse, different blanket. ◆ Save the pieces! ◆ Straighten up and fly right. ◆ Take [it] out of mothballs. ◆ The inaugural address. ◆ The king is dead; long live the king! ◆ The phoenix will rise from the ashes. ◆ The Second Coming. ◆ The South will rise again. [see also Hope] ◆ To be born again. ◆ To bounce back, stronger than ever. ◆ To breathe new life into.

◆ To do a remake of. ◆ To fall/step in sh*t and come up smelling like a rose. [see also Luck] ◆ To feel/look like one's old self (again). ◆ To get a new lease on life. ◆ To get back on one's feet. ◆ To get back to basics. ◆ To get one's second wind. ◆ To get religion. ◆ To make/stage a comeback/rally. ◆ To make a fresh start. ◆ To make a strong comeback. ◆ To go at/pursue [it] with renewed vigor. ◆ To put the spark back into [it]. ◆ To reboot. ◆ To recharge one's batteries. ◆ To reinvent oneself. ◆ To reinvent the wheel. ◆ To restore one's faith in humanity. ◆ To rise from the ashes. ◆ To shift into overdrive. ◆ To start (out) with a clean slate. ◆ To start the new year right. ◆ To turn over a new leaf. ◆ To usher in a new era. ◆ To whip [it] into shape. ◆ To wipe the slate clean. ◆ What has been may be again.

Relativity
(also perspective)

A baloney sandwich may sometimes pass for a square meal. ◆ A father's fortune is often a son's misfortune. ◆ A fool's paradise is a wise man's hell. ◆ A new slant on things. ◆ A sense of proportion. ◆ A willing burden is no burden. ◆ An argument could be made either way. ♦ Ants at a picnic are unwelcome—unless you are an anteater. ♦ At the rate we're going. ♦ At this rate. ♦ Been down so long it looks like up to me. ♦ Better to be a big fish in a little pond than a little fish in a big pond.* ♦ Better to have a smaller piece of a bigger pie. *[see also Adequacy] ♦ Big churches, little saints. ♦ Big fleas have little fleas upon their backs to bite 'em/And little fleas have lesser fleas/And so on ad infinitum. ♦ Crowded elevators smell different to midgets. ♦ E=MC². ♦ Everything's relative. ♦ Form follows function. ♦ From each according to his ability, to each according to his need. ♦ From those to whom much is given, much is expected. ♦ Good health is merely the slowest possible rate at which one can die. ♦ I'll be the judge of that. ♦ If there were no fools, there would be no wise men. ♦ If you like that sort of thing. ♦ In good years, corn is hay; in ill years, straw is corn. ♦ In terms of. ♦ In the grand scheme of things. ♦ In the scheme of nature. ♦ In little churches, the saints look large. ♦ In the stream of life, you are a minnow. ♦ Is it hot in here or is it just me? ♦ It (all) depends. ♦ It's (all in) how you look at it. ♦ It's not how big it is, it's how you use it. ♦ It's not the size of your oar that matters, it's how you paddle your canoe. ♦ It's not the truth that matters, it's what people think the truth is. ♦ It's not whether you win or lose, but how you play the game. ♦ Justice delayed is justice denied. [see also Law] ♦ Morality is what you feel good after. ♦ On a sliding scale. ♦ One if by land, two if by sea. ♦ Open to interpretation. ♦ People are taking the comedians seriously and the politicians as a joke. ♦ Point of view. ♦ Pull devil, pull baker. ♦ Relatively speaking. ♦ Season to taste. ♦ Someday we'll look back on this and laugh. ♦ There is no right or wrong. ♦ To alter one's perceptions. ♦ To have selective memory. [see also Forget] ♦ To mark on a curve. ♦ To put [it] in perspective. ♦ Treat a whore like a queen and a queen like a whore, and you've got it made. ♦ Under the circumstances. ♦ Use determines classification. ♦ What is true by lamplight is not always true by sunlight. ♦ What the traffic will bear. ♦ We do 3 kinds of work: fast, cheap and good. You can have any 2: --If you want it cheap and good, it won't be fast. --If you want it good and fast, it won't be cheap. --If you want it cheap and fast, it won't be good. -[shop sign] ♦ What the traffic will bear. [see also Expense] ◆ When Einstein spoke of relativity, some cried nepotism. ◆ When it comes to fighting I'm a lover; and when it comes to loving, I'm a fighter. ◆ Where one is coming from. ◆ Whether you've got it all ahead of you or you've got it all behind you, you've got it all. — R.D. ◆ Whether you think you can or think you can't, you're right. ◆ Why am I beating myself? Because it feels so good when I stop! ◆ You get what you pay for. ◆ You have to consider the source. ◆ You hear what you want to hear. ◆ You see what you want to see. ◆ You've got to have worse to know better.

Relax

A coffee/lunch break. ◆ A leave of absence. ◆ As you were. ◆ At ease. ◆ Can I get you something to drink? ◆ Don't worry—be happy. ◆ Have a seat. ◆ Life has no rewind button but thankfully, it does have an unwind button. — R.D. ◆ Make yourself comfortable. ◆ Make yourself (right) at home. ◆ Mind if I slip into something more comfortable? ◆ No rest for the weary. ◆ No rest for the weary and the wicked need none. ◆ No rest for the wicked. ◆ Pull up a chair. ◆ Relax and settle in. ◆ Rest one's weary bones/head. ◆ Run your fingers through my hair. ◆ Savor the moment. ◆ Sink into your easy chair. ◆ Sit back and enjoy the show. ◆ Stop and smell the roses. ◆ Take a break/breather. ◆ Take a load off one's feet. ◆ Take five. ◆ Take it down a notch. ◆ To set one's mind at ease. ◆ To spend quality time. ◆ To take the edge off. ◆ Would you care for something to drink/eat/smoke?

Relic

A collector's item. ◆ A knuckle-dragger. ◆ A museum piece. ◆ A thing of the past. ◆ A throwback to prehistoric times. ◆ An old fossil. ◆ Old school. ◆ That's so dated. ◆ That's so nineties. ◆ To go the way of hula hoops and mood rings. ◆ To go the way of buggy whips and high-button shoes. ◆ To go the way of floppy disks and 8-track tapes. [see also Hackneyed]

Religion

A churchgoing man/woman. ◆ A gift from God. ◆ A holy roller. ◆ A man of the cloth. ◆ Almighty God. ◆ An act/article of faith. ◆ And God said to Moses, "take two tablets and call me." ◆ And may the good Lord take a liking to you. ◆ As the Good Book says. ◆ Better God than gold. ◆ Bless this house, oh, Lord, we pray.

Make it safe both night and day. ♦ By Divine Providence. ♦ Divine intervention. ♦ *Dominus vobiscum.* ♦ Give me that old-time religion. ♦ God answers all prayers—but sometimes the answer is "no." – R.D. ♦ God forgot you? You forgot yourself. ♦ God is dead.—Nietsche/Nietsche is dead.—God. ♦ How do I know? The Bible tells me so. ♦ Fingers crossed. [see also Luck] ♦ If God is for us, who can be against us? ♦ In the eyes of God. ♦ In the name of the Father, the Son and the Holy Ghost/Spirit. ♦ It's the Christian thing to do. ♦ Jesus saves. ♦ Jesus saves Green Stamps. ♦ Let go and let God. ♦ Modern religion: sin now pray later. ♦ Now I lay me down to sleep, I pray the Lord my soul to keep; /If I should die before I wake, I pray the Lord my soul to take. ♦ O, ye of little faith. ♦ Prepare to meet thy maker. ♦ Religion is the opiate of the masses. ♦ Say your prayers. ♦ Somebody up there likes/loves me. ♦ That than which nothing greater can be conceived. ♦ The Holy Grail. ♦ The holy of holies. ♦ The house of the Lord. ♦ The immovable mover. ♦ The inner sanctum. ♦ The Lord provides. ♦ The Lord works in mysterious/strange ways (His wonders to perform). ♦ The God within. ♦ The Man Upstairs. ♦ The sanctum sanctorum. ♦ There are no atheists in foxholes. ♦ To answer to a higher call. ♦ To attain/reach nirvana. ♦ To get religion. ♦ To get right with God. ♦ To go to heaven. ♦ To have a religious experience. ♦ To reach the Promised Land. ♦ To read the Good Book. ♦ What would Jesus do? [see also Correct]

Remembrance

A photographic memory. ♦ An elephant never forgets. ♦ Alas, poor Yorick, I knew him (well). ♦ As near as I (can) recall. ♦ I remember it well. ♦ I'll never forget old what's-his-name? ♦ If memory serves (me correctly). ♦ *In memoriam.* ♦ In memory of. ♦ It brings back memories. ♦ It's all coming back to me (now). ♦ Learn it by heart. ♦ Let us never forget what they did to the Jews. ♦ (Lost in) the mists of memory. ♦ Make a mental note. ♦ Memories of days gone by. ♦ Now it all comes back to me. ♦ Remember the Alamo/nine eleven/the Maine/Pearl Harbor. ♦ Remembrance of things past. ♦ Something to remember me by. ♦ Tippecanoe and Tyler too. ♦ To be fresh in one's mind. ♦ To commit [it] to memory. ♦ To have a memory like an elephant. ♦

To have a photographic memory. ♦ To have total recall. ♦ To dimly/ vaguely recall/remember. ♦ To jog one's memory. ♦ To the best of my recollection. ♦ Write that/this down.

Reminiscent

A blast from the past. ♦ A dying/ lost art. ♦ Back in the day. ♦ For old times' sake. ♦ Golden oldies. ♦ I remember it like it was yesterday. ♦ Like old home week. ♦ Oldies but goodies. ♦ Reminiscent of a bygone era. ♦ Sentimental value. ♦ The glorious days of yesteryear. ♦ The memory lingers on. ♦ Those were the good old days. ♦ To stroll down memory lane.

Remote

A backwater. ♦ A drinkwater/jerkwater town. ♦ A (little) hole in the wall. ♦ An out-of-the-way place. ♦ A one-horse town. ♦ A whistle stop. ♦ Bumf*ck, Egypt. ♦ Faraway/far-flung/far-off lands. ♦ In the outback. No-man's land. ♦ Nowheresville. ♦ Off the beaten path/track. ♦ Off the grid. ♦ On the outskirts (of town). ♦ Out back. ♦ Out in the boondocks/ boonies/ hinterlands/outback/ sticks. [see also Rustication] ♦ Out in the middle of nowhere. ♦ Out of the way.

♦ Podunk, U.S.A. ♦ The back forty. ♦ The far reaches. ♦ The outside world. ♦ The Third World. ♦ Uncharted territory/waters. ♦ Words too familiar, or too remote, defeat the purpose of a poet.

Renowned
(also prominence)

A high profile. ♦ A household name/ word. ♦ A legend in his own time. ♦ A living legend. ♦ A reputation to uphold. ♦ A star is born. ♦ A star of stage and screen. ♦ A star on the Hollywood Walk of Fame. ♦ A who's who. ♦ Bask in the limelight. ♦ Burst into the limelight. ♦ Celebrated in story and song. ♦ Come to/ step to the fore. ♦ Front and center. ♦ Front-runner. ♦ In the limelight. ♦ In the public eye. ♦ In the glare of national exposure. ♦ Known far and wide. ♦ Leap to the fore/forefront. ♦ Make a name for oneself. ♦ Mention my name in Sheboygan. ♦ Much bruited (about). ♦ Much publicized. ♦ Star quality. ♦ The cutting/leading edge. [see also Trendy] ♦ The main drag of town. ♦ The stuff that legends are made of. ♦ To be highly regarded/ well respected. ♦ To get top billing. ♦ To lead the pack. ♦ To leave footprints in the sands of time. ♦ To rise to prominence. ♦ To set the standard. ♦ To take center stage. ♦ Top gun. ♦ Top banana. ♦ Top billing. ♦ Who (I'm sure) needs no introduction. ♦ Your reputation precedes you.

Repay

A kindness too quickly repaid is a form of ingratitude. [see also Ingratitude] ♦ Give a beggar a bed and he'll repay you with a louse. ♦ He who wants Lent to seem short should contract a debt that is to be repaid at Easter. [see also Relativity] ♦ How can I ever repay you? ♦ If someone takes your time, it is the only debt that can never be repaid. ♦ It is fraud to accept what you cannot repay. ♦ Make amends. ♦ Make things right. ♦ Repay evil with good, and hell will not claim you. ♦ Repay/reward in kind. [see also Reciprocation] ♦ To live a perfect day, do something for someone who will never be able to repay you. ♦ To redress a grievance. ♦ To repay in like coin. ♦ To reward handsomely. ♦ To right a wrong. ♦ To square up (with).

Repetition

(also frequent, often)

Again and again. ♦ All over again. ♦ All you hear is [n.] this and [n.] that. ♦ As I always say . . . ♦ As they say . . . ♦ Don't repeat yourself. ♦ Double meanings may father second thoughts. ♦ Each and every one. ♦ Every hour on the hour. ♦ Every minute of the day. ♦ For the umpteenth time. ♦ Here we go again. ♦ Hit me again. ♦ How many times do I have to tell you? ♦ I cannot emphasize this too strongly. ♦ I've said it before and I'll say it again. ♦ If I've told you once I've told you a thousand times. ♦ If it happened once, it can happen again. ♦ In rapid succession. ♦ It won't/ wouldn't be the first time (that's happened) (and it won't be the last). [see also Predictable] ♦ It's *déjà vu* (all over again). ♦ Keep 'em coming. ♦ Keep it up. ♦ Many a time. ♦ Many times. ♦ Many's the time. ♦ Now, repeat after me. ♦ One (thing) after another/the other. ♦ One at a time. ♦ One by one. ♦ Once more. ♦ One more once. ♦ Over and over. ♦ People who talk of reincarnation wish to repeat themselves. ♦ Polly wants a cracker. [see also Imitation] ♦ Please hang up and try your call again. ♦ Take it from the top. ♦ Tell them what you're going to tell them; tell them; tell them what you told them. ♦ That makes it [n.] in a row.

♦ Then again . . . ♦ There you go again. ♦ Those who talk doubletalk needn't repeat themselves. ♦ Time after time. ♦ Time and time again. ♦ To demand a recount. ♦ To drive/ hammer the point home. ♦ To dwell on/upon. ♦ To flare up. ♦ To get/ have a do-over. ♦ To get/give a second chance. ♦ To go on and on. ♦ To have second thoughts. ♦ To harp on. ♦ To retrace one's steps. ♦ To revisit the issue. ♦ To see double. ♦ To think better of [it]. ♦ Tune in again next week (same time, same station). ♦ Which is another way of saying . . . ♦ Year after year.

Reputation

A child molester. ♦ A convicted felon. ♦ A (good) track record. ♦ A house of ill repute. ♦ A known offender. ♦ A moral compass. ♦ A rap sheet. ♦ A record as long as your arm. ♦ A red light district. ♦ A registered sex offender. ♦ A reputation to uphold. ♦ A tree is known by its fruit. ♦ All wool and a yard wide. ♦ Above/beyond reproach. ♦ By his work shall ye know him. ♦ Claim to fame. ♦ Give a dog a bad name and he'll deserve it. [see also Prediction] ♦ Have a good/bad rep. ♦ He who hath an ill reputation is half hanged. ♦ I've heard so much about you. ♦ The evil that men do lives after them; the good is oft interred with their bones. ♦ The good that you do is soon gone, but the bad lives on. ♦ To besmirch/sully/tarnish one's image/reputation. ♦ To cast a long shadow. ♦ To get bad/good ink. ♦ To get one's name in the papers. ♦ To live up to one's reputation. ♦ To put one's reputation on the line. ♦ To reflect badly on [so]. ♦ To stake one's reputation on [it]. ♦ Who steals my purse steals trash; who steals my good name takes everything

Rescue
(also prevent)

A(n) eleventh-hour/last-minute reprieve. ♦ Give mouth-to-mouth. ♦ Help is on the way. ♦ Jim Dandy to the rescue. ♦ Nip [it] in the bud. ♦ Pull the fat out of the fire. ♦ Save one's *ss. ♦ Save one's skin. ♦ Saved by the bell. ♦ Snatched from the jaws of death. ♦ The jaws of life. ♦ To bail [so] out. ♦ To break one's fall. ♦ To call for backup. ♦ To come through in the clutch. ♦ To come to [so]'s aid/assistance/rescue. ♦ To come to the rescue. ♦ To cut [n.]/[p.] off at the knees. [see also Attack] ♦ To get/give a reprieve. ♦ To put [so] on life support. ♦ To save the day. ♦ To send in the cavalry. ♦ To stem/turn the tide. ♦ To stick up for [so]. ♦ To throw [so] a lifeline. ♦ Women and children first.

Respectability

A clean-cut, all-American boy. ♦ A cornerstone of civilization. ♦ A down-to-earth person. ♦ A law-abiding citizen. ♦ A meat-and-potatoes man. ♦ A *mensch*. ♦ A no-nonsense person. ♦ A nuts-and bolts-individual. ♦ pillar of society/the community. ♦ A square shooter. ♦ A stand-up guy. ♦ An alright guy. ♦ An honest John. ♦ Honest, hard-working, tax-paying citizen. ♦ On the square. ♦ Solid citizen. ♦ To be straight arrow. ♦ Upright/upstanding member of society.

Restless

A bundle of nervous energy. ♦ Bouncing off the walls. ♦ Flip and flop. ♦ Flopping like a fish. ♦ The natives are restless tonight. ♦ The seven-year itch. ♦ The seventh-inning stretch. ♦ To be antsy. ♦ To have ants in your pants. ♦ To toss and turn. ♦ Twist and turn.

Resume

As I was saying before I was so rudely interrupted. ♦ Back in action. ♦ Back in the saddle (again). ♦ I'm back! ♦ Let's take it from there. ♦ Once again, into the breach. ♦ To get back on course/on track. ♦ To pick up the thread. ♦ To pick/take up where one left off. ♦ We now return to our regularly scheduled program. ♦ Where were we before we were so rudely interrupted?

Return

As MacArthur said, "I shall return." ♦ Back in a flash. ♦ Back in a jiff. ♦ Bring 'em back alive. ♦ Come back, little Sheba. ♦ Don't come back empty-handed. ♦ Here's Johnny! ♦ Home from the hills. ♦ Honey, I'm home! ♦ Return of the Jedi. ♦ Shane, come back! ♦ The prodigal son returns. ♦ To come crawling/running back. ♦ To return to the fold. ♦ To revisit the issue. ♦ We'll be right back after these (important) messages.

Reveal

Come out, come out, wherever you are. ♦ Come out with your hands up. ♦ To blow the lid off. ♦ To blow one's cover. ♦ Come out of the closet. [see also Homosexuality] ♦ Spoiler alert. ♦ To bust/explode a myth. ♦ To come out of one's shell. ♦ To come to light. ♦ To come to the surface. ♦ To expose to the harsh light of reality. ♦ To give the ending away. ♦ To give the high sign. ♦ To let it all hang out. ♦ To put [it] in the glare of the spotlight. ♦ To render an account (of). ♦ To see the light of day. [see also Enlightenment] ♦To show one's stripes. ♦ To show one's true colors. ♦ To show one's unmentionables. ♦ To strip away the veil. ♦ To telegraph one's punches. ♦ To tip one's hand. ♦ To tell the tale. ♦ To whip it out.

Revel

(also dissipation)

A gala affair. ♦ A knees-up. ♦ A pour. ♦ A rollicking good time. ♦ A rootin', tootin', shootin' good time. ♦ A shindig. ♦ A whale of a time. ♦ An after-party. ♦ An after-hours club. ♦ An all-day affair. ♦ Booyah! ♦ Boys'/ girls' night out. ♦ Dancing in the streets. ♦ Fun and frolic. ♦ Get it out of one's system. ♦ Get one's freak/ groove on. ♦ Have the time of one's life. ♦ High jinks (also hi jinks). ♦ Hip, hip hooray! ♦ Hooray and hallelujah! ♦ Hoot and holler. ♦ I can't remember the last time I had such a blast/good time/fun. ♦ Kick up one's heels. ♦ Kill the fatted calf. ♦ Live it up, but don't do anything you can't live down. — R.D. ♦ Make the scene. ♦

Man is a party animal. ♦ My night to howl. ♦ Out on the town. ♦ Party on! ♦ Raise a hullaballo. ♦ Raise a ruckus/rumpus. ♦ Raise Cain/the devil/ hell. [see also Complain] ♦ Rip roaring. ♦ Romp and stomp. ♦ Saturday night and I'm ready to howl. ♦ Shout it from the rooftops. ♦ The evening's festivities. ♦ The evening has only just begun. ♦ The night is young and so are we. ♦ This calls for a celebration. ♦ To bust/cut/let loose. ♦ To cut capers. ♦ To have a blast. ♦ To have a field day. [See also Clean] ♦ To have a good/great time. ♦ To have one's (last) fling. ♦ To make a day of it. ♦ To make whoopie. ♦ To paint the town red. ♦ To sow one's wild oats. ♦ To throw a party. ♦ To whoop it up. ♦ To wine and dine. ♦ Zippity doo dah!

Revenge

All right for you. ♦ An eye for an eye. ♦ An eye for an eye makes the whole world blind. ♦ Divine retribution. ♦ Don't get mad—get even. ♦ Even the score. ♦ Fix you. ♦ Fix [so]'s wagon. ♦ It's payback time. ♦ Let that be a lesson to you. ♦ Living well is the best revenge. ♦ Never seek to be the avenger; God is the avenger. — Angela Maria Delia ♦ No evil deed goes unpunished. ♦ Now we're even. ♦ Payback time. ♦ Revenge is a dish best served cold. ♦ Revenge is sweet. ♦ Settle the score. ♦ Some people do odd things to get even. ♦ That's a game that two can play. ♦ The avenging angel. ♦ The best revenge is massive success. ♦ To be out for blood. ♦ To be out to get [so]. ♦ To do it (just) for spite/out of spite/to spite [so]. ♦ To exact revenge. ♦ To get back at [so]. ♦ To get even (with). ♦ To get payback. ♦ To have the last laugh. ♦ To have the last word. ♦ To make [so] eat her/his words. ♦ To right all wrongs. [see also Organize] ♦ To take it out on [so]. ♦ To turn the tables on [so]. ♦ Two can play (at) that game. ♦ Vengeance is mine, sayeth the Lord. ♦ Who's laughing now?

Rich

A bankroll that would choke a horse. ♦ A get-rich- quick scheme. ♦ A man of means. ♦ A millionaire (many times over). ♦ A rich bitch. ♦ As rich as Fort Knox. ♦ Come into money. ♦ Every person dies rich, leaving millions. ♦ He who would be rich in one year is hanged in six months. ♦ Heavy purse, light of heart. ♦ I don't want to be a millionaire; I just want to live like one. ♦ I'd rather be rich. ♦ If you're rich enough, you can get away with anything. ♦ Independently wealthy. ♦ It is easier for a camel to go through the eye of a needle, than for a rich man to enter the kingdom of God. ♦ Money goes to money. ♦ Mr./Ms. Moneybags. ♦ Of independent means. ♦ Plenty to live on but nothing to live for. ♦ Rich as Rockefeller. ♦ Rolling in dough. ♦ The idle rich. ♦ The rich are different from you and me. ♦ The rich get rich and the poor get poorer. ♦ The road to riches. ♦ Them that has, gets. ♦ There is no one so rich that he does not still want something. ♦ To be born with a silver spoon in one's mouth. ♦ To be filthy rich. ♦ To be in the chips. ♦ To be in the money. ♦ To be made of money. ♦ To be set for life. ♦ To be sitting on a goldmine. ♦ To cry all the way to the bank. ♦ To feel flush. ♦ To have it handed to you on a silver platter. ♦ To have the Midas touch. ♦ To the manor born. ♦ Well off. ♦ Well heeled. ♦ Why wasn't I born rich instead of handsome? ♦ You can't be too rich or too thin. ♦ You'll never get rich by digging a ditch. [see also Poverty]

Ridicule

Call a bald man "Curly." ♦ Call a bespectacled person "foureyes." ♦ Call a stupid person "Einstein." ♦ Call a fat person "Slim." ♦ Call an ugly man "Handsome." ◆ Call a redhead "Carrot Top." ◆ Call a skinny person "Tarzan" (or "Charles Atlas"). ◆ Call a tall person "Stretch." ◆ Laugh up one's sleeve. ◆ Make an *ss of [so]. ◆ Make mock of. ◆ Mock my words. ◆ Mock [so] out. ◆ To dismiss as the rantings/ravings of a lunatic/madman. ◆ To do a send-up (of). ◆ To goof on [sb]. ◆ To have sport with. ◆ To make [so] the butt of jokes. ◆ To make fun/light of. ◆ To poke fun at. ◆ To put [it]/[so] down. ◆ To take the starch out of. ◆ We're laughing with you, not at you.

Right

A right-winger. ◆ Am I right or am I right? ◆ Am I right or what? ◆ Divine right of kings. ◆ For due cause. ◆ Go right and you'll never go wrong. ◆ God is on the side of the largest army. ◆ I'd rather be right than be president. ◆ Isn't that right? ◆ It's only right. ◆ Might makes right. ◆ Nobody's right all the time. ◆ On the side of the angels. ◆ Right as rain. ◆ Right makes might. ◆ Right on the money. ◆ Right you are. ◆ Right-o, guvnor. ◆ Squatter's rights. ◆ That's just it. ◆ The right of first refusal. [see also No] ◆ The right to bear arms. ◆ The right to know/life/work. ◆ The

rightful heir/owner. ◆ Three rights make a left. ◆ To be in the right. ◆ To be (well) within one's rights. ◆ To do what's right (by [so]). ◆ To have a point. ◆ To have every right (to). ◆ To have the right of way. ◆ To read [so] his/her rights. ◆ Two negatives make a positive. ◆ Two wrongs don't make a right. [see also Correct] ◆ Two wrongs may not make a right but three lefts do. - R.D. ◆ You have the right to an attorney. ◆ You have the right to remain silent. (Anything you say can and will be used against you in a court of law). [see also Silence] ◆ You've got it. ◆ You're (so) right. ◆ You've got that right. ◆ What's right is right. ◆ When you're right, you're right.

Ripostes

A pound of fifties/a stack of twenties [in response to bank teller, "Is there anything else I can do for you?"] ◆ And leave/make (some) room for you? [in response to, "Get your mind out of the gutter."] ◆ Better than nothing. [in response to, "How's your husband/wife?" (var. Compared to what?)] ◆ Don't let it happen again. [in response to, "Sorry."] ◆ Don't "sir" me, I'm not an officer. [in response to "no, sir"/"yes, sir."] ◆ Here are the cannonballs—go win the war. ♦ Hay is for horses. [in response to, "hey!"] ♦ I don't know whether to brag because I have nothing to complain about, or to complain because I have nothing to brag about. — R.D. [in response to, "Are you bragging or complaining?"] [see also Brag] ♦ It looks too much like your face. [in response to, "Kiss my *ss."] ♦ It's all up to you. ♦ It's your nickel. ♦ Look that up in your Funk and Wagnall's. ♦ None taken. [In response to, "No offense intended."] ♦ Not much. [in response to, "What are you looking at?"] ♦ Not since Superman died – or, My *ss and your face. [in response to, "Got a match?"] ♦ Oh yeah? Says who? ♦ Over to you. ♦ Return the volley. ♦ So's your mother. ♦ So's your old man. ♦ That's what she said. [in response to a wide variety of statements, e.g. "it won't be long now."] ♦ The ball is in your court. ♦ The turd's on your plate now. ♦ Time to buy a watch. [in response to, "What time is it?"]. ♦ To hell if I don't change my ways. [in response to, "Where are you going?"] ♦ To parry the thrust. [see also Reciprocation] ♦ Very few of us left. [in response to, "You're a good man."] ♦ Who dat say, 'who dat?' ♦ You and whose army? ♦ You got a problem with that? ♦ You have the floor. ♦ Your move.

Risk

(also dangerous, precarious)

A code red. ♦ A delicate balance. ♦ A delicate subject. ♦ A flight risk. ♦ A hairpin turn. ♦ A high-risk industry/occupation. ♦ A high-wire act. ♦ A recipe for disaster. ♦ A threat to life and limb. ♦ A ticking time bomb. ♦ A ticklish situation. ♦ A disaster/tragedy in the making. ♦ A sensitive issue. ♦ About to blow/erupt/explode. ♦ An adrenaline junkie.* ♦ An adrenaline rush. *[see also Excitement] ♦ An occupational hazard. ♦ Asking for trouble. ♦ At gunpoint/knifepoint. ♦ At risk. ♦ Anything you say can and will be used against you (in a court of law). ♦ Behind enemy lines. ♦ Court disaster. ♦ Double jeopardy. ♦ Fraught with danger. ♦ Go into the tank. ♦ Go out on a limb. ♦ Hanging by a thread. ♦ Hanging over one's head, like the sword of Damocles. ♦ He who climbs highest falls farthest. ♦ He who lives by his wits lives on the edge of a precipice. ♦ Here goes nothing. ♦ In jeopardy. ♦ In the line of fire. ♦ Life in the fast lane. [see also Hedonism] ♦ Like walking on eggshells/glass. ♦ Live dangerously. ♦ Nothing ventured, nothing gained. ♦ Nothing ventured, nothing lost. ♦ On a collision course. ♦ Playing with fire. ♦ Proceed at one's own risk. ♦ Riding for a fall. ♦ Risk is the price you pay for opportunity. ♦ Risky business. ♦ Sitting on a powder keg. ♦ Skating on thin ice. ♦ Sometimes you must lose a fly to catch a trout. ♦ Stick one's neck out. ♦ Take a calculated risk. ♦ Take the plunge. ♦ (Teetering) on the brink of disaster.♦ The element of risk. ♦ The higher you climb, the harder you fall. ♦ The perils of Pauline. ♦ There's blood in the water. ♦ Tiptoe through the tulips. ♦ To be asking for it. ♦ To be sitting on a keg of dynamite. ♦ To beard the lion in his den. ♦ To court danger/disaster. ♦ To defy death. ♦ To flirt with danger. ♦ To go for it. ♦ To fly/laugh in the face of danger. ♦ To live on the edge. ♦ To play with dynamite. ♦ To pose a threat. ♦ To push the boundaries/envelope. ♦ To push one's luck. ♦ To put one's life on the line. ♦ To run the risk. ♦ To shoot the rapids. ♦ To take a chance. ♦ To take a flier/flyer (in the market). ♦ To take your chances. ♦ To take your life in/into your (own) hands. ♦ To tempt fate/the fates. ♦ To thumb one's nose at danger/death. ♦ To walk a fine line. ♦ To walk a tightrope. ♦ Treading in deep water. ♦ Under the sword of Damocles. ♦ What've you got to lose? ♦ You'll never know unless/until you try. ♦ You pays your money and you takes your chances.

Romance

A hopeless romantic. ♦ A match made in heaven. ♦ A storybook romance. ♦ A teenage heartthrob. ♦ A pair of lovebirds. ♦ A whirlwind courtship. ♦ (All) lovey-dovey. ♦ An incurable romantic. ♦ And they lived happily ever after. [see also End] ♦ Bill and coo. ♦ Every Jack must have his Jill. ♦ For every him there's a her. ♦ For every match, there's a mate. ♦ For every pot there's a lid. ♦ Hearts and flowers. ♦ Icy fingers up and down your spine. ♦ Kootchy-kootchy coo. ♦ Made/meant for each other. ♦ Soul mates. ♦ Suitor: man after girl's own heart. ♦ To be an item. ♦ To be romantically involved/linked. ♦ To be stuck on/sweet on [so]. ♦ To get her, you have to get together. – R.D. ♦ To hook up (with). ♦ To romance [so]. ♦ To take a fancy/liking/shine to. ♦ Two hearts in three-quarter time. ♦ When your lips meet mine.

Rough
(also tough)

A lean, mean, fighting machine. ♦ A rough idea. ♦ A rough sketch. ♦

Hard as a rock. ♦ One tough cookie. ♦ Rough and ready. ♦ Rough and tough. ♦ Rough and tumble. ♦ Rough around the edges. ♦ Rough as a washboard. ♦ Rough trade. ♦ To give [so] a rough time. ♦ To ride roughshod (over). [see also Dominate] ♦ To rough it. ♦ To rough it up. ♦ Tough as nails.

Routinely

All in a day's work. ♦ An everyday occurrence/ritual. ♦ As a matter of course. ♦ As usual. ♦ Boilerplate. ♦ Cookie-cutter. ♦ In the normal course of action/events. ♦ I'll have the usual. ♦ Just part of our service. ♦ Mass production. ♦ No surprise there. ♦ Standard practice. ♦ The assembly line. ♦ We do it every day. ♦ Your usual self.

Rules

A cardinal rule. ♦ A grandfather clause. A hard-and-fast rule. [see also Law] ♦ An unwritten rule. ♦ Bend the rules. ♦ Everything which is not expressly forbidden is allowed. [converse: everything which is not expressly allowed is forbidden.] ♦ Home rule. ♦ In Hollywood there are no rules, but you break them at your peril. ♦ It is the exception that proves the rule. [see also Exceptions] ♦ Rule Number One

is: [n.]; Rule Number Two is: don't forget Rule Number One. ♦ Rule of thumb.

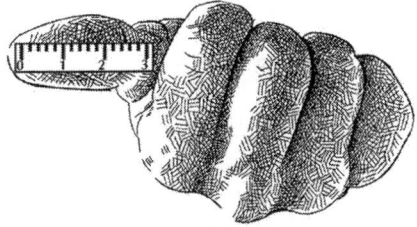

♦ Rules and regulations. ♦ Rules are rules. ♦ Rules are/were made to be broken. ♦ The do's and don'ts. ♦ The five-second rule. ♦ The Rule of Threes—three minutes without air, three days without water, three weeks without food—then you die. ♦ There are two rules in life: 1). There are no rules. 2). See rule #1. ♦ There's an exception to every rule. [see also Exceptions] ♦ To go by the book/rulebook/rules. ♦ To live by the Golden Rule.

Rustication

A clodhopper. ♦ A country bumpkin. ♦ A cracker. ♦ A cracker-barrel philosopher. ♦ A hayseed/hick. ♦ A home-grown beauty. ♦ A mom-and-pop shop/store. ♦ A redneck. ♦ A sh*tkicker. ♦ Cornpone and cornball. ♦ Country as cornflakes. ♦

Down home. ♦ Heigh ho the derry-o. ♦ Hicks 'n' ticks. ♦ Hoedown. ♦ In these parts. ♦ In your neck of the woods. ♦ Local color. ♦ Local yokels. ♦ Old Macdonald had a farm. ♦ Our country cousins. ♦ Our fair city/hamlet. ♦ Out in the boondocks/boonies/ hinterlands/outback/sticks. [see also Remote] ♦ Sticks nix hick pix. [see also Rejection] ♦ The farmer in the dell. ♦ The forest primeval. ♦ The local folk. ♦ The local gentry. ♦ The wide open spaces. ♦ They roll up the sidewalks at night. ♦ This neck of the woods. ♦ To camp out. ♦ To commune with nature. ♦ To pitch a tent.

Safety

A body's not safe, even in his own home. ♦ A safe haven. ♦ Backed by the full faith and credit of the United States government. ♦ Better safe than sorry. ♦ Better to err on the side of caution. ♦ Buckle up for safety. ♦ Children should be seen and not hurt. ♦ Click it or ticket. ♦ Cross at the green and not in between. ♦ Fasten your seat belts. ♦ In one piece. ♦ It's always better to err on the side of safety. ♦ (Just) to be on the safe side. ♦ Keep your mind on your driving and your eyes on the road. ♦ Out of harm's way. ♦ Safe and sound. ♦ Safe

at home. ♦ Safety first (a Boy Scout's motto). ♦ Seat belts save lives. ♦ The coast is clear. ♦ There is safety in numbers. ♦ To be out of the woods. ♦ What've you got to lose? ♦ You have nothing to lose, everything to gain.

Satisfaction

I can't get no satisfaction. ♦ I have very simple tastes; I am easily satisfied with the best of everything. ♦ I'm easily pleased. ♦ If it's [n.] you want, it's [n.] you'll get. ♦ Now are you satisfied? ♦ Now my day is complete. ♦ Satisfaction guaranteed. ♦ Simple minds, simple things. ♦ The pause that refreshes. ♦ The satisfaction of a job well done. ♦ To be completely/fully/thoroughly satisfied. ♦ To one's (complete) satisfaction. ♦ To hit the spot. ♦ To stick to your ribs. ♦ To the hungry soul everything is sweet. ♦ You say you're not satisfied? You say you want more for your money? Tell you what I'm gonna do.

Scarce

(also unavailable)

A dying art. ♦ A good man is hard to find. ♦ (A hard man is good to find.— Mae West) ♦ All booked up. ♦ As elusive as a banana at an old maid's picnic. ♦ Booked solid. ♦ Don't see [it] for dust. ♦

Few and far between. [see also Rarely] ♦ Hard to come by. ♦ Harder to come by than a key on a tuna can. ♦ Haven't seen hide nor hair of. ♦ I never saw anything like it. ♦ In short supply. ♦ Long time no see. ♦ No room at the inn. ♦ No vacancy. ♦ Nowhere in sight. ♦ Nowhere to be found/seen. ♦ Out of network. ♦ Out of range. ♦ Out of reach. ♦ Rare as a square egg. ♦ Scarce as bird sh*t in a cuckoo clock. ♦ Scarce as hen's teeth. ♦ Scarce as rocking horse sh*t. ♦ Supplies are limited. ♦ The [n.] of a lifetime. ♦ The chosen few. ♦ The likes of which the world/this planet has never seen. ♦ Unheard of. ♦ Very few of us left. ♦ While supplies last. ♦ You can count the number of times that's happened on the fingers of one hand. ♦ You can't find decent help nowadays. ♦ You don't see that every day.

Scare

A chamber/house of horrors. ♦ A fright wig. ♦ A good scare is worth more than good advice. ♦ A hair-raising experience. ♦ A white-knuckle flyer. ♦ Enough to make one's blood run cold. ♦ Enough to raise the hairs on the back of one's neck. ♦ Fraidy cat. ♦ Gooseflesh. ♦ Goosepimples. ♦ Jolted right down to one's boots. ♦ Mass hysteria. ♦ More scared than hurt. ♦ Put the fear (of God) into. ♦ Running scared. ♦ Scare tactics. ♦ Scare the (living) daylights out of. ♦ Scared (pretty near) half to death. ♦ Scared sh*tless. ♦ Scared stiff. ♦ Scared witless. ♦ Scaredy cat. ♦ Sh*t scared. ♦ Quivering like a dog sh*tting razor blades. ♦ Shaking like a leaf. ♦ The scare of one's life. ♦ To be chicken. ♦ To be spooked. ♦ To break out in a cold sweat. ♦ To give one the chills. ♦ To have buck fever. ♦ To have one's heart in one's mouth/stomach/throat. ♦ To jump out of one's skin. ♦ To make one's hair stand on end. ♦ To make one's hair stand up on the back of his/her neck. ♦ To put the fear (of God) into. [see also Fear] ♦ To quake/shake in one's boots. [see also Fear] ♦ To scare the dickens out of. ♦ To scare the hide/pants off. ♦ To scare the heck/hell/sh*t out of. ♦ To sh*t one's britches. ♦ To throw a scare into. ♦ White as a ghost/sheet. ♦ You look as though you've seen a ghost. ♦ You might as well kill a fellow as scare him to death. ♦ Your knees are knocking.

Scold

(also admonish, criticize, insult, rebuke)

A slap in the face/ on the wrist. ♦ A dressing down. ♦ Give 'em hell,

Harry. ◆ That's telling them. ◆ To bawl [*so*] out. ◆ To be a ballbuster. ◆ To be/get on [*so*]'s back/case. ◆ To bust balls. ◆ To bust chops. ◆ To call/be called on the carpet. ◆ To call [*so*] out (on). ◆ To catch hell. ◆ To catch/give holy hell. ◆ To chew [*so*] up and down. ◆ To chew [*so*] out. ◆ To come down (hard) on [*so*]. ◆ To come down with both feet in the middle of [so]'s back. ◆ To crack down (on). ◆ To cuss [*so*] out. ◆ To cut/rip [*so*] a new one. ◆ To diss/insult [*so*]. ◆ To dress down [*so*]. ◆ To get/give a dressing-down. ◆ To get/give (a lot of) flak. ◆ To get/give a ration of sh*t. ◆ To get/give (holy) hell. ◆ To get your head handed to you. ◆ To get/give a tongue-lashing. ◆ To get/give a lot of lip. ◆ To get/give static. ◆ To give/take guff. ◆ To give [*so*] a talking to. ◆ To give [*so*] grief. ◆ To give [*so*] what for. ◆ To find fault with. ◆ To have (a few) choice words for [*so*] [sarcastic]. ◆ To hold [*so*] accountable. ◆ To hurl/throw brickbats. ◆ To jump down [*so*]'s throat. ◆ To knock some sense into [*so*]. ◆ To lace/light into. ◆ To let [*so*] have it (with both barrels). ◆ To lower the boom. ◆ To march up and down [*so*]'s back. ◆ To march up one side of [*so*]'s back and down the other. ◆ To never hear the end of it.

◆ To put [*so*] down. ◆ To put [*so*] in her/his place. ◆ To put the screws to. ◆ To rake [*so*] over the coals. [see also Ordeal] ◆ To read [*so*] the riot act. ◆ To ream/tear [*so*] a new *sshole/a new one. ◆ To sell [*so*] short. ◆ To take [*so*] to task. ◆ To tell [*so*] a thing or two. ◆ To tell [*so*] off. ◆ To throw a dig/digs (at) [*so*]. ◆ To throw [it] in [*so*]'s face. ◆ To throw [it] up to [*so*]. ◆ To unload on [*so*]. ◆ To wise off. ◆ What's the (big) idea? [see also Idea] ◆ Verbal assault.

Scoundrel

A bad actor. ◆ A bad apple. ◆ A bad egg/yegg. ◆ A bushwhacker. ◆ A career criminal. ◆ A denizen of the underworld. ◆ A dirty dog/rat. ◆ A four-flusher. ◆ A heel. ◆ A lowdown cuss. ◆ A ne'er-do-well. ◆ A no-goodnik. ◆ A rat bastard. ◆ A real foul ball. ◆ A (repeat) sex offender. ◆ A rotten apple/egg. ◆ A shady character. ◆ A side-winding polecat. ◆ A sleaze ball/slime ball. ◆ An old reprobate. ◆ Dirty son of a so-and-so. ◆ He'd swindle you just as soon as look at you. ◆ Not a shred of common decency. ◆ Of questionable morals. ◆ Rotten to the core. ◆ Scum of the earth. ◆ That dirty, rotten, lowdown son-of-a-b*tch. ◆ You dirty rat, you.

Secret

A cloak of secrecy. ♦ A closely guarded secret. ♦ A closet queen. [see also Homosexuality] ♦ A deep, dark secret. ♦ A military secret. ♦ A private matter. ♦ A secret admirer. ♦ A secret is your slave if you keep it, your master if you lose it. ♦ A secret Santa. ♦ A shadow government. ♦ A star chamber affair. ♦ A trade secret. ♦ A veil of secrecy. ♦ Alcohol preserves everything but secrets. ♦ An open secret. ♦ Behind closed doors. ♦ Behind the scenes. ♦ Between you and your pillow. ♦ Between you, me and the bedpost/ four walls/lamppost. ♦ Can you keep a secret? ♦ Cloak and dagger. ♦ Daisies don't tell. ♦ Deep, dark secrets. ♦ Does Bic tell Schick? ♦ Does Macy's tell Gimbels? ♦ Don't ask, don't tell. ♦ Don't breathe a word of this (to anyone). ♦ Don't let it go any further (than this). ♦ Don't tell a soul. ♦ He who reveals his secret makes himself a slave. ♦ I cannot comment any further on that. ♦ I could tell you, but then I'd have to kill you. ♦ I'll never tell. ♦ If (only) these walls could talk. ♦ If you can't get people to listen to you any other way, tell them it's confidential. ♦ It's/that's for me to know and for you to find out. ♦

(Just) between you and me. ♦ Keep a zipped lip.

♦ Keep it hush-hush. ♦ Keep it/this to yourself. ♦ Keep it under your hat. ♦ Keep this *entre nous*. ♦ Loose lips sink ships. ♦ More than that I cannot say. ♦ Mum's the word. [see also Silence] ♦ My lips are sealed. ♦ My work is so secret even I don't know what I'm doing. ♦ Names are withheld pending notification of the next of kin. ♦ Nobody else needs to know. ♦ Not at liberty to say. ♦ Not for general consumption. ♦ Not for publication. ♦ Off the record. ♦ On the down low. [see also Homosexuality] ♦ On the Q.T. ♦ On the sly. ♦ Out back behind the schoolhouse. ♦ Some things are better done with the lights off. ♦ Sworn to secrecy. ♦ The best-kept secret. ♦ The inner circle. ♦ The only secret a woman can keep is her age. ♦ Three may keep a secret if two are dead. ♦ To be *sub rosa*/subdititious. ♦ To [v.] behind one's back. ♦ To have a skeleton in one's closet. ♦ To keep [it] to oneself. ♦ To keep [it] under wraps. ♦ To keep [so] in the dark. ♦ To keep one's own counsel. ♦ To lead a double life. ♦ To swear [so] to secrecy. ♦ Under cover of darkness. ♦ Under the counter/table. ♦ Under (the) cover of. ♦ Try your friend with a lie and if he keep it a secret tell him the truth by and by. ♦ We've got to stop meeting like this. ♦ Wouldn't you like to know. ♦ You didn't hear it from me. ♦ Your secret is safe with me.

Self

A do-it-yourselfer. ♦ A knowledge of self is priceless, while knowledge of others is dear. ♦ A persecution complex. ♦ A self-imposed [n.]. ♦ A self-made man. ♦ An inferiority complex. ♦ Be yourself; everyone else is taken. ♦ Do your own dirty work. ♦ Do yourself a favor. ♦ Do yourself proud. ♦ Don't B sharp; don't B flat; just B natural. [see also Nature] ♦ He who conquers himself conquers all. ♦ If you want it done right you have to do it yourself. ♦ In your own right. ♦ Just be yourself. ♦ Make it easy on yourself. ♦ Never sell yourself short. ♦ Nobody can make you feel inferior without your consent. ♦ Self aggrandizement. ♦ Self-esteem often asks for a price. ♦ Self-praise stinks. ♦ Respect yourself and others will respect you. ♦ Some things you just have to do yourself. ♦ Speak for yourself (John). ♦ The most pleasing sound to anyone is the sound of one's own name. ♦ There's only one you. ♦ To appear in person/in the flesh. ♦ To be a law unto oneself. ♦ To be a self-starter. ♦ To be self-assured/ self-possessed/self-reliant/self-serving. ♦ To my mind. ♦ To take a selfie. ♦ To thine own self be true. ♦ You're only who I'd be if I wasn't me.

Self-Improvement

As ye sow, so shall ye reap. ♦ As you make your bed you must lie in it. ♦ Cast bread upon waters. ♦ Every man is the architect of his own fortune. ♦ Every man is the captain of his own ship. ♦ He who lives by the sword dies by the sword. ♦ (He who lives by the sword dies swordedly — R.D.) ♦ If you allow yourself to be a worm, don't complain if you get stepped on. ♦ If you do good, forget about it; if you do bad, think about it. — Angela Maria Delia ♦ If you play with a snake, you get bitten. ♦ If you play with fire, you're bound to get burned. ♦ Much shadow of this life is caused by standing in our own sunshine. ♦ Ships don't just come in, someone has to steer them. ♦ To be one's own hardest taskmaster. ♦ To find your true calling. ♦ To man up. ♦ To pull yourself together.

◆ To reinvent yourself. ◆ To take (full) responsibility (for your own actions). ◆ To wear the hair shirt. ◆ You make your own breaks.

Selfishness

A spoiled brat. ◆ Holding out on me, eh? ◆ Hooray for me and f*ck you/ to hell with you. ◆ How am I doing? Anybody I can and the easy ones twice. ◆ If I can't have you, nobody can. ◆ Looking out for Number One. ◆ Mine all mine. ◆ More out of greed than need. ◆ Never give a sucker an even break. ◆ Nice guys finish last. ◆ Selfishness defiles every other quality. ◆ Spoiled rotten. ◆ That's just how I am. ◆ The Me Generation. ◆ This isn't the Good Ship Lollipop, sucker. ◆ To do one's (own) thing. [see also Independent] ◆ What's in it for me? ◆ What's mine is mine and what's yours is mine, too. ◆ What's mine is mine and what's yours is negotiable. ◆ Whether you like it or not. ◆ You know me.

Sensibility

Being of sound mind. ◆ Collect one's thoughts/wits. ◆ Come to one's senses. [see also Enlightenment] ◆ Cracker-barrel philosophy. ◆ Down to earth. ◆ Get/have one's head on straight. ◆ Get with it. ◆ Have your wits about you. ◆ In full possession of one's faculties. ◆ It makes good horse sense. ◆ Plain old common sense. ◆ Snap out of it. ◆ Stone-cold sober. ◆ To be in one's right mind. ◆ To be levelheaded. ◆ To be (thoroughly) grounded. ◆ To come to. ◆ To have both feet on the ground. ◆ To have the presence of mind (to). ◆ To regain consciousness. ◆ Wake up and smell the coffee.

Seriousness

A sobering thought. ◆ All joking/ kidding aside. ◆ Give it top priority. ◆ I cannot overemphasize the importance/seriousness/ urgency of this. ◆ I was never more serious in my life. ◆ I'm serious. [riposte: I'm Roebuck!— who's minding the store?] ◆ I've never been more serious in my life. ◆ No joke. ◆ No kidding (around). ◆ No laughing matter. ◆ To be dead serious. ◆ To give a hoot. ◆ To keep a straight face. ◆ To mean business. ◆ To play for keeps. ◆ To play it straight. [see also Honesty] ◆ To play the heavy. ◆ To say in all seriousness. ◆ To take [it] seriously. ◆ To take [it] to heart. ◆ To take oneself (too) seriously. ◆ To underscore the importance/ seriousness of [it]. ◆ Would I joke about something like that? ◆ You can't be serious!

Setback

A fallback position. ◆ A minor setback. ◆ Back off. ◆ Back to square one. ◆ Back to the drawing board. ◆ Back to the O.R. ◆ Drop/fall back (and punt). ◆ Go back to the beginning. ◆ Going (around) in circles. [see also Pointless] ◆ One step forward, two steps back. ◆ Pick yourself up, dust yourself off and start all over again. ◆ Regroup one's forces. ◆ Retreat, hell! We're just attacking in another direction. ◆ Retreat to a neutral corner. ◆ Right back where we started. ◆ So they've got us surrounded, good! Now we can fire in any direction; those b*st*rds won't get away this time! ◆ Take it from the top. ◆ To do a three-sixty. ◆ To come full circle. ◆ To go to Plan B. ◆ To fall back (on). ◆ To resort to. ◆ To start from scratch. ◆ To suffer a (minor) setback.

Settle

Any port in a storm. ◆ Beggars can't be choosers. ◆ Good enough is sometimes perfect. ◆ Deal with it. ◆ If you can't get it in bushels, take it in spoonfuls. ◆ It'll do in a pinch. ◆ It'll do until something better comes along. ◆ Like it or lump it. ◆ Like it or not. ◆ Settle this once and for all. ◆ Take it or leave it. [see also Choices] ◆ To make do. ◆ To take it any way you can get it. ◆ To tide one over. ◆ When you can't be near the one you love, love the one you're near. ◆ Why settle for less? ◆ You can put out a fire with either cold or hot water. ◆ You take what you can get.

Sex

A cold sweat over a live corpse. ◆ A gang bang. ◆ A *ménage à trois*. ◆ A nooner. ◆ A piece of *ss/tail. ◆ A quickie. ◆ A roll in the hay. ◆ A sex symbol. ◆ A tumble in the sack. ◆ But will you respect me in the morning? ◆ Carnal desires/pleasures. ◆ Do the juicy. ◆ Horizontal collaboration. ◆ Jump [so]'s bones. ◆ Pleasures of the flesh. ◆ Sexual congress/intercourse/ relations. ◆ Sexually explicit. ◆ The facts of life. ◆ The horizontal mambo. ◆ The Mile High Club. ◆ The missionary position. ◆ The old in and out. ◆ The old inny outy. ◆ The sex act. ◆ There is no such thing as bad sex; some is just better than others. ◆ To appeal to the prurient interest. ◆ To ball [so]. ◆ To be intimate with [so]. ◆ To climax/come/get off/reach orgasm. ◆ To dip one's wick. ◆ To do "it." ♦ To (do) sixty-nine. ♦ To do the dirty deed. ♦ To do the nasty. ♦ To dry hump. ♦ To exercise one's love muscle. ♦ To get a little (bit) on the side. ♦ To get a little nookie/poontang/pussy/trim/quiff. ♦ To get into [so]'s pants. ♦ To get it on with [so]. ♦ To get laid. ♦ To get lucky. ♦ To get sloppy seconds. ♦ To get one's ashes hauled. ♦ To get one's pencil wet. ♦ To get one's rocks off. ♦ To go all the way. ♦ To go down on [so]. ♦ To go to bed with [so]. ♦ To have been to the well. ♦ To have make-up sex. ♦ To have one's way with [so]. ♦ To hump. ♦ To knock off a piece. ♦ To have carnal knowledge (of). ♦ To hide the salami/ sausage/weenie. ♦ To know [so] in the Biblical sense. ♦ To make (mad, passionate) love. ♦ To make the beast with two backs. ♦ To make whoopie. ♦ To play stink finger. ♦ To pork [so]. ♦ To pound pubes (with) ♦ To put out. ♦ To put the boots to. ♦ To shag. ♦ To sink one's meat. ♦ To sink the Bismark. ♦ To sleep around. ♦ To sleep one's way to the top. ♦ To sleep together. ♦ To take liberties (with) ♦ To throw a hump/jump into. ♦ To turn a trick. ♦ To varnish one's cane. ♦ Was it good for you? [see also Reciprocation] ♦ X-rated.

Sharp

A sharp tongue is the only edge tool that grows sharper with constant use. ♦ A sharpie. ♦ Cuts through it like a knife through butter. ♦ Look sharp; feel sharp; be sharp. ♦ Razor sharp. ♦ Sharp as a marble/razor/whip. ♦ Sharp as a pig's whistle. ♦ Sharp as a pistol. ♦ Sharp as a sack of wet mice. ♦ Sharp as a tack. ♦ What's the sharpest thing in the world? A fart: it cuts through your pants without tearing them.

Shirk

A deadbeat dad. ♦ A draft dodger. ♦ A goldbricker. ♦ A goof-off. ♦ A sandbagger. ♦ A slacker. ♦ Everybody's job is nobody's job. ♦ I would prefer not to. ♦ It's above my pay grade. ♦ It's not my job. ♦ Let George do it. ♦ Let this cup pass from me. ♦ Play hooky (also hookie/ hookey). ♦ To call in sick. ♦ To cut class. ♦ To dog it. ♦ To drag one's feet. ♦ To fall down on the job. ♦ To featherbed. ♦ To fiddle while Rome burns. ♦ To pass the buck. ♦ To put off till tomorrow what one could do today. ♦ To sandbag. ♦ To shirk one's duty/ responsibility. ♦ To sit on one's hands/haunches. ♦ To weasel/worm one's way out of.

Shock

A bitter pill to swallow. ♦ A real mind-bender. ♦ A real shockeroo. ♦ Didn't know whether to sh*t or go blind. (So I blinked/closed one eye and farted). ♦ In a state of shock. ♦ Shock of one's life. ♦ Shock waves. ♦ To blow you away. ♦ To come as (quite) a blow. ♦ To drop one's teeth. ♦ To have shock value.

Shortsighted

(also overextending)

A false sense of security. ♦ A hollow victory. ♦ Always be nice to people on your way up; you may meet them on your way down. ♦ Can't see beyond the tip of one's nose. ♦ Can't see the forest for the trees. ♦ Don't bite the hand that feeds you. ♦ Don't bite off more than you can chew. [see also Gluttony] ♦ Don't bring a knife to a gunfight. ♦ Don't burn your bridges behind you. ♦ Don't cut off the cat's tail behind its ears. ♦ Don't cut off your nose to spite your face. ♦ Don't get into a p*ssing contest with a skunk. ♦ Don't kill the goose that lays the golden eggs. ♦ Don't put the fox in charge of the henhouse. ♦ Don't set the wolf to guard the sheep. ♦ Don't spit in the well: you may have to drink the water. ♦ Don't spread yourself (too) thin.

♦ Don't start something you can't finish. ♦ Don't win the battle but lose the war. ♦ If you don't feed a cat you will feed many mice. ♦ If you spit into the wind, it will blow back in your face. – Marcantonio Serritella ♦ It's hard for a snorer to know how loud he snores. ♦ In (way) over one's head. ♦ Man overboard! ♦ Narrow-minded. ♦ The cure is worse than the disease. ♦ The wolf may be always hired cheaply as a shepherd. ♦ 'Tis easier to build two chimneys than to maintain one. ♦ To be the richest man in the cemetery. ♦ To have blinders on. ♦ To have tunnel vision. ♦ To throw out the baby with the bath water. ♦ To overextend oneself. ♦ To overstep one's bounds. ♦ To set the bar too high. ♦ When you try to please everybody, you wind up pleasing nobody. ♦ When the lion is attacking is no time to worry about fleas. ♦ When you're knee-deep in alligators is no time to clear the swamp. ♦ You can't be all things to all people.

♦ You can't do everything at once. ♦ You can't please everybody.

Showoff

A barn-burner. ♦ A glory hound. ♦ A know-it-all. ♦ A name-dropper. ♦ A Punch and Judy show. ♦ All eyes are on her/him. ♦ Call attention to oneself. ♦ Don't hide your light under a basket/bushel. ♦ Eat my dust. ♦ Get a load of this. ♦ If my friends could see me now. ♦ If you've got it, flaunt it. ♦ In every actor, there's a little ham. ♦ Look Ma, no hands! ♦ Play it to the hilt. ♦ Play the role. ♦ Razzle-dazzle. ♦ Strut one's stuff. ♦ The bright lights of Broadway. ♦ The center of attention. ♦ The world's a stage. ♦ To barnstorm. ♦ To blow/toot one's own horn. ♦ To get good ink. ♦ To grandstand. ♦ To hail a cab/taxi. ♦ To ham it up. ♦ To have stage presence. ♦ To hot dog it. ♦ To make a grandstand play. ♦ To play to the gallery. ♦ To pull a Brody. ♦ To put on a dog and pony show. ♦ To put on the greasepaint. ♦ To show and tell. ♦ To trot out one's [n.]. ♦ To showboat. ♦ To tread the boards. ♦ Watch my dust/smoke!

Shy

A Casper Milquetoast. ♦ A shrinking violet. ♦ A wallflower. ♦ An inny. ♦ Lacking in confidence. ♦ Painfully shy. ♦ Shy maids end up old maids. ♦ Shy and retiring/unassuming. ♦ To avoid/shun the limelight. ♦ To be camera-shy. ♦ To be publicity shy.

Sidekicks

Abbott and Costello. ♦ Adam and Eve. ♦ Antony and Cleopatra. ♦ Assault and battery. ♦ Batman and Robin. ♦ Beauty and the beast. ♦ Blondie and Dagwood. ♦ Bonnie and Clyde. ♦ Bright and Early. ♦ Burns and Allen. ♦ Caps and gowns. ♦ Cease and desist. ♦ Cheech and Chong. ♦ Crack and Peel. ♦ Crime and Punishment. ♦ David and Goliath. ♦ Death and Taxes. ♦ Don Quixote and Sancho Panza. ♦ Ferdinand and Isabella. ♦ Fibber McGee and Molly. ♦ Flesh and blood. ♦ Flotsam and jetsam. ♦ Frick and Frack. ♦ Fun and Frolic. ♦ Hans and Franz. ♦ Ham and eggs. ♦ Hans and Fritz. ♦ Hansel and Gretel ♦ Hearts and flowers. ♦ Heckle and Jeckel. ♦ Homer and Jethro. ♦ Ike and Tina. ♦ Itch and Scratch. ♦ Jeykll and Hyde. ♦ Kermit the Frog and Miss Piggy. ♦ Laurel and Hardy. ♦ Lewis and Clark. ♦ Ma and Pa Kettle. ♦ Martin and Lewis. ♦ Mary and Joseph. ♦ Masters and Johnson. ♦ Mickey and Minnie. ♦ Moonlight and roses. ♦ Mork and Mindy. ♦ Mutt and Jeff. ♦ Nancy and Sluggo. ♦ Peanut butter and jelly. ♦ Penn and Teller. ♦ Pete and Repeat. ♦ Pots and pans. ♦ Punch and Judy. ♦ Red Ryder and Little Beaver. ♦ Robinson Crusoe and Friday. ♦ Romeo and Juliet. ♦ Rosencrantz and Guildenstern. ♦ Rowan and Martin. ♦ Samson and Delilah. ♦ Scratch and dent. ♦ Scratch and sniff. ♦ Scylla and Charybdis. ♦ Skin and bones. ♦ Smoky and the Bandit. ♦ Sonny and Cher. ♦ Spanky and the Gang. ♦ Starsky and Hutch. ♦ Supply and demand. ♦ Surf and turf. ♦ Sylvester and Tweetybird. ♦ The Bobbsey twins. [see also Alike] ♦ The dynamic duo. ♦ The gruesome twosome. ♦ The Lone Ranger and Tonto. ♦ The odd couple. ♦ Thelma and Louise. ♦ Tristan and Isolde. ♦ Tweedledee and Tweedledum. ♦ Twists and turns. ♦ Wear and tear.

Silence

A deafening/thunderous silence. ♦ A moment of silence. ♦ A pregnant pause. ♦ A silent mouth is sweet to hear. ♦ A silent partner. ♦ A tacit agreement. ♦ A wall of silence. ♦ Better to remain silent and be thought a fool than to open one's mouth and remove all doubt. ♦ Hold your tongue. ♦ I refuse to answer on the grounds that I might incriminate myself. ♦ I'm not talking while the flavor lasts. ♦ In a closed mouth, no flies enter. ♦ (If any person here can show cause as to why these two people should not be joined in holy matrimony) speak now or forever hold your peace. ♦ Keep one's trap/yap shut. ♦ Mum's the word. [see also Secret] ♦ Not a peep out of you. ♦ No comment. ♦ Not a word was spoken. ♦ Plead/take the Fifth. ♦ Silence is assent. ♦ Silence is golden. ♦ Silent as a tomb. ♦ Silent but deadly. ♦ Speak now or forever hold your peace. ♦ Speech is silver but silence is golden. ♦ Take the Fifth Amendment. ♦ The less said the better. ♦ The most formidable weapon against gossip is silence. ♦ The silent majority. ♦ The sound of one hand clapping. ♦ The sound of silence. ♦ The superior man is slow in his words and earnest in his conduct. ♦ They came for the Jews, and I wasn't Jewish so I didn't speak up. They came for the Catholics, and I wasn't a Catholic so I didn't speak up. They came for the Blacks, and I wasn't Black, so I didn't speak up. Then one day they came for me. And there was nobody left to speak up. ♦ To clam up. ♦ To dummy up. ♦ To invoke one's Fifth Amendment rights. ♦ To keep one's mouth shut. ♦ To not open one's mouth. ♦ To not say boo/ peep. [see also Hush] ♦ To not utter a word. ♦ To pause for (dramatic) effect. ♦ To pay hush money. ♦ To suffer in silence. ♦ To zip up one's lip. ♦ Unavailable for comment. ♦ You can sometimes learn more from what was not said than from what was said. ♦ You have the right to remain silent. (Anything you say can and will be used against you in a court of law). [see also Right]

Silly

A silly Billy. ♦ A silly Sally. ♦ A silly grin. ♦ Don't be silly. ♦ How silly of me. ♦ If you ask a silly question you get a silly answer. ♦ Silly boy. ♦ Silly goose. ♦ Silly me. ♦ Slapped silly. ♦ The silly season. ♦ To [n.] oneself silly. ♦ You silly savage.

Sin

A cardinal sin. ♦ A mortal sin. ♦ Be sure your sins will find you out. ♦ He who abides the sin is as guilty as the sinner. ♦ Anyone who looks at a woman lustfully has already committed adultery with her in his heart. ♦ If thine right eye offends you, pluck it out. ♦ It's a sin to tell a lie. ♦ Let he who is without sin among you cast the first stone. ♦ Sin City. ♦ Sins of commission/ omission. ♦ The Seven Deadly Sins. ♦ The sins of the father are visited on the son. ♦ The wages of sin is death. ♦ To sin in one's heart. ♦ To wander from the straight and narrow.

Sincerity

And I mean that sincerely. ♦ Comes from (way) down deep inside. ♦ From the bottom of one's heart. ♦ In all sincerity. ♦ In (all) good conscience/ faith. ♦ In one's heart of hearts. ♦ Sincerely yours. ♦ To act in good faith. ♦ To be in earnest. ♦ To be well-intentioned. ♦ To have every (good) intention. ♦ To have one's heart in it. ♦ To mean well. ♦ With all one's heart (and soul).

Skepticism
(also disbelief)

A bunch of bullsh*t. ♦ A cock and bull story. ♦ A credibility gap. ♦ A crock of sh*t. ♦ A likely story. ♦ A lot of hooey/hot air. ♦ Ain't no such animal. ♦ And the farmer took another load away. ♦ Are you for real? ♦ Are you (f*cking) kidding me? ♦ Are you putting me on? ♦ Balderdash. ♦ Bosh. ♦ Bullfeathers! ♦ Bullsh*t. ♦ Bullsh*t the baker and you'll get a bun; bullsh*t me and you'll get none. ♦ Bushwa. ♦ Can you believe it/this? ♦ Come off it. ♦ Crapola. ♦ Don't hold your breath. [see also Hopeless] ♦ Don't give me that line of bull. ♦ Don't tell me that. ♦ Don't you believe it/that for a second. ♦ Fiddle-faddle. ♦ Full of baloney. ♦ Full of beans. ♦ Full of blarney. ♦ Full of bull/crap/donkey dust/horse manure/ hot air/malarkey/sh*t/wood. ♦ Full of sh*t as a Christmas goose. [see also Christmas] ♦ Get a shovel; it's getting deep in here. ♦ Get outta town! ♦ G'wan/go on. ♦ Get outta here! ♦ Hogwash. ♦ Horsefeathers! ♦ I must be hearing things. ♦ I remain to be convinced. [see also Oppose] ♦ I wouldn't take it as gospel. ♦ I'd better get my hip boots; it's getting deep in here. ♦ I'll believe that when I see it. ♦ If I didn't know any better, I'd say . . . ♦ I'm from Missouri; you've got to show me. ♦ If bullsh*t were electricity, you'd be a powerhouse. ♦ If bullsh*t were nuggets, you'd be a goldmine. ♦ If you were as tall as your stories you'd be the Empire State building. ♦ In a pig's *ss. ♦ In a pig's eye. ♦ It seems I've heard that song before. ♦ It looks/sounds good on paper but. ♦ It taxes the imagination. ♦ It's all in your head/mind. ♦ Like fun. ♦ My eye. ♦

No matter how (thin) you slice it, it's still baloney. ♦ No such thing. ♦ Oh, bull roar. ♦ Oh, come off it. ♦ Oh, dog dung. ♦ Oh, pshaw. ♦ Rave on, catsh*t, and somebody will scratch you under. ♦ Same old story. ♦ Say what? ♦ Sh*t for the birds. ♦ Shut the front door! ♦ So full of sh*t that it's coming out your ears/ that your eyes are brown. ♦ So they'd have you believe/think. ♦ So's Christmas coming. ♦ Stuff and nonsense. ♦ (Surely) you must be joking. ♦ Talking out one's *ss. ♦ Talking through one's hat. ♦ Tell it to Sweeney. ♦ Tell it to the cop on the corner. ♦ Tell it to the judge. ♦ Tell it to the Marines. ♦ Tell me you didn't just say that. ♦ That's hard to swallow. ♦ That'll be the day. ♦ That's a crock (of sh*t). ♦ That's a lot of bull. ♦ That's (absolute/ pure) bullsh*t. ♦ That's double Dutch/ double talk. ♦ This I gotta see. ♦ To be a Doubting Thomas. ♦ To call [it] into question. ♦ To call [so]'s bluff. ♦ To cast doubt on. ♦ To give [so] the hairy eyeball. [see also Flirt] ♦ To put the lie to. ♦ To strain the credibility. ♦ To take [it] with a grain of salt. ♦ Utter nonsense. ♦ Utterly absurd/ridiculous. ♦ Where have I heard that (one) before? ♦ Who do you think you're kidding? ♦ Who's kidding who? ♦ Yeah, right. ♦ Yes sir, no sir, three bags full. ♦ You can't bullsh*t a bullsh*tter. ♦ You can't be serious. ♦ You expect me to believe that? ♦ You only wish. ♦ You've got to be kidding (me). ♦ You've gotta be sh*ttin' me.

Skylark

A little nonsense now and then, is relished by the wisest man. ♦ Clown around. ♦ Fart around. ♦ Fatootz around. ♦ Fun and games. ♦ Futz around. ♦ Horse around. ♦ Monkey around. ♦ Monkey business. ♦ To engage in horseplay. ♦ To fart/fiddle/f*ck/futz around. ♦ To f*ck off. ♦ To play grabass. ♦ To play hanky-panky. ♦ To pull monkeyshines. ♦ To tinker around.

Slander

A backstabber. ♦ A blow from the frying pan if it does not smart, smuts. ♦ A poison pen letter.

♦ A smear campaign. ♦ Defamation of character. ♦ Dig up dirt on [so].

♦ Dish the dirt. ♦ Do a hatchet job (on). ♦ Every knock is a boost. ♦ He who slings mud loses ground. ♦ If you can't say anything nice about a person, don't say anything at all. ♦ Smear tactics. ♦ Take a cheap shot. ♦ The blow of a whip raises a welt, but a blow of the tongue crushes bones. ♦ The truth is not slander. ♦ To back-bite. ♦ To badmouth [so]. ♦ To be a muckraker. ♦ To cast aspersions. ♦ To cast doubt (on). ♦ To cut [so] up. ♦ To dish (the dirt on) [so]. ♦ To diss [so]. ♦ To do a hatchet job on [so]. ♦ To drag [so]'s name through the mud. ♦ To plant/sow the seeds of doubt. ♦ To poison the well. ♦ To poor mouth [so]. ♦ To put the mouth on. ♦ To raise doubt. ♦ To reflect poorly on. ♦ To sling mud. ♦ To take a pot shot. ♦ To talk behind [so]'s back. ♦ To talk trash about [so]. ♦ To tarnish [so]'s image. ♦ To throw shade at [so]. ♦ What goes around, comes around (and when it does, you'd best be sitting down.) - R.D. [see also Deserve] ♦ Yellow journalism.

Sleep

A sleepover. ♦ A slumber party. ♦ A pajama party. ♦ An overnighter. ♦ And so to bed/sleep. ♦ Conk off/out. ♦ Couldn't/didn't sleep a wink.

♦ Counting sheep. ♦ Drift off into dreamland. ♦ Get a good night's sleep. ♦ Get forty winks. ♦ Get one's beauty rest/sleep. ♦ Goodnight, sleep tight, don't let the bedbugs bite. ♦ In lullaby land. ♦ In the Land of Nod. ♦ It's nothing that a good night's sleep won't cure. ♦ Now I lay me down to sleep I pray the Lord my soul to keep. ♦ One hour's sleep before midnight is worth two hours' sleep afterwards. ♦ Out like a light. ♦ Rack out. ♦ Rock-a-bye baby. ♦ Sack out. ♦ See the Sandman. ♦ Saw logs. ♦ Sleep tight. ♦ Sleeping Beauty. ♦ Sleeping like a baby/log/top. ♦ To be dead to the world. ♦ To be fast asleep/sound asleep. ♦ To catch forty winks. ♦ To catch/grab some z's. ♦ To cork off. ♦ To crawl beneath/between the sheets. ♦ To cry oneself to sleep. ♦ To drift off into dreamland. ♦ To get some shut-eye. ♦ To go to sleep with the chickens. ♦ To hit the hay/sack/sheets. ♦ To nod off. ♦ To rack/sack out. ♦ To sleep in. ♦ To sleep it off. ♦ To suffer sleep deprivation. ♦ To take a catnap. ♦ To turn in.

Slippery

A slippery customer. ♦ On a slippery slope. ♦ Slick as a whistle. ♦ Slicker than a dog's/minnow's dick. ♦ Slicker than snail snot. ♦ Slippery as a greased pig. ♦ Slippery as an eel. ♦ Slippery as a polar bear rolled in Miracle Whip. ♦ Slippery as snot (on a greased doorknob). ♦ Slippery when wet. ♦ Slippin' and a-slidin'.

Slipshod

A dollar's not a dollar anymore. ♦ Cobbled together. ♦ Held together with glue and baling wire. ♦ Held together with spit and glue. ♦ Jerry-built. ♦ Put together with spit and baling wire. ♦ Rinky-dink/ rinky-tink. ♦ Slapped together. ♦ They don't make 'em like they used to. ♦ To build one's house of straw. ♦ To build one's castle on sand. ♦ To do the job with a left-handed monkey wrench. ♦ To make a holiday. ♦ To make bricks without straw.

Slow
(also uneventful)

A late bloomer. ♦ A null zone. ♦ A slowpoke. ♦ A time warp. ♦ Absolutely nothing going on. ♦ As slow as molasses (going uphill in January). ♦ Behind the times. ♦ Caught in a time warp. ♦ Got all the time in the world. ♦ In no particular hurry. ♦ In slow motion. ♦ Like watching grass grow/paint dry. ♦ No runs, no hits, no errors, nobody left on. ♦ One day at a time. ♦ One step at a time. ♦ Slow and steady wins the race. ♦ Slow(ly) but sure(ly). ♦ Some things can't be rushed. ♦ They who move like molasses drag their *sses. ♦ Time hangs heavy (on one's hands). ♦ To be a Sunday driver. ♦ To dilly-dally. ♦ To have two speeds: slow and slower. ♦ To move at a glacial pace. ♦ To move at a snail's pace. ♦ To move like Stepin Fetchit. ♦ To take a slow boat to China. ♦ To take the long way around the Horn. ♦ To take the long way home. ♦ To take one's (own) (sweet) time.

Smart

A mind like a steel trap. ♦ A smart Aleck. ♦ An egghead. ♦ Cagey as the K.G.B. ♦ I was born at night—but not last night. ♦ I wasn't born yesterday. ♦ If you were half as smart as you think you are, you'd be twice as smart as you really are. ♦ Not just another pretty face. ♦ To be level-headed. ♦ To have a good/ level head on one's shoulders. ♦ Nobody's fool. ♦ One smart cookie. ♦ Sharp as a tack. ♦ Smart as a whip. ♦ Shrewd as a Philadelphia lawyer. ♦ Sly as a fox. ♦ There is such a thing as being too smart for one's own good. ♦ There's always somebody smarter than you. ♦ To be fast/quick on the uptake. ♦ To be hip/on to/wise to [so]. ♦ To have both feet on the ground. ♦ To know a good thing when you see it. ♦ Too smart for your own good. ♦ What do you take me for? ♦ You have to get up pretty early in the morning to fool me. ♦ You don't fool me for a minute. ♦ You sly dog. ♦ You're a fart schmeller. — Dominick P. Delia

Smile

A cheerful smile makes life worthwhile. ♦ A satisfied smile. ♦ A smile on my face for the whole human race. ♦ An infectious grin/smile. ♦ Grinning/smiling like a Cheshire cat. ♦ If you meet someone without a smile, give him one of yours. ♦ It costs nothing to smile. ♦ It doesn't cost anything to be nice. ♦ Let a smile be your umbrella on a rainy day.

♦ Of all the things you wear, your expression is the most important. ♦ One smile, longer life; one frown, shorter life. ♦ Service with a smile.

♦ Sheepish grin. ♦ Show your pearly whites. ♦ Smile and say cheese. ♦ Smile and the whole world smiles with you, cry and you cry alone. ♦ Smile and the whole world smiles with you, snore and you sleep alone. ♦ Smile for the birdie. ♦ Smile, you're on Candid Camera. ♦ There are hundreds of languages in the world but a smile speaks them all. ♦ When there's a shine on your shoes, there's a smile on your face. ♦ You use fewer muscles to smile than you do to frown.

Smooth
(also soft)

A smooth landing. ♦ A smooth talker. ♦ An old smoothie. ♦ Say something soft and mushy. ♦ Smooth as a baby's *ss. ♦ Smooth as silk. ♦ Smooth sailing. ♦ Soft as the hair on a she-mouse's belly. ♦ To smooth things over.

Solitary

A football widow. [see also Women] ♦ A lone wolf. ♦ A majority of one. ♦ A one-man band. ♦ A selfie. ♦ A voice in the wilderness. ♦ All alone. ♦ (All) by itself. ♦ All by one's lonesome (self). ♦ All together, one at a time. ♦ Am I the only one? ♦ Do it yourself. (DIY) ♦ Fend for oneself. ♦ Go it alone. ♦ He travels fastest who travels alone. ♦ He who lives for no one does not necessarily live for himself. ♦ I for one. ♦ I ain't got nobody. ♦ If you are idle, be not solitary—if you are solitary, be not idle. ♦ In and of itself. [see also Generalizations] ♦ In private life. ♦ In private practice. ♦ In solitary confinement. ♦ Is it hot in here, or is it just me? ♦ Is it just me? ♦ Isn't there anybody else on the air? ♦ It's only me. ♦ Little Miss Lonelyhearts. ♦ Little old/ol' me. ♦ Loneliness is the greatest poverty. ♦ Lonesome as a polecat. ♦ Me, myself and I. ♦ Nobody but you. ♦ None but the lonely heart knows. ♦ The Lonely Hearts Club. ♦ Only you. ♦ Paddle one's own canoe. ♦ Playing solitaire. ♦ Row, row, row your boat, gently down the stream. ♦ Single file. ♦ Solitary confinement. ♦ Sweet solitude. ♦ The cheese stands alone. ♦ The Lone Gunman theory. ♦ To be a wallflower. ♦ To be in one's own world. ♦ To be (out) on one's own. ♦ To fend/shift for oneself. ♦ To go Dutch (treat.) ♦ To go it alone. ♦ To go stag. ♦ To keep to oneself. ♦ To leave one to one's own devices. ♦ What one does in solitude, one must shout from the rooftops. ♦ When you have no observers, be afraid of yourself. ♦ You and nobody but. ♦ You (and you) alone. ♦ You come into this world alone, you live alone and you die alone.

Soon

Any day now. ♦ A.S.A.P. (As soon as possible). ♦ As the moil says, "it won't be long now." ♦ At any minute. ♦ At hand. ♦ At the very latest. ♦ Before long. ♦ Coming (right) up. ♦ Early on (in the game). ♦ In the near/not-too-distant future. ♦ It won't be long now. ♦ Soon enough. ♦ Sooner rather than later. ♦ The sooner the better. ♦ Will be along shortly. ♦ With the next dawn. ♦ Within the hour. ♦ Without further ado/delay/fanfare.

Sort

Eeny, meeny, miney, mo, catch a [n.] by the toe, if he hollers, let him go. Eeny, meeny, miney, mo. ♦ Every other one. ♦ Many are called but few are chosen. ♦ (Many are culled but few are chosen — R.D.). ♦ Mix and/'n' match. ♦ Selective memory. ♦ Separate the wheat from the chaff. ♦ Separate the sheep from the goats. ♦ The Chosen One. ♦ The process of elimination. ♦ This will separate the men from the boys. ♦ To pick and choose. ♦ To single [it]/[so] out. ♦ To take one from column A and one from column B. ♦ To the exclusion of all others.

Speechless

(also mumbling)

A frog in one's throat. ♦ A speech impediment. ♦ (All) talked out. ♦ At a loss for words. ♦ Cat got your tongue? ♦ Don't just stand there with your teeth/tongue in your mouth, say something. ♦ Get the marbles out of your mouth. ♦ Marbles in one's mouth. ♦ More than words can say. ♦ Speak up. ♦ Spit it out. ♦ Tight-lipped. ♦ To clam up. ♦ To get tangled on one's own tongue. ♦ To keep [so] in the dark. ♦ To not breathe a word. ♦ To speak under one's breath. ♦ To withhold evidence. ♦ Tongue-tied. ♦ What am I supposed to say to that? ♦ What else/more is there to say? ♦ When you don't know what you're talking about, mumble. ♦ When you have nothing to say, sing it. – [advertising maxim] ♦ Words cannot describe/express. ♦ Words fail me.

Spoonerisms

A cappy hamper. ♦ A cough of cuppee. ♦ A fine fettle of kish. ♦ A lack of pies. ♦ A lead of hettuce. ♦ A gritty pearl. ♦ A half-warmed fish. ♦ A rough tow to hoe. ♦ A runny babbit. ♦ A thrown's stow away. ♦ A peet of shaper to write on. ♦ At the lead of spite. ♦ Buy a smack of pokes. ♦ Don't fight the band that heeds you. ♦ Fell for it like a bun of tricks. ♦ Hush, you muskies! ♦ In one swell foop. ♦ Is the bean dizzy? ♦ It is kisstomary to cuss the bride. ♦ Life is but a chair of bowlies. ♦ On Memorial Day, they have all the hags flung out. ♦ The Lord is a shoving leopard. ♦ The space of aids. ♦ The yaps are jello. ♦ This must be your ducky lay. ♦ To bead a rook. ♦ To mock a killing bird. ♦ To stow thrones. ♦ Under the alfluence of incohol. ♦ You're too mucking fuch. ♦ You have hissed all my mystery lessons and tasted two whole worms. ♦ You've got it back *sswards. ♦ Your show is slipping. ♦ Yuck foo!

Status

(also occupations)

A bean counter. ♦ A black tie affair. ♦ A desk jockey. ♦ A go-go dancer. ♦ A grease monkey. ♦ A gumshoe. ♦ A headshrinker. ♦ A hoochie coochie dancer. ♦ A legal eagle. ♦ A lot lizard. ♦ A maintenance man. ♦ A numbers jockey. ♦ A paper/pencil pusher. ♦ A private affair. ♦ A private eye. ♦ A redneck. ♦ A short-order cook. ♦ A shrink. ♦ A social climber. ♦ A status seeker. ♦ A status symbol. ♦ A working girl. ♦ An officer of the law. ♦ Blue collar. ♦ By invitation only. ♦ Class distinctions. ♦ Class warfare. ♦ Everybody who's anybody. ♦ Fabric of society. ♦ From the wrong side of the tracks. ♦ High society. ♦ Low man on the totem pole. ♦ Middle management. ♦ One's lot/station in life. ♦ Social strata. ♦ The Beautiful People. ♦ The dregs of society. [see also Dereliction] ♦ The great and the near great. ♦ The *haute monde* [upper class]. ♦ The hoi polloi [lower class]. ♦ The "In" Crowd. ♦ The pecking order. ♦ The rank and file. ♦ The upper crust. ♦ To be status-conscious. ♦ To move in the right circles. ♦ To the manner/manor born. ♦ To sling hash. ♦ Trailer trash. ♦ W.A.S.P. (White, Anglo-Saxon Protestant.) ♦ White collar. ♦ White trash.

Steadfast

A tower of strength. ♦ A Rock of Gibraltar. ♦ An immovable object. ♦ An unwavering sense of purpose. ♦ Don't make waves. ♦ Don't rock the boat. ♦ Don't settle for less. ♦ Don't upset the applecart. ♦ Firmly entrenched.

♦ Hang in there. ♦ Hang tough. ♦ Hard as a rock. ♦ Hold out (for). ♦ Hold that line. ♦ Hold your own. ♦ Hold your own; it's better than holding somebody else's. ♦ Not give an inch. ♦ Not one thin dime for tribute. ♦ On a firm footing. ♦ On an even keel. ♦ Rock solid. ♦ Solid as the Rock of Gibraltar. ♦ Stability is not immobility. ♦ Stand by for the ram. ♦ Stand up for what (you know) is right. ♦ Stand one's (own) ground. ♦ Staunch in (the face of) adversity. ♦ Stay the course. ♦ Steady as she goes. ♦ Steady/ solid as a rock. ♦ That ain't goin' nowhere. ♦ That's my story, and I'm sticking to it. ♦ The pathways are smooth for the captain who runs a tight ship. ♦ The puck stops here. [hockey goalie's motto]. ♦ Through thick and thin. [see also Dependable, Thick, Thin] ♦ To brave the elements. ♦ To dig one's heels in. ♦ To hold one's own. ♦ To nail one's colors to the mast. ♦ To remain on point. ♦ To stand fast/pat. ♦ To stand up for what one believes in. ♦ To stick to one's guns. ♦ To take a hard line. ♦ To tough it out. ♦ To set one's jaw like flint. ♦ We do not negotiate with terrorists.

Stingy

A penny-pincher. ♦ A skinflint. ♦ A tightwad. ♦ A two-bit piker. ♦ Another day, another dollar; squeeze a nickel 'til the buffalo hollers. ♦ Another day, another dollar; squeeze the eagle 'til he holler. [see also Money] ♦ Bargain basement. ♦ Bargain hunters. ♦ Cherry-pickers. ♦ Deep pockets and short arms. ♦ Got the first dollar he ever made. ♦ So tight, he squeaks when he walks. ♦ To be chintzy. ♦ Tighter than a crab's *ss. (And that's watertight!) ♦ To be tight. ♦ To be tight-fisted. ♦ To chintz (on). ♦ To cut corners.

♦ To get every last nickel's worth. ♦ To squeeze a dollar. ♦ To squeeze a nickel till the buffalo turns blue. ♦ To take a shortcut.

Stodgy

A blueblood/bluestocking/bluenose. ♦ A culture vulture. ♦ A slice of life with crust. ♦ A stuffed shirt. ♦ An old codger/fart/fogy/fuddy-duddy. ♦ An old stick-in-the-mud. ♦ Longhair music. [see also Music] ♦ From the old school. ♦ Highfalutin'. ♦ Hoity-toity.

◆ In polite society. ◆ Miss Goody Two-Shoes. ◆ Miss Priss. ◆ Prim and proper. ◆ Snob appeal. ◆ The upper crust. ◆ To be snotty/snooty. ◆ To be straight-laced. ◆ To get (all) uppity. ◆ To have a stick up one's *ss. ◆ To put on airs. ◆ Upper echelon. ◆ Uptight and outta sight.

Straightforward
(also simplify)

A guided missile. ◆ A line drive. ◆ A pointed question. ◆ Address the issue/question. ◆ Could you please be more specific? ◆ Cut out the middleman. ◆ Don't bore me with all the (gory) details. ◆ Cut the crap. ◆ Cut the sh*t. ◆ Cut through the gobbledygook. ◆ Cut through the red tape. ◆ Cut to the chase. ◆ Dispense with the foreplay. ◆ Dispense with the (usual) formalities. ◆ Don't bore me with all the (gory) details. ◆ Find the (least) common denominator. ◆ Get to the point. ◆ Get down to bedrock/brass tacks. ◆ Get down to business. ◆ Get down to the nitty-gritty. ◆ Get right down to it. ◆ Go for the jugular. ◆ Gotta be honest with you. ◆ Have a (direct) bearing (on). ◆ In plain English. ◆ Laser-beam focus. ◆ Lay it on the line. [see also Outspoken] ◆ Let's get something straight (right

from the start). ◆ Look [so] square in the eye. ◆ Put it in lay/laymen's terms. ◆ Quit pussyfooting around. ◆ Reduce it to its simplest terms. ◆ Right to one's face. ◆ Say what you mean, and mean what you say. ◆ Stick to the issues. ◆ Straight as an arrow. ◆ Straight down the middle. ◆ Take the gloves off. ◆ To dispense with [it]. ◆ To do away with [it]. ◆ To dumb [it] down. ◆ To face [it] head-on. ◆ To get right (on down) to it. ◆ To get/give a straight answer. ◆ To reduce [it] to its lowest terms. ◆ To stay on point. ◆ To take care of business. ◆ To talk shop. ◆ Wade through all the b.s. ◆ Who am I/are we/are you kidding? ◆ Without further ado/delay/fanfare/interruption.

Strength

A tower of strength. ◆ Able to leap tall buildings in a single bound. ◆ Enough to knock out a horse. ◆ Heavy duty. ◆ Industrial strength. ◆ It is as easy for the strong man to be strong as it is for the weak to be weak. ◆ It'll put hair on your chest. ◆ It'll put lead in your pencil. ◆ Lord, give me strength. ◆ Man of steel. ◆ Not for the faint-hearted. ◆ Strong as Ackerman forty. ◆ Strong as an ox. ◆ Strong convictions precede great actions. ♦ Strong like bull/ox. ♦ The Rock of Gibraltar. ♦ To have a kick like a mule. ♦ To have oomph. ♦ To pack a wallop. ♦ You don't know your own strength.

Strict

As a matter of principle. ♦ Cross one's t's and dot one's i's. ♦ Do it by the numbers. ♦ Fill out a form. ♦ Orders is orders. ♦ To adhere to/follow the letter of the law. ♦ To be in full compliance. ♦ To do it according to Hoyle. ♦ To do it/go by the book. ♦ To do it up right. ♦ To be chicken sh*t. [see also Cowardice] ♦ To decree from on high. ♦ To follow (proper) procedure/protocol. ♦ To go through (proper) channels. ♦ To give [so] a hard time. ♦ To hard-nose [so]. ♦ To play by the rules. ♦ To stand on ceremony.

Strive

(also effort, exertion)

All or nothing. ♦ An all-out effort. ♦ Blood, sweat and tears. ♦ But that a man's reach may exceed his grasp, or what's a heaven for? ♦ By dint of [n.]. ♦ Do all that's humanly possible. ♦ Do all/everything in one's power. ♦ Do one's darndest. ♦ Do one's level best. ♦ Give it a shot. ♦ Give it one's all. ♦ Go for the gold. ♦ If this doesn't do it, nothing will. ♦ Marshal one's resources. ♦ Move heaven and earth. ♦ Muster all one's strength. ♦ No matter how you struggle and strive, you'll never get out of this world alive. ♦ Only he who attempts the ridiculous can achieve the impossible. ♦ Push/take [it] to the limit/max. ♦ Shoot the moon. ♦ Shoot the works. ♦ Stand on tippy-toe. ♦ Sweating bullets. ♦ Sweating like a pig. ♦ The fruit that falls easiest into hands tastes less sweet than that reached for on the highest bough. ♦ To apply oneself. ♦ To beat one's brains out. ♦ To break a sweat. ♦ To break/bust one's *ss/balls/neck. ♦ To buck for promotion. [see also Up] ♦ To buckle down. ♦ To give it 110%. ♦ To give it all you've got. ♦ To give it your all. ♦ To go for the record. ♦ To go to any/great lengths. ♦ To go to extremes. ♦ To make a concerted effort. ♦ To make every effort. ♦ To marshal/muster one's forces. ♦ To shoulder the burden. ♦ To strain one's milk. ♦ To summon (up) all one's strength. [see also Intensity] ♦ To try too hard. ♦ To do it to the best of one's ability. ♦ To the limits of human endurance. ♦ To work up a sweat. ♦ "When you reach for the stars, you may not quite get one, but you won't come up with a handful of mud either," was adman Leo Burnett's motto. ♦ With all one's heart and soul. ♦ With all one's might. ♦ With might and main.

Stubborn

A hardnose. ♦ A head like a rock. ♦ A head like cement. ♦ A one-way street. ♦ A stubborn cuss. ♦ A tough nut to crack. ♦ Entrenched in one's position. ♦ It's not negotiable. ♦ Like talking to a wall. ♦ Mind is made up. ♦ My way or no way. ♦ My way or the highway. ♦ Set in one's ways. ♦ Stubborn as a bull/donkey/fool/goat/mule/pig/stone/stump. ♦ Stubborn as a thousand born-agains avoiding questions. ♦ To be bull-headed/pig-headed/thick-headed.

Stumped

Beats me (all to hell). ♦ Beats the bejesus out of me. ♦ Beats the pants off me. ♦ Beats the hell/sh*t out of me. ♦ Can't make head nor tail of it. ♦ Can't prove it by me. ♦ Can't say for sure. ♦ Can't say's I do. ♦ Couldn't tell you. ♦ Damned if I can say. ♦ Damned if I know. ♦ Don't know what to make of [it]. ♦ Don't know what you see in him/her. ♦ God only knows. ♦ How should/would I know? ♦ I don't

know; I just work here. ♦ I have no idea. ♦ I haven't got a clue. ♦ I haven't (got) the foggiest (idea/notion). ♦ If I knew the answer to that one, I wouldn't be here (talking to you). ♦ If you don't know, I sure as hell don't. ♦ It's over my head. ♦ It's (way) beyond me. ♦ My mind is (a) blank. ♦ (Now,) that's a good question. ♦ Search me. ♦ There's no telling. ♦ To be befuddled/dumbfounded. To be pigeonholed. ♦ To be sidetracked. ♦ To be stumped. ♦ To defy analysis. ♦ To draw a blank. ♦ To not know where to turn/which way to turn. ♦ Up a blind alley. ♦ Up a dead-end street. ♦ Who can say? ♦ Who knows? ♦ You/you've got me (there). ♦ You're asking me?

Style

Although an owl has large eyes, he can't see as well as a mouse. ♦ Bigger is not necessarily better. ♦ Get it right the first time. ♦ Greatness lies not in being strong but in the right use of strength. ♦ If it's worth doing, it's worth doing right. ♦ If you want it done right, you have to do it yourself. ♦ In the style to which I would like to grow accustomed. ♦ It's not what you do it's how you do it. ♦ It's not what you say it's how you say it. ♦ It's the thought that counts. ♦ Sometimes more is less. ♦ There's a right way and a wrong way to do everything. ♦ There's the right way, the wrong way and the Army way. ♦ To hear it in one's tone of voice. ♦ To support a woman in the style to which she is accustomed. ♦ To support me in the style to which I would like to become accustomed. ♦ You don't have to be a millionaire to live like one.

Subservience

(also beg)

A brown-noser. ♦ Alms for the poor? ♦ An apple-polisher. ♦ As you wish. ♦ At one's beck and call. ♦ At your service. ♦ Buddy, can you spare a dime? ♦ Can you help a guy out with a cup of coffee? ♦ Groveling sharpens the beak. ♦ Here you are. ♦ Here you go. ♦ If begging, unfortunately, be thy lot, knock only at the large gates. ♦ If it's [n.] you want, it's [n.] you'll get. ♦ My name is [n.]; and I'll be your server today. ♦ Oh, there's a brown ring around his nose/and every day it grows and grows. ♦ To answer the call. ♦ To ask on bended knee ♦ To (be a) suck*ss. ♦ To be more than happy (to). ♦ To bow and scrape. ♦ To bootlick/ kowtow/wheedle. ♦ To brownnose [so]. ♦ To come hat in hand. ♦ To do [so]'s bidding. ♦ To do the dirty work. ♦ To freeload/grub/kiss *ss/kowtow/mooch/panhandle. ♦ To make/score (brownie) points. ♦ To petition for a redress of grievances. ♦ To sponge (off). ♦ To suck up (to). ♦ To tote and fetch. ♦ To wait on [so] hand and foot. ♦ We aim to please. ♦ Anything/whatever you say, (boss). ♦ You rang, Madame/Sir? Your obedient servant. ♦ Your wish is my command.

Substance

Brick(s) and mortar. ♦ But where's the hook? ♦ But will it Burke? ♦ But will it play in Peoria? ♦ It's got to have a hook. ♦ It's gotta have a schtick. ♦ Meat and potatoes. ♦ Nuts and bolts. ♦ Something to sink one's teeth into. ♦ Something to hang one's hat on. ♦ Sum and substance. ♦ To bounce it off [so]. ♦ To dip one's toes into. ♦ To get a feel for [it]. ♦ To have something to go on. ♦ To send up a trial balloon. ♦ To test the water. ♦ To run it by someone. ♦ To sound someone out. ♦ What will that little old lady in Iowa think about it? ♦ Where's the beef?

Substitute

A bench warmer. ♦ A place holder. ♦ A stand-in. ♦ An understudy. ♦ Accept no substitutes. ♦ In lieu of. ♦

Nobody is indispensable. ♦ Addressee or current resident. ♦ Pre-school is no substitute for parenting. ♦ There is no substitute for victory. ♦ Technology is no substitute for thinking. ♦ There is no substitute for hard work. ♦ To act in/on [so]'s behalf/stead. ♦ To act on behalf of [so]. ♦ To live vicariously through [so]. [see also Fantasize] ♦ To pinch hit. ♦ To send in a ringer. ♦ To sublimate an instinct/urge. ♦ To work out one's aggressions. ♦ Vulgarity is no substitute for wit. ♦ Whining is no substitute for working. ♦ You can be replaced.

Success

(also efficiency, performance)

A command performance. ♦ A credible performance. ♦ A half-witted success is better than a wholehearted failure. ♦ A hole-in-one. ♦ A howling/ resounding success. ♦ An unqualified success. ♦ And the hits just keep on coming. ♦ Cream rises to the top. [and gets whipped!—R.D.] ♦ Carry it off it fine style. ♦ Come through/pass with flying colors. ♦ Do a bang-up job. ♦ Find fame and fortune. ♦ Coming/ getting/moving up in the world. ♦ Go from rags to riches. ♦ Grab the gold ring on the merry-go-round. ♦ He that would thrive must arise at five; he that has thriven may arise at seven; he who will never thrive may rise at eleven. ♦ (He who has no bread may as well stay in bed. — R.D.) ♦ Hit the big time. ♦ In one's heyday. ♦ Local boy makes good. ♦ Mission accomplished. ♦ Most likely to succeed. [see also Predictable] ♦ No matter where you are on the ladder, there's always somebody one rung ahead of you trying to push you down. ♦ Nothing succeeds like success. ♦ One's body of work. ♦ One's crowning achievement/magnum opus. ♦ Pay one's own way. ♦ Pull off a hat trick. ♦ Reap the fruits of one's labor. ♦ Remember, when you see a man on the top of the mountain, he didn't fall there. ♦ Rise to the occasion. ♦ Safe at home. ♦ Success comes by little degrees (known as Master's and PhD's). — R.D. ♦ Success is valued most highly by those who ne'er succeed. ♦ That does the trick. ♦ The answer to a prayer. ♦ The road to success is always under construction. ♦ The sweet smell of success. ♦ The rules for success only work when you do. ♦ The fulfillment of a lifelong dream. ♦ The big enchilada. ♦ The only place Success comes before Work is in the dictionary. ♦ The rich and famous. ♦ There are many willing people—those willing to work and those willing to let them. ♦ To ace it. ♦ To achieve the desired effect. ♦ To attain a position of prominence. ♦ To amount to something. ♦ To be set for life. ♦ To carry [it] off. ♦ To come across. ♦ To come across with the goods. ♦ To come into one's own. ♦ To come off without a hitch. ♦ To come out/turn out/work out all right. ♦ To come through. ♦ To come through in flying style. ♦ To come to a head. ♦ To come to full flower. ♦ To crack the code. ♦ To cross the finish line. ♦ To deliver the goods. ♦ To do the trick. ♦ To find the silver bullet. ♦ To get one's way. ♦ To go according to plan. ♦ To go off like clockwork. ♦ To go swimmingly. ♦ To have arrived. ♦ To have done well obliges us to do so still. ♦ To have financial security. ♦ To hit a home run. ♦ To hit it out of the ballpark. ♦ To make a go of [it]. ♦ To make a splash. ♦ To make good. ♦ To make it (big). ♦ To make it with room to spare. ♦ To meet one's quota. ♦ To overcome insurmountable obstacles. ♦ To pull [it] out of the fire. ♦ To pull [it] off. ♦ To pull the chestnuts out of the fire. ♦ To come to/ reach fruition. ♦ To realize one's full potential. ♦ To reel in a big one. ♦ To ripen on the vine. ♦ To rise to prominence. ♦ To score a touchdown. ♦ To set the world on fire. ♦ To sleep one's way to the top. ♦ To strike it rich. ♦ To strike oil. ♦ To strike the mother lode. ♦ To succeed, you must proceed. ♦ To try to do something and fail is vastly better than to try to do nothing and succeed. ♦ To work like a champ. ♦ To work like a charm. ♦ Who awakes to find himself famous has not been asleep. ♦ You can't argue with success. ♦ Your raise will become effective when you do.

Sudden

(All) at once. ♦ All of a sudden. ♦ First thing you know. ♦ In a heartbeat. ♦ In a (blinding flash). ♦ In a New York minute. ♦ In one fell swoop. ♦ In the blink of an eye. ♦ In the (very) same breath. ♦ Like a bolt out of the blue. ♦ Never knew what hit him. ♦ On a moment's notice. ♦ Out of left field. [see also Surprise] ♦ Out of nowhere. ♦ Out of the (clear) blue. ♦ Out of thin air. ♦ (Right) out of a clear, blue sky. ♦ Sudden death.

Suicide

A banzai attack. [see also Attack, Surprise] ♦ A Gadarene plunge. ♦ A suicide pact. ♦ Blow one's brains out. ♦ Commit hari-kari. ♦ Commit suicide. ♦ Farewell, cruel world. ♦

Kamikaze. ♦ Self-destruction. ♦ Suicide by police. ♦ To die by one's own hand. ♦ To do away with oneself. ♦ To do oneself in. ♦ To end one's own life. ♦ To fall on one's (own) sword. ♦ To have a death wish. ♦ To kill/"off" oneself. ♦ To open a vein. ♦ To self-destruct. ♦ To sign one's own death warrant. ♦ To take the quick way out. ♦ To take the coward's way out. ♦ To take one's own life. ♦ To take the gas pipe.

Summation

(also basis, essence, foundation)
All the more reason (to). ♦ All told. ♦ And Bob's your uncle. ♦ (And) in conclusion, I'd just like to say: ♦ (And) there you have it. ♦ As a consequence of. ♦ Every story has a moral. ♦ In a nutshell. ♦ In a word. ♦ In brief. ♦ It all boils down/comes down to this. ♦ Let's/we'll leave it at that. ♦ That's about the size of it. ♦ That's all she wrote (there ain't no more). ♦ That's it/the story in a nutshell. ♦ That's the long and short of it. ♦ That's the sixty-four (-thousand)-dollar question. ♦ That's what it's all about. ♦ The blood and guts. ♦ The bottom line. ♦ The crux/heart of the matter. ♦ The end result. ♦ The main thing. ♦ The moral of the story is . . . ♦ The name of the game. ♦ The net-net. ♦ The operative word. ♦ The sum and substance of [it]. ♦ The upshot of [it]. ♦ The warp and woof. ♦ (To make a) long story short. ♦ To sum it up. ♦ To the tune of. ♦ To wrap it up. ♦ What it (all) boils/comes down to. ♦ When you get right down to it. ♦ Where it (all) nets out.

Superlatives

A/an [n.], if ever there were. ♦ A blue ribbon winner. ♦ A keeper. ♦ A killer-diller. ♦ A (little) bit of alright. ♦ A lot to live up to. ♦ A-Okay/A-one. ♦ A poster child for [n.]. ♦ A rootin' tootin' shootin' [n.]. ♦ A socko [n.]. ♦ A tough act to follow. ♦ An A-list actor. ♦ An all-time high/low. ♦ As [adj./adv.] as can be. ♦ As [adj./adv.] as it gets. ♦ As [adj./adv.] as the day is long. ♦ As [adj./adv.] as they come. ♦ As [adj./adv.] as you can imagine. ♦ As [adj./adv.] as you please. ♦ As [adj./adv.] as you've ever seen. ♦ At the peak of perfection. [see also Best] ♦ Awfully nice. ♦ Done to a fine turn. ♦ Done to perfection. ♦ Beyond compare. ♦ Big shoes to fill. ♦ Boff (also boffo, boffola). ♦ Ducky-wuckie. ♦ Far and away/out and away the best. ♦ Far out! ♦ Fine and dandy. ♦ Fine as dandelion wine. ♦ First in Show. ♦ Fit for a king. ♦ He/she is [adj.] in all the right places. ♦ Held in the highest esteem/regard. ♦ I am the greatest. ♦ In all its naked glory. ♦ It doesn't get any better/finer than this. ♦ It's da bomb. ♦ It's the living end. ♦ It's to die for. ♦ Jolly good. ♦ Just ducky. ♦ (Just) out of this world. ♦ Mighty fine/good. ♦ (More) [adj.] than ever. ♦ Not bad, for openers. ♦ Not bad, if I do say so myself. (Sayeth he/she, modestly.) ♦ Not bad is good. ♦ Not (half) bad. ♦ Not too shabby. ♦ Nothing better. ♦ Nothing wrong with that. ♦ Now that's what I call [adj.]. ♦ Of epic/mythical proportions. ♦ Of (recent) note. ♦ Of the first water. ♦ Of the highest order. ♦ Okey-doke.* ♦ Okey-dokey. *[see also Agree] ♦ Peachy keeno. ♦ Peachy-weachy. ♦ Perfectly acceptable. ♦ Pretty fair/good. ♦ Ranked #1 (in customer satisfaction by J.D. Power). ♦ Second to none. ♦ Splendiferous. ♦ Some kinda wonderful. ♦ Super duper! ♦ That takes the cake. ♦ That's (just) Jim Dandy. ♦ That's RAD. ♦ That's zizzy. ♦ The A-Team. ♦ The bee's knees. ♦ The best and the brightest. ♦ The best of the best. ♦ The cat's *ss/meow/ pajamas. ♦ The cream of the crop. ♦ The Great Granddaddy/Mother of All [n.]. ♦ The Greatest Show on Earth. ♦ The greatest [n.] to ever come down the pike. ♦ The height of [n.]. ♦ The likes of which the world has never seen. ♦ The tippity-top/tippy-top. ♦ The (most) [adj.] thing that I ever heard of. ♦ There's none so fair as can compare (to the Marine Corps infantry) [or insert your own preferred military unit – R.D.] ♦ They're grrrrreat! ♦ To have no equal/peer. ♦ Too [adj.] for words. ♦ Totally awesome. ♦ Whammo. ♦ What's not to like? ♦ When only the best will do. ♦ Worth a second look. ♦ You have to go a long way to beat [it]. ♦ You've gotta love it.

Surprise

A banzai attack. [see also Attack, Suicide] ♦ A man surprised is half beaten. ♦ A surprise attack. ♦ An eye-opener. ♦ An unforeseen turn of events. ♦ Bite my hide. ♦ Bless my bones. ♦ Bless my heart. ♦ Blow me down. ♦ Caught off guard. ♦ Caught without one's rollbars. ♦ Fancy that! ♦ Fry my hide. ♦ Goodness gracious. ♦ Guess what? ♦ He's/she's/you're the last person in the world I'd have expected that from. ♦ How about them apples? ♦ How do you like that? ♦ How was I supposed to know? ♦ I almost dropped my teeth. ♦ I could have fallen through the floor. ♦ I damn near (could've) died. ♦ I like to have died. ♦ I'll be a monkey's uncle. ♦ I'll be a son of a gun. ♦ I'll be a whisker's sister. ♦ I'll be damned/darned. ♦ Imagine that. ♦ It happens when you least expect it. ♦ It should come as no surprise. ♦ Jack in the box. ♦ Jeepers creepers. ♦ Judas priest. ♦ Land sakes alive. ♦ Like a deer caught in the headlights. ♦ Lord of mercy. ♦ Mercy me. ♦ My word! ♦ Nothing could have prepared one for [it]. ♦ Now you tell me! ♦ Oh dear. ♦ (Oh) dear me. ♦ Oh me, oh my. ♦ Shiver me timbers. ♦ Sticker shock. ♦ Surprise of surprises! ♦ That takes the cake. ♦ The element of surprise. ♦ Think fast! ♦ To ambush/dry gulch [so]. [see also Attack] ♦ To be in for a shock/surprise. ♦ To be slack-jawed. ♦ To be taken aback. ♦ To catch [so] off guard. ♦ To catch one with one's guard down. ♦ To let one's guard down. ♦ To catch [so] with her/his britches/pants down. ♦ To come as a complete surprise. ♦ To come as a (total) shock. ♦ To come out of left field [see also Sudden] ♦ To do a double take. ♦ To get the surprise of one's life. ♦ To go into shock. ♦ To have dire/unanticipated/ unexpected/ unintended consequences. ♦ To send shock waves through the [n.]. ♦ To set [so] back on her/his haunches/pins. ♦

To spring it on [so]. ♦ To take [so] by (complete) surprise. ♦ To throw [so] a curve/curveball. ♦ (Well), blow me down. ♦ (Well), hush mah mouf'! ♦ (Well), I (do) declare. ♦ (Well), I'll be dadburned/dadgummed/ damned/ dipped (in sh*t). ♦ (Well), I'll be go to hell. ♦ (Well), I'll be hornswoggled. ♦ (Well), never in all my born days. ♦ (Well), ring my chimes. ♦ (Well), what do you know? ♦ What the f*ck? ♦ When you least expect it. ♦ Who knew? ♦ Who woulda thunk it? ♦ Without (any) warning. ♦ Wonder of wonders! ♦ You could have knocked me over with a feather. ♦ You could not pick my jaw up off the floor with a shovel. ♦ You could've floored me. ♦ You could've picked me up off the floor. ♦ You should have seen the look on her/his face.

Surrender

Assume the position. ♦ Buckle under. ♦ Cave in. ♦ Go belly up. ♦ I give (up). ♦ If you insist. ♦ If you must know. ♦ Reach for the sky. ♦ Roll over and play dead. ♦ Stick 'em up. ♦ To admit defeat. ♦ To back down. ♦ To cave in like a house of cards. ♦ To cop out/ fink out. ♦ To give in/give up/give way. ♦ To knuckle under. ♦ To lay down one's arms. ♦ To roll over (and play dead). ♦ To say uncle. ♦ To show the white feather. ♦ To take a dive/nosedive. ♦ To take a fall. ♦ To throw in the sponge/towel. ♦ To throw up one's hands in defeat/despair/dismay. ♦ To turn oneself in. ♦ To wave the white flag (of surrender). ♦ To yield the floor. ♦ To yield the right of way. ♦ You win. You've got me.

Survival

Back from the dead. ♦ Clinging to life. ♦ Every man for himself. ♦ [Every ma'am for herself. – R.D.] ♦ It is better to outlast your teeth than for your teeth to outlast you. – R.D. ♦ He who fights and runs away, lives to fight another day. (But he who is in battle slain, can never rise to fight again.) ♦ In survival mode. ♦ Keep one's head above water. ♦ Last man standing. ♦ Man the lifeboats! ♦ None the worse for wear. ♦ Only the strong survive. ♦ Self-preservation is the first law of nature. ♦ Survival of the fittest. ♦ To live to tell the tale. ♦ To pull through. ♦ To save one's *ss/hide/neck/ skin. ♦ To save one's soul.

Suspicion

A dead cat on the line. ♦ A fly in the ointment. ♦ A rattler in the woodpile. ♦ A sneaking suspicion. ♦ Caesar's wife must also be above suspicion. ♦ Can't put my finger on it. ♦ It does not compute. ♦ Of doubtful/dubious/questionable origin. ♦ Raises more questions than answers. ♦ Round up the usual suspects. ♦ Something fishy is going on. ♦ Something is radically wrong. ♦ Stinks on ice. ♦ There's a skunk/ snake in the woodpile. ♦ There's something rotten in Denmark. ♦ Things just don't add up. ♦ To have a funny feeling. ♦ To have qualms (about). ♦ To have serious misgivings. ♦ To reek/smell/stink to high heaven. ♦ To smell a rat. ♦ Under a cloud. ♦ Under (a cloud of) suspicion. ♦ Under suspicious circumstances. ♦ Where there's smoke there's fire.

Sympathy

A bleeding heart (liberal). A crying shame. ♦ Ain't it/that a shame? ♦ Heartfelt condolences. ♦ Get well soon. ♦ I wouldn't wish it on my worst enemy. ♦ In our thoughts and prayers. ♦ It shouldn't happen to a dog. ♦ My heart bleeds for you/goes out to you/pumps (purple) p*ss for you. ♦ The snake charmer who is bit must expect no sympathy. ♦ This is the world's tiniest violin (playing you hearts and flowers). ♦ To feel bad/

sorry for [so]. ♦ To have a heart. ♦ To have a lump in one's throat. ♦ To have/take pity (on). ♦ Tsk, tsk, tsk. ♦ You have my (deepest) sympathy.

Taboo

A (big) no-no. ♦ A sacred cow. ♦ Don't even go there. ♦ Everything I like is either illegal, immoral or fattening. ♦ It's just not done. ♦ Keep your hands off. ♦ Look but don't touch. ♦ Off limits. ♦ Out of bounds. ♦ Strictly taboo. ♦ That's a no-no. ♦ The forbidden fruit is the sweetest. (But the most dangerous). ♦ There are laws against that. ♦ To cross over to the dark side. ♦ To have zero tolerance (for). ♦ Totally unacceptable. ♦ Unhand me, you cad! ♦ We don't use that word.

Taciturnity

A man of few words. ♦ A whistling girl and a crowing hen never come to any good end. ♦ A word and a stone once let go cannot be recalled. ♦ Don't put your foot in your mouth. ♦ Engage brain before opening mouth. ♦ Epigrams succeed where epics fail. ♦ Hold one's tongue. ♦ Least said, soonest mended. ♦ Never let your heart rule your head. ♦ One wrong wisecrack could become the chink in one's armor. ♦ Silent men, like still water, deep and dangerous. ♦ Speak softly but carry a big stick. ♦ Still water runs deep. ♦ The brighter the moon, the more the dogs howl. ♦ The less said, the better. ♦ The tongue attacks and the ear gets clapped. ♦ There's no taking back what you've said. ♦ Those who live too conspicuously tempt the notice of fate. ♦ To keep a low profile. ♦ Wouldn't say sh*t if he/she had a mouthful (of it).

Tact

A soft answer turneth away wrath. ♦ An iron hand in a velvet glove. ♦ An ounce of discretion is worth a pound of wit. ♦ Be tactful; overlook not your own opportunity. ♦ Break it (to me) gently. ♦ Don't dip your pen in the office inkwell. ♦ Don't rub it in. ♦ Don't sh*t where you eat. ♦ I mean no disrespect. ♦ Gunboat diplomacy. ♦ Handle with kid gloves. ♦ He who would be spoken of well himself must not speak ill of others. ♦ Keep a civil tongue. ♦ If I may be so [adj.] as to say. ♦ Most of us know how to say nothing but very few of us know when. ♦ Never burn your bridges behind you. ♦ (Please) don't take this the wrong way. ♦ Some things are better left unsaid. ♦ Southern hospitality. ♦ Speak not of rope to the hanged man's wife. ♦ The art of brinksmanship. ♦ To choose your words wisely. ♦ To couch [it] in gentler/softer terms. ♦ To know all the right things to say. ♦ To know how to work the room. ♦ To know when to keep one's mouth shut. ♦ To let [so] down easy/gently. ♦ To pull one's punches. ♦ To put it mildly. [see also Agree] ♦ To respectfully decline. ♦ To spare [so]'s feelings. ♦ To sugarcoat [it]. ♦ You catch more flies with honey than you do with vinegar.

Talkative

A babbling brook. ♦ A blow-by-blow description. ♦ A chatty Cathy. ♦ A lively tongue speaks for a quick mind. ♦ A motor mouth. ♦ A pain can be more disagreeable to your listener than to you. ♦ A running commentary. ♦ A talking jag. ♦ A torrent of words. ♦ All the gory details. ♦ Can talk the hind legs off a dog/donkey/horse. ♦ Can't get a word in edgewise. ♦ Doesn't come up for air. ♦ He/she could talk under water. ♦ Her/his tongue was hung in the middle and ran at both ends. ♦ It is only too easy to confuse a presumed need for information with the urge to impart it. ♦ Like to hear oneself talk. ♦ My, how you do go/run on. ♦ Talk till you're

blue in the face. ♦ Talk till the cows come home. ♦ The gift of gab. ♦ There is no tax on the mouth. ♦ To bandy about. ♦ To be vaccinated with a phonograph needle. ♦ To bat/beat one's gums. ♦ To bend [so]'s ear. ♦ To flap one's yap. ♦ To run off at the mouth. [see also Complain] ♦ To talk a blue streak. ♦ To talk one's (fool) head off. ♦ To talk the ears off a brass monkey. ♦ To talk [so]'s arm/ear/head off. ♦ To talk the bark off a tree. ♦ To wag one's jaw. ♦ Wise men speak because they have something to say; fools, because they have to say something.

Tall

A big galoot. ♦ A man never stands so tall as when he stoops to help a child. ♦ A tall drink of water. ♦ *ss high to a tall Indian. ♦ Growing like a weed. ♦ Tall and skinny like a weed: built for pleasure not for speed. [see also Thin] ♦ Tall as giraffe nuts. ♦ Tall, dark and handsome. ♦ Tall trees catch much wind. ♦ To be able to eat spaghetti off [so]'s head. ♦ To stand on tiptoe. ♦ To tower over [so].

Teach

(also indoctrination, inspiration)
A classic case (of). ♦ A guiding light. ♦ A role model. ♦ A textbook example.

♦ A working model. ♦ Allow me to demonstrate. ♦ As the twig is bent, so grows the tree. ♦ Awe inspiring. ♦ Get a clearer fix on. ♦ Get into the swing of things. ♦ Get up to speed. ♦ Give a man a fish and you will feed him for a day; teach him to fish and you will feed him for a lifetime. ♦ I taught him everything he knows. ♦ Let that be a lesson to you. ♦ Let your conscience be your guide. ♦ Like so. ♦ Teacher's pet. ♦ The teachers are afraid of the principal; the principal is afraid of the Board of Education; the Board of Education is afraid of the parents; the parents are afraid of the kids; and the kids are afraid of no one. ♦ Those who can, do; those who cannot, teach. ♦ To baptize by fire. ♦ To fire/fuel/spur/ stir the imagination. ♦ To make one's spirits soar. ♦ To shed light on (the subject). ♦ To show [so] the ropes. ♦ To walk [so] through [it]. ♦ What you teach is twice learned. ♦ Words to live by. ♦ You can't teach an old dog new tricks. [But you can learn new tricks from an old dog!] — R.D.

Tease

Bait the wolf with a taste, then keep him at bay. ♦ Give [sb] a rough time. ♦ Give [sb] the business. ♦ I was just funning you. ♦ Only joshing. ♦ The royal runaround. ♦ To bust [so]'s agates/balls/chops. ♦ To do a number on [so]. ♦ To drive [so] to distraction. ♦ To fun [so]. ♦ To get a rise out of [so]. [see also Irk] ♦ To get into [so]'s henhouse. ♦ To get/give the runaround. ♦ To give [sb] a hotfoot. ♦ To give [sb] the business. ♦ To jerk [sb] around. ♦ To pull/yank [sb]'s chain. ♦ To pull [so]'s leg. ♦ To put [sb] on. ♦ To rattle [sb]'s cage. ♦ To rib [sb]. ♦ To take a ribbing.

Telephonese

Could you spell your name for me, please? [rejoinder: Sure, I've been doing it for years — R.D.] ♦ Give me a buzz. ♦ He/she is gone for the day. ♦ He/she is not available at the moment. Would you like to be connected to his/her voicemail? ♦ I just (now) got off the phone with him/her. ♦ I'm sorry, he/she has stepped away from his/her desk (for a moment). [see also Absence] ♦ If a man answers, hang up. ♦ Is he/she expecting your call? ♦ Just a phone call away. ♦ Please listen carefully as our menu has changed. ♦ Ring me up sometime. ♦ Sorry, wrong number. ♦ This call may be monitored (or recorded) for quality or training purposes. ♦ To get on the horn. ♦ To give [so] a buzz/call/jingle/ring. ♦ To have telephonitis. ♦ To play telephone tag. ♦ To ring [so] up. ♦ What is the nature of your call? ♦ Who shall I say is calling? ♦ Will he/she know what this is in reference to? ♦ You just (now) missed her/him. ♦ Your call is important to us (and will be answered in the order in which it was received).

Television

A vast wasteland. ♦ Aimed at a 12-year-old mentality. ♦ And now a word from our sponsor. ♦ As seen on TV. ♦ Chewing gum for the eyes. ♦ Edited for television. ♦ The boob tube/idiot box. ♦ The ever-loving Vast Wasteland. ♦ The ratings game. ♦ The story at eleven. ♦ We'll be back after this important message.

Temper

A little pot is soon hot. ♦ Before you lose your temper count to ten. ♦ Keep your temper, nobody else wants it. ♦ Temper, temper. ♦ To be a hothead. ♦ To be hot-headed. ♦ To blow a fuse. ♦ To blow one's cool/cork/ stack/top. ♦ To fly into a rage. ♦ To fly off the handle ♦ To go through the roof. ♦ To have a hair trigger. ♦ To have a short fuse. ♦ To have a temper tantrum. ♦ To lose it. ♦ To lose one's cool. ♦ To lose one's composure/ head/ patience/ temper. ♦ Who loses his temper is defeated.

Temporary
(also casual, impermanent)

A cameo appearance. ♦ A commercial break. ♦ A flash in the pan. ♦ A fleeting glance/moment. ♦ A one-night stand. ♦ A passing glance. ♦ A sidelong glance. ♦ A passing reference. ♦ A short shelf life. ♦ A temporary restraining order. ♦ A tip of the hat. ♦ A weekend warrior. ♦ All is transitory. ♦ As the need arises. ♦ At first blush/ glance. ♦ Beside the point. ♦ By the bye. ♦ By the way. ♦ Casual sex. ♦ Do you believe in casual sex, or should I dress? ♦ Everybody will be famous for 15 minutes. ♦ Flavor of the month. ♦ For a spell. ♦ For now. ♦ For the nonce. ♦ For the time being. ♦ Here today, gone tomorrow. ♦ It's a long road which knows no turning. ♦ It's a nice place to visit, but I wouldn't want to live there. ♦ Just going through a phase/stage. ♦ Just passing through. ♦ Living out of a suitcase. ♦ Nothing lasts forever. ♦ On the surface. ♦ *Sic transit gloria mundi.* ♦ Something's gotta give. ♦ Subject to change. ♦ The bubble's going to break. ♦ There are no roads without end. ♦ This too shall pass. [see also Forbearance] ♦ To be short-lived. ♦ To entertain the idea/ thought. ♦ To have one's moment in the sun. ♦ To make a pit stop. ♦ To make mention of. ♦ To mention [it] in passing. ♦ To not last long. ♦ To pencil [it] in. ♦ To speak off the cuff. ♦ To touch on/upon. ♦ To toy with the idea.

Temptation

A preview of coming attractions. ♦ Get thee behind me, Satan. ♦ Give a wolf a taste, then keep him at bay. ♦ I can resist anything but temptation. ♦ Looks good enough to eat. [see also Attractive] ♦ Nobody is above temptation. ♦ Offer the carrot on a stick. ♦ See-through clothing. ♦ The only way to get rid of a temptation is to yield to it. ♦ The spirit is willing but the flesh is weak. ♦ To bait the trap. ♦ To have drool appeal. ♦ To hike one's skirt. ♦ To make one's mouth water. ♦ To show some skin. ♦ To whet one's appetite. ♦ To wrestle with one's demons.

Theft

A cradle snatcher. ♦ A sneak thief. ♦ A thief would rather steal a purse than find one. ♦ Cops and robbers. ♦ Get a 5-finger discount/a 100% discount. ♦ Grand larceny. ♦ Highway robbery. ♦ I pity the river; I pity the brook; I pity the one who steals this book. — Angela Maria Delia ♦ Illegal search and seizure. ♦ Petit/petty larceny. ♦ They can't steal what they can't find. ♦ Thieves think others fools who play by the rules. ♦ To be light-fingered/have light fingers. ♦ To boost [it]. ♦ To have sticky fingers. ♦ To "liberate" [it]. ♦ To make off with. ♦ To mug [so]. ♦ To pull a heist/ job/robbery. ♦ To rob the cradle. ♦ To rob [so] blind. ♦ To roll a drunk. ♦ To spirit [it] away. ♦ To take the bread out of [so]'s mouth. ♦ To wrest the viands. ♦ Use an Oklahoma credit card.

Thick

As thick as one's wrist. ♦ Blood is thicker than water. [see also Water] ♦ In the thick of it. ♦ So thick, you could cut it with a knife. ♦ Thick as a brick/ditch. ♦ Thick as flies/pea soup/thieves. ♦ Thick as the hair on a dog's back. ♦ Through thick and thin. [see also Dependable, Steadfast, Thin] ♦ To be thick-headed/ have a thick head. ♦ To come thick and fast. ♦ To lay/spread it on thick.

Thin

A bag of bones. ♦ A skinny malink. ♦ A Skinny Minnie. ♦ Nothing but skin and bones. ♦ Skinny as a weed. ♦ Tall and skinny like a weed/built for pleasure, not for speed. [see also Tall] ♦ Slim as one's pinkie. ♦ Slim chance. ♦ The walls are so thin, if you sneeze your neighbor says, "God Bless You." ♦ Thin as a rail. ♦ Thin as six o'clock. ♦ Through thick and thin. [see also Dependable, Steadfast, Thick]

Think

(also ponder)

A battle of the wits. ♦ A blue-sky session. ♦ A brainstorming session. ♦ A think tank. ♦ A wise man reflects before he speaks; a fool speaks and reflects upon what he spoke. ♦ Bear in mind. ♦ Chew the cud. ♦ Collect your thoughts. ♦ Come to think (about/of it). ♦ Contemplate your navel. ♦ Don't let your tongue cut your throat. ♦ Don't put your foot in your mouth. ♦ Engage brain before opening mouth. ♦ Food for thought. ♦ Give it some thought. ♦ I think, therefore I am. ♦ If you don't use your head, you'll have to use your feet. ♦ In deep reverie. ♦ In the back of one's mind. ♦ Keep (it) in mind. ♦ Kick it around (a bit). ♦ Listen to reason. ♦ Nothing is either good or bad but thinking makes it so. ♦ Paralysis by analysis. ♦ Pause to reflect. ♦ To think it through. ♦ Sleep on it. ♦ So I said to myself ('Self,' I said). ♦ Something to think about. ♦ Soul-searching. ♦ That's using the old noodle. ♦ The first rule of think well is to write well. ♦ There must be a logical explanation. ♦ They can't put you in jail for what you're thinking. ♦ Thimk. ♦ Think ahea D. ♦ Think all you say but do not say all you think. ♦ Think before you speak. ♦ Think first and speak afterwards. ♦ Thought-provoking. ♦ To bandy it about. ♦ To blue-sky. ♦ To brainstorm. ♦ To come to mind. ♦ To cross one's mind. ♦ To do it in one's head. ♦ To enter one's mind. ♦ To entertain the thought. ♦ To factor [it] in. ♦ To follow the thread of [so]'s argument. ♦ To give it a think. ♦ To mull/think it over. ♦ To occur to one. ♦ To pop into one's head. ♦ To put on one's thinking cap. ♦ To rack/wrack one's brain. ♦ To reach a (logical) conclusion. ♦ To take [it] into account/under advisement. ♦ To think [it] out/over/through/up. ♦ To think long and hard about [it]. ♦ To think outside the box. ♦ To toy with the idea. ♦ To use one's grey matter. ♦ To use one's head/noodle/smarts. ♦ Train of thought. ♦ Weigh the options/pros and cons. ♦ Weigh one's words (carefully). ♦ Within reason.

Thorough

All the nits and gnats. ♦ All the whys and wherefores. ♦ And everything in between. ♦ Attention to detail. ♦ Climb every mountain /ford every stream/follow every rainbow/till you find your dream. ♦ Every jot and tittle. ♦ Hash and re-hash. ♦ In clinical/minute detail. ♦ Leave no stone unturned. ♦ They use everything on the pig but the whistle. ♦ To be all over it. ♦ To cover all the bases. ♦ To dot all the i's and cross all the t's. [see also Comprehensive] ♦ To dig into [it]. ♦ To drill down. ♦ To exhaust every possibility. ♦ To follow through. ♦ To get granular. ♦ To go through [it] with a fine-tooth comb. ♦ To go through with [it]. ♦ To hang on [so]'s every word. ♦ To hash it over. ♦ To read from cover to cover. ♦ To read the fine print. ♦ To the ends of the earth. ♦ To use every means at one's disposal. ♦ To work it over. ♦ Word for word.

Thrift

A shoestring budget. ♦ A staycation. ♦ Daylight saving time. ♦ Economy is the wisdom of the rich and the riches of the poor. ♦ Get what you can, and what you get hold; 'tis the stone that will turn all your lead into gold. ♦ Getting and spending, we lay waste our powers. ♦ Husband one's resources. ♦ If you keep something for seven years, you're sure to find a use for it. ♦ Industry is fortune's right hand—frugality her left. ♦ It's not what you earn, it's what you save. ♦ Keep and you shall have. ♦ Make it on a shoestring. ♦ Nothing should be bought that can be mended or done without. ♦ Salt [it] away. ♦ Save a tree—eat a beaver. ♦ Save [it] for a rainy day. ♦ Sock it away. ♦ Squirrel it away. ♦ Take care of your pennies, and the dollars will take care of themselves. ♦ 'Tis too late to spare when the pocket is bare. ♦ Tighten (up) one's belt. ♦ To build a nest egg. ♦ To build sweat equity. ♦ To live within one's means. ♦ To patch is honorable, to patch a patch is an abomination. ♦ To pinch pennies. ♦ To scrimp and save. ♦ To tighten the purse strings. ♦ Trim the lamps. ♦ Two can live as cheaply as one. ♦ Waste not, want not. ♦ Willful waste makes woeful want. ♦ Without frugality none can be rich; and with it very few would be poor. ♦ Year-end savings. ♦ Your life savings.

Tight

As tight as a cramp. ♦ Good night, sleep tight, and don't let the bedbugs bite. ♦ Sit tight. ♦ So tight he squeaks when he walks. ♦ Tight as a drum. ♦ Tight as a tick. ♦ Tight as the bark on a tree. ♦ Tighter than a crab's *ss (and that's watertight). ♦ Tighter than a duck's *ss—and that's waterproof. ♦ Tighter than a gnat's *ss in fly time. ♦ Tighter than Dick's hat band. ♦ Tighter than the skin on a hot dog. ♦ Tighter than two coats of paint. ♦ Up tight (and outta sight). ♦ Wound up tighter than an 8-day clock.

Time

A minute wasted is ne'er replaced. ♦ All the time. ♦ All the while. ♦ At all times. ♦ At one time. ♦ At one time or another. ♦ Day after day. ♦ Day in, day out. ♦ Day to day. ♦ Every single day. ♦ Half-past the cow's *ss; a quarter to his balls. ♦ Hour after hour. ♦ Not a moment to lose. ♦ On time. ♦ *Tempus fugit.* (Time flies)! ♦ The march of time. ♦ The only reason for time is so everything doesn't happen at once. ♦ The whole time. ♦ There's no time to lose. ♦ There's not a moment to waste. ♦ Time after time. ♦ Time and tide wait for no man. ♦ Time and time again. ♦ Time flies when you're having a good time. ♦ Time heals all wounds. ♦ Time wounds all heels. ♦ Time is of the essence. ♦ Time is running out. ♦ Time marches on. ♦ Time means nothing to a hog. ♦ Time there is plenty of. ♦ Time well spent. ♦ Time will tell. ♦ Time's a-wasting. ♦ To buy time. ♦ To do time. ♦ To gain time. ♦ To have the luxury of time. ♦ To keep time. ♦ To kill time. ♦ To lose time. ♦ To mark time. ♦ To save time. ♦ To serve time. ♦ To set aside time. ♦ To spare time. ♦ To spend time. ♦ To squander time. ♦ To take time. ♦ To take one's (own sweet) time. ♦ To waste time. ♦ Waste of wealth is sometimes retrieved but waste of time, never. ♦ We shall see what we shall see. ♦ What time is it? It's Howdy Doody time! ♦ When you are winding your watch, you have time on your hands. ♦ Where does the time go? ♦ Work expands to fill the time allotted to it. ♦ Year in, year out.

Timeliness
(also finally)

About that time. ♦ After wit belongs to all. ♦ After the fact. ♦ Along about now. ♦ Are you happy now? ♦ As time goes by. ♦ At a decent hour. ♦ At (long) last. ♦ At the appointed hour. ♦ Don't try to turn the clock back; wind it again. ♦ Foresight is better than hindsight. ♦ Hindsight is (always) 20/20. ◆ Hindsight: the view from the backside of a mistake. ◆ I thought you'd never ask. ◆ If only our hindsight were as good as our foresight (we'd all be a damn sight better off). ◆ If you throw a stone into a pack of dogs, the one that is hit barks. ◆ In retrospect. ◆ In the interim. ◆ It's about time. ◆ It's been a long time coming. ◆ It's high time. ◆ Looking back in hindsight. (Is there any other way to look back? — R.D.) ◆ (Just) in time. ◆ Long overdue. ◆ Meanwhile, back at the ranch. ◆ Monday-morning quarterback. ◆ Now is the hour. ◆ Now is the time. ◆ Now it can be told. ◆ Postman: You're only as good as your last drop. ◆ Right away. ◆ Right now. ◆ Right on schedule/time. ◆ Right on the dot. ◆ Speak not of what you were— it's what you are today. ◆ That's what I've been trying to tell you (all along). ◆ The biggest ones always get away. ◆ The one that got away is always the biggest. ◆ The time has come. ◆ The time has come, the Walrus said, to speak of many things. ◆ 'Tis the season. ◆ To get one's priorities straight. ◆ To set one's priorities. ◆ To have one's finger on the pulse of things. ◆ To tell time. ◆ To this (very) day. ◆ Today's the day. ◆ What have you

done for me/us lately? ◆ What time do you have? ◆ What time is it? It's Howdy Doody time! ◆ What time you got? ◆ What took you so long? ◆ When you're up to your *ss in alligators is no time to clear the swamp. ◆ With every day that goes by. ◆ With every passing day. ◆ You can't win today's ballgame with yesterday's home runs. ◆ You never know how many rats are on a ship until it's sinking. ◆ You should've seen the one that got away. ◆ You're only as good as your last home run.

Tired

(About to) drop in one's tracks. ◆ *ss is dragging/ sucking buttermilk/ sucking wind. ◆ Bleary-eyed. ◆ Bone weary. ◆ Can't keep one's eyes open. ◆ Crapped out. ◆ Dead tired. ◆ Dead on one's feet. ◆ Dog tired. ◆ Done in. ◆ Fading fast. ◆ Going downhill fast. ◆ Huffin' and a-puffin'. ◆ Like an ant dragging an anchor. ◆ (Plumb) tuckered out. ◆ Thank God it's Friday (TGIF).

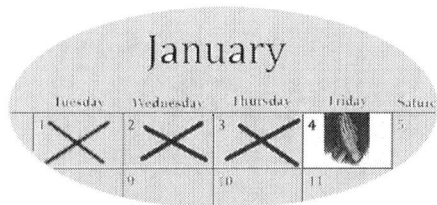

♦ Tired out. ♦ To be bushed. ♦ To be whacked out. ♦ To burn out. ♦ To fade in the stretch. ♦ To fizzle out. ♦ To lose one's mojo. ♦ To peter out/ poop out. ♦ To run out of steam. ♦ To shoot one's wad. ♦ To trail off. ♦ Too pooped to pop. ♦ Worn to a frazzle.

Toasts

Bottoms up! ♦ Down the hatch. ♦ Good luck! ♦ Here goes nothing. ♦ Here's looking at you. ♦ Here's looking at you, kid. ♦ Here's looking up your old address. ♦ Here's mud in your eye. ♦ Here's to [n.]. ♦ Here's to you. ♦ Live long and prosper. ♦ May the road always rise to your feet; may the wind always be at your back; may the sun always shine on your face. ♦ May the dreams you hold dearest, be those which come true; the kindness you spread, keep returning to you. - [Irish blessing] ♦ May we kiss whom we please, and please whom we kiss. ♦ May you be in heaven a (full) half hour before the devil knows you're dead. ♦ May you live as long as you want to, and want to as long as you live. ♦ May you run out of deposit slips before you run out of checks. - R.D. ♦ Through the lips and over the gums, lookout, stomach, here she comes! ♦ To love, to money, and to the time to enjoy them. ♦ To propose a toast. ♦ To your health!

Tomorrow

Eat, drink and be merry for tomorrow we die. ♦ Feast today makes fast tomorrow. ♦ Here today, gone tomorrow. ♦ If we can't forget yesterday there will never be a tomorrow. ♦ Nobody knows tomorrow. ♦ One today is worth a thousand tomorrows. ♦ Plan for tomorrow but don't live for it. — Angela Maria Delia ♦ There's always tomorrow. ♦ Tomorrow is another day. ♦ Tomorrow never comes. ♦ Today [n.], tomorrow, the world.

Tongue Twisters
(also doggerel, etc.)

A diller, a dollar, a ten-o'clock scholar. ♦ A funny little bird is the pelican. His beak can hold more than his belly can! ♦ A selfish shellfish made an enemy of an anemone. - R.D. ♦ Ashes, ashes, all fall down. ♦ A woman who is long chased may not long remain chaste. — R.D. ♦ As Venus said, "Look, Ma—no hands!" — R.D. ♦ Assault: to add injury to insult. — R.D. ♦ Beans, beans, are good for your heart; the more you eat, the more you fart. ♦

Beans, beans, the musical fruit; the more you eat, the more you toot. The more you toot, the better you feel; so let's have beans with every meal! ◆ Bend over and touch your toes and I'll show you where the wild goose goes. ◆ Betty Boughter bought a bit of bitter butter, put this bit of bitter butter in her batter, made her batter bitter; Betty bought a bit of better butter, put this bit of better butter in her batter, made her bitter batter better! ◆ Bouncy, bouncy, ballie; your sister's name is Paulie. ◆ Chicken in the car, car won't go; that's how you spell Chicago. ◆ Composure self. ◆ Every party has a pooper, that's why we invited you, party pooper! Party pooper! ◆ Fat and Skinny had a race, up and down the pillowcase. Fat fell down and broke his crown—and Skinny won the race! ◆ Fat, fat the water rat; fifteen bullets in his hat. ◆ For some, life is but a dream; for others, life is a dream of butts. ◆ From here . . . to there . . . to Gramercy Square. When I get there, I'll pull your hair! ◆ Fuzzy Wuzzy was a bear, Fuzzy Wuzzy had no hair; Fuzzy Wuzzy wasn't fuzzy, was he? ◆ Gene, Gene, made a machine; Joe, Joe, made it go; Art, Art, blew a fart and knocked the whole damned thing apart. ◆ Genessee *quoi*.

◆ Glory, glory hallelujah, teacher hit me with the ruler. Now she's sittin' in the cooler while I go marching on! ◆ Great God almighty, the wind flew up her nightie. ◆ Gynecologist: an orifice worker. ◆ Here we go 'round the mulberry bush. ◆ Hip, hip, puree. ◆ Homing bird/humming pigeon. ◆ How much wood would a woodchuck chuck if a woodchuck could chuck wood? ◆ Henhouse: an egg plant. ◆ How, now, brown cow, grazing in the green, green grass? ◆ "I" before "E" except after "C" (or when sounded as "A" as in neighbor or weigh). ◆ I scream, you scream, we all scream for ice cream! ◆ I see London, I see France, I see [n.]'s underpants. ◆ In days of old when knights were bold and condoms weren't invented/Men wrapped their c*cks in woolen socks and humped away contented. ◆ Inka binka bottle of ink; the cork fell out and you stink. ◆ Jack and Jill went up a hill to fetch a pail of water. ◆ Jack and Jill went up a hill; they both had a buck and a quarter/Jill came down with two and a half/Do you think they went up for water? ◆ James Johnson jumped off the end of a jolly boat. Jiminy what a jump! ◆ Jingle bells, Batman smells, Robin laid an egg; the Batmobile lost a wheel and

Joker took ballet. ♦ Listen, listen, the cat's p*ssin'; where, where?—Under the stair. Run, run, get your gun; hurry up, he's/she's all done. ♦ Merrily we roll along, roll along . . . ♦ Mother, may I go out to swim?/Yes, my darling daughter/Hang your clothes on a hickory limb/But don't go near the water. ♦ My country 'tis of thee, I come from Italy, my name is Schmidt. I own a barber shop; they call me guinea wop; I run to tell the cop; he says shaddap. ♦ No more pencils, no more books, no more teacher's dirty looks! ♦ Not because you're dirty, not because you're clean, just because you kissed a boy/girl behind a magazine. ♦ Now is the time for all good men to come to the aid of their country. ♦ One little, two little, three little Indians, four little, five little, six little Indians, seven little, eight little nine little Indians: ten little Indian boys! ♦ One two, button my shoe; three four, shut the door; five six, pick up sticks; seven eight, lay them straight; nine ten, a good fat hen; eleven, twelve, who will delve? thirteen, fourteen, maids a-courting; fifteen, sixteen, maids a-kissing; seventeen, eighteen, maids a-waiting; nineteen, twenty, my stomach's empty. ♦ Red Rover, Red Rover, send [n.] over. ♦ Roll me over in the clover. ♦ Rubber baby buggy bumpers. ♦ The [n.] that America made great. ♦ The house that Jack built. ♦ Peter, Peter, pumpkin eater, had a wife and couldn't keep her. ♦ Peter Piper picked a peck of pickled peppers. ♦ Prostitute: a busy body. ♦ Prostitution: a widespread practice. ♦ Said the bow-legged rooster to the knock-kneed hen: I ain't had a piece since 1910. ♦ Seven slimy snakes slowly slithered southward. ♦ Shakespeare, it ain't. ♦ She sells seashells by the seashore. ♦ The horse Marines were eating beans, *parlez vous*; The horse Marines were eating beans, *parlez vous*; The horse Marines were eating beans and pooped all over the submarines; Hinkey dinkey *parlez vous*. ♦ The quick brown fox jumps over a lazy dog. ♦ They named a tower after you: eyefull. ♦ This is the church, this is the steeple; open the door and you'll see all the people! [illustrated by interlocked fingers] ♦ Toe, knee, chest, nut! ♦ Two bits, four bits, six bits, a dollar; all for [n.] stand up and holler! ♦ Two picaninnies, sitting on the fence, trying to make a dollar out of ninety-nine cents. ♦ Underhand, overhand, pennies, pennies, pitch, slaps, off the beach, Johnny high-dive. ♦ Well, she jumped in bed and covered up her head and she said I couldn't find her; I knew damn well she lied like hell, I jumped in right behind her. ♦ When the weather's hot and sticky, that's no time for dunkin' dickie/When the frost is on the pumpkin, that's the time for dickie dunkin'! ♦ Yinglish is half Yiddish, half English. ♦ You and me, sittin' in the tree K-I-S-S-I-N-G.

Tools

A poor workman always blames his tools. ♦ Any job is easier when you have the right tools. ♦ Children and fools should not play with sharp tools. ♦ Give me a lever long enough, and I will move the world. ♦ If the only tool you have is a hammer, you tend to see every problem as a nail. ♦ It's not how big it is, it's how you use it. ♦ Keep a cool tool, fool (I'm wise to that rise in your Levis). ♦ The best tool is a pipewrench and the second best tool is another pipewrench. You can break anything with 2 pipewrenches. ♦ Tools of the trade.

Travel

A little traveling music. ♦ A puddle-jumper. ♦ A tropical paradise. ♦ Along the highways and byways. ♦ Heaven on earth. ♦ It's fine to go traveling, but it's so nice to come home.

♦ Join the Navy and see the world. ♦ Living out of a suitcase. ♦ (Miss you and)wish you were here. ♦ On the road. ♦ Over hill and dale. ♦ Over the bounding main. ♦ Over the river and through the woods to grandmother's house we go. ♦ See the U.S.A. in your Chevrolet. ♦ Ride the rails. ♦ Sail the high seas/Seven Seas. ♦ The call of the open road. ♦ The road less traveled by. ♦ The Toonerville Trolley. ♦ They came/gathered from near and far. ♦ To be well traveled. ♦ To get away from it all. ♦ To go back and forth. ♦ To go door to door. ♦ To have wanderlust. ♦ To make house calls. ♦ To make the rounds. ♦ To ride the rails. ♦ To roam/travel far and wide. ♦ To roam/wander the streets. ♦ To see the sights. ♦ To travel light. ♦ To use public transportation. ♦ To wend one's way. ♦ Where you headed?

Trendy

A cool cat. ♦ A fashion plate. ♦ *A la mode.* ♦ Ahead of the curve. ♦ All the rage. ♦ Get with it. ♦ In fashion/ vogue. ♦ In the swim. ♦ It's mainstream. ♦ It's right now. ♦ It's the last word in [n.]. ♦ It's the thing to do. ♦ It's what's happening, (baby). ♦ It's what's happening/ "hot"/"in." ♦ On the bleeding edge. ♦ On the cutting/ leading edge.

[see also Renowned] ◆ State of the art. ◆ The *dernier cri.* ◆ The ("in") thing. ◆ The last word. ◆ The latest and greatest. ◆ The latest in a long line of [n.]. ◆ The latest thing. ◆ The next big thing. [see also Future] ◆ The temper/tenor of the times. ◆ The tide of current events. ◆ To be a trend-setter. ◆ To be *au courante.* ◆ To be trendy. ◆ To be up to the minute. ◆ Way cool.

Trickery
(also magic)

A parlor trick. ◆ Bag of tricks. ◆ Close your eyes and open your mouth. ◆ Materialize out of thin air. ◆ Notice, the fingers never leave the hand. ◆ Pick a card, any card. ◆ Pick a number, any number. ◆ Pick a number from one to ten. ◆ Pull a rabbit out of the hat. ◆ Simon says. ◆ Sleight of hand. ◆ The hand is quicker than the eye. ◆ Trick or treat. ◆ Tricky Dickie.

Trouble

Could I trouble you for a match? ◆ Double trouble. ◆ Earthly care(s) and woe(s). ◆ Everybody has their troubles. ◆ Got trouble right here in River City. ◆ If it has tits or tires, you're going to have trouble with it. (female version: If it has testicles or tires, you're going to have trouble with it.)

[see also Women] ◆If it's trouble you want, it's trouble you'll get. ◆ Nobody knows the trouble I've seen; (nobody knows but Jesus). ◆ Now you're asking for it. ◆ Struggle and strife. ◆ The troubles of the pot only the spoon that stirs it knows. ◆ To be a troublemaker. ◆ To look for trouble. ◆ Trouble with a capital T, which rhymes with P. and that stands for pool. ◆ We all have our own cross to bear. ◆ We've all got our troubles. ◆ Woe is me. ◆ Woe (be) unto you. ◆ You don't need any references to borrow trouble. ◆ You're asking for trouble. ◆ You've got your troubles; I've got mine.

Truisms
(also superstitions)

A body at rest, tends to remain at rest; a body in motion, tends to remain in motion. ◆ A cat always lands on its feet. ◆ A cat has nine lives. ◆ A four-leaf clover is good luck. ◆ A killed snake squirms until sundown. ◆ A moving target is harder to hit. ◆ A rabbit's foot brings good luck. ◆ A star shines brightest right before it burns out. ◆ Ain't ain't in the dictionary. ◆ Airplane crashes happen in threes. ◆ An itchy nose means you're going to have a fight/kiss a fool. ◆ An itchy left palm means money is coming to you. [see also Money] ◆ An itchy right palm means you're going to spend money. ◆ At the end of every rainbow is a pot of gold. ◆ Birds fly south for the winter. ◆ Bread always falls with the buttered side down. ◆ Breaking a mirror means seven years bad luck. ◆ Carrots are good for your eyesight: did you ever see a rabbit wearing glasses? ◆ Chicken in the car, car won't go; that's how you spell Chicago. ◆ Christopher Columbus discovered that the world is round. ◆ Don't wear brown shoes with a blue suit. ◆ Don't mix stripes with polka dots. ◆ Don't wear white after Labor Day. ◆ Finding a penny with heads up is good luck. ◆ Flowers bloom in the spring. ◆ God created Eve from Adam's rib. ◆ Good things come in threes. ◆ Great art: a cough, a sneeze and a fart. ◆ Hold a seashell to your ear and you will hear the ocean. ◆ If you dig a hole straight down, you will reach China. ◆ If you dream of snakes you will have a fight that day. ◆ If you drop a fork, expect male company, a spoon, female company. [see also Expectation] ◆ If you exit through a different door than you entered, it's bad luck. ◆ If you kill a spider it will rain. ◆ If you put a tooth under your pillow, the Tooth Fairy will replace it with money while you sleep. ◆ If you spill salt, you must throw a pinch of it over your left shoulder to avoid bad luck. ◆ If when driving in a car you spot an oncoming car with only one headlight, you can yell "padiddle!" and kiss whoever's next to you. ◆ In the eye of the hurricane it is calm. ◆ *In vino veritas*. (In wine there is truth). ◆ It takes more than a teaspoon of water to wash a teaspoon. ◆ Knock (on) wood for good luck. ◆ Lightning never strikes twice in the same place. [see also Destiny] ◆ Masturbators develop hairy palms. ◆ Nero fiddled while Rome burned. ◆ Never put anything smaller than your elbow in your ear. ◆ Newton discovered gravity when an apple fell on his head. ◆ No matter how high a station one achieves in life, everyone begins as a little squirt. – R.D. ◆ Nothing from nothing leaves nothing. ◆ Nothing minus nothing equals nothing. ◆ Old wives' tales. [see also Lore] ◆ One year of a dog's life equals seven human years. ◆ Santa Claus lives in the North Pole. ◆ Sneezes come in threes. ◆ Spring forward; fall back. [a mnemonic to remember daylight saving time] ◆ The clouds are always darkest before the storm. ◆ The criminal always returns to the scene of the crime. ◆ The moon is made of green cheese. ♦ The Mounties always get their man. ♦ The Russians invented it. ♦ Thirty days hath September, April, June and November; all the rest have thirty-one, except February. ♦ Till Columbus discovered America, everybody thought the world was flat. ♦ The whole is not equal to the sum of its parts if you can't find some of its parts. — R.D. ♦ To make the world safe for democracy, we must first make democracy safe for the world. ♦ To open an umbrella indoors is bad luck. ♦ Water seeks its own level. ♦ We bought Manhattan from the Indians for twenty-four dollars. ♦ When is a door not a door? When it's ajar! ♦ Which came first, the chicken or the egg? ♦ Why did the chicken cross the road? To get to the other side! ♦ William Tell shot an arrow through an apple atop his son's head. ♦ You should always wear clean underwear, in case you get hit by a car and wind up in the hospital.

Trust

An act of faith. ♦ Be nice to everyone but trust no one. — Angela Maria Delia ♦ Between trust and distrust lies the safe road. ♦ Blind trust. ♦ Don't trust anybody over 30. ♦ He who trusts nobody is never deceived. ♦ In God we trust—all others must pay cash.-- (sign). [see also Lend] ♦ Love all, trust a few. ♦ Put stock in. ♦ Set a peck of salt with a man before you trust him. ♦ To be good for the money. ♦ To have every confidence (in). ♦ To have street cred. ♦ To set (great) store by. ♦ To trust [so] implicitly. ♦ Trust me on this one. ♦ Wouldn't put it past her/him/them/you.

Truth

A nugget of truth. ♦ A seeker of truth. ♦ A truth well said is well repaid. ♦ Be true to your teeth, or they'll be false to you. [dentist's maxim] ♦ Do you solemnly swear that the testimony you are about to give is the truth, the whole truth, and nothing but the truth so help you God? ♦ Don't kid yourself. ♦ Face (the) facts. ♦ Grain of truth. ♦ If the truth be known. ♦ If you tell the truth you don't have to remember what lies you told. ♦ It's a sin to tell a lie. ♦ It all comes out in the wash. ♦ It is easier to remember the truth than a lie. ♦ Let's face it. ♦ Many a truth is spoken in jest. ♦ Many a truth is spoken through false teeth. — R.D. ♦ Obedience to the truth. ♦ The absolute truth. ♦ The God's honest truth. ♦ The Gospel truth. ♦ The naked truth. ♦ The (plain) unvarnished truth. ♦ The truth as we know it. ♦ The truth hurts. ♦ The truth is not libel. ♦ The truth, the whole truth and nothing but the truth, so help me, God. ♦ The truth will out. ♦ The truth will set you free. ♦ To be painfully honest. ♦ To get one's story straight. ♦ To have the ring of truth. ♦ To ring true. ♦ To tell (you) the truth. ♦ Tried and true. ♦ Truth be told. ♦ Truth in lending. ♦ Truth is stranger than fiction. ♦ Truth or consequences/dare. ♦ What you do in secret will be shouted from the housetops/rooftops. ♦ Which nobody can deny. ♦ You can't make this stuff up. ♦ You have my (solemn) word. ♦ You/your saying it doesn't make it true.

Try

Give it a go/shot/try/whirl. ♦ Give it the old college try. ♦ Go up to bat. ♦ Have a go (at it). ♦ Have at it. ♦ If at first you don't succeed, try and try again. [see also Perseverance] ♦ No one who endeavors is lost. ♦ Once you go black you'll never go back. ♦ Take a crack/ shot/stab/whack at [it]. ♦ Take a flier/flyer (in the market). ♦ Take your best shot. ♦ To make an attempt. ♦ Try as I might. ♦ Try it, you'll like it. ♦ Try [it]/this on for size. ♦ Try one's hand/ luck (at). ♦ Try one's mightiest. ♦ You can sit on the log and die or you can try to move it. ♦ You never know unless you try. ♦ You've tried all the rest, now try the best!

Turnabout

A cornered rat may attack. ♦ A reversal of fortune. ♦ A role reversal. ♦ It works both ways. ♦ It's the other way around. ♦ No more Mr. Nice Guy. ♦ Now that's a switch. ♦ Off the schneid. ♦ Sometimes the worm turns; mostly it just wriggles. ♦ To turn on a dime. ♦ The frog turns into a prince. ♦ The shoe is on the other foot. ♦ The ugly duckling becomes a swan. ♦ The worm turns. ♦ To alter alliances. ♦ To change one's mind. ♦ To commute [so]'s sentence. ♦ To do a flip-flop. ♦ To make a screwy U. ♦ To overturn [so]'s conviction. ♦ To overturn the (Supreme) Court's decision. ♦ To step through the looking glass. ♦ To switch sides. ♦ To turn [it] inside out. ♦ To turn [it] upside down. ♦ To turn the tide. ♦ To turn turtle. ♦ Topsy-turvy. ♦ Turnabout is fair play.

Typical

Conform to the norm. ♦ It's/that's typical. ♦ It's to be expected. ♦ Joe Average. ♦ Joe Blow. ♦ Joe Schmo.

♦ Joe 6-pack. ♦ Just what you'd expect. ♦ Man-on-the-street. ♦ Par for the course. ♦ Straight out of Central Casting. ♦ Your average Joe/schlub. ♦ Your basic/standard [n.].

Ugly

A face like a clenched fist. ♦ A face only a mother could love. ♦ A face that would stop a clock. ♦ A great/perfect face for radio. ♦ Beat with an ugly stick (and hit with the whole tree). ♦ Beauty is only skin deep, but ugly goes clean through. ♦ Butt ugly. ♦ Did you take your ugly pills today? ♦ How much do you charge to haunt a house? ♦ I wouldn't f*ck her with your dick. ♦ I wouldn't want to meet him in a dark alley. ♦ I've seen better heads on a glass of beer. ♦ I've seen better legs on a piano. ♦ If my dog had a face like that I'd shave his *ss and teach him to walk backwards. ♦ In an ugly mood. ♦ It ain't pretty. ♦ Just looking at him is enough to give you the creeps/willies. ♦ Pretty ugly. ♦ Pug ugly. ♦ The ugly duckling becomes a swan. ♦ So ugly the tide wouldn't take her out. ♦ This is not going to be pretty. [see also Warning] ♦ To be no oil painting. ♦ To be/get beat with the ugly stick. ♦ Throw a flag over her head and f*ck for Old Glory. ♦ Ugly as a mud fence. ♦ Ugly as sin.

Uncertainty

A crisis of confidence. ♦ A grey area. ♦ A Hail Mary pass. ♦ An identity crisis. ♦ An unknown quantity. ♦ As far as we know. ♦ Catch-as-catch-can. ♦ Don't be so sure. ♦ Don't count on it. [see also Skepticism] ♦ For all we know. ♦ For one reason or another. ♦ God/Lord only knows. ♦ Has its ups and downs. ♦ Hit or miss. ♦ It/that remains to be seen. ♦ Nagging doubts. ♦ Nip and tuck. ♦ Not necessarily. ♦ Not sure. ♦ Nothing is certain. ♦ On a hiding to nothing. ♦ On again, off again. ♦ One never knows, do one? ♦ She loves me, she loves me not. ♦ Some men have it, some don't. ♦ Sometimes I wonder. ♦ Sometimes you bite the bear; sometimes the bear bites you. ♦ Somewhere along the way. ♦ The blind leading the blind. ♦ The element of doubt. ♦ The jury's (still) out on that one. ♦ The only thing certain is that nothing is certain. ♦ The results are inconclusive. ♦ There are no guarantees in life. ♦ There are no right or wrong answers. ♦ There's no such thing as a sure thing. ♦ There's no telling. ♦ Time will tell. ♦ To have (one's) doubts. ♦ To have questionable morals/motives. ◆ To have the dubious distinction. [see also Notoriety] ◆ To scratch one's head. ◆ To take pot luck. ◆ Touch and go. ◆ Trial and error. ◆ Up in the air. ◆ What makes you so sure? ◆ We have no way of knowing (for sure). ◆ What's a body/mother to do? ◆ When in doubt, punt. ◆ When is enough enough? ◆ Where do we go from here? ◆ Where do you draw the line? ◆ Where does that leave me/us? ◆ Who is to say? ◆ You have to wonder. ◆ You never can tell. ◆ You never know. ◆ You never know from day to day. ◆ You never know what's coming next/what's in store/what to expect/what tomorrow may bring.

Unchangeable

A dwarf on a mountain is still a dwarf. ◆ A leopard cannot change its spots.

◆ Any way you look at it. ◆ Apes remain apes though you clothe them in velvet. ◆ Bred in the bone will out in the flesh. ◆ Breeding will tell. ◆ Crows everywhere are equally black. ◆ Dyed-in- the-wool. ◆ Garbage in, garbage out. ◆ Matter can neither be created nor destroyed. ◆ Once a thief, always a thief. ◆ No matter how (thin) you slice it, it's still baloney. ◆ Snow, whether baked or boiled, gives only water. ◆ The crow's never whiter for washing. ◆ The onion produces no roses. ◆ The wolf loses his teeth but not his appetite. ◆ The wolf may turn grey but not kind. ◆ To be set in one's ways. ◆ To show one's upbringing. ◆ You can take the boy out of the country, but you can't take the country out of the boy. ◆ You can't make a silk purse from a sow's ear. ◆ You must walk a long while behind a wild goose before you find an ostrich feather.

Uncle Baronisms

(original malapropisms)

A Chevy Impaladin. ◆ A circular pump. [circulating]. ◆ A game of chest. ◆ A social leopard. ◆ I couldn't believe my eyes; I must have been seeing a barrage. ◆ I didn't mean to do it; I made an errand. ◆ He's been so good to me; I want to do something to retaliate. ◆ I feel fine as a fiddle. ◆ I get a lot of headaches; I'm afraid that

I may have a clock in my brain. ♦ I hear that Richard made the demon's list at college. ♦ I know the name of that song: it's "I Love You for Seven Hundred Reasons." ♦ I liked the suit but the propellers were too big. ♦ I saw the pasture; he was sitting out in front of the church. ♦ I went out to dinner with Monk. We ordered two dozen clams and he polished off all thirty-two of them. ♦ In the mere future. ♦ It takes two to tangle. ♦ It's his own fault; he'll get no symphony from me. ♦ It's part of the course. ♦ Money is the rules of old eagles. ♦ Oops; I almost dropped it. Good thing I've got good reflections. ♦ Poison ivory. ♦ Richard, can you come down and fix this thing? This thing's got a thing in it. [the TV] ♦ That diamond can't be real; it must be an invitation. ♦ The doctor told me that I have hemorrhoids but I think he's wrong; I think they're just piles. ♦ The Long Ranger. ♦ They say that she's an infant: you know, she loves to f*ck. ♦ They want to give me a physical and an I.Q. test; I'm not worried about the physical but I am worried about the IQ test; I am kinda weak in the eyes. ♦ They beat him to a Pope. ♦ To curve your appetite. ♦ We've all got our quirps. ♦ What did the teacher say as her glass eye rolled across the room? "There goes my favorite pupil!"

Uncontrolled
(also bedlam)

A cluster f*ck. ♦ A free-for-all. ♦ A gangbang. ♦ A loose cannon. ♦ A mad scramble. ♦ A media circus. ♦ A shoot-'em-up. ♦ A wild card. ♦ All hell broke loose. ♦ All over the lot/place. [see also Comprehensive] ♦ Anything goes. ♦ Hit or miss. ♦ Hurry up and wait. [see also Hurry] ♦ It's not up to me. ♦ It's out of my hands. ♦ Like a horse with no rider. ♦ Mob rule. ♦ No hard and fast rules. ♦ No telling when (or where). ♦ On again, off again. ♦ Out of control. ♦ Sheer bedlam/lunacy/mayhem/pandemonium. ♦ The inmates have taken over the asylum. ♦ The roof caved in. ♦ The sh*t hit the fan. ♦ The wind blew and the sh*t flew. ♦ To be ruled by one's impulses. ♦ To create a scene. ♦ To get out of hand. ♦ To go haywire. ♦ To go on a spree. ♦ To have created a monster. ♦ To go on a rampage. ♦ To go postal. ♦ To make a big hullabaloo. ♦ To make a racket. ♦ To move by fits and starts. ♦ To run amok. ♦ To run rampant. ♦ To run wild. ♦ To set up a great hue and cry. ♦ To spiral out of control. ♦ To tubthump. ♦

To weave in and out. ♦ Utter chaos. ♦ When the spirit moves you. ♦ Where were you when the lights went out/the sh*t hit the fan?

Understanding

Be in the know. ♦ Be levelheaded. ♦ Be well-versed [in]. ♦ Can you dig it? ♦ Commit [it] to memory. ♦ Copy that. ♦ Do I make myself clear? ♦ Do you get my drift? ♦ (Do you) kapeesh? ♦ Do you see my point? [rejoinder: Yes, it's on the top of your head.—R.D.] ♦ Do you read me?—(Over). ♦ Don't cha know. ♦ I dig. ♦ I get your drift; you do not have to snow again. ♦ I heard you the first time. ♦ I read you (loud and clear). ♦ [p.] wrote the book (on). ♦ If you get my drift. ♦ If you know what I mean. ♦ In her/his/their infinite wisdom. ♦ Is that understood? ♦ It's not what you know it's who you know. ♦ It's not who you know, it's what you know (var. It's not who you know it's who you nose). [see also Knowledge] ♦ Know it backward and forward. ♦ Know it by heart. ♦ Know it inside and out. ♦ Know [it]/[so] like a book. ♦ Know it like the back of one's hand. ♦ Know the ins and outs. ♦ Know the ropes/the score. ♦ Know thyself. ♦ Know what I mean, jellybean? ♦ Know whereof you speak. ♦ Know one's oats/sh*t/smoke/stuff. ♦ Roger Dodger. ♦ Roger that. ♦ Sage advice. ♦ Street smart/wise. ♦ Ten-four, good buddy. ♦ To be hip. ♦ To be in the loop. ♦ To be fast/quick on the uptake. ♦ To be savvy. ♦ To be up on [it]. ♦ To be with it. ♦ To get it through one's head. ♦ To get the idea. ♦ To go into it with one's eyes wide open. ♦ To have a bird's eye view. ♦ To have a good head on one's shoulders. ♦ To have (a lot of) smarts. ♦ To have it down cold/pat. ♦ To have more degrees than a thermometer. ♦ To have street smarts. ♦ To know better. ♦ To know right from wrong. ♦ To know the drill. ♦ To know the whys and wherefores. ♦ To know what's happening. ♦ To know what's what. ♦ To know where he/she is coming from. ♦ To know where it's at. ♦ To know where the bodies are buried. ♦ To know where one stands. ♦ To make sense of it. ♦ To see (right) through [it]/[so]. ♦ To see the big picture. ♦ To take [it] literally. ♦ To take [it] to mean. ♦ To wrap one's mind around it. ♦ What did [p.] know and when did [p.] know it? ♦ You dig (what I'm saying)? ♦ You get the (general) idea. ♦ You get the picture. ♦ You hear? ♦ You know (what I mean)? ♦ You know what I'm saying?

Undoubtedly

All the more reason. ♦ Do bees like honey? ♦ Do donuts have holes? ♦ Do pigs oink/squeal? ♦ Does a bear sh*t in the woods? ♦ Does a beaver slap water with a flat tail? ♦ Does a one-legged duck swim in circles? ♦ Does an owl sh*t through feathers? ♦ If you go to a graveyard, you will see tombstones. ♦ If you go to a seder, you will find *matzat*. ♦ If you go to Alaska, you will see Eskimos. ♦ If you go to Rome, you will find Italians. ♦ If you go to the racetrack, you will see horses. ♦ If you lift a hen, you may find an egg. ♦ If you open a hive, you should see bees. ♦ If you visit a dairy, you are bound to see cows. ♦ If you visit a jail, you will find prisoners. ♦ If you visit a kennel, you will find dogs. ♦ Is a frog's *ss watertight? ♦ Is all around a pig's *ss pork? ♦ Is the Pope Catholic? ♦ It goes without saying. ♦ It's (like) the 800-pound gorilla in the room. ♦ No sh*t, (Dick Tracy). ♦ Not a doubt in anyone's mind. ♦ So what else is new? [ironic/sarcastic] ♦ That's exactly what I mean. ♦ That's what I'm talkin' about. ♦ Where does an 800-pound gorilla sleep? Anywhere it wants! ♦ You've answered your own question.

Unemployed

♦ Between jobs. ♦ Collecting unemployment. ♦ In the breadline. [see also Poverty] ♦ Kicked upstairs. ♦ Lacking gainful employment. ♦ On the bench/sidelines/skids. ♦ On the street. ♦ Out in the cold. ♦ Out of a job. ♦ Out of work. ♦ Pounding the pavement. ♦ To file for unemployment. ♦ To wear out shoe leather.

Unfair

A (gross) miscarriage of justice. ♦ An unfair advantage. ♦ Foul is foul and fair is fair. ♦ I demand a recount. ♦ Life is unfair. ♦ No fair. ♦ Teacher's pet. ♦ That's not (exactly) cricket. ♦ The boarding house reach. ♦ The brother-in-law effect. ♦ The odds are stacked against you. ♦ The race is not always to the swift (nor victory to the strong). ♦ To cry foul. ♦ To give preferential treatment. ♦ To play favorites. ♦ To show partiality. ♦ Two wolves and a sheep voting on what to have for dinner. ♦ Uncalled for. ♦ We wuz robbed. ♦ Who ever said life was fair?

Unfamiliar

A complete/perfect/total stranger. ♦ A nodding/passing acquaintance. ♦ It doesn't ring a bell. ♦ Never saw the guy before in my life. ♦ Ships passing in the night. ♦ Some guy I once met. ♦ Stranger in a strange land. ♦ To be out of the loop. ♦ To be out of touch. ♦ To not know [so] from Adam/Adam's off ox. ♦ We went to different schools together.

Unflattering

A butthead. ♦ A dickhead. ♦ A creep/geek/nerd/weirdo. ♦ Klu Klux Klan member: a sheethead. ♦ To be a goofball/goof-off/f*ck-up. ♦ To be a pinko communist. ♦ To be a real turkey. ♦ To be a/an sh*thead/sh*theel/ *sshole. ♦ To be odd man out.

Unity

A house divided against itself must fall. ♦ A house divided cannot stand. ♦ A rising tide lifts all boats. ♦ A team player. ♦ All for one and one for all. ♦ All hands on deck. ♦ All together now. ♦ All together, one at a time. ♦ Band together. ♦ He who eats alone, chokes alone. ♦ In the same breath. ♦ In unity there is strength. ♦ It's easy to steal from a cut loaf. ♦ Man is a social animal. ♦ Male bonding. ♦ Many hands make light work. ♦ No man is an island. ♦ So say you all? ♦ Team spirit. ♦ The father must make the table round. ♦ The herd instinct. ♦ The mob has many heads but no brains. ♦ The whole is equal to the sum of its parts. ♦ [The whole is equal to the sum of its parts—unless you can't find some of its parts. – R.D.] ♦ There is safety in numbers. ♦ To a man. ♦ To act in concert. ♦ To be of one mind. ♦ To close ranks. ♦ To present a unified front. ♦ To think as one. ♦ The Blue Wall of silence. ♦ There is strength in numbers. ♦ Together/united we stand, divided we fall. ♦ Two heads are better than one. ♦ We are all one. ♦ We must all hang together or surely we will all hang alone. ♦ We're all in the same boat. ♦ We're all passengers aboard this space ship Earth. ♦ We're all traveling down the same road. ♦ Who drinks his ale alone let him catch his horse alone. ♦ (Who drinks his Beck's alone, let him jump start his Mercedes alone – R.D.). ♦ With one voice.

Unlucky

A bad break. ♦ A reversal of fortune. ♦ Behind bad luck comes good luck. ♦ Better luck next time. ♦ Good luck in placing your manuscript elsewhere. ♦ Can't catch a break. ♦ If a black cat crosses your path, it's bad luck. ♦ If it weren't for bad luck, I'd have no luck at all. ♦ If you break a mirror it's seven years bad luck. ♦ If you spill salt, it's bad luck. [To avert it, throw some of the spilled salt over your left shoulder].

♦ If you walk under a ladder, it's bad luck. ♦ Ill-gotten gains bring bad luck. ♦ Lucky at cards, unlucky in love. ♦ Most unfortunate. ♦ No such luck. ♦ S.O.L. (sh*t out of luck). ♦ Star-crossed. ♦ Three on a match are bad luck. ♦ Three little kittens lost their mittens. ♦ To be down on one's luck. ♦ To be in the wrong place at the wrong time. ♦ To lose one's shirt. ♦ To have the Midas touch in reverse. ♦ To open an umbrella indoors is bad luck. ♦ Too bad. ♦ When one's luck runs out.

Unpredictability

A lot can happen overnight. ♦ A year often does not bring as much as an hour. ♦ At the mercy of. ♦ Everything happens at once. ♦ Feast or famine. ♦ From one extreme to the other. ♦ Has its highs and lows/ups and downs. ♦ Here and there. ♦ It can/could go either way. ♦ It just as easily could have gone the other way. ♦ On again, off again. ♦ Originality is unexpected in certain places. ♦ Peaks and valleys. ♦ The vicissitudes of life. ♦ To be [adj./adv] one minute and [adj./adv.] the next. ♦ To blow/run hot and cold. ♦ To have hot and cold flashes. ♦ To seesaw/teeter-totter. ♦ To wax and wane. ♦ What a difference a day makes. ♦ When it rains, it pours. ♦ Whim and caprice.

Unrestrained

A clear shot. ♦ A free-for-all. ♦ All's fair in love and war. ♦ All you can eat. ♦ All you could ask/hope for. ♦ All you want. ♦ An unobstructed view. ♦ Anything (and everything) goes. ♦ As you please. ♦ At full gallop/speed/throttle/tilt. ♦ By fair or foul means. ♦ Damn the torpedoes, full speed ahead. [see also Hurry] ♦ Do everything humanly possible. ♦ No holds barred. ♦ Open season. ♦ Pull out all the stops. ♦ Shed one's inhibitions. ♦ The sky's the limit. ♦ To allow unlimited/unrestricted access. ♦ To bring/call up the reserves. ♦ To give/have a blank check. ♦ To give/have carte blanche. ♦ To give/have free rein. ♦ To give [so] his/her head. ♦ To give [so] wide latitude. ♦ To go whole hog. [see also Zeal] ♦ To have the run of the place. ♦ To know no bounds. ♦ To one's (little) heart's content/desire. [see also Happiness] ♦ To take full liberty (to). ♦ To write one's own ticket. ♦ Unbridled passion. ♦ Wide open. ♦ Wild man of Borneo.

Unsightly

A milk moustache. ♦ A sorry sight. ♦ A unibrow. ♦ A widow's peak. ♦ Baggy pants. ♦ Bags/circles/rings under one's eyes. ♦ Beady eyes. ♦ Buck teeth. ♦

Bushy eyebrows. ♦ Droopy drawers. ♦ Get a stick and I'll kill it. ♦ Having a bad hair day. ♦ High-water pants/ trousers. ♦ Kill it before it spreads. ♦ Looks like it came out of the wrong end of a rabbit. ♦ Looks like sh*t. ♦ Looks like the part of the chicken that went over the fence last. ♦ Looks like the part of the Polaroid you throw away. ♦ Run-down at the heels. ♦ To have a dumb look on one's face. ♦ To have schmutz on [it]. ♦ To look like death has set in. ♦ To look like death warmed over. ♦ To look like hell. ♦ To look like something the cat dragged in. ♦ To look like the wrath of God. ♦ To look like the wreck of the Hesperus. ♦ Torn and tattered. ♦ You look like a monkey f*cking a football. [military] ♦ You look like you've been shot at and missed, sh*t at and hit. ♦ Your eyes look like a roadmap. ♦ Your eyes look like two p*ssholes in the snow. ♦ Your hair looks like an explosion in a hayloft.

Unsuited

A fish out of water. ♦ A square peg in a round hole. ♦ Can't hack it. ♦ Doesn't have it in her/him. ♦ Don't bring a knife to a gunfight. ♦ Ill equipped/prepared/ suited (to). ♦ Not built that way. ♦ Not in one's

nature. ♦ Not one's bag. ♦ Not one's thing. ♦ Not one's cup of tea. ♦ Not to one's liking. ♦ Out of one's element/ league. ♦ Out of place. ♦ Over one's head. ♦ To have no heart/ stomach for [it].

Unsympathetic

Ain't that a shame. ♦ Cry me a river. ♦ I feel for you . . . but I can't reach you. ♦ I have better things to do with my time. ♦ I wouldn't give him the (right) time of day. ♦ I wouldn't give him the sweat off my balls. ♦ I wouldn't lift a finger/pinkie to help him. ♦ I wouldn't p*ss on him if he were on fire. ♦ My heart bleeds for you/goes out to you. ♦ My heart pumps p*ss for you. ♦ Rough on rats. ♦ Tough beans. ♦ Tough sh*t. ♦ Tough titty. ♦ Tough tucas. ♦ You made your bed, now lie in it. ♦ You'll get no sympathy from me. ♦ You'll find your sympathy in the dictionary between sh*t and syphilis.

Unthinkable

Beyond belief. ♦ Bite your tongue. ♦ Don't even think about parking here. ♦ God/heaven forbid/help us. ♦ Hard to imagine. ♦ I shudder to think about [it]. ♦ I would hate to see that happen. ♦ It never entered my mind. ♦ It's the furthest thing from my mind. ♦ Let it never be. ♦ Let this cup pass from me. ♦ May it never come to that/pass. ♦ Never in a million years. ♦ Perish the thought. ♦ To think the unthinkable. ♦ What a catastrophe/horror that would be.

Untrustworthy

A fly-by-night operation. ♦ A snake in the grass. ♦ A two-timer. ♦ He'd just as soon [v.] you as look at you. ♦ He'd try to sell you the Brooklyn Bridge. ♦ He'll steal anything that's not nailed down. ♦ Of questionable character. ♦ To be up to something. ♦ To have ulterior motives. ♦ To not put it past [so]. ♦ Up to no good. ♦ With malice aforethought. ♦ Would you buy a used car from this man? ♦ Wouldn't trust him as far as I could throw him.

Unwelcome

(also inappropriate, intrude, unpleasant)

A gate-crasher. ♦ A match made in hell. ♦ A May-December romance. ♦ An unlikely pair. ♦ As welcome as a fart in church ♦ As welcome as a ham sandwich at a bar mitzvah. ♦ As welcome as a shadow on Groundhog Day. ♦ As welcome as something moving in your Waldorf salad. ♦ Feel like the third wheel. ♦ Foreign matter. ♦ I can take a hint. ♦ I know when I'm not wanted. ♦ If you are unexpected and uninvited, you are also unwelcome. ♦ It's enough to gag a maggot. ♦ Not on the guest list. ♦ Odd man out. ♦ P.U. – that stinks! ♦ To be off-putting. ♦ To go over like a fart in church/lead balloon/turd in the punch bowl. ♦ To horn in (on). ♦ To overstay/wear out one's welcome. ♦ Unpleasant truths are never popular.

Up

Everything goes up, except wages. ♦ I shot an arrow into the air, it fell to earth I know not where. ♦ Onward and upward. ♦ Sky high. ♦ Steep as a horse's face. ♦ To buck for promotion. [see also Strive] ♦ To the tippity-top. ♦ To the tippy-top. ♦ Up like a rocket, down like a stick. ♦ Upsy-daisy. ♦ Upwardly mobile. ♦ What goes up must come down. ♦ Whoopsy-daisy.

Used

A retread. ♦ Formerly owned by a little old lady who only drove it on Sunday. ♦ Gently worn. ♦ Good as new. ♦ In working order. ♦ It is only used on bonfire nights. ♦ Low mileage. ♦

None the worse for the wear. ♦ On the rebound. ♦ Previously owned. ♦ Second hand. ♦ Second-hand Rose. ♦ Sloppy seconds. ♦ Things are not what they used to be.

Useful

A little [n.] goes a long way. ♦ All is grist which comes to the mill. ♦ Crooked logs make straight fires. ♦ Even a single hair casts a shadow. ♦ Even the hairs on your head are numbered. ♦ Food for thought. ♦ It's all grist for the mill. ♦ They also serve who only stand and wait. ♦ To come in handy. ♦ To serve a purpose. ♦ To do/stand one in good stead.

Useless

A (complete) waste of money. ♦ A fifth wheel. ♦ A white elephant. ♦ All is not grist which comes to the mill. ♦ Good for nothing. ♦ How's that working for you? ♦ Like paying for a dead horse. ♦ Odd man out. ♦ Of no earthly use. ♦ That dog don't/ won't hunt. ♦ That won't be necessary. ♦ That won't wash. ♦ There's no call for/to. ♦ To outlive its/one's usefulness. ♦ Useless as a chimney in July. ♦ Useless as a chocolate teapot. ♦ Useless as a lizard in a blizzard. ♦ Useless as balls on a priest. ♦ Useless

as a gun with no trigger. ♦ Useless as a one-legged man in a butt-kicking contest. ♦ Useless as a screen door on a submarine. ♦ Useless as the "O" in opossum. ♦ Useless as tits on a boar hog/nun. [N.B. Entries that begin with "useless as" may be also stated ironically by substituting "useful as," e.g. "Useful as a chocolate tea pot."] ♦ Won't do any good.

Vague

A high fog index. ♦ A flimsy/tenuous argument. ♦ Circumstantial evidence. ♦ It gives about as much light as a white bean up a black bear's *ss. ♦ It's clear as mud. ♦ Pure as the driven slush. ♦ Shrouded in mystery. ♦ Sketchy details/facts. ♦ To gloss over the facts/issue. ♦ To speak in generalities. ♦ What are you telling me? ♦ Your argument gives off more heat than light.

Valuable

A chunk of change. ♦ A lot of cabbage/ wood. ♦ A lot of shekels. ♦ A lot of simoleans. ♦ A lot of skins. ♦ A respectable sum. ♦ A healthy/tidy sum. ♦ Good as gold. ♦ Mucho moola. ♦ Not exactly chicken scratch. ♦ Nothing to sneeze at. ♦ Prize/prized possession. ♦ That ain't hay. ♦ To be worth one's salt. ♦ Worth a king's ransom. ♦ Worth his/her/its weight in gold.

♦ Worth (some) heavy coin. ♦ Worth the price of admission.

Varied

(also diversity)

A change of pace. [see also Change, Different] ♦ A checkered past. ♦ A crazy quilt. ♦ A high yellow. ♦ A little bit of this, and a little bit of that. ♦ A melting pot. ♦ A mixed bag. ♦ A rogue's gallery. ♦ A sailor has a girl in every port. ♦ And what have you. [see also Etcetera] ♦ Bits and pieces. ♦ Cast of characters. ♦ For a change. ♦ Four and twenty blackbirds baked in a pie. ♦ I'm in the mood for something different tonight. ♦ In one's choice of colors. ♦ It takes all kinds (of people to make a world). ♦ It takes all sorts. ♦ Little bit of this, and a little bit of that. ♦ Mix it up. ♦ Mixed reviews. ♦ Odds and ends. ♦ Of all shapes and sizes. ♦ Of all sorts. ♦ One from Column A and one from Column B. ♦ Results may vary. ♦ Roman hands and Russian fingers. ♦ Sour, sweet, bitter, pungent—all must be tasted. ♦ This, that, and the other thing. ♦ To have many irons in the fire. ♦ To have other fish to fry. ♦ To mix apples and oranges. ♦ To run the gamut. ♦ Variety is the spice of life. ♦ Variations on a/the theme. [see also Imitation] ♦ Various and sundry. ♦ You can have any color you like—as long as it's black. ♦ You meet all kinds. ♦ You name it, we've got it.

Venality

A bag man. ♦ A little vigorish. ♦ Anything for a buck. ♦ Cross my palm (with silver). ♦ Every man has his price. ♦ Everything goes on green. ♦ Grease the mahogany. ♦ Here's a little something for yourself. ♦ Hush-money. ♦ In it for the bucks. ♦ Insider trading. ♦ The almighty dollar. ♦ To accept bribes/kickbacks/ payola. ♦ To be in golden handcuffs. ♦ To be on the dole/take. ♦ To grease [so]'s palm. ♦ To take a golden parachute. [see also Generosity] ♦ To take kickbacks. ♦ Working for the Yankee Dollar.

Versatile

A catch-all. ♦ A double-duty beauty. ♦ A good multitasker. ♦ A man for all seasons. ♦ A man of many talents. ♦ A Procrustean bed. ♦ A switch-hitter. [see also Homosexuality] ♦ A triple threat. ♦ A renaissance man. ♦ All rolled into one. ♦ An all-around guy. ♦ An all-around [n.]. ♦ Covers a multitude of sins/things. ♦ Doing everything is doing nothing well. ♦ In more ways than one. ♦ It does everything but part your hair. ♦ Jack of all trades (master of none). ♦ One size fits all. ♦ To wear many hats. ♦ [adj./n.] is as [adj./n.] does.

Virtue

A clear conscience is the greatest armor. ♦ A clear conscience is usually the sign of a bad memory. ♦ A paragon of virtue. ♦ A virtuous woman is a crown to her husband. ♦ He who sows virtue reaps fame. ♦ There is no pillow so soft as a clear conscience. ♦ Virginity is like a soap bubble; one prick and it is gone. ♦ Virtue is its own reward. ♦ Wealth adorns the house, virtue the person. ♦ With virtue you can't be entirely poor; without virtue you can't really be rich. ♦ Woman's virtue is man's greatest invention. ♦ Worry not that no one knows of you; seek to be worth knowing.

Volunteer

Don't all raise your hands at the same time. ♦ Don't everybody answer at once. ♦ He who accepts to carry the goat on his shoulder will soon be asked to carry the cow. ♦ I need one volunteer. ♦ Never volunteer. ♦ Nobody's holding a gun to her/his/your head. ♦ Of one's own accord/free will/volition. ♦ On one's own steam. ♦ To do [it] pro bono/on spec. ♦ To roll up one's sleeves and pitch in. ♦ That would be me.

Voluptuous

A body that won't quit. ♦ A classy chassis. ♦ All her curves are in the right places. ♦ All that meat and no potatoes. ♦ All tits and teeth. ♦ Amply endowed. ♦ An hourglass figure. ♦ Built like a brick sh*thouse. ♦ I'd eat a mile of her sh*t just to get to her *ss/to see where it came from. ♦ Legs up to her armpits. ♦ Of ample bosom. ♦ Of generous proportions. ♦ Shake it, shake it but don't break it; wrap it up and I'll take it. ♦ What a set of bazooms/ choppers headlights/ high beams (on that). ♦ What a pair of ta-tas.

Vote

A straw poll. ♦ A vote for [n.] is a vote for [n.]. [e.g. *A vote for Jones is a vote for progress.*] ♦ All in favor say aye. ♦ Every vote counts. ♦ Hold your nose and vote. ♦ Let's have show of hands. ♦ Let's put it to a/the vote. ♦ On the campaign trail. ♦ One man, one vote. ♦ Show of hands, please. ♦ The ayes have it. [see also Acceptance] ♦ The nays have it. [see also Oppose] ♦ To cross party lines. [see also Betray] ♦ To get out the vote. ♦ To poll the jury. ♦ To turn out at the polls. ♦ To win the popular vote. ♦ Unfair restrictions. ♦ Vote early and often. ♦ Voter turnout.

Vulnerable
(also defenseless)

A chain is only as strong as its weakest link. ♦ A sitting duck. ♦ A chink in one's armor. ♦ A fatal flaw. ♦ A sitting duck/pigeon. ♦ A soft spot in one's heart (for). ♦ A weakness (for). ♦ An Achilles heel. ♦ At [so]'s mercy. ♦ Belly up. ♦ Caught in a weak moment. ♦ Easy prey. ♦ Fair game. ♦ Like a fish out of water. ♦ Like a turtle on its back. ♦ Not a leg to stand on. ♦ On the flat of one's back. ♦ Stranger in a strange land. ♦ To be in [so]'s crosshairs/peepsights. ♦ To be out of one's element. ♦ To be putty in someone's hands. ♦ To be spread-eagled. ♦ To have a glass jaw/soft underbelly. ♦ To lead with one's chin. ♦ To leave oneself (wide) open. ♦ To throw oneself on the mercy of the court. ♦ Wandering around like a lost puppy/sheep.

Wait

A cooling-off period. ♦ A station break. ♦ An interminable wait. ♦ And now, for these important announcements. ♦ Any day now. ♦ But wait! There's more! ♦ Coming right up. ♦ Coming up next. ♦ Coming soon to a theater near you. ♦ Don't do a thing/anything till you hear from me. ♦ Hold it (right there). ♦ Hold your horses. ♦ Hurry up and wait. [see also Uncontrolled] ♦ I'll wait to hear from you. ♦ In case of a knockdown, cease fighting and move to a neutral corner. ♦ It's ill waiting for dead men's shoes. ♦ It's on back order. ♦ Just a minute. ♦ Just passing the time of day. ♦ Just you wait. ♦ Keep your shirt on. ♦ Killing time. ♦ Leave them alone and they'll come home. ♦ Let me find/get a pencil. ♦ Nothing better to do. ♦ Now hold on just one second (there). ♦ Now wait just a cotton-picking minute. ♦ On deck. ♦ On hold. ♦ On standby. ♦ Some other time. ♦ Stand by. ♦ Stand by for the ram. ♦ Stand by to stand by. ♦ Take a number. ♦ The jury is still out (on that one). ♦

The pause that refreshes. ♦ To bide time. ♦ To bide one's time. ♦ To call/ take (a) time out. ♦ To cool one's heels. ♦ To hang around. ♦ To hang out. ♦ To hold off. ♦ To lie in wait. ♦ To march in place. ♦ To mark time. [see also Delay]

To play the waiting game. ♦ To reserve/suspend judgment. ♦ To see which way the wind blows. ♦ To sit on the sidelines. ♦ To sit this one out. ♦ To sleep on it. ♦ To stop the clock. ♦ To wait in/on line. ♦ To wait until the (very) last minute. ♦ To warm the bench. ♦ Until further notice. ♦ Wait a minute/sec/ second. ♦ Wait a while. ♦ Wait and see. ♦ Wait, don't tell me; let me guess. ♦ Wait it out. ♦ Wait one. ♦ Wait one's turn. ♦ Wait till next year. ♦ Wait until one's ship comes in. ♦ Wait up! ♦ Waiting in the wings. ♦ We shall see what we shall see. ♦ (Well) worth the wait. ♦ We'll get back to you. ♦ While away the hours. ♦ When the time comes. ♦

Whoa, boy, whoa. ♦ Whoa, Nelly. ♦ Your call will be answered in the order in which it was received.

Walk

A walk around the block. ♦ Baby steps. ♦ Get there on my own two feet. ♦ Go for a walk. ♦ Hit the bricks. ♦ Hoof it. ♦ I walk the line. ♦ Pound the pavement. ♦ To stretch one's legs. ♦ To take a hike. ♦ To walk it off. ♦ To walk with a halting gait. ♦ Travel by shank's mare. ♦ Travel by Shoe Leather Express. ♦ Shaky/unsteady/wobbly on one's feet/ pins. ♦ Walk this way. ♦ Why walk when you can ride? ♦ You talk the talk, but can you walk the walk?

Warning

A cautionary tale. ♦ A credible threat. ♦ A rap on the knuckles. ♦ A shot across the bow. ♦ A slap on the wrist. ♦ A (thinly) veiled threat. ♦ A wake-up call. ♦ An idle threat. ♦ Bad/evil omen. ♦ (Better) smile when you say that. ♦ Consider yourself warned. ♦ Do you know cancer's seven deadly warning signals? ♦ Does not bode well. ♦ Don't f*ck with me. ♦ Don't get any ideas. ♦ Don't get me going/started. ♦ Don't mess with me. ♦ Don't say I didn't warn you. ♦ Don't tread on me. ♦ Don't try anything foolish. ♦

Go ahead, make my day. ♦ Halt or I'll shoot! ♦ Hands off. ♦ Fire a warning shot (into the air). ♦ Fire in the hole! ♦ Fore! ♦ I wouldn't do that if I were you. ♦ I'll see you in court. ♦ I'll sue you for every dime you're worth. ♦ Keep off the grass. ♦ Keep your hands in the air (we've got you covered). ♦ Keep your hands where we can see them. ♦ No trespassing. ♦ Not to be trifled with. ♦ On/under pain of. ♦ Red on black, venom lack; red on yellow kills a fellow. [coral snake warning] ♦ Slippery when wet. ♦ Spoiler alert. ♦ Stop! In the name of the law. ♦ Stop! Or I'll shoot! ♦ This call may be recorded for quality purposes. ♦ This means you. ♦ This is not a good sign. ♦ This is not going to be pretty. [see also Ugly] ♦ This program contains material that may be offensive to some people. (Viewer discretion is advised.) ♦ To bare one's fangs/teeth. ♦ To be upfront about [it]. ♦ To flex one's muscles. ♦ To go easy on [so]. ♦ To let [so] off with a warning. ♦ To make a show of force. ♦ To raise/send up a red flag. ♦ To rattle sabers. ♦ To read [so] his/her rights. ♦ To tell you up front. ♦ To tip [so] off. ♦ Violators will be prosecuted. ♦ Violators will be towed at their own expense. ♦ We have ways to make you talk. ♦ We know where you live. ♦ We're going to let you off easy/ with just a warning this time. ♦ You'll hear from my/our lawyer(s). ♦ You've been warned.

Weakness

A Casper Milquetoast. ♦ A fruit. ♦ A mama's boy. ♦ A namby-pamby. ♦ A pantywaist. ♦ A pushover. ♦ Can dish it out but can't take it. ♦ Every suit of armor has its Achilles Heel. ♦ It is the tiny rift in the lute/that by and by will make the music mute. ♦ Limp-wristed. ♦ Mealy-mouthed. ♦ Tied to his mama's/mother's apron strings. ♦ To be a namby-pamby/niminy-piminy. ♦ To be wishy-washy. ♦ To have a glass jaw. ♦ To have round heels.

Weapons

A billy club. ♦ A blade. ♦ A Bowie knife. ♦ A night stick. ♦ A peacemaker. ♦ A Saturday-night special. ♦ A shank. ♦ A shiv. ♦ A six-shooter. ♦ A pig-sticker. ♦ A toad-sticker. ♦ A weapon of opportunity. ♦ A zip gun. ♦ Brass knuckles. ♦ The murder weapon. ♦ The weapon of choice. ♦ The smoking gun. ♦ Weapons of mass destruction.

Weather

A torrential downpour/rain. ♦ April showers bring May flowers.

♦ Cloudy morning, fair evening. ♦ Coming down pretty hard out there. ♦ Did you order this weather? ♦ Evening red and morning gray, send a traveler on his way. Evening gray and morning red, brings the rain upon his head. ♦ Everybody talks about the weather but nobody does anything about it. ♦ If March comes in like a lamb it goes out like a lion; or if March comes in like a lion it goes out like a lamb. ♦ If snowflakes are big, the snow won't last. ♦ If the snow is like meal, the storm will be real/there will be a great deal. ♦ If winter comes can spring be far behind? ♦ In the driving rain. ♦ It was a dark and stormy night. ♦ It's raining, it's pouring (the old man is snoring). ♦ Lovely weather for ducks. ♦ Nice weather we're having, isn't it? ♦ Not a fit night out for man nor beast. ♦ Ol' Man Winter. ♦ Rain, rain, go away; come again another day. ♦ Raining cats and dogs. ♦ Red sky in the morning, sailor take warning; red sky at night, sailor's delight. ♦ Ring around the sun, time for fun. Ring around the moon, storm coming soon. ♦ Snow like cotton, soon forgotten. Snow like meal, will give a great deal. ♦ Temperature is mild, in the low [n.]

with a chance of scattered showers. ♦ The weather, like the government, is always in the wrong. ♦ Think the rain'll hurt the rhubarb this year? ♦ This isn't the weather we ordered. ♦ To ride out/weather the storm. [see also Endurance] ♦ When it rains, it pours. ♦ When smoke descends, good weather ends. ♦ Whether it's cold or whether it's hot, we've got to have weather, whether or not. [see also Inexorable] ♦ Winter won't come until the brooks are full.

West

All quiet on the Western Front. ♦ California, here I come. ♦ From east to west, [n.] is the best. ♦ Go West, young man, go West. ♦ Out West. ♦ Somewhere west of Laramie. ♦ The fastest gun in the West. ♦ The wicked witch of the West. ♦ The wild (and wooly) west. ♦ West of the Mississippi/Pecos/Rockies.

Wife

A light wife makes a heavy husband. ♦ A trophy wife. ♦ An ideal wife is any woman who has an ideal husband. ♦ He knows little who will tell his wife all he knows. ♦ Q: How's the wife? A: Better than nothing. ♦ Of earthly goods the best is a good wife.

A bad, the bitterest curse of human life. ♦ She who must be obeyed. ♦ My old lady. ♦ The old battle-axe. ♦ Who was that lady I saw you with last night? That was no lady, that was my wife! ♦ To fulfill one's wifely duties. ♦ Your better half.

Win

A signal victory. ♦ A slam dunk. ♦ A triumph of the human spirit/soul/will. ♦ A victory dance/lap. ♦ A win-win situation. ♦ A winning hand. ♦ A winning streak. ♦ An arm/fist pump. ♦ And may the best man win. ♦ Flush with victory. ♦ He'll win it in a minute. ♦ If you can't join 'em, beat 'em. ♦ In the winner's circle. ♦ It's their game to lose. ♦ Let's win this one for the Gipper. ♦ Look no further. [see also Best] ♦ Make a clean sweep. ♦ Run away with the pack. ♦ The loser gets the boot; the winner gets the booty. - R.D. ♦ The object of the game is to win. ♦ The spoils of war. ♦ To be ahead on points. ♦ To be magnanimous in victory. ♦ To beat out all the competition. ♦ To break the bank. ♦ To carry the day. ♦ To come out ahead (of the game). ♦ To conquer all. ♦ To emerge victorious. ♦ To finish in the money. ♦ To get the best/better of. ♦ To have [it] one's way. ♦ To

hit a grand slam. ♦ To hit paydirt. ♦ To hit the jackpot. ♦ To nose [so] out. ♦ To run the table. ♦ To snatch victory from the jaws of defeat. ♦ To take top honors. ♦ To the victor belong/go the spoils. ♦ To walk away/off with [it]. ♦ To win by a comfortable/tidy margin. ♦ To win by a nose. ♦ To win by a wide margin. ♦ To win by default. ♦ To win hands down. ♦ To win out. ♦ To win the day. ♦ Undisputed champion of the world. ♦ Victory is at hand. ♦ Victory has a thousand fathers; defeat is an orphan. ♦ Victory is sweet. ♦ Victory is sweet but sugar is not victory. ♦ We have a winner! ♦ Win by a landslide. ♦ Winner and still champion. ♦ Winner take all. ♦ Winners never quit and quitters never win. ♦ Winning isn't everything; it's the only thing. ♦ You can't win 'em all. [see also Forbearance]

Wine

A meal without wine is a day without sunshine. ♦ Drink wine, and you will sleep well. Sleep, and you will not sin. Avoid sin, and you will be saved. Ergo, drink wine and be saved. ♦ Good wine ruins the purse; bad wine ruins the stomach. ♦ He who likes drinking is always talking of wine. ♦ Life is too short to drink bad wine. ♦ Take a little wine, for thy stomach's sake. ♦ The vinegar may taste of wine, but not the wine of vinegar. — R.D. ♦ There are more old wine drinkers than old doctors. ♦ Who loves not women, wine and song remains a fool lifelong. ♦ Wine, women and song. ♦ Wine improves with age: the older I get, the more I like it. ♦ Wine is a mocker, strong drink is a brawler. ♦ Yesterday it was wine, women and song; today it's beer the old lady and TV.

Wise
(also older, mature)

A nugget of wisdom. ♦ A senior citizen. ♦ A wisenheimer. ♦ A wise man keeps his own counsel. ♦ A wise man knows everything; a shrewd one everybody. ♦ An old rat in the barn. ♦ An older crowd. ♦ Full of wise saws. ♦ He is a fool who cannot be angry; but he is a wise man who will not. ♦ It is better to sit with a wise man in prison than a fool in paradise. ♦ Knowledge is knowing a tomato is a fruit; wisdom is not using tomatoes to make a fruit salad. ♦ Never digest a kernel of wisdom without a grain of salt. ♦ Old birds are not caught with chaff. ♦ Sufficiently wise words, sufficiency to the wise. ♦ The frog is wiser than the tadpole. ♦ The wise man relies on his backbone, not his wishbone.

♦ Too soon we get oldt and too late schmardt. ♦ What are you, a wiseguy or a truck driver? ♦ You're getting smart in your old age. ♦ Wisdom of the ages. ♦ Wise beyond one's years. ♦ Wise men learn more from fools than fools from wise men. ♦ Wise to the ways of the world. ♦ Wise up and grab a pick. ♦ You better wise up. ♦ Your wisdom has kept you far away from dangers. (fortune cookie)

Wish

A wish list. ♦ Be careful what you wish for—you might get it. ♦ He with the larger half of the wishbone gets to make the wish. ♦ If wishes were horses, beggars would ride. ♦ If wishes were fishes, you'd be a school of whales. ♦ If ifs were water, you'd be a wishing well. ♦ Make a wish. ♦ Once upon a star. ♦ Star light, star bright, first star I've seen tonight. ♦ To lock pinkies. ♦ Toss a coin into a fountain and your wish will come true. ♦ When you wish upon a star your dreams come true. ♦ Wish I may, wish I might, make my wish come true tonight. ♦ Wish in one hand, spit in the other; see which one fills up first. ♦ Wishful thinking. ♦ Wishing doesn't make it so. ♦ Your wish is my command. ♦ You get three wishes.

Withdraw

(also reversal)

All bets are off. ♦ Breach of promise. ♦ Coitus interruptus. ♦ "Dammit I'm mad" is "Dammit I'm mad" spelled backwards. - Joe Conforti ♦ I take back every word/everything I said. ♦ To back down. ♦ To back out/bow out (gracefully). ♦ To back-pedal. ♦ To be an Indian giver. ♦ To break/go back on one's word. ♦ To cop out/fink out. ♦ To contradict oneself. ♦ To cut one's losses. ♦ To do a one-eighty. ♦ To do an about-face. ♦ To double back (on one's tracks). ♦ To have a change of heart. [see also Change] ♦ To issue a retraction. ♦ To make a screwy U/U-ie. ♦ To make a U-turn. ♦ To step back from. ♦ To suffer withdrawal symptoms. ♦ To swear off. ♦ To take a step back. ♦ To tear oneself away. ♦ To think better of (it). ♦ To throw it into reverse. ♦ To turn around and go back. ♦ To turn back. ♦ To weasel out.

Womanize

(see also Bachelorhood)

A c*nt hound. ♦ A Don Juan. ♦ A gigolo. ♦ A ladies' man. ♦ A lady-killer. ♦ A lothario. ♦ A male prostitute. ♦ A man about town. ♦ A playboy. ♦ A player. ♦ A prince charming. ♦ A skirt-chaser. ♦ A swordsman. ♦ A T

and A man. ♦ Beaver fever. ♦ Find 'em, feel 'em, f*ck 'em and forget 'em. ♦ Go wenching. ♦ To be on the make. ♦ To chase two-legged deer. ♦ To have a wandering eye. ♦ To hunt poontang.

Women

A biatch. ♦ A bitch on wheels. ♦ A fallen woman. ♦ A frustrated old maid. ♦ A girl has got to have her own principles. ♦ A girly-girl. ♦ A football widow. [see also Solitary] ♦ A grass widow. ♦ A kept woman. ♦ A man may toil from sun to sun; but a woman's work is never done. ♦ A scarlet woman. ♦ A son's a son till he gets a wife but a daughter's a daughter for life. ♦ A stay-at-home mom. ♦ A woman's place is in the house. The White House. (political poster) ♦ A woman's place is in the home. ♦ A woman's work is never done. ♦ Behind every great man is a great woman. ♦ [Behind every great woman is a great behind.] — R.D. ♦ Belle of the ball. ♦ Blonde bombshell. ♦ Damsel in distress. ♦ *Femme fatale.* ♦ Girl talk. ♦ Girls gone wild/wrong. ♦ Hell hath no fury like a woman scorned. ♦ I usually don't do this on the first date. ♦ I'm not that kind of girl. ♦ If it has tits or tires, you're going to have trouble with it.

(female version: If it has testicles or tires, you're going to have trouble with it.) [see also Trouble] ♦ If she lets you, she'll let somebody else. ♦ If you were a man, (I'd punch you in the mouth/smack you in the teeth.) ♦ In search of Mr. Right. ♦ In the dark they're all alike. [see also Alike] ♦ Is that any way to treat a lady? ♦ It's a woman's prerogative to change her mind. ♦ It's not the men in your life; it's the life in your men. ♦ Just another pretty face. ♦ Keep 'em barefoot and pregnant. ♦ Ladies in waiting. ♦ Ladies of the evening. ♦ Lying down/upside down they're all alike. ♦ Never underestimate the power of a woman. ♦ Nice girls don't. ♦ Queen of the hop. ♦ The distaff side. ♦ The fair sex. ♦ The female of the species. ♦ The girl next door. ♦ The tender gender. ♦ There she is, Miss America. ♦ To go through the change (of life). ♦ To maintain her girlish figure. ♦ To treat a woman as a sex object. ♦ To use her feminine wiles. ♦ What kind of a girl do you think I am? ♦ You can't live with 'em and you can't live without 'em. ♦ You may call a woman a kitten but never a cat /You may call a woman a mouse but never a rat/You may call a woman a chick but never a hen/You may call a woman a duck but never a goose/You may call a woman a vision but never a sight.

Work

A busman's holiday. ♦ A honey-do list. ♦ A labor of love. ♦ A nine-to-fiver. ♦ All work and no play (makes Jack a dull boy). ♦ All work and no play makes jack. ♦ Anyway, it's a living. ♦ Choose a job you love and you will never have to work a day in your life. ♦ Gainfully employed. ♦ Gigolo: a working stiff. ♦ Hard work never killed anybody. ♦ It's too much like work. ♦ Keep up the good work. ♦ I'm not afraid of work; I can lie down right next to it and go to sleep. ♦ Nice work if you can get it. ♦ Nine to five. ♦ Slave (all day) over a hot stove. ♦ Sweat bullets. ♦ The quality of work done for nothing is equal to the fee. ♦ To freelance. ♦ To hold down a job. ♦ To hold down two jobs. ♦ To moonlight. ♦ To sling hash. ♦ To sweat blood. ♦ To do double duty. ♦ When they told me I would have a ball at work, they didn't tell me there would be a chain attached. ♦ Whistle while you work. ♦ Work hard, play hard. ♦ Work is the curse of the drinking man. (Sign). ♦ Work smarter, not harder. ♦ Write if you get work. ♦ You do nice work—(only damned little of it). ♦ You've gotta be doing something. ♦ Your life's work.

Worry

A worrywart. ♦ It's enough to keep you awake nights. ♦ The misfortunes hardest to bear are those which never come. ♦ There are more people in cemeteries from thinking than from fasting. ♦ To knit one's brow. ♦ Were the diver to think on the jaws of the shark, he would never lay hands on the precious pearl. ♦ Worry is interest you pay on troubles that you don't have yet. [see also Carefree] ♦ Worried sick. ♦ Worrying doesn't change a thing. ♦ Worrying helps nothing. ♦ Your worries are over.

Writing

A man of letters. ♦ A potboiler. ♦ A work of fiction. ♦ Critic: one who puts it down in writing. ♦ Deathless prose. ♦ Easy writing makes vile hard reading. ♦ Everybody has at least one book in them. ♦ *Furor scribendi.* ♦ Gems of wisdom. ♦ If you put a monkey in a room with a typewriter, given an infinite amount of time the monkey will write a novel/the complete works of Shakespeare. -[the Infinite Monkey theory] ♦ It is written. ♦ Kill (all) your darlings. [see also Kill] ♦ Pen: a stick with a point on one end and

a fool at the other. ♦ Pearly words. ♦ Put it in black and white. ♦ The Great American Novel. ♦ The pen is mightier than the sword. ♦ To dash off a note. ♦ To jot [it] in your little black book. ♦ To put [it] in writing. ♦ To put [it] into words. ♦ To put pen to paper. ♦ To reduce [it] to writing. ♦ To take copious notes. ♦ To write it down. ♦ What's not put in writing is written on the wind.—Dominick P. Delia

Wronged

A royal screwing. ♦ Get it in the end. ♦ He done her wrong. ♦ Screwed, blued and tattooed. ♦ The aggrieved/injured party. ♦ The purple/royal shaft. ♦ To be/feel put out. ♦ To be/feel put-upon. ♦ To get a bum/raw deal. ♦ To get burned. ♦ To get it in the neck. ♦ To get the shaft. ♦ To get the sh*tty/short/wrong end of the stick. ♦ To get/give short shrift. ♦ To get shortchanged. ♦ To get stabbed in the back. ♦ To take sh*t from/off. ♦ To wind up with one's hand on one's *ss. ♦ You've been had. ♦ You've had it. ♦ You've had the cock/course/green weenie.

Yes

Absitively, posilutely. ♦ Absolutely perfect. ♦ Absolutely. ♦ Aye aye, Captain/sir. ♦ Be my guest. ♦ By all means. ♦ But of course. ✦ Can do. ✦ Charmed, I'm sure. ✦ Don't mind if I do. ✦ Feel free. ✦ Fine by/with me. ✦ Go right ahead. ✦ I don't mind in the slightest. ✦ I thought you'd never ask. ✦ If you got 'em, smoke 'em. ✦ It would be my pleasure. ✦ Knock yourself out. ✦ Neat. ✦ Nifty. ✦ No problem. ✦ Permission granted. ✦ Sure thing. ✦ (That's) for sure. ✦ To answer/ reply in the affirmative. ✦ To yes you to death. ✦ Twist my arm. ✦ Very much so. ✦ Why, (most) certainly. ✦ Why, I'd be delighted. ✦ Why sure. ✦ Why the f*ck not. ✦ Yes indeed. ✦ Yes indeedy. ✦ Yes, and you may take two giant steps. ✦ You bet. ✦ You betcha. ✦ You'll get no argument from me.

Youth

At a tender (young) age. ✦ In the bloom of youth. ✦ In the prime of (one's) life. ✦ Peach fuzz. ✦ Salad days. ✦ The Fountain of Youth. ✦ You're only young once. (Remember that, young ones. – R.D.) ✦ Young, dumb and full of come. ✦ Young maids, "who,"—old maids, "when." ✦ Youth is wasted on the young. ✦ Youth must be served. (But only with proper I.D. – R.D.) ✦ Youth possesses the gift of time, age, the gift of wisdom. ✦ Youth would be great if only it came late in life. ✦ You'll never be younger than you are today.

Zeal

All out. ✦ A [v.]-ing fool. ✦ All fired up. ✦ A get-rich- quick scheme. ✦ Do [it] like it's going out of style. ✦ Do [it] like there's no tomorrow. ✦ Go to any extreme/ lengths. ✦ Gung ho. ✦ Like a house afire. ✦ Like Grant took Richmond. ✦ Like nobody's business. ✦ Like one possessed. ✦ Never let your zeal affect your weal. ✦ On a [n.] "kick." ✦ To [v.] left and right. ✦ To [v.] like crazy/like mad. ✦ To [v.] up a storm. ✦ To be a ball of fire. ✦ To be a(n) [adj./n.] freak. ✦ To be all caught/wrapped up in [it]. ✦ To be really into it. ✦ To beat all (get out). ✦ To beat the band. ✦ To come on like Gangbusters. ✦ To come on strong. ✦ To eat, sleep and breathe [it]. ✦ To get carried away (with). ✦ To give it the works. ✦ To go all out. ✦ To go for broke. ✦ To go hog wild. ✦ To go to town. ✦ To go whole hog. [see also Unrestrained] ✦ To play it to the hilt. ✦ To raise one's sights. ✦ To raise the bar. ✦ To swing for the fences. ✦ To shoot for the moon. ✦ To turn out in full force. ✦ To wade in with both feet. ✦ To whale away. ✦ Zeal is fit only for wise men, but is found mostly in fools. ✦ Zeal without knowledge is fire without light.

TABLE OF CLASSIFICATIONS

Armed	Boys
Arrival	Brag
Arrogance	Brave
Ass	Brief
Assault	Britain
Association	Bureaucracy
Assurance	Burn
Astonishment	Business
Attack	Busy
Attitude	Capability
Attraction	Carefree
Attractive	Catch
Authority	Causality
Available	Caution
Avoid	Cavil
Bachelorhood	Censored
Bald	Certainty
Beauty	Challenges
Begin	Change
Behavior	Chat
Behind	Child
Belief	Chitchat
Best	Choices
Bet	Christmas
Betray	Church
Big	Cigar
Birth	Clarification
Blab	Clean
Blame	Clear
Bonus	Close
Bore	Clumsy
Borrow	Coincidence
Boss	Cold

Collaboration

Combat

Command

Commonplace

Comparison

Compel

Complain

Complicity

Comprehensive

Compromise

Conceal

Confide

Conflict

Confused

Consideration

Contract

Contrive

Cool

Cooperation

Confucius

Correct

Courage

Cowardice

Cozy

Crazy

Credit

Crime

Critical

Criticism

Crowding

Curiosity

Cute

Cyber-Slang

Dance

Dark

Dearth

Death

Debt

Decisive

Deduce

Defeat

Defy

Dejection

Delay

Demeaning

Demur

Departure

Dependable

Dereliction

Deserve

Desire

Destroy

Detect

Deteriorate

Determination

Devil

Difference

Different

Difficulty

Dilapidated

Dilemma

Disappear

Disappointment

Disapprove

Disbelief

Discomfiture

Discovery	Escape
Dishonest	Etcetera
Dismay	Eternal
Disrupt	Euphemisms
Distance	Eventually
Divide	Everyone
Dogs	Everywhere
Dominate	Exaggeration
Doomed	Exasperation
Drenched	Excel
Drink	Exceptions
Drunk	Excess
Dupe	Excitement
Duty	Exemplary
Early	Expectation
Earn	Expediency
Easy	Expense
Eat	Experience
Egotism	Extemporaneous
Embarrassment	Extravagant
Emergency	Extremes
Emotion	Extroverted
Enamored	Failure
Encore	Faith
End	Fall
Endearments	Familiarity
Endurance	Familiarize
Enjoyment	Family
Enlightenment	Fanfare
Enough	Fantasize
Envy	Far-reaching
Err	Farewells
Erroneous	Fat

Fear	Gossip
Finagle	Gratitude
Finality	Grooming
First	Grudge
Flat	Guess
Flattery	Guilt
Flee	Gullibility
Flexibility	Guns
Flirt	Habit
Flourishing	Hackneyed
Fly	Handicapped
Fool	Happen
Forbearance	Happiness
Forget	Harmless
Forgive	Haste
Fours	Hate
Frail	Health
Free	Heaviness
Fresh	Hedonism
Friend	Hell
Fugitive	Henpecked
Fun	Hero
Futility	Hint
Future	History
Gambling	Home
Gardening	Homosexuality
Generalizations	Honesty
Generosity	Honor
Genius	Hope
Glare	Hopeless
Glory	Horse
Gluttony	Hospitality
Good	Hot

Humanity	Inexpensive
Humiliate	Inferiority
Humorous	Influence
Hunch	Ingratitude
Hurry	Inherit
Hush	Inimitable
Hypocrisy	Initiative
Idea	Injury
Idle	Innocence
If	Inoperative
Ignorance	Insecurity
Ignore	Insincere
Illegal	Insist
Illness	Insults
Illusion	Intensity
Imitation	Intimacy
Immaterial	Investigate
Immediacy	Investment
Impasse	Invitation
Impolite	Irk
Impossibility	Irrelevant
Imprisonment	Judgment
Improve	Kill
Improvise	Kindness
Incite	Kiss
Inconspicuous	Knowledge
Increase	Language
Incredulity	Late
Independent	Laughter
Indeterminate	Law
Industrious	Lazy
Inept	Leadership
Inexorable	Learn

Lend	Motion
Lengthy	Motionless
Liberty	Music
Lie	Mystery
Life	Nag
Lifelong	Naked
Limited	Names
Listen	Nature
Long	Nausea
Lore	Necessity
Loser	Negotiate
Loss	Nervous
Love	Nervy
Low	New
Loyalty	News
Luck	No
Manners	None
Marginal	Nose
Marriage	Notoriety
Masculine	Now
Maybe	Obedience
Mean	Objectivity
Meddle	Oblivious
Medical	Obsequies
Meek	Obvious
Menstruation	Oddball
Merciless	Official
Messy	Ogle
Misbehavior	Open
Moderation	Opinion
Money	Opportunity
More	Oppose
Mother	Optimism

Ordeal	Poverty
Organize	Power
Ostracism	Powerless
Outcry	Praise
Outspoken	Preach
Outwit	Precaution
Overseas	Predictable
Oversee	Prediction
Paltry	Preference
Participate	Pregnant
Patience	Prejudice
Patriotic	Premature
Peace	Preparation
Penny	Pressured
Penultimate	Pretend
Perfection	Pride
Permanence	Problem
Perquisites	Profanity
Perseverance	Profit
Personalities	Progress
Persuasion	Promise
Pessimism	Proof
Pictures	Protection
Placate	Proverbs
Pleading	Public
Poetry	Pun
Pointless	Puns
Politics	Punishment
Popularity	Pure
Position	Purpose
Possession	Pursue
Postpone	Quality
Potential	Question

Quickly

Quiet

Quit

Quote

Rarely

Readiness

Reality

Rebukes

Reciprocation

Reckless

Recuperation

Reduce

Refinement

Regret

Rejection

Rejoinders

Rejuvenation

Relativity

Relax

Relic

Relief

Religion

Remembrance

Reminiscent

Remote

Renowned

Repay

Repetition

Reputation

Rescue

Respectability

Restless

Resume

Return

Reveal

Revel

Revenge

Rich

Ridicule

Right

Ripostes

Risk

Romance

Rough

Routinely

Rules

Rustication

Safety

Satisfaction

Scarce

Scare

Scold

Scoundrel

Secret

Self

Self-Improvement

Selfishness

Sensibility

Seriousness

Setback

Settle

Sex

Sharp

Shirk

Shock

Shortsighted

Showoff	Style
Shy	Subservience
Sidekicks	Substance
Silence	Substitute
Silly	Success
Sin	Sudden
Sincerity	Suicide
Skepticism	Summation
Skylark	Superlatives
Slander	Surprise
Sleep	Surrender
Slippery	Survival
Slipshod	Suspicion
Slow	Sympathy
Smart	T.V.
Smile	Taboo
Smooth	Taciturnity
Solitary	Tact
Soon	Talkative
Sort	Tall
Speechless	Teach
Spoonerisms	Tease
Status	Telephonese
Steadfast	Temper
Stingy	Temporary
Stodgy	Temptation
Straightforward	Theft
Strength	Thick
Strict	Thin
Strive	Think
Stubborn	Thorough
Study	Thrift
Stumped	Tight

Time
Timeliness
Tired
Toasts
Tomorrow
Tongue Twisters
Tools
Travel
Trendy
Trickery
Trouble
Truisms
Trust
Truth
Try
Turnabout
Typical
Ugly
Uncertainty
Uncle Baronisms
Unchangeable
Uncontrolled
Understanding
Undoubtedly
Unemployed
Unfair
Unfamiliar
Unflattering
Unity
Unlucky
Unpredictability
Unrestrained
Unsightly

Unsuited
Unsympathetic
Unthinkable
Untrustworthy
Unwelcome
Up
Used
Useful
Useless
Vague
Valuable
Varied
Venality
Versatile
Virtue
Volunteer
Voluptuous
Vote
Vulnerable
Wait
Walk
Warning
Weakness
Weapons
Weather
West
Wife
Win
Wine
Wise
Wish
Withdraw
Womanize

Women
Work
Worry
Writing
Wronged
Yes
Youth
Zeal